ANATOMY
of a BANKING
SCANDAL

ANATOMY
of a BANKING
SCANDAL

The Keystone Bank Failure–
Harbinger of the 2008 Financial Crisis

Robert S. Pasley

Transaction Publishers
New Brunswick (U.S.A.) and London (U.K.)

Library of Congress Catalog Number: 2016006375
ISBN: 978-1-4128-6279-0 (hardcover); 978-1-4128-6334-6 (paper)
eBook: 978-1-4128-6229-5
Printed in the United States of America

Library of Congress Cataloging-in-Publication Data

Names: Pasley, Robert S., author.
Title: Anatomy of a banking scandal : the Keystone Bank failure--harbinger of the 2008 financial crisis / Robert S. Pasley.
Description: New Brunswick : Transaction Publishers, [2016] | Includes bibliographical references and index.
Identifiers: LCCN 2016006375 (print) | LCCN 2016013541 (ebook) | ISBN 9781412862790 (hardcover) | ISBN 9781412863346 (pbk.) | ISBN 9781412862295
Subjects: LCSH: First National Bank of Keystone (W. Va.) | Bank failures--United States--History. | Banks and banking--United States--History. | Subprime mortgage loans--United States--History. | Financial crises--United States--History.
Classification: LCC HG2613.K494 F577 2016 (print) | LCC HG2613.K494 (ebook) | DDC 332.1/2230975449--dc23
LC record available at http://lccn.loc.gov/

2016006375

To my beautiful wife, Gay, and to our two wonderful daughters, Virginia and Heather.

Contents

Preface		ix
Author's Note		xi
Acknowledgments		xiii
Cast of Characters		xv
Entities Involved		xxi
List of Acronyms		xxiii
1	Burying the Documents	1
2	J. Knox McConnell and the Rise of the Bank	9
3	Billie Cherry, Terry Church, and the Town of Keystone, West Virginia	23
4	Death of Knox McConnell	33
5	A Train Wreck A Comin'	49
6	The Examinations of the Bank, 1990–1997	81
7	1998 Examination	115
8	The Last Year of the Bank	127
9	The Criminal Cases	165
10	The Civil and Administrative Cases	193
11	The Case Against the Attorneys	209

12   The Case Against the Bank's Accounting
     Firm—Grant Thornton   219

13   The Sad Story of Gary Ellis   257

14   Aftermath of the Failure of the Bank   269

15   Harbinger of the 2008 Financial Crisis   279

16   Lessons Learned   293

17   Consolidation of the Federal Banking Agencies   301

18   Conclusion   321

Appendix A   Additional Information Concerning
             the Criminal and SEC Cases Brought
             Against the Insiders of the Bank   323

Appendix B   Additional Information Concerning
             the Civil Cases Brought in Connection
             with the Bank   329

Bibliography   335

Index   337

Preface

This is a true story about a bank failure in 1999. The case involved a series of unusual characters who caused the bank's failure and engaged in a dizzying array of fraud and deceit. The fraud included embezzlement, bank executives stealing from one another, and even cooking the books to cover up massive losses from the securitization of subprime mortgages. The bankers yelled and screamed at the bank examiners, lied to their own attorneys and auditors and threatened a series of lawsuits. They hired fake bodyguards to intimidate the examiners; brought an injunction against the regulators based on forged emails; wrote threatening letters to the banking agency supervising the bank; and even buried bank documents in a large ditch outside of town to avoid them from being discovered by the examiners. The bank's failure was also a harbinger of the 2008 financial crisis, but it went mostly unnoticed and understudied.

The bank—the First National Bank of Keystone—was a tiny bank located in an economically depressed area of an already poor state—West Virginia; not too far from where the Hatfields and McCoys feuded.

The people running the bank were able to grow it from $17 million in total assets to over $1 billion. Along with this growth came amazing earnings. For three years in the 1990s, the bank was touted as the most profitable large community bank in the entire country—out of more than 5,000 similarly situated banks. It was phenomenal.

It was also fraudulent.

None of the numbers were real.

The bank's purported earnings came from the securitization of subprime mortgages. The earnings were so great that the management of the bank was able to embezzle millions of dollars from the bank without being noticed. They hid their embezzlement—and the much larger fraud related to the securitizations—from the federal bank examiners, its shareholders, the outside directors, and the nationally prominent auditors and attorneys working for the bank.

There were three primary managers of the bank: Knox McConnell, Ms. Billie Cherry, and Ms. Terry Church. McConnell became the president of the bank in 1977, and brought along his lifelong companion and secret lover, Cherry.

Church came with the pair in 1977 and became the senior executive vice president of the bank. Even though Cherry became the president of the bank after McConnell died in 1997, Church was the person who actually ran the bank—and had been running the bank even prior to McConnell's death.

McConnell and Church grew the bank by getting it involved in the securitization of subprime mortgages between 1993 and 1999. However, none of the securitizations was profitable and the bank was falsifying its books to hide this fact. Ironically, the bank was assisted first by Lehman Brothers and then Bear Stearns—who reaped huge fees, knowing that the securitization deals were worthless.

When the bank finally failed in 1999, the FDIC thought it would be one of the ten largest bank failures since the Great Depression. It turned out to be the sixty-ninth largest failure between 1934 and the present, out of more than 4,000 failed banks.

As the result of the frauds, numerous civil and criminal cases were brought in the aftermath of the bank's failure. One criminal case was brought against Cherry and three criminal cases were brought against Church. They were convicted or pled guilty in all of the cases. Cherry died in prison. Church was released from prison in September, 2015.

The bank ended up as the subject of congressional hearings and an Inspector General's review. In spite of the riskiness of the bank's line of business, and the stark and surprising failure of the bank, the regulators and Congress failed to adequately learn from the lessons the failure of this bank could have taught, especially in connection with the subsequent 2008 financial crisis. There are, however, more lessons that could still be learned.

Author's Note

This book is based primarily on court records – depositions, sworn testimony at trial and court exhibits, as well as congressional hearings, scholarly books and interviews of people involved in the case. The book also draws from material obtained through the Freedom of Information Act, including banking agency memoranda, letters, reports of examination, and even suspicious activity reports filed with the Department of Justice. The original manuscript contained a myriad of footnotes to all of this, but the footnotes were too voluminous and made it too distracting to read, so most of the footnotes were eliminated. Explanatory footnotes and footnotes related to copyrighted and congressional sources have been kept. The quotations in the book are primarily from sworn testimony in court cases and depositions. Rather than repeating "alleged," or "it was testified that," or "court records reflect" throughout the book, the reader should understand that that is the case and read the book accordingly. When I have drawn conclusions, I have done my best to provide reasonable interpretations of the record, primarily from cases in which the defendants in issue were found to be guilty of crimes or civilly liable for their alleged wrongdoing.

Acknowledgments

This project has been a very long one and there are a number of people and entities I would like to thank for their assistance, guidance and good wishes. They include the following:

- Bill Archer
- Aleta Barie
- American Banker
- Ron Barnhart
- Joshua Barrett
- Jean Battlo
- Janet Beasley
- Fran Belcher
- Anne Benham
- Janice Bickham
- Sgt. Bievins
- Mark Blair
- John Byrne
- Michael Callahan
- Michael Carey
- Jane Carney
- Owen Carney
- Joe Ciccarelli
- Robert L. Clarke
- Steve Cocheo
- Charles Davis
- Richard Delmar
- Donna Dickerson
- Jeffrey Dorrell
- John Dow
- Charles Dunbar
- Dana Eddy
- John Elmore
- Jacqueline England
- Judge Faber
- Ray Froy
- Catherine Ghiglieri
- Michael Gibson
- Jean Grant
- John D. Hawke, Jr.
- Charlotte Hays
- Bryan Heath
- Judy Henderson
- Marc Hochstein
- Arild Johassen
- Dennis Jones
- Bernard Kaufman
- Kenneth Krattenmaker
- Dennis Lormel
- Jerry Martin
- Jonathan Matthews
- Michael McGlothlin
- Billy Joe McPeak
- Barbara Meade
- Larry Messina
- John Michelich
- Marc Hochstein
- National Archives
- Wendy Sue Pack
- Mary Jane Pennington
- William Powell
- Barbara Rehm
- Philip Robertson
- Susan Arnold Robinson
- Richard Romero
- Ken Rosen
- Ron Schneck
- Vondelere Scott
- Robert Selbe

- Robert Serino
- Allison Skinner
- Rick Spelsberg
- Peggy Spradling
- Laura Sweeney
- Nelson Travis
- William T. Weber, Jr.
- West Virginia Board of Accountancy
- Penny Wright
- Jennifer Zudonyi

While I owe a debt of gratitude to all of the above, I would like to single out Owen and Jane Carney and Mark Blair for special thanks. I could not have written this book without you.

Last, I would particularly like to thank my daughter, Virginia, who used her skills as an English major from the College of William and Mary and as a graduate from the master's program at the Missouri School of Journalism to copy edit the manuscript and who offered invaluable advice for the organization of the book.

Cast of Characters

OCC

- Mark Blair, national bank examiner; examiner-in-charge of the 1999 examination of the bank
- Leann Britton, senior deputy comptroller for bank supervisory operations
- John Chopel, national bank examiner
- Don Coonley, chief national bank examiner
- Doug Daugherty, national bank examiner; examiner-in-charge of the examinations of the bank, 1994–98
- Frank Forrest, licensing analyst, Atlanta office
- Joey Johnson, national bank examiner
- Rodney Gearheart, national bank examiner
- Kathy Gerardy, national bank examiner; analyst, Division of Special Supervision/Fraud
- Catherine Ghiglieri, field office director
- Sam Golden, ombudsman
- John D. (Jerry) Hawke, Jr., comptroller of the currency, 1998–2004
- Bryan Heath, national bank examiner
- Mark Jacobsen, senior advisor to the comptroller of the currency
- Ann Jaedicke, deputy comptroller for Special Supervision and Fraud
- Tim Knaak, national bank examiner; examiner-in-charge of the 1998 examination of the bank
- Tim Long, deputy comptroller of multi-national banks
- Eugene Ludwig, comptroller of the currency, 1993–98
- Morris Morgan, national bank examiner
- Karen Murtagh, national bank examiner
- Ron Schneck, director, Division of Special Supervision/Fraud
- Robert B. Serino, deputy chief counsel
- Rick Spelsberg, assistant deputy comptroller
- Cindy Wilson, national bank examiner

FDIC

- Michael Morgan, examiner

First National Bank of Keystone

- Diane Bailey, compliance officer
- Justin Bays, certified public accountant
- Victor Budnick, director
- Virginia Burks, senior loan officer
- Jane Carney, acting chief financial officer, January 1999–March 1999
- Owen Carney, president, January 1999–March 1999
- Billie Cherry, president and chairman of the board, 1997–98
- Terry Church, senior executive vice president, 1995–99
- Sandy Dalton, internal auditor
- Gary Ellis, president, April 1999–September 1999
- Connie Evans, certificate of deposit clerk
- Michael Gibson, director
- Michael Graham, executive vice president and chief operating officer of Keystone Mortgage Corporation (KMC)
- Gail Graham, wife of Michael Graham
- Scott Griffith, head of IT
- Meredith Hale, assigned to the IT Division
- Daniel Halsey, director
- Evelyn Herron, employee at the bank's Bradshaw branch
- Dee Hughes (Mama Dee), janitor
- Bernard Kaufman, director
- Penny Kosa, employee of KMC
- J. Knox McConnell, president and chairman of the board, 1977–97
- Lora McKinney, vice president, proof operator
- Vickie Mickles, senior vice president and manager of loan department
- Ron Mitchell, chief financial officer; associate of Melgar's
- Barbara Nunn, employee of KMC
- Patricia Orell, switchboard operator
- Wendy Sue Pack, executive administrative assistant to Church
- Louis Pais, director
- Melissa Quizenbeury, executive vice president, cashier, and director
- Deborah Shrader, vice president, assistant cashier
- Ellen Turpin, vice president, head bookkeeper
- Nancy Vorono, secretary for McConnell
- Deborah Watkins, drive-up teller
- Jeanie Wimmer, employee at the bank's Bradshaw branch
- Gracie Wooldridge, bookkeeping

Employees on Terry Church's Ranch

- T. G. Church
- Warren Johnson
- Bill Miles
- Doug Penny

Grant Thornton

- Susan Buenger
- Stan Quay, lead auditor

Kutak Rock

- Michael Lambert, primary counsel to the bank

Other Attorneys and Advisors to the Bank

- Harald Bakkebo, owner of Prime and Clearview; associate of Melgar's
- Robert L. Clarke, partner, Bracewell & Giuliani; comptroller of the currency,1985–92
- Robert Krasne, partner, Williams & Connolly
- Dan Melgar, advisor to the bank on securitizations

Clearview

- Milton Drageset

Prime

- Shannon Doyle, assistant vice president

Terry Church's Family Members and Friends

- Jeff Church, Church's stepson
- Hermie (Junior) Church, Church's husband
- Tony Church, Church's step-grandson
- Larry Fisher, Church's older brother
- Jerry Haynes, friend of Jeff Church

Government Agencies

- Joe Ciccarelli, special agent, FBI
- Dean Lauffer, special agent, FBI
- Robert Selbe, special agent, FBI

Others

- Roy Barnett, Waynesburg College
- Billy Conn, heavyweight prize fighter
- Steven Copolo, friend of Michael Graham
- Joseph Ray Davidson, attempted to get McConnell's antique car
- Jeffrey Dorrell, attorney for Bakkebo

- David A. Faber, Senior District Court Judge
- Clifton Lewis, CapMac
- Scott Mannes, ContiTrade
- Matt McConnell, Waynesburg College
- Michael McGlothlin, an associate of Graham's; sued by the FDIC
- Harry J. Potter, forensic accountant for the FDIC
- Andrew Radoff, second husband of Billie Cherry
- David Sexton, friend of Michael Graham
- Scott Sizemore, employee of Keystone Hardware Store
- Mack Wright, uninsured depositor of bank

Associated with Harald Bakkebo

- Brian Bakkebo, Bakkebo's son
- Felipa Chadwick, Bakkebo's girlfriend
- Gary Jackson, indicted with Bakkebo in New Orleans
- David Mackarness, co-owner of F.S. Holdings, SA, which purchased Bakkebo's company, Prime
- Patrick McGee, purchaser of F.S. Holdings, SA
- Pieter Oosthuizen, co-owner of F.S. Holdings, SA, which purchased Bakkebo's company, Prime
- Bobby Shamburger, indicted with Bakkebo in New Orleans

Loan Servicers

- John LaRose, president, Compu-Link
- Dan Pearson, Compu-Link
- Patricia Ramirez, Advanta
- Dee Romero, Advanta

Law Firm Representing FDIC

- Mullin Hoard Brown LLP

Government Figures

- Alfonse D'Amato, U.S. Senator (R-NY), 1981–99
- Sheila Bair, chair of the FDIC, 2006–11
- Lloyd Bentsen, secretary of the Treasury, 1993–94
- Ben Bernanke, chairman of the Federal Reserve Board, 2006–14
- Tim Geithner, president of NY Federal Reserve Bank, 2003–09; secretary of the Treasury, 2009–13
- Henry B. Gonzalez (D-Tx.), chairman, House Banking Committee, 1989–95
- Alan Greenspan, chairman of the Federal Reserve Board, 1987–2006
- John P. LaWare, governor of the Federal Reserve Board, 1988–95

- James Leach (R-Iowa) member of the U.S. House of Representatives, 1977–2007; chairman of the House Committee on Banking and Financial Services, 1995–2001
- Laurence Meyer, member, Board of Governors of the Federal Reserve Board, 1996–2002
- William Proxmire, U.S. Senator (D-Wis.), 1957–89
- Donald Riegle, U.S. Senator (D-Mich.), 1976–95; chairman of the Senate Committee on Banking, Housing, and Urban Affairs, 1989–95
- J. L. Robertson, vice-chairman of the Federal Reserve Board, 1966–73
- Ellen Seidman, director of the OTS, 1997–2001
- William Seidman, chairman of the FDIC, 1985–91
- Donna Tanoue, chair of the FDIC, 1998–2001
- Paul Volcker, chairman of the Federal Reserve Board, 1979–87

Entities Involved

- Advanta—loan servicer for Keystone bank

- Bear Stearns—replaced Lehman Brothers; co-sponsor of nineteenth (and last) securitization deal with Keystone bank

- Capital Markets Assurance Corporation (CapMac)—replaced FSA, but withdrew in 1996

- CEDE—clearing house for certificates of deposit

- City National Bank—partnered with Keystone bank in buying and holding loans to be put into securitization deals

- Clearview Capital Corporation—loan originator for Keystone bank

- Coast Partners Securities, Inc.—Melgar related company

- Compu-Link—loan servicer for Keystone bank

- ContiTrade Services Corporation (Conti)—replaced Master Financial; co-sponsor of securitization deals 1 to 4 with Keystone bank

- Euro-Play B.V.—had option to buy Prime

- Federal Deposit Insurance Corporation (FDIC)—federal insurer of deposits held by financial institutions

- Federal Savings & Loan Insurance Corp. (FSLIC)

- Financial Securities Assurance Company (FSA)—provided additional insurance for Keystone bank for securitization deals 1 to 5 for Keystone bank

- F.S. Holdings, S.A.—purchased Prime and sold it to Keystone bank

- Grant Thornton—accounting firm working for Keystone bank

- Kutak Rock—law firm representing Keystone bank

- Lehman Brothers—replaced Conti; co-sponsor of securitization deals 5 to 18 with Keystone bank

- Master Financial—was to be initial co-sponsor of securitization deals for Keystone bank; also provided and serviced a number of the initial loans

- Office of the Comptroller of the Currency (OCC)—supervisor of Keystone bank

- Prime Financial Corporation—loan servicer for Keystone bank

- Ronhardan, Inc.—corporation formed by Ron Mitchell, Harald Bakkebo, and Dan Melgar to buy residuals from Conti

- Royal Consulting Group—Melgar-owned company

- United National Bank—replaced City National Bank; partnered with Keystone bank in buying and holding loans to be put into securitization deals

List of Acronyms

ALLL: Allowance for Loan and Lease Losses

CAMELS: Capital, Assets, Management, Earnings, Liquidity & Market Risk Sensitivity

CD: Certificate of Deposit

C&D: Cease and Desist Order

EIC: Examiner-in-Charge

FDIC: Federal Deposit Insurance Corporation

FHA: Federal Housing Authority

GAAS: Generally Accepted Auditing Standards

GAAP: Generally Accepted Accounting Principles

HLTV: High Loan-to-Value

HUD: Department of Housing and Urban Development

KMC: Keystone Mortgage Corporation

OCC: Office of the Comptroller of the Currency

OIG: Office of Inspector General

OTS: Office of Thrift Supervision

ROE: Report of Examination

ROAA: Return on Average Assets

ROAE: Return on Average Equity

TCD: Temporary Cease and Desist Order

TRO: Temporary Restraining Order

1

Burying the Documents

Oh, what a tangled web we weave,
When first we practice to deceive.
—Sir Walter Scott

Thursday, August 12, 1999

The bank examiners had just left the tiny town of Keystone, West Virginia, for a long weekend. They had been examining the only bank in town—the First National Bank of Keystone—since June 21, 1999, and the process had become more and more contentious.

After the examiners left, Terry Church, the head of the bank, called Bill Miles, an employee at her ranch outside of town. She wanted him and the other men at the ranch to dig a hole large enough to hold two truckloads of bank documents. Miles asked, "Aren't we going to burn the documents?" But Church responded: "There is not enough time, and there are too many to burn."

Church directed Miles to have some men dig the hole and to send the "TopKick"—a GMC truck that could hold approximately fifteen tons of gravel—down to the abandoned schoolhouse where the bank stored some of its documents. The TopKick had never been used to move bank documents, but this day was going to be different.

T. G. Church, a distant relative of Terry Church's husband, drove the TopKick down to the schoolhouse. When he got there, he backed the TopKick up to the front of the schoolhouse, positioning the truck right under a third floor window. Then, senior bank officers and a crew of men started throwing bank documents out of the window onto the flatbed of the truck. There was no effort to keep the boxes of bank records intact as they hit the truck. As T. G. later recounted, "They just throwed them out the window."

The previous day, Terry Church had sent two officers of the bank up to the schoolhouse to draw a big "X" on boxes that could be thrown out

1

in accordance with the bank's two-page "document destruction policy." They were in the process of doing that when Church and Michael Graham—the number-three person at the bank—showed up and started to indiscriminately mark boxes with "Xs." The two officers, Lora McKinney and Ellen Turpin, just looked at each other, shrugged and let them be. The activity was especially unusual because, according to Turpin, the bank "had never thrown anything away." The bank had documents dating back to the 1950s, and was leasing both the schoolhouse and another site to store documents.

When the TopKick was finally loaded, T. G. drove it back up Burke Mountain to Terry Church's C&H Ranch. He then got the track loader— a huge caterpillar, but with tracks instead of wheels—and proceeded to dig a ditch a hundred feet long, thirty feet wide, and ten feet deep. He sloped the ditch at one end so he could back the TopKick all the way down into the hole. After dumping the truckload, he drove back into town to pick up a second full load of documents from the schoolhouse.

Meanwhile, Warren Johnson, another employee of Terry Church's, had taken the "One Ton" truck (which actually could hold several tons of gravel) to the neighboring town of Kimball to pick up even more documents. These documents were from a house recently purchased by Ms. Billie Cherry, the chairman of the board of the bank, from the estate of the late Dr. Fickins. The house needed cleaning out, and the fact that the doctor's old papers were thrown out along with the bank documents would later be used to argue that the removal and burial of all of the documents was simply done in the normal course of affairs.

After Johnson dumped his truckload into the hole that T. G. had dug, he returned to town, parked the One Ton at the hardware store, which was right next to the bank, and walked the three and a half blocks up the steep hill to the schoolhouse. Once the TopKick was loaded for the second time, Johnson and T. G. drove it back to the ranch. When they got there, they learned that Church had called Miles a second time. She wanted someone to drive back into town and pick up the One Ton—which was being loaded with still more documents at the bank. So T. G. left the TopKick for Johnson to dump, and drove to the bank in another vehicle.

Graham, a bank officer and operating head of the bank's thriving mortgage securitization subsidiary, had driven the One Ton from the hardware store, across the parking lot, to the bank, and had positioned the truck under a balcony at the bank. He had Scott Sizemore, a hardware store employee, help him throw bank documents off the balcony onto the back of the One Ton. Sizemore had never done this before, so he asked Graham why they were doing it. Graham said that the bank could destroy documents after two years. The minimum retention period for bank documents, however, is actually five years, and, further, this bank had been placed under a specific directive—from its federal banking regulator, the Office of the Comptroller of the Currency (OCC)—to suspend all document destruction.

After Graham and Sizemore finished throwing bank documents off the balcony, Turpin went into the storage room where the documents had been kept and saw that there was very little left. To her, the room looked "naked."

T. G. picked up the One Ton's second load (the fourth truckload of the day) and drove it back to the ranch; it was about 5:30 PM. Because it was late, the men were thinking they could wait until the next day to dump this last load and cover up the documents. However, Church called Miles a third time and said, "No, cover it today." So the men dumped the load, filled the hole with dirt and smoothed it out. Later on, they seeded the area to make it look like it had never been disturbed.

Friday, August 13th

The day after the initial burial of four truckloads' worth of documents, Church asked bank employees if they or anyone they knew "could come in [over the weekend] and help toss some deposits and different things [out] and not ask any questions." Turpin volunteered and asked her sister-in-law, Amber, to assist. When asked later why she suggested her sister-in-law, Turpin simply said, "I mean, she could use the money." Amber, seeing that Church wanted to destroy microfilm tapes, suggested putting them in the microwave. Church tried it, but it started "stinking really bad" and the effort was abandoned.

Sunday, August 15th

Doug Penny had just returned from work on the Churches' boat marina in Bristol, Tennessee, and was visiting Miles on the ranch. It was shortly after lunch when the message came through that Church needed them to dig a second hole and bury more documents.

This time, the material to be buried included microfilm. Penny, who knew Church from childhood and who was the co-manager of her ranch, dug a hole next to the much larger first hole and, with Church's help, threw the bags in. He then "tracked them in" by adding dirt and "smoothed her up real good." He then seeded the area.

Afterward, they talked about the possibility of digging up some other areas of the ranch and seeding them so that "it wouldn't be like just one area was disturbed." But they never got around to doing that.

When the bank examiners returned from the weekend, they did not realize that the bank documents and microfilm were missing. But, during the next two weeks, they discovered that half of the bank's assets were missing.

Wednesday, September 1st

Due to this discovery, the OCC closed the bank early in the morning and handed it over to the Federal Deposit Insurance Corporation (FDIC) as receiver.

The First National Bank of Keystone was chartered in 1903 and had survived the Great Depression. To reflect this accomplishment, the bank had its motto, "Time Tried—Panic Tested," engraved on the side of the bank. But the bank could not survive the senior management's embezzlement and fraud, and the bank's extensive operating losses that had—up to that time—been hidden from the examiners.

That evening, in spite of the bank's closure, the document destruction continued. Church wanted eight to ten boxes of documents and microfilm that she had taken from her office at the bank put into the C&H Ranch's incinerator. The process took a number of hours, and Doug Penny, who was helping her, did not finish the job until 9:30 or 10 that night.

Thursday, September 2nd

The next morning, the document destruction started up again. Early in the morning, two women—one of whom was Church's aunt-in-law, Dee Hughes or "Mama Dee"—shredded five to six bags of documents. When they were done, they gave the bags to Miles to put in the incinerator.

Later that day, law enforcement moved in. No one in the government—neither law enforcement nor the bank examiners—knew about the burning and burying of documents and microfilm, but it was reported to the authorities that Church had been seen the weekend before removing two Suburban loads' worth of records from her office in the bank. Based on that tip, law enforcement obtained a search warrant for a number of the buildings on the C&H Ranch. The warrant was executed with the help of six FBI agents, one FBI financial analyst, a Treasury agent, and an FDIC Inspector General agent. Six state troopers were assigned to secure the residences.

The search of the ranch was no small undertaking. The property included a house for Terry Church and her husband, Hermie; a house for each of Church's two stepsons; a house for Church's brother, Larry

Fisher; a house for Church's father and stepmother; and a house for Mama Dee. Actually, all of the "houses" were double-wide trailers, except for the house that Church and her husband lived in. The ranch also had a horse barn for the quarter horses Church owned; a small shop; a six-car garage; and a large building complete with a gymnasium, a basketball court, grill facilities, and a solarium. There was also a pool house, eighty-five feet by fifty-four feet (with a 55,000 gallon kidney-shaped swimming pool).

At the end of the day, after having been engaged in the search for five hours, law enforcement officials took away fifty-five items, comprising twenty-two boxes, twenty-seven envelopes, five notebooks, and a safe. Still, they did not come close to finding the buried documents.

Friday, September 3rd

Undaunted by the federal law enforcement search the previous day, Church handed a blue cooler to her stepson, Jeff Church, and asked him to hide it in a safe place. She claimed it contained documents and materials that would serve to protect her against the vendetta she believed the government had against her.

Jeff enlisted the help of his best friend, Jerry Haynes. At first, they hid the cooler in a cave by a ball field, but thought a woman had seen them. So they retrieved the cooler and took it up beyond Haynes' home and put it in an old river bed. (It was later discovered that among the contents of the cooler were OCC internal emails from a national bank examiner disparaging the officers of the bank and discussing how to close the bank on spurious grounds.)

A month later, three FBI agents appeared at Jerry Haynes' home and started questioning him. They wanted to know if he knew anything about the location of any bank records. They told him he had a narrow window of opportunity to cooperate—an opportunity that would close if the agents turned around and left. Haynes started to talk, and led the agents to the blue cooler.

At about the same time, Bill Miles—at his wife's urging—called the FBI and told them about the documents buried on the ranch, and, based on that confidential tip, the FBI was able to obtain a second search warrant for the ranch.

Wednesday, October 13th

Prior to searching the ranch for a second time—and in order to further bolster the application for the search warrant—the FBI took a helicopter ride over the ranch to see if they could determine where the digging had occurred and if the documents had been unearthed and moved.

The FBI got the State Police to fly a helicopter out of Charleston, West Virginia, all the way down to Keystone (about a three-hour car drive) and circle over the ranch. It was the first helicopter ride for one of the FBI agents and he felt sick whenever he looked out the window directly down at the ground, so he tried to keep his eyes trained on the horizon.

They determined that some areas of the ground on the ranch were different and could be where the ditches had been dug. So the next day, armed with a warrant, they arrived in force at the ranch.

Thursday, October 14th

Law enforcement executed the search warrant with twenty-seven agents from five different agencies. They brought a ground-penetrating radar device that would determine where the ground had been disturbed and where it was not as compact as it should have been. They also brought a backhoe to dig up the documents.

After using the radar device for over an hour—even with the benefit of having seen the land the day before from the helicopter—the FBI was getting nowhere. They could not find where the documents were supposedly buried. The backhoe operator, though, who had been sitting on his backhoe and chewing tobacco, called out to the FBI agents, asking them whether they were looking for where the ground had been dug up. They said they were. The operator, a local man who had more experience in digging than the agents evidently did, said, "It's right over there."

Joe Ciccarelli, the supervising agent on the scene, told the agents using the radar to get out of the way and let the backhoe do its work. On the first try, the backhoe operator came up with buried bank documents. The agents then took over with hand shovels—in order not to harm the documents—and proceeded to dig up the entire area.

The first area they uncovered held most of the microfilm, and they later found the larger burial area that contained hundreds of account records, ledgers, and other bank documents. There was so much buried that law enforcement officials had to send out for more boxes from U-Haul, Wal-Mart, and Lowes in Bluefield and Princeton, twenty-two and twenty-seven miles away, respectively. They also obtained some additional boxes from a dumpster owned by the bank itself. As it got dark, they still had not finished and had to secure the property in order to come back the following day and complete the excavation.

In all, they carried away 469 boxes of paper documents, as well as bank proof tapes and microfilm as recent as June 30, 1999—just sixty days before the bank failed. In the annals of bank failures, this was unprecedented.

For Church, this period of time was particularly difficult. The bank's failure and the searches of her ranch were clearly an ordeal, but they were not the only source of stress in her life. The day before the second search commenced, Church was in Pennsylvania making the decision to take her stepmother off life support. Church's stepmother died on the first day of the massive excavation of the ranch. Law enforcement did not know of Church's absence, or the reason for it, until they started to execute the search warrant.

Friday, October 15th

Right after her stepmother's wake, Church got a frantic call from the wife of Michael Graham. Gail Graham was crying and Church asked, "What's the matter?" Gail responded, "They arrested Mike and took him away." She added, "Terry, there is a warrant out for your arrest, too."

Church returned to the Keystone area, and was arraigned on October 18, 1999. She was formally indicted on November 10th for obstruction of a federal bank examination.

Building where the First National Bank of Keystone was located. It now houses the Keystone City Hall and Police Department. On the side of the building is the bank's motto, "Time Tried – Panic Tested."

Keystone Hardware Store, located next to the First National Bank of Keystone. It was purchased by Terry Church for her husband.

The abandoned Keystone schoolhouse where the bank stored some of its documents.

2

J. Knox McConnell and the Rise of the Bank

Be not afraid of greatness;
some are born great,
some achieve greatness and
some have greatness thrust upon them.
—Malvolio, *Twelfth Night*

J. Knox McConnell arrived at the First National Bank in Keystone, West Virginia, as its new president in 1977. McConnell was a controlling person, but colorful and ambitious.

McConnell claimed to have grown up poor, but his father was a merchant, and apparently had enough money to send Knox to prep school and then on to college. According to Knox, his father was also the mayor of their little town outside of Pittsburgh—Clairton, which was later the setting for the movie *The Deer Hunter*. However, the town of Clairton has no record of a McConnell ever having been mayor. There is a McConnell listed in the archives, but that individual ran for mayor in 1929 and lost.

Not only did McConnell not grow up poor, when he died, his estate was recorded as being worth more than $23 million. By all accounts, though, he lived like a poor person. Some people said he frequently wore the same inexpensive suit. Up until the last six months of his life, he lived in a small, rented apartment, after which he moved to a small, one-story house. The house was sparsely furnished, with a low-end couch and a TV in one room and a bed in another. He usually just drove a Buick—nothing fancy.

McConnell's obituary would later claim that he had graduated from Stanford University with a graduate degree. However, it did not specify what year he graduated, the type of graduate degree he received, or his field of study. Furthermore, Stanford has no record of his ever having attended, let alone having graduated.

His obituary also claimed that he "Served as Company Commander of the 82nd Airborne." However, it did not list what company, battalion, or brigade he was attached to. His discharge papers indicate that he was inducted into the army on December 14, 1945—after the conclusion of World War II—became a corporal on May 29, 1946, and was honorably discharged at that rank on November 4, 1946, having served ten months and twenty days and having seen no foreign service. As a noncommissioned officer, whose highest rank was that of corporal and who served for less than one year, it is not possible for him to have been a "Company Commander," a rank reserved for commissioned officers.

* * *

Even his banking career had some question marks. In 1960, after working for a number of different banks, McConnell became involved in organizing a new bank by the name of the Conemaugh Valley Bank in Blairsville, Pennsylvania. However, the bank across the street from where the new bank was to be located filed a formal complaint, asserting that the new bank should not be allowed to open. The contesting bank argued that the town had a "pitifully small population" of only 9,091, was too small to support a second bank, and, further, was decreasing in size. In addition, it noted that both the state banking regulator and the OCC had previously disapproved branch bank applications due to the poor economy of the area. The contesting bank argued that the economic conditions had only gotten worse since then.

In spite of the arguments against establishing a new bank, the State Department of Banking approved the application—disregarding the department's chief examiner's recommendation to deny it. In doing so, the department amassed a 474-page record, but failed to explain its decision in any way and failed to set forth even the most cursory of findings or conclusions. These deficiencies, at a minimum, should have caused the case to be remanded to the banking superintendent for a written explanation. However, the reviewing court—the Supreme Court of Pennsylvania—upheld the Banking Department's decision based solely on the fact that the banking superintendent had approved the application. There was no real judicial review—just a rubber stamp.

McConnell's version of the story of how the Pennsylvania Supreme Court reviewed the case and decided in his favor underscores the questionable nature of his actions.

In his autobiography, McConnell noted that the chief judge of the Supreme Court of Pennsylvania was John C. Bell, Jr., and that his brother, Bert Bell, was the Commissioner of the National Football League. McConnell said that he went to see a friend in the professional sports world—the former boxer Billy Conn—to ask if he could intercede. According to McConnell, Conn took him to see Art Rooney, the president of the Pittsburgh Steelers:

> We went down to see Mr. Rooney at the Steelers' office in the Pittsburgher Hotel . . . After a while, Mr. Rooney sat back in his chair and said, "Young man, something like this cannot be fixed and I can tell you now I would not fix anything even if I could, but I do believe you are worth working with. Now leave me alone and let me see what I can do." I told Mr. Rooney I did not want anything fixed for I, too, did not work that way. I just wanted a fair deal. . . .
>
> Exactly fourteen weeks later, the Pennsylvania Supreme Court ruled in my favor. . . .

Of course, the whole story was most likely completely made up by McConnell. The idea that the president of the Pittsburgh Steelers would get involved in a case like this for someone he did not know (even though Rooney knew Billy Conn) strains credulity. That the Bells would discuss the case and would somehow conspire to "fix" the case is even more unbelievable. But the notion that McConnell, while professing unbounded integrity, would think that these conversations reflected an appropriate way to conduct business, not to mention judicial proceedings, is not at all difficult to believe. Curiously, it was Chief Justice Bell who authored the decision allowing the new bank to open—a fact that may have led McConnell to retroactively concoct the story. There is no way of knowing for sure.

* * *

In June, 1975, after working as a banker in the Pittsburgh area, McConnell went to Saipan for two years to be the president of the Micronesia Development Bank. He was accompanied by his friend, companion—and secret lover—Billie Cherry. She expected him to marry her—but he never did. Many of her friends thought that they were nothing more than "very good friends" (she did his laundry, bought his clothes, cooked his meals, and helped him entertain), but court records indicate that their relationship was much more—it just never resulted in marriage. When he returned from Saipan, he landed the position with the First National Bank of Keystone in Keystone, West Virginia, and brought her along again, as well as her friend, Terry Church.

McConnell, if nothing else, was a great networker, and relied heavily on personal connections—especially political connections. McConnell was a staunch Republican and, in fact, was a friend of President George H. W. Bush. McConnell was, apparently, the finance chairman for the State of West Virginia for Bush's 1988 and 1992 presidential campaigns. McConnell also served on the 1988 George Bush for President National Steering Committee. In turn, Bush appointed McConnell to the National Small Business Advisory Council of the Small Business Administration in 1989. The closeness of the friendship is reflected in a handwritten note from Bush to McConnell on White House stationery on April 19, 1989:

> Dear Knox—I'm now caught up with your correspondence. I can't reply to each note; but as I told you I do enjoy hearing from you— Great seeing you! Warm Regards from all Bushes—George

One of McConnell's other big claims to fame was knowing the light heavyweight/heavyweight boxer Billy Conn, mentioned above. Given McConnell's propensity for tall tales, some of the bank directors did not know whether to believe the story until Conn showed up for dinner in Keystone once. McConnell said that his father took him to a prize fight in 1935, when McConnell was eight years old. He said he met the boxer then and they became life-long friends. McConnell always said that he emulated Conn.

In fact, McConnell claimed that it was Conn who encouraged him to go into a career of banking. As recounted in his autobiography, titled *The Boxer and the Banker*, McConnell states that he was having difficulty deciding what to do with his life:

> I went up to see the Champ one night and told him I was really mixed up; I didn't know what to do. Out of the clear blue sky, he said, "If I were you, kid, I would be a banker. They go to work at 9:00 AM and leave at 2:00 PM and all day long they sit and look at the most wonderful stuff in the world—money."

Unfortunately, McConnell pursued this advice more like a follower of the infamous bank robber, Willie Sutton, than Billy Conn. Sutton, of course, when asked why he robbed banks, reportedly answered, "Because that is where the money is."

Conn, McConnell's hero, was an honest man. Although most people do not recognize his name now, he was a boxing icon. Almost like a Hollywood story, Conn showed up at a gym in Pittsburgh at the age of fourteen, weighing only 125 pounds with a 6′1″ frame.[1] He had no experience, but caught the eye of the boxing trainer, and, at the age of sixteen, had his first professional fight—which he lost.[2]

Despite a rocky start, Conn went on to have a 46-10-1 record by the time he captured the light heavyweight crown at the age of twenty-one.[3] He successfully defended the title three times, and gave up his title to go into the heavyweight division.[4] Conn won all seven of his heavyweight bouts before getting a chance to fight the great Joe Louis on June 18, 1941, at the New York Polo Grounds.[5]

The Pittsburgh Pirates, Conn's hometown team, were playing that night, but the team's management decided to interrupt the game in the third inning to broadcast the fight live to the baseball fans.[6] It is the only time in Major League Baseball history that a game has been interrupted in this fashion.[7]

In one of the ten best professional boxing fights of all times, Conn outfought Louis for most of the first twelve rounds.[8] Conn was lighter and faster than Louis; Louis was sluggish and seemingly out of training.[9] Going into the thirteenth round, Conn was ahead on the scoring cards of the referee and two judges: 7-5, 7-4-1, and 6-6.[10] However, between the twelfth and thirteenth rounds, Conn announced to his handlers that he wanted to go for a knockout: "I can take this sonuvabitch out this round."[11] They told him, "No, no, Billy."[12]

Conn came out in the thirteenth round and was dominating Joe Louis, but it was never a good idea to go toe-to-toe with Joe Louis. Eventually, Louis, with a thirty-pound advantage,[13] got through Conn's defenses and landed a series of right–left combinations. Conn knew if he could just fall and take most of the count, he would lose the round, but, perhaps, could go on to win the fourteenth and fifteenth rounds.[14] He told himself, "Fall! Fall!"[15] But for some reason he could not, and Louis hit him again and again. Conn finally went down and the count began. He started to stagger to his feet at about the count of eight, but he was called out, with two seconds left remaining in the round.[16]

The Pirates resumed play against the N.Y. Giants, but the game was called due to a rule at that time that no inning could start after 11:50 PM. It ended up as a 2-2 tie.

Conn lost the fight, but had succeeded in making the world stand still—or at least the Pittsburgh Pirates and their fans—at least for one night.

McConnell wanted to be like Billy Conn and to be number one, but McConnell had neither the talent nor integrity to do so legitimately.[17]

* * *

Between 1977 and 1992, McConnell operated the First National Bank of Keystone as a typical, small community bank. The only regulatory issue was that he made a lot of out-of-area loans to doctors in Pittsburgh. Out-of-area loans can be a problem because they are indicative of a bank not serving its community and because the loans are harder to monitor. But there was very little business or money in the Keystone area, the loans to the doctors were sound, and McConnell had strong connections to Pittsburgh. Mostly through this out-of-area lending, McConnell was able to grow the bank from a very small size, with total assets of $17 million in 1977, to a bank of moderate size, with $102 million in total assets by 1992.

Early on, one relatively small-time fraud McConnell became involved in related to the sale of $100,000 certificates of deposit (CDs). In order to avoid paying the high interest rates prevalent at that time for the CDs, McConnell would agree to give the depositor a Cadillac instead of the going return on the CD. The local Cadillac dealer was willing to go along with the scheme because the high interest rates had caused the automobile market to become stagnant, and the dealer was behind in paying for his financing at the bank for the "floor planning," or purchasing, of the cars he was trying to sell.

Pursuant to the scheme, at the end of five years, the depositor got the Cadillac and the principal from the CD. However, due to the fact that the market value of the car was greater than what the car dealer owed on his loan for the car, the bank had to refund him the difference. What happened, though, was the dealer and McConnell personally split the refund. So McConnell ended up pocketing $2,000 to $3,000 for each car deal, based on services provided by the bank.

It was not until McConnell and the bank got involved in the business of subprime mortgages, though, that the fraud at the bank really took off.

* * *

In 1992, the bank started to become involved in the purchase of subprime mortgages. In February of that year, McConnell and Cherry went to a conference in California conducted by an expert in the area, Daniel Melgar. The conference touted the merits of Title One loans,[18] and McConnell became intrigued.

The purpose of the Title One program is to encourage lending institutions to finance home improvement projects to preserve the nation's existing housing market and to support the construction industry. The loan proceeds can only be used for "property improvements that protect or improve the basic livability or utility of the property." In addition, the loans are limited to $25,000 in amount and twenty years in duration. There are additional, complicated limitations concerning loan-to-value ratios and the borrowers' fixed income versus gross income. The Federal Housing Administration (FHA) provides some insurance for the loans, but the insurance is limited and is subject to various technical restrictions.

Neither McConnell nor anyone else at the bank knew anything about Title One loans or their intricacies. Nonetheless, he had his number-two person, Terry Church, look into the possibility of having the bank become involved in purchasing these kinds of loans from all over the country. He gave her Melgar's card and said, "Call this man. I want to know in ten words or less if we can make money using him."

The next month, March, 1992, Church traveled to California to review potential loans for purchase. She ended up purchasing $3 million worth of Title One loans from Master Financial, a loan originator which Melgar allegedly touted as a "qualified FHA Title I lender and an excellent marketing organization."[19]

Upon review of this acquisition, the OCC—the federal banking regulator in charge of supervising the bank—determined that the bank's purchase violated the law. The bank had exceeded the amount a national bank can loan to any one person (or the amount of loans it can acquire from one entity). In order to remedy the violation, Melgar suggested that, instead of selling the Title One loans outright to another institution, the bank could sell them through the process of securitization.

This process involves buying a certain number of similar loans (in this case, subprime mortgages); analyzing them; packaging them together as a security; having them rated by a rating agency; retaining an underwriter, a trustee, an insurance company (to supplement the FHA insurance), and a loan servicer; and then dividing up the package of loans into tranches or segments that can be sold to sophisticated investors. It is not an easy or inexpensive task. In addition, it requires a number of people, including financial experts, attorneys and accountants.

It is a method of making many more loans than the bank could otherwise make. If it held the loans itself, the bank would be required to hold a sufficient amount of capital to protect against potential losses. However, by selling the loans into a securitization deal, the bank moves the loans off its own books and, thus, is freed up to make additional loans, almost on an endless basis. In theory, because the securitization process involves the accumulation of a large pool of loans, the risk of default associated with individual loans is dispersed among the many loans.[20]

The problems pertaining to the securitization process include the fact that it involves the acquisition and analysis of many more loans than is normal; is a very complicated process, as noted above; and involves a lot of up-front fees and expenses—to pay the loan originators, the trustee, the loan servicers, the entity providing insurance for the securitization, the lawyers and the accountants, not to mention to pay for the loans themselves. It can prove to be very risky, especially for the uninitiated, and especially when it involves already risky assets, such as subprime mortgages.

In spite of all of this—or perhaps just due to ignorance—McConnell told Church to review the securitization process and to see if the bank could get involved in this high-risk type of sophisticated investment. Church allegedly had to look up the term "securitization" before she started.

McConnell thought he had finally found a way for him—and his bank—to become number one.

* * *

Between 1993 and 1998, the bank entered into nineteen securitizations, starting at $33 million for the first deal and ending up at $565 million for the last deal; comprising $2.7 billion altogether in purchased and securitized loans. As a result of these securitizations, the bank grew from $102 million in total assets in 1992 to $280 million in total assets by 1995.[21] That was not enough for McConnell. By the next year, the bank had increased its total assets to $528 million.[22] By 1997, its total assets were $836 million and, at the time the bank failed in 1999, its reported total assets were $1.1 billion.[23] That represented more than a sixty-fold increase since McConnell took over the bank in 1977.

Based on something known as "gain-on-sale" accounting, the bank, starting in 1993, was able to immediately book its anticipated profits from the securitizations, without waiting to see how the deals actually panned out. Unfortunately, all but one of the securitizations were unprofitable.[24]

In spite of that, the bank continued to report huge earnings. Throughout most of the 1990s, the bank was named by the *American Banker* as one of the most profitable large community banks in the entire country.[25] Specifically, as set forth in the footnoted chart, the bank was reported to be the most profitable large community bank in the entire country for three years in the 1990s—1994, 1995, and 1998—out of more than five thousand banks.[26] The likelihood of this happening legitimately was miniscule, especially at a small, insignificant bank in rural West Virginia, but the marketplace never seriously questioned it.

The Keystone bank was not even on the list of the top hundred earning banks in 1992. In the very next year, however, the bank was number two. The following year, it was number one. This growth in income and assets was astronomical. The regulators were aware of it and thought that something was wrong, but did not know exactly what it was.

In fact, the bank was falsifying its assets and its income. The extent of this fraud was so great that the senior management was able to embezzle millions of dollars from the bank without being detected. They were taking out unauthorized fees and spending the money on houses, ranches, bed and breakfasts, marinas, vehicles, motorcycles, guns—just about everything.

* * *

The fraud that was uncovered at the bank—and that caused the bank to fail—was committed against the OCC, the FDIC, the bank's shareholders, and the bank's depositors; especially the uninsured depositors. In one particularly sad case, an uninsured depositor, Mack Wright, committed suicide on June 5, 2001, at the age of 57. He had begun working right after college. At the age of 35, he had already started saving for his retirement. His parents had been very frugal, and he, in turn, wanted to leave his children an inheritance. He had two accounts at the bank at the time of its failure, each with more than $100,000. He had previously asked the bank if he should move part of his money out of the bank to keep the funds within the FDIC-insured deposit limit of $100,000,[27] but was assured by management that the bank was strong and that his funds were safe. After the bank failed, he started to become very concerned about money. He had planned to retire, but he felt he could not. He simply continued to work. But he never stopped talking about the bank and he tried to watch every penny. He and his wife stopped going out to eat and he even started to complain when his family used paper towels, because they were not reusable. He slipped into depression and jumped to his death from a bedroom window fifty feet off the ground. He left behind a wife of thirty-five years, a son, a daughter, a son-in-law, and two grandchildren.

The fraud was also against the outside directors of the bank. Most of the directors had long-standing ties to the bank and to the community. Director Victor Budnick's father had been a director of the bank for thirty-one years, and his father before him had been a director since 1929. Director Louis Pais' brother was also a director and was the chairman of the board of the bank until his death. The Pais family had been connected with the bank since it was chartered in 1903.

After the bank's failure, the outside directors were devastated. According to Director Michael Gibson, "it certainly shortened the lives of Pais and Budnick, both of whom had impeccable reputations in the community and who had done great service to the community and were successful business people."

Gibson, in turn, wondered if—instead of a Scarlet A—he had a Scarlet K, for Keystone, affixed to his reputation. He had thought about resigning from the board because the business of the bank was just too complex and was too far outside the realm of his experience, but he thought he could continue to assist the bank and the community. As he noted, most directors of a small bank are simply members of the community and do not have expertise in banking, let alone securitizations:

> They're traditionally not banking experts. They are traditionally not accountants. They are members of the community who ostensibly have good heads on their shoulders and are dedicated to promoting the safety and soundness of the bank, and, what they don't know, they get qualified experts.

However, the experts let the bank down. The bank's outside accounting firm, Grant Thornton, did not find the fraud. And the one capable expert briefly employed by Keystone, Owen Carney, was fired.[28] The board was helpless with regard to the former situation and was not strong enough to prevent the latter.

The fraud at the bank and its failure also affected the public in general, especially the impoverished town of Keystone, which had become reliant on the bank as the second largest employer in the county.

* * *

It was initially projected by the FDIC that the failure of the First National Bank of Keystone was to be one of the ten largest commercial bank failures since the Great Depression. In the end, it was the sixty-ninth largest failure out of the 4,083 banks that failed between 1934 and December, 2015.[29]

With its subprime mortgages and securitizations, it was also a harbinger of the 2008 financial crisis—but it went virtually unnoticed and unstudied.[30]

Notes

1. Angelo Prospero, "Billy Conn—The One and Only Pittsburgh Kid," http://www.billyconn.net/articles/BILLY_CONN_the_one_and_only_Pgh_kid.htm; BoxRec, http://boxrec.com/list_bouts.php?human_id=009007&cat=-boxer. BoxRec.
2. Id.
3. BoxRec.
4. Id.; Sam Gregory, "Billy Conn—Joe Louis fight," *East Side Boxing*, June 4, 2007, http://www.eastsideboxing.com/news.php?p=10504&more=1.
5. BoxRec; Frank Deford, "The Boxer and the Blonde," *Sports Illustrated*, June 17, 1985.
6. Id.
7. Confirmed by Major League Baseball, April 24, 2012.
8. Deford, "The Boxer and the Blonde," ("Men had been slugging it out for eons, and there had been 220 years of prizefighting, and there would yet be Marciano and the two Sugar Rays and Ali, but this was it. This was the best it had ever been and ever would be, the 12th and 13th rounds of Louis and Conn on a warm night in New York just before the world went to hell."); Mike Casey, "Sometimes a great notion: Billy Conn," *East Side Boxing*, March 14, 2009, http://www.eastsideboxing.com/news.php?p=19061&more=1; Gregory, "Billy Conn—Joe Louis fight."
9. Casey, "Sometimes a great notion."
10. Deford, "The Boxer and the Blonde."
11. Id.
12. Id.
13. Id.
14. Id.
15. Id.
16. Id.
17. Another famous individual who wanted to be like Billy Conn was Marlon Brando's character in the 1954 classic, "On the Waterfront." In the famous

scene toward the end of the movie, just before Brando says, "I coulda been a contender," his brother, played by Rod Steiger, says, "You could have been another Billy Conn."

18. The loans are called "Title One" loans due to the fact that Title One of the National Housing Act in 1934 authorized the loans as part of a property improvement loan program. It is the oldest such program in the country.

19. The Title One loan program is administered by the FHA, which is part of the Department of Housing and Urban Development (HUD). So, frequently, people will refer to Title One loans as FHA Title One loans and/or HUD Title One loans.

20. However, this, in fact, is misleading in terms of the entire financial system. As Lawrence Lindsey, a former Federal Reserve governor explained, securitization can diversify the risk, but it does not reduce the risk. He said, "You as an individual can diversify your risk. The system as a whole, though, cannot reduce the risk. And that's where the confusion lies." The Financial Crisis Inquiry Report, "Report of the National Commission on the Causes of the Financial and Economic Crisis in the United States," January, 2011, 45.

21. *American Banker* article, June 10, 1996.

22. *American Banker* article, June 3, 1997.

23. *American Banker* articles, June 11, 1998, June 8, 1999.

24. The one small exception was a deal that broke even, described later in the book.

25. *American Banker* articles, June 8, 1993, June 10, 1994, June 7, 1995, June 10, 1996, June 3, 1997, June 11, 1998 and June 8, 1999. All of the ensuing data is derived from these *American Banker* reports.

26.

Year	Key-stone ROAA (Return On Average Assets)	Key-stone ROAE (Return On Average Equity)	Key-stone standing (based on ROAA)	Mean ROAA for all large community banks	Mean ROAE for all large community banks	Key-stone net income ($000)	Number of large community banks
1992	1.87	18.44	Not in the top 100	1.09	12.69	1,817	5,578
1993	6.66	55.75	2	1.20	13.27	7,233	5,564
1994	7.53	47.85	1	1.18	12.62	10,084	5,587
1995	9.51	62.55	1	1.23	13.02	20,817	5,395
1996	8.96	66.11	4	1.22	12.86	40,600	5,760
1997	3.90	21.81	3	1.31	15.72	25,111	N/A
1998	7.24	42.98	1	N/A	N/A	69,300	N/A

As shown in the chart, the bank's ROAA increased by over 500% between 1992 and 1995. The bank's ROAE increased by approximately 360% between

1992 and 1996. Also, the bank's 1995 ROAA was over 770% greater than the average for all large community banks. Its 1996 ROAE was over 500% larger than the average for all large community banks.

The bank's net income increased four-fold in one year, between 1992 and 1993, after it started securitizing subprime mortgages. Between 1993 and 1996, the bank's income increased another 560%.

27. The FDIC insurance limit has subsequently been raised to $250,000.
28. As explained in Chapter Eight, Owen Carney was the president of the Keystone bank for a very short time.
29. FDIC statistics. At the time it failed, the bank was the forty-second largest failure, based on its actual losses of approximately $532 million, which were down from the original estimate of over $800 million in losses. If the latter number had held true, the failure would have been the twenty-first largest bank failure at the time it failed. According to FDIC figures, the losses initially attributable to the Keystone failure represented almost 35% of all losses the FDIC incurred between 1997 and 2002.
30. Although the financial crisis technically started in 2007 and continued into 2009, for sake of ease, it will be referred to as the 2008 financial crisis.

3

Billie Cherry, Terry Church, and the Town of Keystone, West Virginia

Nearly all men can stand adversity,
but if you want to test a man's character,
give him power.
—Francois Duc de la Rochefoucauld

Billie Cherry arrived in Keystone on Halloween night in 1977, as Knox McConnell's assistant and companion. Later, she became a prominent local patron of the arts. In April, 1991, with McConnell's backing, she was appointed by President George H. W. Bush to the President's Advisory Committee on the Arts for the John F. Kennedy Center in Washington, D.C. She was Keystone's first female—and first Republican—mayor. She also owned a bed and breakfast just outside of town, called the Cherry Key Inn.[1]

Behind her bed and breakfast, Cherry had built something of a replica of London's Globe Theatre for the benefit and use of a local artist and playwright she was supporting. The theatre, however, never looked much like Shakespeare's original theatre and was built only a couple hundred yards from the train tracks, making it difficult to hear the actors—and adding an anachronistic dimension to such plays as *Julius Caesar*—when the trains passed by.

A few towns away, Cherry also owned a beautiful, historic house called Jones Mansion. The house is known for its lavish features, including twenty-eight Omega-shaped windows in a 112-foot long ballroom. The windows contain original lead glass and were created, in part, with sixty-six stained glass windows imported from Scotland.[2] The house is situated high up on a hill and was built by one of the original coal barons of the area, James Elwood Jones, whose father had come over from Wales.[3] The house is also known as "Murder Mansion" due to a grisly triple murder that occurred in the house on February 14, 1998.[4]

Starting in 1978, Cherry was, at various times, the bank's comptroller, head cashier, and head of the bookkeeping department.

At the time the bank failed, Cherry was seventy-five years old, and was viewed as a venerable grandmother. She was a generous benefactor to many and was loved by the bank employees and many in the town.

* * *

Terry Church arrived in Keystone with Cherry in 1977. She started as the bank's internal auditor, and then became the compliance officer and eventually a loan officer. In 1980, she was made an assistant vice president and, in 1992, after working at the bank for fifteen years, she became a senior vice president. In 1995, she acquired the exalted and incomprehensible title of senior executive vice president.

Beginning in 1993, she ran the securitization business of the bank and, by at least 1995, was running the bank. McConnell, by this time, had become a figurehead at the bank, spending most of his time writing letters to the OCC complaining about almost everything and writing letters to state and national political figures. According to his secretary, he was writing to former President George H. W. Bush almost every day.

When McConnell died in 1997, the issue arose as to who would succeed him as president and chairman of the board of the bank. Even though Church was really running the bank, she, for some reason, did not want these titles.

Church and the other senior management knew that if McConnell's positions were given to the wrong person—that is, someone they could not control—their whole enterprise would be in jeopardy. So Church decided that Cherry would be a good choice. She was well known in the community and had been affiliated with the bank for two decades. The fact that she was aging and knew nothing about the bank's primary business—securitizing subprime mortgages—was not important to Church.

As Barbara Nunn, an employee of the bank, explained:

> Ms. Church had told Mr. Graham . . . what were they going to do now that McConnell was dead, that she could not afford for anyone else to come in the bank and be on the board, they would have . . . to get

Ms. Cherry to take the president's position, because then [Church] could control her and tell her what she needed done.

* * *

Like Cherry, Church was very generous, but many believed that her generosity was intended, at least in part, to buy loyalty and to pay for silence.

Church also instilled a strong element of fear in the bank employees. As Ellen Turpin noted:

> Terry could put the fear. She could scare your—Terry was very—I don't know how to put it. She was scary. You respected her, but if you didn't do what she said, you knew you were out the door.

Penny Kosa, a bank employee, put it simply, "She was kind of intimidating." McKinney, who helped mark the boxes initially at the schoolhouse, acknowledged that she would do pretty much anything Church asked because she was afraid not to. She explained, "Ms. Church hired me, and Ms. Church could fire me."

Deborah Shrader, another employee at the bank, said:

> You didn't tell her no. . . . You did not tell her no. She was my boss. She didn't ask, she just told you to do it, and you never said no. I don't think there was anyone in the bank that would tell her no. . . .
>
> I said no one told her no. I was scared to tell her no. . . . She was my boss. You didn't question her. When she told you to do something, you did it.

This went for the ranch employees too. As T. G. Church, the employee who dug the hole and buried many of the documents on the ranch, said, "Well, when Terry would call to have something done, you really would just do whatever was told—you know, they would tell you to do."

There was also a large degree of paranoia, as Turpin testified:

Q. Did you have an understanding of what would happen to you or your fellow employees if you told Grant Thornton [the bank's auditors] that you suspected the financial records contained false information?

A. Yes, sir.

Q. What would have been the consequence?

A. You would have been fired or worse.

Q. Firing I understand. "Or worse" is a subjective thing. Or worse, you might have been subjected to some sort of physical reprisal?

A. Rumor was at that time that Terry was in the Mafia and that she had people that had left there or that she had gotten rid of or whatever, that she had threatened them physically.

There was never any proof of ties to the Mafia. While there was plenty of money floating around, the bank was located in the desolate, backwater of West Virginia. The senior bank managers were simply embezzling money and dummying up the books of the bank. There was no other known type of fraud or criminal activity. Yet the fear persisted. There was even talk of someone called "The Sheik" who might visit you if you did something to upset the senior bank management. These were all rumors, though. Nothing could be proven.

But, reinforcing the paranoia, the employees started to believe that the bank's walls had ears. According to Turpin, Church heard everything, knew everything:

> Again, you were scared of losing your job. No matter who you told, they were going to [tell] Terry. Terry would know who told them like that. It was often said that our walls had ears because it never failed, when you talked about something not happening or something happening, it—I don't know how to explain it.
>
> Whenever you would talk about something that Terry said would happen or something, then it hadn't happened for six months, then all of a sudden, Terry came up with this idea, like she said, "We're going to have a staff meeting next week." Well, six months later, we don't have one and somebody brings it up, "Why didn't we have that staff meeting Terry talked about six months ago?" That evening we had it. I mean, it was just weird things that happened.

Whether it was keeping a job, fear, or outright paranoia, bank employees did as Church told them—even when it was illegal. Turpin succinctly reflected the sentiment of many of the bank employees when she testified as follows:

Q. Did you ever agree with them to do illegal things?
A. I done what I was told.

Doing what you were told was exactly what Church seemingly wanted and expected.

She owned the one convenience store in town, the one hardware store in town, a construction company, and the large ranch on top of Burke Mountain. She was the head of the only bank. Aside from

Cherry's bed and breakfast, there was not much else in or around Keystone. Many people were beholden to Church—especially the employees of the bank.

In this regard, bank employee Patricia Orell explained why she signed a falsified document for Church as follows:

> Because when Terry told you to do something, you did it. And, you know, nobody argued or—you know, if she told you to do it, you did it. If not, you know—if I didn't sign this, I knew I'd have been fired on the spot.

Unfortunately for Church, right after Orell testified to this, Church's attorney violated a cardinal rule of cross-examination by having Orell repeat her testimony, only in a more damaging fashion for his client:

> Q. [A]s you testified . . . you said you would have been fired on the spot. Did you ever see anybody fired on the spot—
> A. No.
> Q. by Ms. Church?
> A. No, because nobody ever did anything against her.

Actually, that was not true. One brave soul, Meredith Hale, dared. And she was fired on the spot.

Hale had only made it through the eighth grade, but later got her high school Graduate Equivalence Diploma and attended various colleges, though she never got a college degree. She went to work for the bank in 1994, without any previous banking or financial experience, and was assigned to the IT section of the bank, but without any title. However, Hale was exceedingly bright. She learned a lot about the bank's securitization business—enough to help another bank, United National Bank, in Wheeling, West Virginia, put together a securitization deal after the Keystone bank stopped doing its own securitizations.

One day in May or June of 1999, Terry Church came to Hale and asked her to fill in the data gaps in an inventory list of Keystone loans that Church had prepared. Hale knew that United had purchased many of the loans from Keystone and was holding them in anticipation of Keystone buying the loans back for a potential securitization. In reviewing and updating the inventory list, Hale noticed that the vast majority of the loans—approximately $360 million out of $400 million—were really owned by United and should not have been on a list purporting to represent Keystone's loans. So she deleted United's loans from the list and handed the inventory back to Church:

> I give this back to Terry. Terry comes up to my desk and says, "This is not the file that [I gave you], what happened to all of the loans?" I said, "Well, I took off all those loans because they belong to United," and she said, "They don't belong to United, they belong to Keystone," and I said, "Well, United paid the principal balance on the [loans], United paid the premium on the [loans], and United paid the accrued interest on the [loans]." I said, "As far as my books are concerned, United National owns . . . those loans."[5]
>
> She told me that I needed to do what I was told and stop thinking that I know everything. She told me to "Put the file back the way she had it." I told her "No." I said, "I'm not doing it." I said, "It's not inventory [owned by Keystone] and I'm not going to call it inventory [owned by Keystone]." She told me "Either do what [you're] told or go away," and I said, "Well, I can get my stuff and leave now," and she said, "No, let's make it official; yesterday was your last day." I just picked up my stuff and left.

As Hale left, Church issued the following threat: "I will see you dead first before I let you destroy what I've worked all these years to build."

What Hale had no way of knowing is that she had uncovered the heart of a massive fraud that Church and others in the bank were perpetrating, which, in a few months, would result in the failure of the bank and a massive loss to the FDIC deposit insurance fund.

* * *

Other than Hale, no one had dared to stand up to Church because there were few, if any, other job alternatives—and the women at the bank could not afford to lose their jobs.[6] McKinney's husband was not employed at that time; she, with three children at home, was the only one working. Turpin was supporting three families. And Orell had a new baby at home, a seven-year-old son, and a husband who had been laid off from the coal mines and who was close to going on permanent disability.

* * *

Coal mining was what had made Keystone a boomtown. But with the decline of coal mining, it had become a small and economically depressed town.

The first load of coal was carried out of the Keystone area on the Norfolk and Western Railway in 1883, and McDowell County, where Keystone is situated, was relatively prosperous for a long time afterward.[7] Keystone itself was named in 1892 for the Keystone Coal & Coke Company out of Greensburg, Pennsylvania. Prior to that, it had been known as Cassville. The town was incorporated in 1909, and its population went from 1,088 in 1900 to 2,942 in 1940—a 270% increase.

The town of Keystone is only about seventy miles from the infamous area where the Hatfields and McCoys feuded. Keystone itself was a wild mining town with the particular distinction of having had a notorious red-light district known as Cinder Bottom, apparently named for the accumulation of cinders in that area of town from the coke ovens.[8] It was also known as the "Sodom and Gomorrah of McDowell County's early coal fields."[9]

According to an oral history, the town of Keystone and, in particular, Cinder Bottom, was a crazy place:

> Well, someone was killed down there about every week. There was gambling, hustling, numbers playing, prostitution. You could buy whiskey, any kind you wanted: Scotch, bourbon, good moonshine, bad moonshine, almost-good moonshine. And home brew. Every other door, or every three or four doors there was a house you could buy whiskey, or something else. And if that's not wide open, I don't know what you would call it.[10]

However, after the 1940s, Keystone started to decline in population and in income. In 1960, Keystone's population was only 1,457—less than half of what it was in 1940—and was inexorably declining. By 2000—the year after the bank failed—there were only 453 people residing in the town.

The town of Keystone continued to decline. In 2010, a little more than ten years after the bank failed, the town's population was down to 282, less than 10% of what it was in its heyday.

At the time the bank failed, Keystone's per capita income was only $7,033, the second lowest in the state of West Virginia, already a poor state. Approximately 46% of the town's population lived below the poverty line. One newspaper account after the bank's failure said that the town "looks like a movie set left over from Coal Miner's Daughter."[11]

* * *

The entire county where Keystone is located was also economically depressed and had experienced the same population boom and bust as Keystone. McDowell County's population in 1890 was 7,300. In 1900, it had mushroomed to 18,747, an increase of 257%. By 1950, the population reached 98,887, a further increase of 527%. It was the third most populous county in the state.

But then it started to decline in population, and its descent was the most rapid in the state. Between 1950 and 1990, the county's population went from 98,887 to 35,233, a decline of 64%. In the 1960s, the county was a focus of President Lyndon Johnson's "War on Poverty."[12] And in the 1980s, more than 70,000 coal mining jobs were lost—representing more than 50% of the industry's jobs. By 2000, just after the bank failed, the population of the county was only 27,329, a decline of 72% from the 1950s.

In terms of income, McDowell struggled throughout the 1990s. The median household income in the county was far less than the median income not only for the United States, but also for West Virginia. As it turned out, for each year during this time, McDowell County's median income was the lowest of the entire state.

The corresponding level of poverty in McDowell County was approximately twice that of the state of West Virginia and 2.5 to 3 times the poverty level of the United States. In fact, the poverty level in McDowell County was the highest in the state each year during this time period. In 1999, the year the bank failed, there were only six counties in the entire country whose median income level was lower than McDowell County's.

McDowell County's level of poverty, while extremely high, was decreasing between 1993 and 1999. This may have been based on the profitability of the bank. However, from 1999 on, the poverty levels started to go back up. In 2009, the poverty level in McDowell County grew to a high of 40%, again the highest in the state.

* * *

With this consistent degree of low incomes and high levels of poverty, it is no wonder that the trapped bank employees would do almost anything Terry Lee Church told them to do in order to please her and to keep their jobs.

Notes

1. She was also on the nonprofit board that owned the schoolhouse where the bank stored some of its documents and personally owned another storage place which the bank used to store additional documents—at the exorbitant cost of $420,000 a year.

2. Bill Archer, "Historic McDowell County coal baron home is B&B, ATV lodge," *Bluefield Daily Telegraph*, Bluefield, WV, May 27, 2012; Jean Battlo, "Jones Mansion, The Checkered History of a McDowell County Landmark," West Virginia Traditional Life, *Goldenseal*, Summer, 2005.
3. Id.
4. The Valentine's Day murders stemmed from a ten-year love affair between Stanford (Tony) Allen, who lived in a nearby mobile home, and Jeanette Henderson, who lived in the mansion with her husband, David Henderson. David worked nights as a custodian and did not get home until 2 AM, and Jeanette's mother, Ms. Barber, who lived with them, went to bed early. So, about once a week, Allen would sneak up between those times to see Jeanette. On February 14th, Allen was high on crack cocaine and went up to the house when David, Jeanette, and her mother were all there. Allen shot them sixteen times, ten of the shots being fatal. When the state police arrived, they did not have too much trouble focusing their attention on Allen because, when one of the troopers hit the redial button on the living room phone, the call went directly to Allen's home. Allen was tried and convicted on three counts of murder and was sentenced to three consecutive life sentences.
5. Basically, what Hale is saying here is that United National Bank laid out the money to purchase the loans—usually paying a premium for the loans, as well as paying for the accrued interest.
6. Almost all of the employees at the bank were women because Knox McConnell was concerned about distracting romances within the workforce. The women were frequently referred to as "Knox's Foxes." Christopher Rhoads, "West Virginia Bank is Little Big Man of Profitability," *American Banker*, March 5, 1996.
7. Study performed by editors and authors for the Federal Reserve Banks, the Federal Reserve System, and the Brookings Institution, "The Enduring Challenge of Concentrated Poverty in America: Case Studies from Communities Across the U.S.," 2008 (Brookings Study), 110–11.
8. Jean Battlo, "Cinder Bottom, A Coalfields Red-Light District," West Virginia Traditional Life, *Goldenseal*, Summer, 1994.
9. Id.
10. Michael Kline, "'Wide Open,' Nat Reese Remembers Cinder Bottom," West Virginia Traditional Life, *Goldenseal*, Summer, 1994.
11. Timothy Roche, "Poor Town, Rich Bank," *Time*, November 1, 1999.
12. Brookings Study, 109.

4

Death of Knox McConnell

Of all escape mechanisms,
death is the most efficient.
—H. L. Mencken

Although Knox McConnell helped start the bank down the road of securitizing subprime mortgages, was involved in the falsification of the bank's earnings, and was embezzling from the bank, he did not live long enough to see the resulting failure of the bank. He died on October 26, 1997, two years before the bank failed.

On that day, McConnell had driven by himself from Keystone to Morgantown, West Virginia, for a meeting of the state's pari-mutuel betting commission. He collapsed in his hotel room shortly after checking in.

McConnell was seventy years old when he died, had not really ever taken care of himself, and was a diabetic. Consequently, his death could have easily been attributable to natural causes. However, there was a lingering suspicion on the part of many people that there may have been foul play.

Nothing could be proven, but there were some unusual circumstances surrounding his death. First, the death was unexpected. Second, someone could have easily replaced his insulin with something else. Third, his companion and lover, Billie Cherry, had secretly gotten married on June 14, 1997, just four months before, and had not told McConnell. Fourth, in spite of Cherry having just gotten married, she went with McConnell on a romantic Caribbean cruise and had returned with him only a week before his death. Who knows, but something could have gone wrong during the cruise. Fifth, beginning the day after McConnell died, Cherry and Church started to loot his estate of millions of dollars. That is not something ordinarily done to a trusted friend and mentor—and, in Cherry's case, lover.

* * *

McConnell's will, dated April 9, 1993, designated Church as the executrix of the estate. But, other than getting a possible fee for being the executrix, she was to receive nothing. Cherry was to only get a small and temporary stipend.

The stipend for Cherry was to be created through the purchase of a government security in the amount of $250,000, but she was to be given only the interest from the security and only for a period of ten years. It was estimated that this was to be about $12,500 a year. At the end of the ten years (or earlier if Cherry died), the stipend would stop.

The will left the rest of McConnell's estate to his college, Waynesburg College, in Waynesburg, Pennsylvania, to establish a scholarship in his name.

According to the probate filings, McConnell's estate was worth more than $23 million. So, in spite of this large amount of money, the woman who expected to marry him; the woman who entertained for him and who did his shopping and cooking for most of his adult life; the woman with whom he was romantically involved for forty years; and the woman with whom he went on a Caribbean cruise the week before he died—was to get only $12,500 a year and only for ten years.

Church and Cherry decided to change this.

They proceeded to pillage his estate—his safe deposit boxes; his banking accounts; his company; his bank stock; and his real estate. They changed his will by creating two backdated codicils; lied to the probate court in the process; and paid "bonuses" to various bank employees out of the estate—some bonuses being for their assistance in the process.

McConnell's Safe Deposit Boxes

McConnell died on a Sunday. The very next day, Monday, October 27th, just after lunch, Church had her employees bring in McConnell's safe deposit boxes—which she had keys to. As they were doing an inventory of the boxes, they came across McConnell's mother's diamond engagement ring.

Church said, "Here is Mr. McConnell's mother's ring." Cherry responded, "He told me he had lost it." And Church told her, "Well, here, you can have it."

So Cherry took it. Simple as that.

McConnell's Bank Accounts

The next day, Tuesday, October 28th, they started going through McConnell's four bank accounts.[1] The accounts were each in his name only, but Church had Barbara Nunn, an employee of the bank, take all the signature cards and the saving passbooks and add "or Billie Cherry" to all of the accounts. Using "or" (instead of "and") meant that the accounts would be considered as alternatively owned by either McConnell or Cherry, and, thus, the accounts could pass directly to Cherry without going through probate. It amounted to $4,282,588 that was simply transferred out of McConnell's estate for Cherry's benefit. According to Church, this was done "to correct the mistake that Knox had [made] when he left Billie's name off the accounts."

In order to accomplish the change, Nunn practiced typing "or Billie Cherry" on an electric typewriter. She used a photocopy of the signature cards and passbooks to see exactly where things lined up on the paper and how the addition would fit. In some instances, the insertion fit on the same line as McConnell's name; other times, Nunn had to put Cherry's name on the next line. The whole process took several hours, with Church standing over Nunn, and Cherry sitting silently in the room.

Then, Church had Melissa Quizenbeury, the executive vice president and cashier of the bank, add Cherry's name to the computer entries relating to McConnell's accounts. Church again explained away the change by saying "Billie's name should have been on there anyway. . . ."

When it was finished, Quizenbeury closed the joint McConnell/Cherry accounts and opened new ones in Cherry's name only—with all of the money transferred to the new accounts, to the penny.[2]

Quizenbeury knew that this was wrong and thought that, if McConnell wanted Cherry to be on his accounts, he would have added her name to them. She knew that Church's excuse was not valid.

When Church told Cherry that McConnell's accounts had been transferred to her, Cherry simple-mindedly asked, "Oh, you can do that?" Later, during her testimony in the ensuing criminal trial involving the looting of McConnell's estate, Cherry vacillated between claiming that she knew she was on the accounts, but just did not know how much was in the accounts, to admitting that she did not know anything at all about the accounts until Church told her.

She also claimed to not even know why the funds were being transferred from McConnell's accounts to hers. As she testified:

> Then Melissa [Quizenbeury] brought in three withdrawals that were related to the four savings accounts that had my name on it. And I didn't know why it went from four to three, so I asked Terry, and she said, "Well, you're to sign these."

The withdrawal slips were in the amounts of $2,071,101.37, $1,103,040.35, and $1,025,223.82, but she did not know where they were from, where they were going, or why they were being handed to her:

Q. So is it your testimony that, unbeknownst to you, these savings withdrawal slips had already been filled out by someone else?
A. Yes, sir.
. . . .
Q. Well, ma'am, if these bank accounts had your name on them all along, what were these other people doing filling out withdrawal slips for you?
A. I don't know.

It was clear, though, from subsequent questioning in the criminal trial that Cherry had never had any ownership or financial interest in the accounts:

Q. Can you explain why none of the records of the First National Bank of Keystone shows your name on any of those accounts prior to the death of McConnell?
A. I didn't know that.
Q. So you have no explanation?
A. No.
. . . .
Q. [C]an you explain why your name does not appear on any of the 1099s until after Mr. McConnell is dead?
A. No, I can't explain that.

After taking McConnell's mother's diamond ring on Monday and then silently watching as more than $4 million was transferred from his estate to her accounts Tuesday morning, Cherry calmly went out to the funeral parlor and selected McConnell's casket later that Tuesday afternoon.

The wake for McConnell was the next day, Wednesday, October, 29th. That morning, prior to what should have been a solemn, sad occasion, involving the death of a man she had been romantically connected with, Cherry went out shopping for a car. Using the ill-gotten proceeds from McConnell's bank accounts, Cherry bought a $30,000 Honda Passport for her son, Michael, from her first marriage.

McConnell's Sole Proprietorship—Marbil

Marbil was a company that McConnell created in 1993 with the assistance of Michael Graham. It was a shell company. It conducted no business; held no real estate; had no employees—except for McConnell; and did not purchase or sell any goods or provide any services. Yet it held some very valuable assets—two very large certificates of deposit.

Because McConnell's share of the funds embezzled from the bank[3] had been funneled through Marbil, it is likely that Church knew about the company. However, even though McConnell had named Marbil after his late mother, *Mar*ie, and *Bi*llie Cherry, it does not appear that Cherry knew much about it. As she put it: "[Marbil] was a company that Knox started for—I'm not really sure the purpose of it."

After McConnell died, Church, Cherry, and Graham discovered the existence of the CDs and set about to claim them for themselves. The first thing they did was to declare themselves as having been equal one-quarter owners of the company with McConnell. They then declared themselves officers of the company. Cherry became the president; Church became the vice president/secretary; and Graham the treasurer.

After that, they prepared bylaws which set forth the unusual—if not unheard of—clause that stated, upon the death of any one of the four shareholders, his or her shares would automatically be divided among the remaining shareholders, with no payment or compensation to the estate of the deceased. So the assets of Marbil owned by McConnell did not pass through probate and did not get distributed in accordance with the dictates of his will. Rather, the assets instantly became the property of the three co-conspirators.

One of the CDs owned by Marbil was in the amount of $1,838,650.89, and was held at the First State Bank and Trust Company of Rainelle, West Virginia—a small bank about a hundred miles north of Keystone. Church contacted the bank on November 3, 1997, and asked for the CD to be released, but the bank objected. If the CD had been in the name of an individual, the bank's practice would have been to release the CD upon death, with no penalty being charged for early withdrawal. However, the CD was in the name of a company, so there was going to be a penalty of about $70,000 to $80,000 for early withdrawal. The co-conspirators—Church, Cherry, and Graham—wisely decided to wait the two months until the CD matured, on December 29, 1997.

The Rainelle bank also explained to Church that, in addition to requiring the owners of Marbil to wait for the CD to mature, the bank would need some corporate records, including board minutes and a duly authorized resolution requesting the disbursement of the CD. So Church typed up minutes of board meetings that never occurred, bylaws that never existed, and a resolution that was never approved.

Once the check from the Rainelle bank was received and deposited into the Marbil account, Church had the name of the Marbil account changed to Hog Pen—the name of her husband's shell company—so the proceeds of the CD, in effect, went to Church.[4] The number of the account was not even changed.

The second CD Marbil held, in the amount of $2,836,156.23, was also cashed and transferred via the Marbil account into the Hog Pen account on the same day as the first CD. So between the two CDs, Church gained $4,674,807.12.

The question is why—given the fact that the three co-conspirators purportedly each owned a third of the Marbil company after McConnell died—Church got all of the money?

Church provided one answer to this riddle when asked about the Marbil transactions:

> Q. So is it your testimony that your friends and business associates, Mr. Graham and Mrs. Cherry, said to you, "Terry, here's $4.6 million. You've worked hard. You can keep it." Is that your testimony?
> Church: Yes, sir, it is.
> Q. You, Mrs. Church, have some very nice friends.

A second possible explanation was put forth by Nunn, who said:

> Ms. Church made a comment that Ms. Cherry took all of McConnell's money and did not give her any of it after she had made the change, so she said she was going to take the money that was in . . . Marbil's account.

In other words, Church had arranged for Cherry to get $4 million in cash from McConnell's accounts, but was annoyed that Cherry had not shared any of the money with her and so this was her way of getting back at Cherry.

According to Graham, there was a third alternative explanation—that she just took it:

> She basically said that she was taking Marbil.
>
> . . . .
>
> She just took it and we said nothing, you know.
>
> . . . .
>
> Because we didn't own any of Marbil.

He added that Church explained that McConnell "set it up [because McConnell] wanted [Church] to have Marbil and the money in the Marbil account, and that's what basically [she] set all this [the minutes and resolution, etc.] up for."

If this did not make perfect sense, there was yet a fourth explanation that, because it was primarily McConnell's share of the embezzled funds—the "appraisal" fees and the "due diligence" fees[5]—that went into the Marbil account, Church felt that she was owed the money because she was instrumental in obtaining the fees. In fact, Church—through her attorney—admitted this:

> Subsequent to the [criminal trials], Ms. Church was debriefed by agents and attorneys for the government. When asked why she took the Marbil account, whether she took that because Ms. Cherry had taken the savings accounts, Ms. Church said that no, she took it because it was hers, it was the account she and Knox used to disguise his "due diligence" fees. . . . Any services were performed by Ms. Church; she had had to share the "fees" with McConnell, and she felt that the money in the account "belonged" to her (while acknowledging that the receipt of a "due diligence" fee had not been authorized by the board of directors).

There is no way of being sure which version, or combination of versions, is correct.

With regard to the disbursement of the money in the Marbil account, Cherry, as with most everything else, was simply clueless. She admitted—even though doing so was against her interest—that there was no board meeting authorizing the cashing of the CDs and transferring them to the Hog Pen account. Further, she claimed that she did not even know about the accounts or the money, despite the fact she was the one who signed the letter to the Rainelle bank asking for the first CD to be released:

> Q. So, there wasn't a board meeting of Marbil to take a vote and say, "Let's change the name of Marbil to Hog Pen," was there?
> A. No, sir.
> Q. And on the same day there was a deposit of $2.8 million; right?
> A. Yes, sir.
> Q. Do you have any idea where that came from?
> A. No, I don't, sir.
> Q. Despite the fact that you were supposedly President of Marbil; is that right?
> A. Yes, sir.

Q.   And there is no doubt this was the Marbil account before January 2?
A.   Yes, sir.
Q.   So all of a sudden the Marbil account has $4.6 million in it; am I right?
A.   Yes, sir.

The Codicil to McConnell's Will

Having taken his mother's diamond engagement ring, misappropriated over $4 million in cash deposits from his accounts, and stolen two CDs worth $4.6 million from his company, the three co-conspirators set out to take most of the rest of McConnell's $23 million estate. They did this through the simple means of a codicil—a legal term for an addendum or amendment to a last will and testament. In order to be valid, a codicil, of course, has to be written when the person is still alive and the person has to sign it. But those issues were not insurmountable.

The funeral was in Pittsburgh, on Halloween, October 31, 1997, exactly twenty years after Church and Cherry first arrived in Keystone. This was a Friday. The following Monday, November 3rd, Church typed up the codicil.

As stated earlier, McConnell's will left his entire estate (aside from the small stipend for Cherry) to his college, Waynesburg College. The will was broken down as follows: paragraph one of the will provided for the payment of McConnell's debts; paragraph two set up the stipend for Cherry; and then paragraph three gave everything else to the college:

> The residue of my estate after being liquidated and all debts and taxes are paid shall be given to **WAYNESBURG COLLEGE, WAYNESBURG, PENNSYLVANIA TO BE USED FOR THE J. KNOX McCONNELL SCHOLARSHIP FUND**. This fund is for deserving students regardless of race, color or creed.
>
> (Emphasis in the original.)

That was it. The rest of the will had to do with the appointment of Church as the executrix and what would happen if the college ceased to exist. The will was only two and a half pages long.

So Church and her fellow conspirators decided to keep it simple in devising the codicil. It was only one page in length and modified only paragraph three of the will:

PLEASE CHANGE PAGE TWO—NUMBER 3 TO READ AS FOLLOWS:

THE RESIDUE OF MY ESTATE AFTER ALL MY DEBTS AND TAXES ARE PAID SHALL BE DIVIDED AS LISTED BELOW:

A. TRANSFER 40% OF MY STOCK IN THE FIRST NATIONAL BANK OF KEYSTONE TO WAYNESBURG COLLEGE, WAYNESBURG, PENNSYLVANIA.

B. TRANSFER 40% OF MY STOCK IN THE FIRST NATIONAL BANK OF KEYSTONE TO HARGRAVE MILITARY ACADEMY, CHATHAM, VIRGINIA.

C. TRANSFER THE REMAINING SHARES OF MY STOCK IN THE FIRST NATIONAL BANK OF KEYSTONE EQUALLY TO MY LIFETIME FRIENDS FOR THEIR HARD WORK AND DEVOTION TO ME, BILLIE J. CHERRY AND TERRY L. CHURCH OF KEYSTONE, WEST VIRGINIA.

D. MY DEVOTED SECRETARY, NANCY C. VORONO, I LEAVE $1,000.00 FOR EACH YEAR THAT SHE HAS SERVED ME.[6]

So Church and Cherry wrote themselves into the will, arranging for each to get 10% of McConnell's Keystone bank stock. In coming up with these percentages, they used a calculator to carefully figure out how much they needed—in addition to their own stock—to retain control over the bank. They could not risk the possibility of the schools—either separately or jointly—gaining control over the board and possibly replacing the officers of the bank. It took them about thirty minutes to do the necessary calculations.

It is unclear to this day why Church and Cherry added Hargrave Military Academy—McConnell's prep school—to the codicil. Church claimed that McConnell meant to include the school in his will, but the simple fact is he did not. In addition, it is unclear why Church and Cherry did not simply write Waynesburg College out of the will entirely or give it an extremely small amount of the bank stock so it would have no control over the bank or so they could easily buy the school out.

The last paragraph of the codicil, giving money to McConnell's secretary, Nancy Vorono, came about because, as they were creating the codicil, Cherry said, "Well, we need to add Nancy Vorono's name on this because of all her work and time she's done putting up with Knox." So they added McConnell's secretary to the codicil.

This greatly surprised Vorono when she learned about it. She had worked for McConnell for twenty years, but he was a difficult boss and

Vorono did not think that McConnell even liked her, let alone enough to put her in his will. So she was pleasantly surprised—until she found out the truth:

> I think it was a few weeks, or maybe a week or so after Mr. McConnell's death, Mrs. Church and I were in the lobby and we were coming up to my office, and it was like a walkway. When we got into the office, she was going through the door and she glanced over her shoulder and said, "Did you know that you are in Mr. McConnell's will?"
>
> And I said, "I am?"
>
> . . . .
>
> I was shocked, because I didn't think Mr. McConnell liked me well enough to put me in his will, and it pleased me very much that he thought of me in that way, but now I know that he didn't.

The whole process of writing and editing the codicil took about two to three hours. Church typed; Cherry read over the document; and Graham corrected some typos. However, they made a huge error which went unnoticed by the probate court and all of the attorneys involved in the subsequent litigation pertaining to the estate.

The fact that the will left almost all of McConnell's estate to his college was very straightforward and clear. The codicil, though, only addressed McConnell's stock in the First National Bank of Keystone, and none of the rest of his assets.

According to the court filings submitted by Church in probating the will, McConnell's Keystone bank stock was valued at approximately $10.5 million. His whole estate, though, was valued at over $23 million, not counting the $4.6 million in CDs held by Marbil.

Specifically, he had the bank accounts worth more than $4 million, which Cherry took. He had stock (aside from the Keystone bank stock) worth more than $1.1 million; IRAs, annuities, and insurance policies valued at $6.8 million; other checking accounts and CDs (aside from the Keystone bank accounts and the Marbil CDs) worth $430,000; and two condominiums valued at $185,000.

All of this was lost, though, when Church and Cherry failed to mention these other assets in the codicil. Paragraph three of the original will disposed of McConnell's entire estate. The codicil nullified this paragraph, and replaced it with a paragraph that only addressed McConnell's stock in the First National Bank of Keystone. The rest of the assets went into some kind of legal limbo. Later, it would be decided that it was all irrelevant, as Judge Faber (who presided over almost all of the subsequent litigation) correctly held that "McConnell did not legitimately possess the funds in his estate."[7]

* * *

According to witnesses, once the codicil was drafted, Church practiced signing McConnell's signature and then put pen to paper. After it was done, she collected up and shredded the excess copies. Graham and Nunn both signed as witnesses. Graham explained that he did so because Church asked him to. In admitting to his involvement, he noted that:

> I'd done a lot worse things than this and just never entered a protest. I just did it. I was asked to do it, and I did it.

Nunn explained that she did not want to witness the codicil, but that Church told her that she didn't trust anybody else and that it was being done to protect the bank.

Vickie Mickles, a bank employee, was then called in to notarize the codicil. In advance of this, though, Church or someone had covered up all of the document with pieces of paper taped in place so that only the signature lines were visible. The nature of the document was not visible; the content of the document was not visible; and the date of the document was not visible. It did not matter, though. Mickles wondered why everything was covered up and viewed it as unusual, but did not ask any questions. She later said that, if she had seen that the document was backdated from November 3, 1997 to May 7, 1996, she would have notarized the document anyway, "because [she] was instructed by Terry Church." Such was the kind of control Church had within the bank.

Two weeks later, on November 18, 1997, Church, Cherry, Graham, and Nunn drove from Keystone to Princeton, West Virginia, to submit the will and codicil for probate. They understood what they were about to do and were very nervous. In the car ride to the courthouse, Nunn said, "I hope everything goes okay with this and it gets recorded correctly, or we're all in trouble." Church and Cherry agreed they would be in trouble if it were ever discovered that the papers they were submitting were not McConnell's true will. Church said, "I hope this goes through so we, you know, we don't have—we don't end up going to jail for this." And Nunn responded, "I do too." As it turned out, Church and Cherry were indicted and prosecuted for embezzling from McConnell's estate, while Graham and Nunn were listed as unindicted co-conspirators in the case.

For the short term, though, the will and codicil were accepted by the clerk's office and Church was designated as the executrix of the estate.

The Second Codicil to McConnell's Will

Not content with all she had taken so far from McConnell's estate, Cherry decided that she would also like the two condominiums McConnell owned: one in Orlando, Florida and the other in Pittsburgh, Pennsylvania. Church said that it would not be a problem. As Nunn explained:

> One day, Ms. Cherry told Ms. Church that she wished that she could have [McConnell's] condos, that she was the one who used them. And Ms. Church told her it was no problem; she said she could fix a paper that said Mr. McConnell had left them to her.

So Church and Cherry created a second codicil conveying the two condos out of the estate to Cherry. As Church typed, Cherry was right there, standing next to Church's desk. As with the first codicil, Church was the one who signed McConnell's name to the document.

The codicil read, in part, "In the event of my death, I, J. Knox McConnell, do hereby bequeath to Billie Jean Cherry, my lifelong friend, the following properties": the Orlando and the Pittsburgh condos. What was a bit comical about the document was that the co-conspirators backdated it to August 16, 1996, Cherry's 72nd birthday. Cherry disingenuously later testified that she thought it "was nice" that McConnell would be so thoughtful as to convey over to her the two condos on her birthday. As she well knew, McConnell was not that nice at all.

In creating this second codicil, though, Church made another mistake—she forgot to have it notarized. So, after the second codicil was submitted to the court, the clerk rejected it and mailed it back.

Church's response to this setback was to tell Cherry to not worry; that Church would value the condos at a low amount so that Cherry could purchase them easily. Of course, Cherry now had more than enough money to pay for almost anything she wanted and she bought the condos on April 22, 1998.

So Cherry now owned two more condos—in addition to her house in Keystone; her bed and breakfast outside of Keystone, the Cherry Key Inn;[8] her storage facility; and a condo she bought in Lady Lake,

Florida, about fifty miles north of Orlando, for herself and her new, secret husband—her former high school sweetheart, Andrew Radoff.

Bonuses for Various Bank Employees

The money given to Vorono was written into the first fake codicil. However, on November 7, 1997, shortly after McConnell's death, there were other payments made to various employees of the bank. According to Nunn:

> Ms. Church had given me the piece of paper with names and dollar amounts on it and told me to call each person, and get their checking account number and make a deposit. . . . She said after the [last] securitization, which was the largest one they had, that she was giving people a bonus.

Graham was paid $100,000; Nunn was paid $75,000; Quizenbeury was paid $35,000; and Mickles was paid $10,000. Five other people received $5,000 each, including McKinney and Turpin. Some were told the money was a bonus resulting from the bank's last securitization deal; others were told it was from McConnell's estate. It was unclear which it really was supposed to be. However, to the extent it was a payment from the estate, the checks could not have been processed that quickly. The probate process was going to take much longer—it had been less than two weeks since McConnell's death and his will had not even been submitted to the court. But not many questions were asked.

Unlike Vorono, who appears to have been completely blameless, some of the others were involved in one way or another in the various schemes. Graham, for instance, acknowledged that he thought his payment was, in part, for his having witnessed the codicil. Church's relatively bland explanation to him implicitly bore that out: "I'm giving you $100,000 for all your work and everything you've done for myself and Knox McConnell."

Nunn, who got $75,000 ($5,000 more than her underlying annual salary), acknowledged that "[o]ther than the fact that [Church] said it was a bonus for [the last] securitization, it was for changing the signature cards and signing as a witness on the codicil." Nunn also assumed that the payment was for her "to be quiet."

Quizenbeury was told the money came from McConnell's estate and was very surprised:

> I didn't really believe that I was in his will. There was no reason for me to be in his will. He wouldn't have left me anything.

. . . .

> Terry gave me [the $35,000] out of his will for all that we had done, all that me and other people . . . [had done] at the bank. Changing the accounts, putting up with Mr. McConnell, you know, putting up with her, putting up with everything that went on there.

Like Vorono, she was soon disabused of her shaky belief that McConnell had been uncharacteristically generous to her. Shortly before Quizenbeury was due to go into a deposition relating to a lawsuit brought by Waynesburg College and Hargrave Academy about McConnell's will and estate, Church approached her:

> Ms. Church told me . . . did I realize that I was not in his will; and I assumed that's so that I wouldn't say that in the deposition that I was left in his will.
>
> . . . .
>
> I didn't think that Mr. McConnell would leave me any money. There would have been no reason for him to have left me money.

Church, at the last minute, wanted to make sure that Quizenbeury did not claim that she was in the will or codicil when she clearly was not.

Mickles, who was not accused of any wrongdoing, was also initially told that the money was from McConnell's estate. It occurred to her that the probate process should have taken longer, but she did not raise any questions. Like Vorono and Quizenbeury, she was very surprised to learn that McConnell had provided for her in his will:

> Terry Church asked me if I knew that Mr. McConnell had left me $10,000 in his will.
>
> . . . .
>
> I didn't say anything for quite a bit of time, because I was confused and maybe in a state of shock.
>
> . . . .
>
> Well, of course, if someone wants to leave you $10,000, you're going to be happy about it, but still I was a bit confused why he would have left me $10,000.
>
> . . . .

I was not very personable with Mr. McConnell and did not feel he
would have wished for me to have had $10,000 of his money.

It was too good to be true. Just as Mickles was about to go into her
deposition relating to the lawsuit brought by the two schools, Church
revealed to her the truth, in a sort of backhanded way. According to
Mickles:

> Terry Church entered into the room, and she walked up to Melissa
> Quizenbeury, closer to Melissa Quizenbeury than actually to myself,
> and she spoke to Melissa Quizenbeury, but she spoke about me. And
> she said something to the effect: "Does she know that she really was
> not left any money in the will?" Which she was referring to the "she"
> being me.

So, McConnell, who was known as being miserly during his life, continued to be proven so after his death.

Notes

1. Church's "Appraisement of the Estate," filed in connection with McConnell's
    estate, listed five bank accounts at the Keystone bank totaling $4,356,582.
    The ensuing indictment against Church and Cherry listed only four accounts,
    totaling $4,282,588. Three of the accounts listed in the appraisement and the
    indictment have the same account numbers. However, the remaining accounts
    do not line up exactly. This chapter will use the accounts and figures in the
    indictment. (The reason for the variances is not known.)
2. Church and Cherry were so venal that they also took McConnell's $18,000
    in EE Bonds and rewrote them to read "Knox McConnell or Billie Cherry."
3. These funds were in the form of "appraisal" fees and "due diligence" fees that
    were split between Church and him, as discussed in Chapters Five and Six.
4. As noted later in Chapter Eight, Church's husband was not involved with the
    CDs or the deposits. Everything was under Terry Church's control.
5. See footnote 3, above.
6. The will itself was typed, for the most part, in normal type, but the codicil
    was all in capital letters—a style that Church preferred.
7. It also seemed to escape scrutiny the anomalous fact that Cherry was to only
    get a small stipend pursuant to the will, but a large amount of McConnell's
    Keystone bank stock pursuant to the codicil.
8. Cherry did not buy the Jones Mansion—which she was going to convert into
    a second bed and breakfast—until June, 1998.

5

A Train Wreck A Comin'

The first man says to the second man,
"You lose money on every transaction."
The second man responds,
"Yes, but I make it up in volume."
—Old joke

As set forth earlier, when McConnell and Church began the process of purchasing loans and selling them into the market, neither of them knew anything about Title One loans or the securitization process. According to Church, even up to the time McConnell died—over five and a half years later—he still did not understand the securitization process.

Church's own financial background was not extensive. She graduated from a two-year college, Duff's Business College in Pittsburgh, with an associate degree in stenography. Then she went to work as the comptroller for an apartment complex in Pittsburgh. After she followed McConnell to Keystone, West Virginia, she obtained a bachelor's degree in Appraisal Technology and a master's and a Ph.D. in Business Administration; but these were correspondence degrees from Western State University in Doniphan, Missouri. In addition, all three degrees were issued on the same day. By Wall Street standards—and most people's standards—these degrees were not very meaningful. Eventually, in 1980, at the age of twenty-seven, she obtained a college degree in banking from Bluefield State College in Bluefield, West Virginia, a small college located about twenty-one miles from Keystone.[1]

Church recognized that she needed assistance in handling the complicated and risky process of purchasing subprime loans from all over the country, analyzing them, bundling them into securities and then selling them in segments to sophisticated investors. This process is usually engaged in by only the very largest banks and Wall Street investment houses. So Church turned to three people to assist her.

First was Wendy Sue Pack. Pack had gone to a religious college in California where she majored in music. She had absolutely no background in banking or finance. She was a stay-at-home mom raising four children. She was in Keystone because her husband was the minister of the local Worldwide Church of God, which Church's aunt-in-law attended. In 1992, Church hired Pack to work for the bank part-time, from her home, to review some loan files, and identify missing documents. In 1993, Church hired her to do some bookkeeping at the Keystone Hardware Store (which Church had purchased for her husband, a local former coal miner from Keystone who had retired on disability). Eventually, Pack was hired to work at the bank full-time.

When Pack heard about the trips to California, she jokingly said, "Oh, wow, someday I'm going to jump onboard with you all, because I'm from California." The next thing she knew, Church asked her to go on a trip to California to review loan files—even though Pack admitted that she "didn't know much about a loan file." Church compensated Pack generously for this assistance—paying her about $550,000 over the course of three years. Curiously, these payments did not come directly from the bank, but flowed through the hardware store. Church also paid off Pack's mortgage, and, at least one time, took Pack's entire family to California on vacation.

The second person Church called upon for assistance was Mama Dee—Church's aunt-in-law (who attended the Worldwide Church of God and introduced Pack to Terry Church). Mama Dee worked for the bank as a janitor, cleaning and also shredding bank documents. For her expertise and background, Church paid her more than $800,000 over a period of four years.

The third person Church used to assist her in the securitization process was Deborah Watkins, the bank's drive-up teller. None of them, needless to say, had any experience with subprime mortgages or securitizations.[2]

When the first securitization package was ready to be finalized, the bank staff did not know what they were doing and there was a lot of yelling and screaming. Consequently, Melgar, who was the primary individual assisting the bank, stepped in and said, "Look, we got to get this done. I'll pull it together for you." He did so and predicted high returns for that securitization deal and for the ones that would follow. Unfortunately, his predictions turned out to be incorrect. According to an expert testifying in one of the many cases brought after the bank failed, not only were Melgar's predictions throughout the securitization process wrong, he had to have known they were wrong:

> Keystone's securitization program was a failure. . . .
>
> You know, from the start, they had problems that either they were paying too much for the loans, or that the loans were of insufficient quality, or that the whole program was mismanaged to the point where it couldn't work. Keystone had, you know, innumerable problems with either the loans or the administration of this contract of insurance, and so the basic reason it didn't work is that they spent a lot of money to buy loans which were no good, and they knew it early on, that there was a problem.
>
> Mr. Melgar knew there was a problem early on, and they continued to grow a losing program. . . .
>
> I'm sure [Melgar] knew the program wasn't working.

One of the issues with Keystone's securitization program was that the bank allegedly allowed Melgar to virtually run the entire securitization process. Specifically, according to the evidence at trial, the bank allowed him to select the loan originators; set the price for the loans; choose the loan servicers; designate the insurance company; provide valuations for the deals; and create pricing matrices. As set out by a reviewing court:

> Keystone's loan securitization transactions were orchestrated by Dan Melgar. . . . Neither Keystone's officers nor its directors . . . had experience with loan securitization, and Melgar effectively exercised sole control over the securitization program in which Keystone engaged. . . . Significantly, he provided projections of future loan performance on which Keystone relied in making its high-stakes foray into loan securitization.

With regard to the directors, they were not involved. None of them was familiar with the esoteric world of subprime mortgage securitizations, and some of them were elderly or did not have a background in banking at all. In 1999, when the bank collapsed, one director was sixty-nine years old; another was seventy-eight years old. Cherry herself was seventy-five years old. One director was a local attorney; one was a doctor from the Philippines; and one was a retired beer distributor. While all of them had ties to Keystone, several were living far away— one in New England and one on the West Coast.[3] Consequently, these directors were not actively involved in the supervision of the bank and its high-risk venture.

* * *

The very first securitization deal that Keystone put together was supposed to have had a company by the name of Master Financial serve as a co-sponsor. Master Financial was also the provider and servicer of nearly a third of the loans in the deal. In addition to this apparent conflict of interest, there was another problem.

In February of 1993, HUD brought charges against Master Financial for failing to verify the source of borrowers' first payments; for using false verifications of employment—fraudulent W-2s and pay stubs—to qualify borrowers; and for advising borrowers to finance their initial payments with the loan proceeds. According to a complaint subsequently filed by the FDIC, Melgar was aware of these charges when he recommended that the bank use Master Financial.

According to the complaint, Melgar and the bank eventually realized that Master Financial could not participate in the securitization deal while under such a cloud, so they replaced Master Financial with ContiTrade Services Corporation, a large New York entity, as the co-sponsor. In addition, as set forth in the complaint, Prime Financial Corp., a company owned by one of Melgar's associates, Harald Bakkebo, took over the loan servicing for Master Financial. In order to persuade Master Financial to withdraw from the deal, however, the bank allegedly had to make it "an offer Master Financial couldn't refuse."

Initially, Prime was both a loan originator and a loan servicer for the bank. But the OCC objected to that arrangement as being a conflict of interest. So another company, Clearview Capital Corporation, was created for the purpose of providing loans to Keystone, and Prime became the main loan servicer. What the OCC did not know was the fact that Bakkebo, a Norwegian citizen living in the United States, who owned and ran Prime, also owned and ran Clearview after it was created. So the conflict was never resolved.

Clearview, as a loan originator, produced an unusually high percentage of the loans for the bank—as much as 60% for some of the deals. Typically, a bank purchasing loans for securitizations uses a variety of different loan originators, but Keystone did not.

In addition to the conflict of interest and the excessive number of loans from one source, the loans themselves proved to be of very poor quality. Everyone understood that the loans were mostly to subprime borrowers. However, Clearview greatly accentuated the problem of dealing with subprime loans by approving them without regard to proper credit quality standards. Pack noted that the loans were "completely and totally abysmal."

Milton Drageset, who worked first at Prime and then at Clearview, said the people at Clearview knew that the Keystone bank was going to buy the loans, so they simply did not care. From his perspective, "the environment was one in which loans were funded for production sake, not for credit or quality sake." Because proper credit standards were ignored in this fashion, the default rate on the loans was high and the resulting overall value of the securitizations was put in jeopardy. In Drageset's words, it was "A train wreck a comin'."

Drageset believed that Bakkebo knew of the poor quality of the loans. When asked whether he thought Bakkebo "was a person of good character and honesty and integrity . . . or something different," Drageset replied:

> My perception was that he, unfortunately, fell on the wrong side of the fence. He always seemed to have a penchant for finding ways to skirt the system, take advantage, those types of things.

Drageset finally left Clearview in 1996 because "senior management's way of originating loans . . . was just continuing beyond unethical." He just "couldn't take it anymore".

When the Keystone bank failed in 1999, Drageset's only reaction was to wonder why it had taken so long.

Drageset was not the only one who noted problems. Shannon Doyle was another. She was beholden to Bakkebo for having given her a job when she was unemployed and desperate. She had started as a receptionist and had advanced to become an assistant vice president of Prime. But after a while, she began to notice some problems.

Prime had purchased approximately four hundred loans from a failed financial institution and had sold the loans to a bank in northern California. That bank complained that the loans were of poor quality, and insisted that Prime repurchase them. The day this happened, there was a big shouting match in the office over the issue. After work that day, Doyle was with some friends at J.D.'s Bar and Grill, located downstairs from Prime's office. She noted that Bakkebo was with Melgar just a few tables away and she could hear Bakkebo complaining in a loud voice about buying the loans back: "I'll be a son of a bitch if I am just going to sit and eat this."

But Prime was forced to repurchase the loans. Later, a lot of cash payments started to come in to make some of the repurchased delinquent loans current. Doyle processed these payments, and started to send all of the money collected on the loans to the finance department. However, she was stopped from doing so. One of the managers at Prime said:

> No, no, no, no, no, no. Shannon, no. You're only supposed to give those to the finance department like one or two every other day. I never gave you that money. You can't talk about this.

So Doyle was directed to keep the cash in a vault and to spoon feed it to the finance department so that the cash payments—which were very unusual—would not be as noticeable. This went on for a period of months. One day, Doyle commented to someone else at Prime that they were doing a good job collecting on the delinquent loans. The person got very quiet and then said:

> Shannon, you can't talk about this with anyone. You can't have anyone else involved with this at all. This is not a joke. Harald can lose his [HUD] license for this. . . . Just don't discuss it or Harald could be in a lot of trouble.

Subsequent to Doyle asking about the cash payments, only wire payments came in to make the loans current. In addition, Doyle was unceremoniously cut out of the process.

Fraudulently making delinquent loans appear current through third-party payments was bad enough. But Doyle was confronted with a further development. She has a semi-photographic memory, and, when a series of folders came to her from Clearview for filing, she recognized them as being part of the original four hundred loans that had been begrudgingly repurchased by Prime and shipped to Clearview. She quickly noted that the loans had all been reassigned new numbers and that the loan files were not complete. The folders contained only negative information, such as "delinquency letters, bankruptcy notices, [and] default notices" relating to the loans. This meant that the original files, wherever they were, had all of the negative documentation purged from them. This was painfully obvious to Doyle, and she realized that she was dealing with, in her words, "America's dumbest criminals." As it turned out, the sanitized files had been sent on to Keystone and were ready to be placed into a securitization.[4]

* * *

After the first securitization deal was completed, it became apparent that neither Church nor any of her assistants could read or understand the reports that the securitization trustee sent them. If they had been able to, perhaps they would have been able to discern earlier on that the process was not profitable for the bank. As it was, when they got the reports—known as Master Service Certificates—they first let them pile up on their desks, and then put them in the "closet under the stairs." So, the bank was purchasing millions of dollars' worth of subprime loans throughout the country, and was placing the key reports indicating the status and value of the loans in the closet—without reading or understanding the reports.

As an additional problem, the bank did not have a computer database with which to manage the securitizations. The bank did get computer disks that reflected the loans it had purchased, but the staff frequently misplaced them. Moreover, they had no understanding of how to combine or sort the information on the disks in order to determine if they truly owned the loans they thought they had purchased. In other words, the people running this high-risk, sophisticated securitization program did not understand the first thing about it.

However, even considering their ignorance, the bank management should have realized that the process was a losing proposition when Conti, after co-sponsoring the first four deals, declared the process a failure and withdrew. In a letter dated December 22, 1994, slightly more than one year after the bank started the securitization process, Conti listed four areas of concern which caused it to withdraw:

- the administration of the securitization process was faulty;
- the quality of the loans making up the securitizations—the crux of the deals—was deficient;
- the bank had paid too much for these poor quality loans; and
- the anticipated profits had not materialized.

Conti wanted out.

Curiously, even though both the bank and Melgar received Conti's letter, Melgar—according to Church—was able to convince the bank that Conti was not telling the truth. Melgar allegedly indicated that Conti was trying to hide the fact that it actually viewed the deals to be so profitable that it wanted to withdraw from the joint venture in order to go into competition with the bank. According to Conti, this was false, but, as Church stated later, Melgar was "the best BSer" she knew.

After Conti resigned, Lehman Brothers stepped in to replace them. This was a move that foreshadowed Lehman's later problems. Even at this time, though, Lehman's decision was nothing short of remarkable. Lehman, an apparently sterling Wall Street firm, was willing to join with a small, inexperienced bank in rural West Virginia in a securitization program which Lehman's predecessor, Conti, had said was a losing proposition.

* * *

One reason why Lehman Brothers may have been willing to work with Keystone is that the two Lehman officials in charge of preparing the securitization deals had received preferential thirty-year fixed loans from the bank at 7%—with no points and no fees—for second residences in New Jersey. The loans were in the amount of $400,000 and $500,000. This was a time when such loans should have commanded as much as 9.5% to 10%. So, in order to please—and keep—Lehman Brothers, the bank was making unusually large, out-of-area, preferential loans to Lehman Brothers executives for luxury second homes. To say this was a conflict of interest and improper is an understatement. The OCC uncovered these loans in 1997, but apparently did not do anything about them. It neither took any action against the bank nor any action against the Lehman Brothers officials.

The OCC, unfortunately, was under the belief that it had no legal jurisdiction over the Lehman Brothers officials. Even if that were the case, the OCC could have taken disciplinary action against the bank or could have referred the matter to the SEC. The OCC did neither.

In fact, the OCC could have easily taken an action against the Lehman Brothers officials. The basis for any such action would have been evidence that the officials—as independent contractors:

> "knowingly or recklessly participate[d]" in:
>
> - any violation of law,
> - any breach of fiduciary duty, or
> - any unsafe or unsound banking practice
>
> "which caused or [was] likely to cause" a loss to the bank or a significant adverse effect on the bank.

Given how the bank clearly did not know what it was doing, the fact it was losing money, and the fact that Conti (and then other companies as described below) exited the program due to blatant operational and financial problems, it is hard to believe that the OCC could not have established the existence of an "unsafe or unsound banking practice" that was "likely to cause" a loss or other damage to the bank. As it turned out, of course, the securitization program did not just result in losses, it caused the failure of the bank.

Further, the fact that the Lehman Brothers officials were obtaining preferential loans would, by itself, constitute an "unsafe and unsound banking practice" that was costing the bank money and depriving it of sound, impartial counsel from a leading Wall Street firm.

At a minimum, one way or the other, the OCC should have brought a halt to this blatant conflict of interest.

While all of the shortcomings of the bank's securitization program were not completely apparent until after the bank failed, the OCC—or the FDIC as receiver—could, at least at that time, have taken action against the Lehman Brothers officials, but they never did.

* * *

The only saving grace from the perspective of Lehman Brothers was that, unlike Conti, Lehman did not share in the profits—or risk—with the bank. Lehman Brothers worked strictly on fee income—which was substantial. Specifically, Lehman Brothers received a fee of 1% on approximately $1.96 billion in deals. This, of course, translated into over $19 million—not bad for taking no risk.

Ironically, however, after Lehman finally woke up and pulled out after fourteen deals, Bear Stearns, the other eventual poster child of the 2008 financial crisis, took its place in the very last securitization deal that Keystone put together.

* * *

Conti had shared the expenses and the potential profits—known as the residuals—with the bank in the first four deals. The residuals represent the equity in the deals that is paid out only after all the expenses have been covered and all of the investors have received their return. Thus, the residuals are the riskiest aspect of the securitizations. Profit from them is most likely not to be realized if there are problems. And there had been plenty of problems with each of the first four securitizations. The loan quality was poor, the loan servicing was poor, the bank did not know what it was doing and none of the four securitizations had been profitable.

Not only did Conti determine that the first four deals had not performed as expected, Conti threatened Melgar with a lawsuit "for furnishing false default, delinquency, and residual value information." Accordingly, Conti demanded to have its 50% interest in the residuals (the bank owned the other 50%) bought out. This amounted to slightly over $6 million. Melgar and the bank agreed to Conti's demand—perhaps out of fear of having the lack of profitability of the deals become apparent to the world.

In spite of Conti's revelations with regard to the poor performance of the securitizations, the bank was showing a profit because it was recording an estimated "gain-on-sale" relating to the securitizations. The "gain-on-sale" concept is designed to represent the present value of the profit that the bank reasonably expects to obtain from the securitizations. However, the bank's projections represented an overly optimistic—if not totally exaggerated—version of what the securitizations might someday bring.

Melgar and his compatriots organized a company called Ronhardan, whose sole purpose was to buy out Conti's interest in the residuals. The "Ron" in the name came from Ron Mitchell, who worked with Melgar; the "har" from Harald Bakkebo; and the "dan" from Dan Melgar. Ronhardan borrowed $4 million for this acquisition; and—all in their individual capacities—Bakkebo borrowed $1.6 million; Melgar borrowed $1.6 million; and Ron Mitchell borrowed $800,000. All of these borrowings came from the Keystone bank and totaled $8 million. It is not clear why the bank loaned more than the asking price for the residuals, but what is known is that all of these loans were later forgiven by the bank.

The loans themselves represented a conflict of interest for the bank in the first place given the fact they were made to assist the bank, and were made to individuals and entities in business with the bank. In fact, Church acknowledged that the loans were designed to enable the bank—not Ronhardan—to obtain control over the residuals. Furthermore, the loans were out-of-area and were falsely described as consumer loans. The loan to Ronhardan itself was improperly made out as a loan to "Ron Hardan, Inc."—most likely to further disguise the true nature, purpose, and recipient of the loan.

* * *

Shortly after Conti withdrew from the securitizations after the fourth deal, Financial Securities Assurance Company (FSA)—the entity that was providing insurance above and beyond the FHA insurance—withdrew after the fifth deal. In its letter of withdrawal, FSA bluntly stated:

> With this letter, [we] confirm the obvious. Performance of the above-referenced transactions has been abysmal.

FSA was replaced by CapMac (Capital Markets Assurance Corporation, a large Wall Street insurance entity). Yet, it too withdrew by the end of 1996. CapMac explained that the performance of the securitizations was poorer than expected, that the default rates were higher than expected, and that losses were higher than expected.

So, two major insurance firms had withdrawn and the primary co-sponsor of the deals had withdrawn, only to be replaced by a Wall Street entity that was unwilling to share in the risk of what was being touted as an incredibly profitable enterprise. Something was wrong, but the bank chose to ignore the obvious.

* * *

Perhaps the bank's continuing with the securitizations had something to do with the fact that the senior management of the bank was extracting massive and illegal "due diligence" fees for supposedly reviewing and approving the poor quality loans the bank was purchasing for the securitization deals.

McConnell authorized these fees for Church and himself starting in 1992. Initially, the due diligence fees were set at $75 for each loan reviewed. As set forth in the minutes of the Executive Committee of the Board signed by McConnell, and dated April 16, 1992:

> Mr. McConnell brought before the Board the importance of completing a review or due diligence on each FHA Title One loan being purchased. Mr. McConnell indicated with the experience and expertise of both himself and Mrs. Church that the due diligence fee of $75 per loan for each of them is well within reason *due to the type of loan involved* and *the extraordinary income these loans generated* to the bank.
>
> (Emphasis added.)

Of course, at this time—early 1992—the bank was only beginning to purchase loans. The first securitization deal did not even come about until 1993. So there was no "extraordinary income" generated. Further, the "type of loan involved" was subprime or worse—the loans were poor-quality, out-of-area, Title One loans that would create extraordinary losses for the bank—not income. Further, McConnell, contrary to the implication of the minutes, was not involved in the review of any loans.

The fees were increased a little more than a year and a half later, on December 22, 1993, by adding a bonus of twenty-five basis points (BPS) (or one quarter of 1%) of the securitization deals onto the already improper $75 per loan charge. According to minutes signed by McConnell:

> Mr. McConnell indicated that he thought the bank was now in line to start generating an enormous amount of income. . . .
>
> Due to the increase of responsibility and the increase of the work load, the due diligence fee per loan will remain at $75, however, for every securitization that is successfully completed . . . a bonus of 25 BPS of the amount securitized [will] be paid to each Mr. McConnell and Mrs. Church.

As an example of what this meant: for the last deal, which totaled $565 million in loans, this additional "bonus" alone extracted by McConnell and Church would have been 0.25% of $565 million, or $1.41 million—for each of them.

There were 15,869 loans in this deal, so the $75 per loan fee would have added an extra $1,190,175. So McConnell and Church would have received $2.6 million—each—as a result of this one securitization.

However, on that particular deal, McConnell and Church actually made even more.

On April 30, 1996, the bank dropped the $75 per loan fee, but increased the "bonus" being paid to McConnell and Church from twenty-five basis points each to fifty basis points each. So, again, using the example of the last securitization deal, this actually netted McConnell and Church $2.82 million—each.[5]

All told, McConnell and Church took out $29 to $30 million in "bonuses" and "due diligence" fees, a term which Church later acknowledged was simply a euphemism for embezzlement. No wonder they did not want to give up the bank's securitization program, no matter what the risk was to the bank, the FDIC deposit insurance fund, or the many people who would eventually lose their stock in the bank and/or their uninsured deposits.

The payment of the fees represented an obvious conflict of interest in light of the fact McConnell was approving fees to be paid to himself, and the fact that reviewing the loans should have been part of their well-paid duties at the bank.

Moreover, the fees were not disclosed to the board of directors of the bank, let alone approved. The minutes quoted above were, in fact, fake. They were manufactured in order to provide McConnell and Church some degree of cover should they ever be questioned about the fees.

To further hide the payments, McConnell and Church had the fees paid directly out of the general ledger of the bank instead of from an appropriate expense account. Not only were the payments disguised by being sent through the general ledger, they were further disguised by being sent through ten different accounts within the general ledger, including Miscellaneous Liabilities; Premium FHA Title One; Loans Held for Sale; Savings Contra; Securitization Expense; Pass-Thru Expense; Federal Home Loan Bank; Interest Income Real Estate; Trading Account; and Prime Financial. So it is a small wonder the fees were never found.

No 1099s or W-2s were issued to either McConnell or Church for these fees, and they paid no taxes on the fees.

* * *

In addition to the bonuses and fees that bank management was extracting from the deals, the entities originating and servicing the loans appeared to be receiving very large fees. For example, the following chart sets forth some of the fees that were charged by Coast Partners Securities, Inc., one of Melgar's affiliated companies,[6] for some of the securitization deals.

Deal Number	Coast Fees
1994–1	$295,993
1994–2	$259,224
1995–2	$581,875
1995–3	$743,610
1995–4	$962,355
1995–6	$1,794,109
1996–2	$2,444,188
1996–3	$1,432,170
1998–P2	$2,000,000

In addition to these fees pegged to the specific securitization deals, the bank also paid Coast a monthly fee. This fee started out at $40,000 to $50,000 a month and was later increased to $100,000 a month.

There were also potential conflicts of interest between the various entities owned by Bakkebo and Melgar. As noted previously, Bakkebo owned both Prime and Clearview, two organizations that should have been separate and independent. Further, Bakkebo had a 10% interest in Melgar's affiliated company, Coast, and Melgar thought, at one point, that he himself was a part-owner of Bakkebo's company, Clearview. Bakkebo later told him that he was mistaken. Perhaps no one was sure. Perhaps things were so intertwined it did not matter.

There were also fees that were charged between and among these entities, as well as other inter-company financial transactions. As an example, on February 13, 1995, Royal Consulting Group—a company owned by Melgar—sent Prime a bill for $400,000. There was no explanation in the bill as to what it was based on; only that four hundred hours were purportedly worked at a cost of $1,000 an hour. When asked, Melgar could not remember what services were provided to Prime. Royal itself was a shell company with a mail drop in Carson City, Nevada. Melgar was the sole owner of Royal, and yet had never been to Carson City.

On March 1, 1995, Royal sent Clearview a bill for $250,000. The basis for the bill was vague—purportedly for services for developing a program for cost containment, establishing "systems & procedures for [a] *master servicing loan administration system*," and assisting with the development of a disaster recovery program. (Emphasis added.) What is funny about this bill is that Clearview was only involved in supplying loans to Keystone—not in servicing them. So the bill did not even make sense; Clearview had no need of a loan servicing system. When asked, Melgar stated that he did not know of any services Royal provided to Clearview or what he did to deserve the payment.

On January 1, 1996, Coast sent a bill to Clearview for $250,000. The bill indicated that Coast was helping Clearview to, among other things, sell Title One loans to "an accredited lender"—presumably Keystone. On the same day, the bill was reissued for the same services, but, this time, in the amount of $300,000. There was no explanation in the bills how either the $250,000 or the $300,000 was arrived at, let alone why the amount suddenly changed. Further, Melgar initially testified under oath that Clearview was not a client of Coast—but changed his story when shown the bills.

On top of the fees, there was a $250,000 loan from Clearview to Royal on April 1, 1996. Melgar also testified that there were loans that went the other way as well. That is, his company, Royal, borrowed money from Keystone in order to give to Clearview. This apparently was to make it look like the bank was not lending directly to the company supplying the bank with loans.

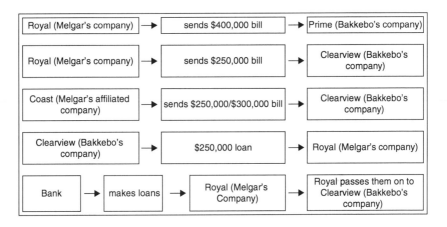

Of note, three weeks after Royal sent the bill of $250,000 to Clearview, Melgar wrote to the bank that Clearview had done an outstanding job and was "the key to success." Melgar urged the bank to pay Clearview even more money—which the bank did. In addition, Melgar proposed that Keystone pay Clearview a fee for loans produced by other loan providers even when those providers stopped using Clearview and went directly to Keystone to provide loans for the securitizations—which, again, Keystone did.

These fees and other transactions between the interlocking or connected companies represented, at a minimum, the appearance of a conflict of interest. These transactions are not how business is normally conducted, to say the least.

Essentially, according to court testimony, Melgar and companies he owned or was connected with were being paid by the bank to find companies to originate loans for the various securitizations, and to find companies to service those loans while, at the same time, they were also being paid by the loan origination and loan servicing companies themselves. But the bank was not aware of these payments or the potential conflict.

As one of the FDIC experts explained:

> So [Melgar] was involved with the process of selling the loans . . . as well as [with the entity that was] the buyer of the loans, so he would

make money from the person who was selling loans at the same time he was making money from Keystone, who was buying the loans. . . .

In some cases, he got commissions. Some cases, he . . . got money from both Clearview and Prime, and so he had relationships or sources of money from the seller, as well as representing the buyer. And so that means that he is not acting in the best interests of the buyer, because he has a conflicted position.

A reviewing Court of Appeals piled on by noting:

Melgar directed much of Keystone's securitization business to two entities controlled by Bakkebo: Prime Financial Corporation ("Prime") and Clearview Capital Corporation ("Clearview"). Acting on Melgar's advice, Keystone purchased hundreds of millions of dollars in loans—most at premium prices—from Clearview, and also hired Prime to service loans worth several hundred million dollars. Keystone was unaware, however, that Prime and Clearview were paying Melgar hundreds of thousands of dollars in fees that nominally were for consulting services, but for which Melgar performed no work. Neither Melgar nor Bakkebo disclosed to Keystone that Melgar had a financial incentive to assist Bakkebo's companies in obtaining business.

Church later said—in reference to the overlapping fees and dual allegiances—"Well, that would have been a conflict of interest, and [we wish] we could have found out a little bit earlier that Keystone was getting screwed."

* * *

At about this same time, Church found out about the illegal cash payments being made by Bakkebo and others to bring the delinquent loans current.[7] She also found out that some of these loans might be part of two securitizations that were about to be finalized in two days. She was furious. She got Bakkebo on the phone and yelled, "Harald, what in the hell is going on?" Church claims that she then disclosed the situation to Lehman Brothers and CapMac. The upshot was that the one securitization deal, which was not infected by these loans, was allowed to go forward, but that the other securitization deal had to be cancelled.

Curiously, while Church had gotten very mad about the fronting of cash for delinquent loans in securitizations that were already replete with uncreditworthy loans, at the same time, she defended the illegal bonuses and fees she and McConnell were extracting from the deals:

Well, what Mr. McConnell and I were doing in the bank was one thing, but selling the loans on the secondary market was involving a whole lot more people. We had the investors; we had the Securities and Exchange Commission, because it was a securitization on the secondary market; we had the big brokers; and we were dealing with big boys.

Things finally came to a head in August, 1996, when Church attended a conference with Melgar in Phoenix, Arizona. Over the previous months, Church had found out about the fees that Clearview and Prime had paid to Coast and Royal. She had also found out about the cross-ownership between the companies. So, during the conference, she called Melgar up to her hotel room:

> I had our attorney, Mike Lambert, who was in the hotel room along with Wendy Pack and myself, and I asked Dan [Melgar] to come up to the room so we could discuss these new findings that we had and . . . [w]hen Dan came up, we were starting to have words back and forth, and I approached him and asked him why he lied to us . . . or didn't tell us that he was getting fees from Clearview and fees from Prime and going behind Keystone's back, out bad-mouthing Keystone, and going to our sellers and telling them Keystone was going out of business. . . . And he just kind of laughed and said that Keystone was a little country bank and didn't know too much, and . . . he called me a "stupid bitch," and I lost my temper, and I decked him.

Terry Church was a very large, heavy-set woman[8] and was not someone to be crossed. The bank stopped doing business with Melgar after this incident—but only temporarily.

* * *

In spite of the reality of poor quality loans, high level of past due payments, securitization deals that were losing money, and Wall Street partners that were withdrawing from the arrangement, Melgar claimed to Church that "the 'sky is the limit'" in terms of future profits and success.

In April, 1994, and then again in January, 1995, Melgar set forth his structuring assumptions for upcoming securitization deals, predicting an 8% default rate on the loans that went into the deals. He also noted that the loans from Clearview—the company owned by Bakkebo—were in the B+ to A range. Church later noted that the quality of the loans was not even close to that. Pack was not so kind, and sarcastically said that the loans were more in the D to F range—ratings lower than what the rating agencies even use.

As it turned out, Melgar's predicted default rate of 8% was way too low. In October, 1995, in a letter to the bank, even he had to acknowledge that the bank was experiencing "substantial defaults"—estimated at 18% for the first two deals and 12% for the next five deals. As a result, the bank had to increase the required cushion of extra collateral (or additional loans placed in the deal) for the first three deals from 7% to 21%.[9] This huge difference in originally projected numbers should have been a red flag recognized by all. But Melgar, in the same letter, indicated that the "newer deals are performing much better" than the earlier deals, and that even the earlier deals "could generate substantial cash if the default [rates] fall." This was unlikely and, in fact, did not happen.

In the October, 1995 letter Melgar sent to the bank—in addition to being generally upbeat—he set forth glowing projected residual values for the first seven securitizations, as set forth in the chart below.

Deal Number	Estimated Net Present Value of Residuals
1993–1	$2.8 mm
1994–1	$1.6 mm
1994–2	$2.1 mm
1994–3	$2.4 mm
1995–2	$10.1 mm
1995–3	$8.4 mm
1995–4	$18.0 mm

This was to represent the present value of the profits the bank could expect to realize. The following year, the bank itself filed similarly favorable financial notes appended to its consolidated financial statements for 1996 for the thirteen securitizations deals undertaken by that time:

Deal Number	Estimated Net Present Value of Residual (95–96)
1993–1	$4,685,692
1994–1	$7,729,390
1994–2	$5,715,362
1994–3	$2,539,039
1995–2	$6,377,673
1995–3	$5,982,727

Deal Number	Estimated Net Present Value of Residual (95–96)
1995–4	$10,774,269
1995–6	$21,012,863
1996–1	$11,058,287
1996–2	$30,514,620
1996–3	$17,614,810
1996–P1	$12,197,598
1996–P2	$24,446,613
Total	$160,638,943

All of these estimates were wildly incorrect. In fact, by the end of 1996, the bank was already insolvent.

Knowing this, the bank had started booking assets it did not have, in order to make itself appear solvent. First, instead of simply recording the value of the overcollateralization on its books, the bank fraudulently doubled the amount. Then the bank started booking loans that it did not own. By this time, these fraudulent assets amounted to $165 million, or roughly the amount the bank was projecting in profits.

* * *

Pack, Church's right-hand person within the bank, started to sniff out the problems. One night after work in early 1997, Pack and Church were alone in the bank. Church called to Pack and said, "Wendy, come here. I want you to come in here." Pack was leaving, passing through the kitchen area, but went over to where Church was, sitting on the edge of one of the bookkeepers' desks. Church said, "Wendy, we're $100 million out."

It was totally out of character for Church to ever admit to anything like this. The news stunned Pack. She went home, but could not sleep. She had begun to catch on that the securitizations were not earning any money, and she was considering leaving the bank as a result—but she had not thought that things were that bad. Now she did.

Pack came to the bank the next morning and started to ask other people about the missing $100 million. She talked to Justin Bays, a CPA at the bank; Diane Bailey, the bank's compliance officer; Sandy Dalton, the bank's internal auditor; Melissa Quizenbeury, the executive vice president and cashier of the bank; and Vickie Mickles, vice president and manager of the bank's loan department. None of them admitted to knowing anything. However, Bays reportedly said, "Well you know how they play with the general ledger." Bailey apparently said, "I don't know . . . but you know things are funny around here." Dalton, however, cautioned her, "You better watch who you talk to around here." But Pack continued to ask around, almost every day, trying to find out who knew about the bank's situation.

Pack believes that word of her persistent questioning got back to Church. One or two months later, Church fired Pack, allegedly claiming that she was acting under orders from McConnell.

A little while before this happened, Pack, with permission from the bank, had started her own inspection company to contract for site visits of the houses related to the subprime loans the bank was buying. However, Church claimed that McConnell had determined, after the fact, that it was a conflict of interest and that Pack should be fired. It was clearly a conflict of interest, but it is not certain whether that was the reason that Pack was fired or even that McConnell knew anything about it.

After Pack was fired, more strange things started to happen. Bays, who rented property from Pack and her husband, approached Pack at one point, reportedly saying that he could no longer pay his rent in person:

> Wendy, your place of business is being watched, because Terry knew that I was there [paying the rent] and she called me and wanted to know what I was doing.

Pack took this monitoring as a threat to keep her quiet.

Later, Church herself went to Pack's husband's church, took Pack aside, and allegedly told her:

> I just want you to know that I defended you. [The OCC is] examining you for embezzlement.

Pack was scared out of her mind. She was frightened for her own personal safety and for that of her husband and children:

> I knew how much crap she could create. I was terrified. I knew I hadn't embezzled anything. But I knew she could create something. I was terrified. I mean, you just have to appreciate the position I'm in.

It took Pack years to get over her fear.

* * *

To make matters worse, in January, 1996, three years into the bank's seven-year securitization program, Bakkebo was indicted on federal charges for a massive fraud. The indictment came out of New Orleans and involved nine defendants altogether. It was a fifty-count indictment, and Bakkebo was involved directly or indirectly in all fifty counts. If the bank had taken the time to read the indictment, it could have determined that it was dealing with someone who was alleged to have engaged in very serious criminal activity, part of which related directly to Keystone's securitization deals.

There were nine transactions covered in the indictment, involving activity that took place in the late 1980s and early 1990s. The transactions involved conspiracy, fraud, deception, and the multimillion dollar bilking of insurance companies.

A review of just three of the transactions reflects the seriousness of the allegations.

In the first transaction, Bobby Shamburger and Gary Jackson—the two main defendants in the case—allegedly borrowed $750,000 in securities from the Louisiana Insurance Premium Assistance Corporation (IPAC) in return for a promissory note from their company, Southshore Holding Corporation. They used the securities to borrow $500,000 from a bank in Florida and used $300,000 of that loan to buy Riverside Holding Company. The important thing about Riverside is that it owned two insurance companies, Midwest Life Insurance Company and Fidelity Fire and Casualty Insurance Company. To complete the circle of fraud, they allegedly used $1.3 million from Midwest's assets

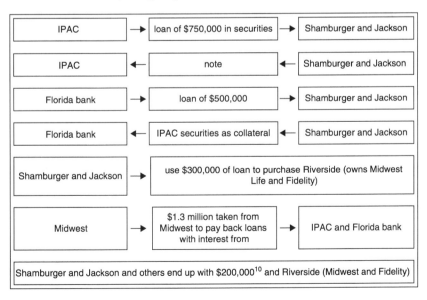

to pay off the loan from the Florida bank and to pay for the securities borrowed from IPAC. Bakkebo was named a vice president and director of Midwest Life Insurance in order to facilitate the various transactions.

In the second transaction, a third party, with Jackson's assistance, allegedly purchased a building known as the Parkway Plaza in San Antonio, Texas, from the Federal Savings and Loan Insurance Corporation (FSLIC—the then sister agency to the FDIC) for a little over $1.5 million in December, 1988. Approximately eleven months later, in November, 1989, the property was conveyed to Jackson and Shamburger, themselves, for $3 million—twice the purchase price. Then—over a period of five months—after another series of conveyances between companies owned by Southshore, the property was conveyed to Fidelity Insurance Company[11] for $10 million. None of these conveyances involved the transfer of real money. However, the next one did. In May, 1990, Parkway Plaza was sold—through a shell company—to Midwest for $16.5 million. So, the upshot of the allegation was that a piece of property bought from the government in 1988 for $1.5 million was converted into eleven times that much in cash—$16.5 million—sixteen months later.

In the third transaction, Jackson and Shamburger allegedly used a shell company partially owned by Bakkebo to purchase loans from Grant Street National Bank, Denver, Colorado for $7.3 million. They then allegedly inflated the value artificially by $1 million, selling the notes to Midwest for $8.3 million. To add further injury to Midwest, they allegedly conveyed only approximately half of the loans to Midwest that had been paid for. Then, for additional compensation, they sold to Midwest—a second time—some of the loans that were held back from Midwest. As a result of the transactions alleged in this third transaction, Jackson, Shamburger, and Bakkebo made a profit of $4 million. Their accountant concluded that they owed federal taxes of $1.2 million on the transaction, but, not liking that conclusion, Bakkebo sought out another accountant in a different state who miraculously concluded that no taxes were owed. Then, in order to service the loans that were sold to Midwest, the conspirators created the company Prime Financial Corporation.

Prime was one of the companies used to originate and service loans for the Keystone securitizations. If the bank had simply read through the indictment, they could have discovered this and acted accordingly.

* * *

Although Melgar was not implicated in the Louisiana charges, he agreed to post $200,000 toward Bakkebo's bail. Two years later, however, Melgar lost his money when Bakkebo jumped bail and fled to his home country of Norway—which had no extradition treaty with the United States.

Subsequent to his return to Norway, Bakkebo was shot and killed at point-blank range by a business associate, outside the city of Bergen. This happened on March 3, 2006, during a meeting between Bakkebo and three business associates.

The purpose of the meeting was to discuss a planned business project. After about fifteen minutes, one man excused himself from the meeting to go to the bathroom. Instead of going to the bathroom, he went out to his car and got a shotgun, loaded it, and returned to the small cabin where the meeting was being held.

This person had previously seen some threatening emails that Bakkebo had written, implying that Bakkebo might be in the process of hiring someone to kill him. He claimed that he felt intimidated by Bakkebo, and wanted to threaten him in return, but not harm him. However, the court did not find this defense to be credible because the man had been in the military, knew how to handle firearms, held the shotgun only two and a half feet away from Bakkebo's head, and had only one round of ammunition in the shotgun. This meant that, if he had just fired a warning shot into the air, he would have been defenseless against Bakkebo—whom he was apparently afraid of.

The court also found the fact that the defendant immediately fled the scene in his car and stopped to throw the shotgun into a lake was incompatible with the defense that he had not intended any harm. If it had been an accident, the court reasoned, it was more likely that he would have stayed to assist Bakkebo, who died almost immediately from the short-range shot that went through his jaw, rupturing a jugular vein and the carotid artery. In addition, the defendant initially denied knowing where the shotgun was and waited three days after being questioned by the police before revealing that he had thrown the shotgun into the lake. In the end, the man was convicted and sentenced to ten years.

The case was notorious in Norway, especially in light of the fact that, at the time, very few murders took place in the country.[12]

* * *

With regard to the other defendants in the Louisiana case, five of the eight defendants pled guilty in 1999, received sentences ranging from probation to more than fifteen years' imprisonment, and were ordered to make reimbursement ranging from $25,000 to $48 million. Also in

1999, two defendants went to trial and were convicted. They received sentences of four years' and fourteen years' imprisonment and were required to make reimbursement of $1.4 million.

One of the primary conspirators, Bobby Shamburger, became a fugitive and was the subject of a segment of the popular TV show, "America's Most Wanted." He was finally captured in 2001 and pled guilty in 2003. He received a sentence of ten and a half years and was ordered to make reimbursement of $70.2 million.

* * *

Even though Bakkebo had been indicted in January, 1996, Melgar did not tell the bank about it until March. Church was with Melgar at a seminar in Charlotte, North Carolina, when Melgar broke the news. Church was scared and concerned, but Melgar apparently claimed that Bakkebo could "get out of it and that it was just a lit-tle snafu." They decided to wait until after the seminar was over before telling McConnell for fear that he would explode and say something in front of representatives of the OCC, who were also at the seminar.

When he learned of the development, McConnell was, in fact, furi-ous and wanted Bakkebo taken completely out of the program due to concern that the OCC might find out. McConnell and Church were scheduled to go to another seminar in April on the West Coast, and planned to confront Bakkebo at that time. However, the day before they were to leave, Church's husband suffered two severe seizures and a mild stroke, so Church could not go. McConnell proceeded on his own.

When he returned, he simply told Church to continue to deal with Bakkebo the same as before, and gave no explanation. As it turned out, the volume of loans the bank purchased from Bakkebo's company, Clearview, increased significantly.

The bank went even further to please Bakkebo. The same month that Bakkebo was indicted, January, 1996, his wife died. They had been separated for six years. However, five months later, in June of 1996, Bakkebo went to the Keystone bank, apparently still upset about his wife's death and seeking a loan for his girlfriend so she could purchase a million-dollar house in California. By this time, the bank knew of the indictment, yet went ahead with the out-of-area loan to the alleged felon.

Church's testimony on the subject of this loan was almost humorous:

A.   In [June] of '96, Harald [Bakkebo] came to the bank. . . . and he was requesting a loan for his fiancée . . . Felipa Chadwick. . . . They were buying a home for a million dollars . . .

Q.   Now, in [June] of '96, though you had already learned about his indictment; isn't that right?

A.   Yes. . . . I was told by Mr. McConnell to give Harald whatever he needed . . . . Harald sat in my office, and he broke down and started bawling, and needed the loan for Felipa. And after he broke down, and then settled down, we went ahead and made the negotiations for the million-dollar loan.

Q.   Now, why was he crying? I mean if you know.

A.   He said he was sad over his wife's death and that everything was, you know, piled up on him, and the indictment and losing his wife, and so he cried.

Q.   Okay. I don't mean to come across as flippant, but let me see if I understand this. When did his wife die?

A.   Some time the first part of '96, is what I remember.

Q.   So he comes to Keystone . . . upset about his wife?

A.   Yes.

Q.   And the million-dollar loan to his girlfriend is going to make him feel better?

A.   I'm not going to sit here and judge. All I can tell you is what happened.

This loan, which McConnell had directed Church to make—knowing that Bakkebo was under federal indictment and that the loan was out-of-area—was approved without any apparent on-site visit or credit quality review, was not written up on the bank's loan forms, and, four months later, was totally forgiven by the bank, along with a number of other loans. One explanation for these actions is that Bakkebo and others were possibly threatening to expose the bank's mismanagement of the securitizations.

* * *

In light of the indictment against Bakkebo, it was determined that Prime's license to service Title One loans would be in jeopardy if Bakkebo continued to be its owner. Consequently, Melgar was appointed to sell Prime, and was made trustee of Bakkebo's other company, Clearview (reflecting once again how close the bank's supposedly independent advisors really were). Through a series of unusual and seemingly sham transactions, the ownership of Prime went from Bakkebo to his son, Brian Bakkebo, and then to a Luxembourg company by the name of

F.S. Holdings, S.A. This company was owned by Pieter Oosthuizen, a Canadian citizen living in London, and his friend, David Mackarness, a resident of Brussels, Belgium. F.S. Holdings was formed purely for the purpose of buying and selling Prime—presumably to the Keystone bank—at what turned out to be an exorbitant price. Of note is the fact that Oosthuizen had been introduced to Bakkebo by Gary Jackson, one of the primary defendants in the Louisiana indictment.

Before the negotiations for the sale of Prime to Keystone were completed, a group of unknown investors—represented by a Patrick McGee from Belfast, North Ireland—purchased F.S. Holdings. McConnell liked McGee because he was on the Northern Irish boxing commission, and McConnell himself was on the boxing commission for the state of West Virginia. In McConnell's world, this was more important than sound banking procedures.

Yet another entity, a Dutch corporation by the name of Euro-Play B.V., paid for an option to buy Prime. However, the option was issued before Euro-Play was even created. In addition, Oosthuizen, whose shell company owned Prime, did not even know who the investors of Euro-Play were.

Rather than buying Prime outright, the Keystone bank had initially tried to get the company to simply release the loans it was servicing so that they could be given to a different, untainted servicer and be placed into an upcoming securitization deal. The bank made a number of phone calls and had its outside lawyer, a partner with a large law firm, Kutak Rock, send demanding letters. All to no avail.

While presiding over the resulting civil trial against Bakkebo in 2004, Senior U.S. District Court Judge David A. Faber asked the following:

> The Court: This may be a dumb question,[13] but you tried to terminate [Prime] for the misconduct. Why didn't you just fire them for the funny business and misconduct?
> Church: We tried to, sir.
> The Court: What did your lawyers tell you about it?
> Church: Mike Lambert supposedly was one of the best attorneys, and he fired these letters off, and they just wouldn't give the loans up. They would not give the loans up or relinquish their servicing. . . . Knox did not want to sue. If we went on to sue them, then he knew the Comptroller would be alerted to the lawsuit.

The court actually hit on the key issue. If the bank had sued, the bank's primary regulator, the OCC, would have become aware of the lawsuit, the underlying indictment, and the various machinations by all involved, and might have been able to unravel what was going on at the bank.

Faced with an inability to sue, the bank became a victim of what turned out to be one-sided negotiations. Initially, the bank offered $3.5 million for Prime. On October 3, 1996, F.S. Holdings countered with an offer of $5 million. Both figures were far in excess of what Prime was worth. However, knowing that the bank was forced to accept whatever price was proffered, and, thus, unfettered by normal business constraints, F.S. Holdings held the bank up for even more. Four weeks later, on October 31, 1996, after having offered to sell Prime for $5 million, F.S. Holdings sold it to the bank for $8 million in cash. In addition to this price, the bank agreed to forgive the $1 million loan to Bakkebo's girlfriend, to forgive his $1.6 million Ronhardan-related loan, to repay the $260,000 in interest payments Bakkebo supposedly had made on his Ronhardan-related loan (payments which, strangely, the bank could not even verify) and to forgive the other Ronhardan-related loans as well. McConnell had directed Church to buy Prime at any cost and that, apparently, was what happened. According to Church, "Knox told me he didn't give a crap what had to be done, just get it done."

As summarized by the judge:

> It seems to me that what happened here is Keystone overpaid for Prime as a result of Knox McConnell's determination to hide the results of the bad securitization program from the regulators, and he overpaid as basically a result of the fraud. . . .
>
> McConnell knowingly overpaid for it to hide—because his objective was to hide from the regulators the fact that the securitization program was going in the tank, and everybody involved in the deal knew that the price was too high. McConnell knew he was paying too much. His agent in working out the deal, Terry Church, knew the bank was paying too much. Melgar and Bakkebo knew it. Bakkebo took advantage of that vulnerability to get more money than he was entitled to, so it wasn't an arm's length deal at all resulting in a bad bargain; it was a situation where everybody involved knew that the contract price was way too high, and the objective was not to pay a fair value for the company they were buying, but to make sure the regulators didn't sniff out the problem here.

After paying much more than $8 million for Prime, the bank, only two months later, sold the servicing rights of the loans held by Prime to City Holding, Inc. for $2 million on December 31, 1996. There was not much else of value relating to Prime. According to the FDIC expert's calculations, the total loss to the bank connected with the purchase of Prime amounted to $14.6 million (after taking into consideration such things as lost interest).

In addition to the bank paying an exorbitant price for Prime so the bank could continue its securitizations, Oosthuizen, McGee, and Jackson took out extremely large fees. Oosthuizen was paid $50,000 to find a buyer—which, it would seem, was known to be the bank from the outset; was paid a director's fee of $10,000 a month for about six to seven months; and was paid $100,000 when F.S. Holdings was purchased. Some of these payments went into a Swiss bank account. Mackarness, his friend and partner, also got $100,000 when F.S. Holdings was sold.

Jackson, the person who was indicted with Bakkebo in the Louisiana case and who made the initial introductions between Bakkebo and Oosthuizen, received $300,000. The reason he received this fee is not completely clear, although Oosthuizen claimed that Jackson spent seven to eight months in California working on the deal. Given how the "deal" worked out, it does not seem to have required much work on the part of anyone. Of note, according to Oosthuizen, none of the payments for Jackson actually went directly to him. Instead, they went to his relatives: his ex-wife, his son, his brother, and his parents. In addition, they flowed through the Swiss account Oosthuizen had established.

After Prime was sold, Melgar came back into the picture for the last securitization deal the bank did, which was called 1998-P2. The deal was the largest ever for the bank—$565 million—and the bank desperately needed help. Unfortunately, the deal was very bad. To begin with, even though—according to Church—Melgar had assured her that all of the segments, or tranches, of this securitization had been sold, that turned out not to be the case. The "A" tranches had been sold, but two other segments of the securitization, known as the "B-1" and "B-2" tranches, had not been sold, so the bank had to buy them back from the securitization pool on the day of the closing.

* * *

Overall, between 1993 and 1998, the bank had placed $2.7 billion in loans into nineteen securitizations. The only deal that had broken even was the deal known as 1996-1, which contained no loans from Prime or Clearview. All in all, the bank's securitization program was a colossal failure.

The bank knew that the securitization process was a failure early on. However, the bank's reaction to this reality was not to pull out—as Conti, FSA, CapMac and eventually Lehman Brothers did—but, instead, it was to double-down. From 1993 to 1998, except for a dip in volume in 1997, the volume of the deals got larger each year.

Deal Number	Deal Amount
1993–1	$33,485,689
Total for 1993	$33,485,689
1994–1	$33,505,655
1994–2	$29,342,258
1994–3	$33,130,106
Total for 1994	$95,978,019
1995–2	$70,402,773
1995–3	$84,984,357
1995–4	$112,227,946
1995–6	$209,226,091
Total for 1995	$476,741,167
1996–1	$67,733,848
1996–2	$287,226,162
1996–3	$163,676,624
1996–P1	$75,390,512
1996–P2	$143,014,661
Total for 1996	$737,041,807
1997–P1	$24,998,049
1997–P2	$126,506,154
1997–P3	$182,109,614
1997–P4	$122,127,687
Total for 1997	$455,741,504
1998–P1	$292,359,060
1998–P2	$565,201,221
Total for 1998	$857,560,281
Grand Total	$2,656,548,467

In order to increase the size of the deals, the bank had migrated from Title One loans to high loan-to-value (HLTV) loans. By definition,

HLTV loans are highly leveraged, meaning that the value of the underlying asset or collateral (in this case a home) represents a relatively large percentage of the loan. Thus, a $90,000 loan secured by a home appraised at $100,000 would be an HLTV loan.

The important point here is that the constraints applicable to Title One loans do not apply to HLTV loans, so a bank can make larger loans, and can make them for debt consolidation, for instance, and not just for home improvement. There is less of a margin for error in making and collecting such loans, but the return can be higher. Starting in about the middle of 1996, after about twelve securitizations, Keystone expanded its portfolio by buying HLTV loans, in addition to Title One loans.

Even though the bank was losing money and was falsifying its books and records to hide that fact, it continued to put together larger and larger securitization deals in the hope that it could somehow make up the losses and turn a profit. This procedure was seemingly just following Melgar's reasoning: "It is apparent that the profitability . . . is a direct result of the increasing volume." This was his view in 1995, but, even then, there was no income from the deals. And there never was going to be.

According to Church, the increased size and number of securitization deals was a matter of desperation:

> Well, at that point in time,[14] we were in it too deep. . . . And everybody seemed to think that [there was a] possibility of Keystone making money on larger deals, better quality product, better loans, that we had a chance of making it, so we continued to pursue it.

Unfortunately, the quality of loans did not get better. Instead, the bank continued to lose even more money. In addition to this hopeless gamble, Church explained that the bank persisted in purchasing loans and entering into securitizations in order to be able to continue to manipulate the books and records of the bank:

> We had to continue to do the securitization [deals] in order to hide the fact that the loans and the residual on the books [were] not accurate. And by continuing to do more securitizations, that gave Mike [Graham] the ability to have more loans come in and, once they were sold, he was able to change account numbers and . . . to keep the books and the subsidiary ledgers coinciding so that would look like they were balancing. . . .
>
> I had no choice at that time. It was just a monumental error. . . .

I think deep down I was hoping that, through a miracle, the residuals would start to pay. I was hoping that Mike [Graham] was right, that the loans were out there somewhere and they had been charged off, and there was some out there. And Knox [McConnell] was on us like—with a bullwhip, and you didn't backfire on that.

This reasoning of doing more losing deals in order to turn a profit was, of course, a Catch-22, and eventually it caught up with the bank.

The Keystone bank's securitization business was doomed from the outset. The primary players in the bank had to have known that not too far into the process. What they probably also knew toward the end was that the walls were crumbling down all around the subprime securitization market. As a result of the Russian debt crisis in August, 1998, and the bailout of Long-Term Capital Management in September, 1998, there was a "flight to quality" and a corresponding steep reduction in demand for investments in securitization deals involving subprime mortgages.[15] Nationwide, the rate of such securitizations went from 55% in 1998 to 37.4% in 1999.[16] In addition, the originators of subprime mortgages saw interest rates skyrocket so they ended up being squeezed between the high interest rates they had to pay to obtain the subprime loans and the declining revenue streams from securitization deals. This was one reason why the Keystone bank suddenly stopped doing any additional deals in late 1998. However, this also meant that they no longer had additional deals to help mask the poor performance of the earlier deals.

Notes

1. With regard to her education, an ironic point is the fact that Church graduated from Keystone High School in Knox, Pennsylvania.
2. Once the securitization process began in earnest, the bank built an addition and hired about twenty-five to thirty employees—almost all women—to handle back-office type work, including handling loan files, collecting data, checking credit scores, and preparing documents for the securitization deals.
3. One director, Victor Budnick, who was from Keystone, graduated from Yale University and then Harvard Law School and had a background in finance, but he was living in Connecticut. Bernard Kaufman, another director, was born and raised in the adjoining town of Kimball, West Virginia, went to college at the University of New Mexico and graduated from Brooklyn Law School. However, he was retired at the time the bank got involved in securitization and was living in California.
4. There was some confusion as to whether the loans that were sanitized and/ or artificially made current amounted to five or six loans, twenty-nine to thirty-nine loans, or the four hundred that Doyle testified to. While Doyle's

testimony seems to be the most specific and credible, the FDIC's expert explained that it did not matter:

> A little fraud is completely intolerable in the market. There is no such thing as a little fraud when it comes to things like advancing payments for borrowers or falsifying loan records. Once you have fraud, you have to—you don't really know how far the fraud extends, and so even one instance of fraud is, you know, equivalent to a massive amount of fraud.

5. At least through the end of 1997, McConnell's share of the due diligence fees was deposited into his company, Marbil, or his estate after he died in October, 1997.

6. Coast was involved indirectly with the Keystone securitizations. It is unclear who actually owned Coast, but it seems to have been connected with Melgar, and it had the same address as Melgar's company, Royal Consulting Group. In addition, Melgar signed various memos under Coast's letterhead.

7. These were the loans that Shannon Doyle, working at Prime, had identified.

8. After the bank failed, one examiner joked that someone ought to make a movie of the story—and get John Goodman to play the part of Terry Church.

9. This is referred to as the "overcollateralization" or OC. So for a $100 million deal with an OC of 7%, that would mean that the bank would create a securitization containing $100 million in securitized loans to be sold to the investors, but it would actually be backed by $107 million worth of loans.

10. The $200,000 is the difference between the $500,000 loan from the Florida bank and the $300,000 used to purchase Riverside.

11. Fidelity was purchased in the first transaction described above.

12. The mass murder of seventy-seven people in Norway by Anders Behring Breivik did not occur until July, 2011.

13. In point of fact, none of Judge Faber's questions was dumb—he presided over all but one of the numerous criminal and civil cases resulting from the failure of the First National Bank of Keystone, and did a superb job.

14. Her statement was made in 1997, but the same view point was consistent throughout the process.

15. The Financial Crisis Inquiry Report, "Report of the National Commission on the Causes of the Financial and Economic Crisis in the United States," January, 2011, 74–75.

16. Id.

6

The Examinations of the Bank, 1990–1997

J. P. Morgan lamented in the months before his death in 1913,
"The time is coming when all business
will have to be done with glass pockets."
Beverly Gage, "The Boss of Bosses."
—Slate, May 23, 2012

Banking is a highly regulated industry. The Office of the Comptroller of the Currency (OCC), a bureau created within the Department of Treasury in 1863, is tasked by law with examining all national banks on a periodic basis. Typically, it is a rather straight-forward matter. However, examining the First National Bank of Keystone was never routine or easy. By all accounts, it was a nightmare for both the examiners and the bank.

It was a given that the bank, located in the tiny town of Keystone, had nowhere to eat and, aside from Billie Cherry's Bed and Breakfast, had no place to stay.[1] The examiners had to travel east from Keystone approximately forty-five minutes on Route 52, a winding, precarious, mountain road, to Bluefield or Princeton, West Virginia, for a hotel, and had to drive west to Kimball, West Virginia, about five miles from Keystone, to either the convenience store or the Kentucky Fried Chicken for something to eat for lunch—there was nothing else. However, the poor location of the bank was not the only problem.

Whenever an examination at Keystone was about to start, the staff of the bank was instructed to put up numerous pictures taken of the president of the bank, Knox McConnell, with different state and national political figures, presumably to impress—if not intimidate—the examiners. In addition, McConnell would place a full-size, cardboard cutout picture of George H. W. Bush in the board room—in case there were any examiners who were so obtuse as to not know of the close personal friendship between McConnell and Bush. That not being enough, McConnell sometimes paraded around inside the bank with a rifle, pretending to guard the visiting examiners. The examiners were not pleased with McConnell's antics.

When criticized, McConnell would react by going to extremes. For instance, when the examiners noted that the bank did not have sufficient signs posted indicating that the bank's deposits were federally insured by the FDIC—a very minor infraction—McConnell directed that FDIC stickers be put everywhere, including on the toilets. More commonly, McConnell would fire off letters to the OCC's senior management complaining about the conduct and the requests of the examiners. He also appealed the examination ratings of the bank a number of times to the OCC's ombudsman, who had the authority to overrule the examiners. McConnell railed against the examiners, asked the OCC to remove those examiners whom he viewed as disrespectful, and threatened a multimillion dollar lawsuit against the OCC and the examiners. It was not a typical bank for the examiners to deal with.

McConnell was actually successful a number of times in having certain examiners removed from the examining team at the bank. In one instance, there was an examiner, Rodney Gearheart, who collected pocket knives as a hobby. He and McConnell regularly played a game called "dropping knives," which entailed each person holding a folded pocket knife in his fist and then placing—or dropping—it on a table and each person taking the other one's knife. The person who started with the less valuable knife would come out ahead.

During one examination, Gearheart was reviewing the possible impropriety of the bank giving Cadillacs rather than interest payments—with McConnell getting a personal kickback—discussed in Chapter Two. Wanting to thwart that investigation, McConnell complained to the OCC that Gearheart had pulled a knife on him. McConnell even had bank employees swear that it happened. Of course, it was all fabricated, but Gearheart was removed from the examination team.

When Rick Spelsberg started as the assistant deputy comptroller for the area that included Keystone, he received a call from the Federal Reserve saying the bank might be involved in a Nigerian advance-fee scam. So Spelsberg called the bank only to be informed that McConnell and Cherry were out of the country on a trip and that Spelsberg would have to wait for them to return before getting an answer. Knowing that the higher-ups wanted a status report, Spelsberg wrote a short memo stating that McConnell and Cherry were on a trip together out of the country. McConnell obtained a copy of this internal memo and exploded. He accused Spelsberg of improperly suggesting that McConnell and Cherry were having an affair—which, of course, they were, but Spelsberg knew nothing about it.

This was simply McConnell's way of establishing a record of alleged improprieties that he could later use against an examiner who became troublesome. As a result, a number of examiners asked not to be sent to the bank out of concern over how they would be treated and for fear that their reputations would be sullied. Eventually, it became very difficult to staff an examination team for the bank.

* * *

Once an examining team was put together and got to the bank, the struggle continued. Church had the bank employees take an adversarial position toward the bank examiners. As Penny Kosa, a bank employee, recounted, Church told the bank employees:

> They are not your friend. You do not talk to them by yourself, because they will twist and turn your words. You always have someone there with you while you talk to them.

Deborah Shrader, another bank employee, reiterated this by noting that Church instructed the employees: "never talk to [the examiners] by yourself, you always talk in groups of two."

In addition, examiner access to documents and employees was impeded in that all requests had to go through senior bank management—either Church or Graham—who were frequently unavailable, sometimes for an entire day. Responses to requests were delayed. Simple reports took seven to fourteen days to receive. Documents had to be requested a number of times. Many times, the documents produced were not what had been requested. Documents were reported to be missing or lost. The examiners themselves were sometimes accused of having lost the very documents they were seeking.

The fact is the bank knew that the examiners were allotted only a certain amount of time to complete each examination and to get on to the next assignment. Consequently, the bank intentionally stalled the examination process and frequently succeeded in having the examiners leave the bank with issues unresolved.

When the examiners were in the bank, their work space was videotaped. In spite of the protestations of the bank, the examiners, at the direction of Washington, D.C., put a Styrofoam coffee cup over the lens of the camera to thwart the bank. However, the bank also surreptitiously tape-recorded phone conversations with the OCC. Further, while the examiners were at lunch, the bank would take their laptops and would download the hard drives. At night, the bank would take the work papers that the examiners had torn into little pieces and thrown away, and would spend the night taping the pieces of paper back together. According to Church:

> Church: We went through the trash since 1980 on every examination.
> Q.   You've always collected the trash from the federal bank exam-
>   iners?
> Church: Yes, sir, we find very interesting reading.
> Q.   And you tape their torn up documents back together, don't you?
> Church: Yes, on several occasions in my office, Mr. Ellis became very
>   good at taping upside down, because he could find them
>   quicker and piece them together.

The idea of Gary Ellis, who was the president of the bank during the last examination, and other senior managers of the bank going through the trash of the OCC bank examiners is virtually unheard of.[2] The process was unethical and, on a personal level, very messy, requiring the bank staff to pull out torn up pieces of paper from among "apple cores, coffee grounds, and so forth."

There was even a camera over the copier so that the bank could tell what the examiners were copying. In one instance, when an examiner copied a manual pertaining to how the bank's securitization model operated, the bank complained about it almost immediately and demanded the copy be surrendered.

When things did not go its way, the bank called upon third parties to intercede. Specifically, it had West Virginia's two U.S. Senators, Robert Byrd and John D. "Jay" Rockefeller IV, send lengthy, aggressive letters to the OCC which the bank had drafted. The bank also hired a former comptroller of the currency, Robert L. Clarke, to try to mediate between the bank and the OCC, and hired the prestigious law firm of Williams & Connolly, located in Washington, D.C. The partner from Williams & Connolly who helped represent the bank was an OCC alumnus, having spent several years in the OCC's Enforcement and Compliance Division—the part of the OCC's Law Department that negotiates and litigates administrative actions and deals with problem banks.

According to OCC senior officials, the "attempts [to influence the OCC] did not affect OCC's supervision of the bank." However, the many complaints and accusations took a toll on the examiners, used up precious time, and put the examiners on the defensive. Even before a report of examination was finalized, it would be subject to intense scrutiny in anticipation of what the bank might complain about. The District Office in Atlanta would ask the examiners to defend every critical remark in the report. Then, after the report was sent to the bank and McConnell sent in his typical letter complaining about the report, the examiners would have to defend their conclusions to Atlanta again and, often, to the Washington, D.C. office and to the OCC's ombudsman.

As the examiner-in-charge (EIC) of the last examination of the bank, Mark Blair, noted:

> Once we started identifying problems in Keystone in the early 90s, our staff was unsure of the support provided by senior OCC management. This was due to constant diversions created by the senior management of Keystone. Many members of the examination staff over the years felt that whenever Keystone made allegations of wrongdoing, we would be required to respond to senior management as if we were the problem. For example, we were required to respond to several accusations of harassment and examiner bias—which were completely unfounded—at the majority of the onsite examinations.

As the bank became more enmeshed in the business of securitizing subprime mortgages in the 1990s, the OCC did become more persistent. Its examinations became longer, its staffing of the examinations became stronger, and its responses to identified problems included informal and then formal administrative actions. However, due to the resistance and recalcitrance of the bank, the regulatory process became more difficult and, in hindsight, the OCC should have done a lot more and should have acted much earlier.

1990

At this time, based on an examination dated December 18, 1989, approximately three years before the bank's securitization program started, the OCC rated the bank as an overall "2" in its CAMEL ratings. The acronym, CAMEL, stands for Capital, Assets, Management, Earnings, and Liquidity—the five primary components by which the banking agencies evaluate the health and soundness of the banks they regulate. An "S" for Market Risk Sensitivity was added in 1997. The examiners give each bank a rating of 1 to 5 (1 being the best; 5 being the worst) for the adequacy of each of these components, and then arrive at a composite rating.

An overall rating of "1" is excellent, reflecting strong performance and risk management practices. A rating of "2" is very good, but reflective of some moderate weaknesses. These weaknesses, however, should be within the board's and bank management's ability and willingness to correct. A "2" rated bank should also be in substantial compliance with laws; overall risk management practices should be satisfactory; and there should be no material supervisory concerns. A rating of "3" indicates that the bank is beginning to have some problems, ranging from moderate to severe. The bank may also be in significant noncompliance with laws; have less than satisfactory risk management practices; and need more than the normal amount of regulatory supervision. A "4" rated bank has serious financial or managerial deficiencies and its problems range from severe to critical. There may be significant noncompliance with laws and the failure of such a bank is a distinct possibility. A "5" rating is reserved for the most serious problem banks whose failure may be imminent.

1991

Based on the November 30, 1991 examination, the OCC again gave the bank an overall "2" rating, but rated the bank's management as a "3." In addition, the OCC found significant deficiencies in the bank's internal controls, problems with the bank's internal audit, and a violation of the statute requiring the bank to publicly issue complete and accurate quarterly financial reports. These are known as "call reports," because they are subject to being "called," or requested, by the regulator. However, for decades banks have been required to simply file these reports on a quarterly basis.

A call report violation is reflective of the fact that the bank is not keeping good records. It is fairly serious because the public—both investors and depositors—rely on these figures. Even the examiners rely to a large extent on what the bank reports as its capital, assets, earnings, and so forth. The examiners will test the bank's assumptions, will sample transactions, will review the bank's loan portfolio, and will examine the bank's books and records, but, if the bank's underlying financial figures are inaccurate, the examiners can be misled or will have to spend too much time trying to rectify the numbers. Determining the accuracy of the bank's figures is usually the job of the bank's external auditor. Examiners, on the other hand, conduct examinations to determine the overall health of the bank, whether it is in compliance with laws and regulations and whether the bank's policies and procedures are sound.

As a result of the 1991 examination, the OCC required the bank to refile two call reports—for the quarters ending September 31, 1991 and December 31, 1991—and advised the board of directors of the bank that future violations could lead to the assessment of civil money penalties.

1992

As a result of the November 30, 1991 examination, the OCC had the bank enter into a "commitment letter" on March 19, 1992. This is an informal administrative action, is not released to the public, and is designed to address problems before they become more serious. Commitment letters are not enforceable, meaning that the OCC cannot assess the bank a penalty for noncompliance and cannot otherwise force the bank to comply with it. However, noncompliance is certainly a factor in determining the overall condition of the bank and deciding whether to bring a formal administrative action.

In this case, the commitment letter addressed the bank's management and staffing requirements, investment and lending policies, and the need for an adequate internal and external audit. It also required the bank to correct the outstanding violation of law.

1993

Based on the examination dated May 31, 1993, the OCC continued to rate the bank as a "2" overall, but again rated management as a "3." This examination was the first to review the bank's Title One securitization program. While the OCC concluded that the overall financial condition of the bank remained satisfactory, the OCC again cited internal and external audit deficiencies and noted that the bank lacked systems, policies, and procedures for its Title One program. In addition, for the second time, the OCC found that the bank's internal controls were unacceptable. Further, the OCC found a violation of the bank's legal lending limit, discussed in Chapter Two.

During the 1993 examination, the OCC also found violations of the Truth in Lending Act. This is the law which requires a financial institution to provide a borrower with specific disclosures pertaining to the nature of the loan he or she is receiving, including information about the overall interest rate charged on the loan, as reflected by an "annual percentage rate" or APR. The law is implemented through a regulation commonly referred to as "Reg. Z."

The Reg. Z violations resulted from the bank having failed to properly disclose to borrowers the various "points" and other financing charges the bank was assessing—making it seem to the borrowers that their loans were less expensive than they really were. As a result of the finding, the OCC required the bank to review all of its consumer loans for the previous two years to determine the extent of the bank's misrepresentations and, thus, the bank's liability. Instead of doing that, the bank went back and falsified its records to make it seem like the borrowers had actually received accurate disclosures in the first place. The OCC eventually discovered this during its next examination in 1994, as discussed below.

After the 1993 examination, McConnell wrote one of his many letters directly to Comptroller Eugene Ludwig, trying to explain to him how banks should be examined, why they fail, and why the savings and loan crisis of the 1980s occurred. Given McConnell's limited background, he was not qualified to speak on these topics and clearly could not articulately cover these topics in a two-page letter. Nonetheless, McConnell went on to propose in the letter that there should be no bank examiners and that all reviews of banks should be done by certified public accountants. This contention flew in the face of 130 years of OCC examinations which had historically been proven to be very good.

Ironically, as explained later in this book, it was the bank's own external accountants who did a miserable job in auditing the bank, failing to uncover a massive fraud even though it was virtually right in front of them. Further, many of the examiners reviewing Keystone's books and records were, actually, also certified public accountants.

In the letter, McConnell summed up his philosophy as follows:

> Let's get to the point of doing good examinations. I have always said that a good bank has good loans, and a bad bank has bad loans. It is as simple as this.

Unfortunately, it is not that simple. In addition, what McConnell forgot to say is that a good bank does not attempt to carry on its books loans it does not own—which is what the Keystone bank ended up doing.

In his letter, McConnell went on to complain about the examiners "nitpicking"—and concentrating on minor violations of law. McConnell contended that, if examiners focused, instead, on the quality of loans, there would be far fewer bank failures. What McConnell did not understand—or chose to ignore—was the fact that the examiners' primary focus in most examinations is on the quality of loans—because a bank's loan portfolio is usually its largest asset. The fact that examiners are also required to check for compliance with rules and regulations does not detract from this primary duty.

In closing his letter, McConnell tried to be folksy and personal, saying, "I want you to know that it is good communicating with you. KEEP THE FAITH, and ON TO VICTORY!" (Emphasis in the original.)

* * *

As a result of the poor findings in the 1993 examination, the OCC had the bank enter into a revised commitment letter on October 28, 1993. This updated administrative action carried forward many of the provisions of the original commitment letter, but, importantly, added two new articles. The first required the bank to develop a comprehensive policy to guide its Title One securitization program.

The second new article in the revised commitment letter required the bank to update and confirm the status of all certificates of deposit (CDs)—which are large deposits placed in a bank for a set period of time in order to receive a large, specified interest rate. This issue became extremely important for the bank. As set forth in Chapter Eight, the bank eventually went so far as to falsify the dates and existence of some of its CDs. It did this in order to illegally evade stringent restrictions on the use of brokered CDs—restrictions which were imposed due to the bank's poor level of capital.

1994

In the April 11, 1994 examination, the examiners continued to express concerns about the bank's accounting for its securitization program; criticized the bank for significant loan administration weaknesses; found deficiencies in interest rate and liquidity management; and determined that the bank had an unacceptable audit. In fact, on this last point, the OCC correctly concluded that the bank's internal audit process was seriously compromised because Terry Church, who was running the bank, was also reporting the results of the audit to the board—instead of the independent auditors themselves.

In addition to all of this, the OCC found call report violations for the second time. The call report violations were extensive—affecting the call reports for December 31, 1993 and March 31, 1994—and involved misstating past due loans, improperly capitalizing loans to keep interest current, treating loans as current when the bank was receiving only partial payments, and not recognizing that many loans were delinquent or should have been put on a nonaccrual status.[3] In addition, the OCC was critical of the bank's "gain-on-sale" accounting, which was supposed to provide an accurate and commercially reasonable estimate of the value of the bank's financial interest in the outstanding securitizations.

In the 1994 examination, the examiners followed up on the Reg. Z violations uncovered in the previous examination. The OCC wanted to determine the results of the bank's review or "look-back" of consumer loans that was designed to determine the extent of the problem involving incorrect disclosures. In response to the examiners' inquiries, the bank presented documents that it claimed were the original Reg. Z disclosures given to borrowers, stating that they were accurate and that they reflected the borrowers' signatures. If this were true, it meant that there were no violations to begin with and, thus, the bank had no liability to any consumers.

The bank, though, had made three mistakes. First, some of the borrowers' signatures did not match other copies of their signatures and, consequently, did not appear to be authentic. Second, the disclosure forms that the bank had used did not even exist when the loans were made. Third, the documents did not match the copies of the disclosures that the examiners had actually made during the previous examination. When confronted, the bank could not explain these obvious discrepancies.

As it turned out, of course, the bank's proffered documents were forgeries. As one field examiner subsequently stated in an email back to OCC headquarters:

> Also, were you aware of the fact that bank personnel falsified some consumer records . . . to avoid reimbursement issues? Seems they spent the weekend signing and back dating various disclosures only to have the examiners point out that the dates predated the printing of the form. Nothing was ever done about this but obviously criminal referrals should have been filed for a falsification of bank records. I bring this up to point out just what measures these people will go to to misrepresent things to us.

The OCC eventually did file criminal referrals,[4] but no criminal prosecutions ever materialized. Similarly, the OCC never took any administrative action against the bank or the individual bankers for this blatantly illegal conduct. It seems the OCC did not reflect on or sufficiently heed the examiner's comments to the effect that the bank's senior management would lie about almost everything.

* * *

To make matters worse, during the 1994 examination, OCC bank examiner Karen Murtagh discovered possible embezzlement and tax evasion on the part of McConnell and Church. Apparently, Church was acting as a real estate appraiser for the bank—in addition to all of her other duties—and was charging the bank $400 for her services, when the going rate was only $200 for such appraisals.

To further compound the problem, Church was splitting the fee with McConnell (similar to the way she and McConnell split the securitization fees—as discussed in the previous chapter). While Church was arguably conducting the appraisals, McConnell had minimal involvement in the process—simply approving the loans at the end.

To add to the problem, the bank did not issue a 1099 or W-2 to either Church or McConnell for the fees. Moreover, the bank did not even pay the money directly to either of them. Half of the payments made by the bank went to the Keystone Hardware Store—the company that Church had purchased for her husband—and the other half went to McConnell's company, Marbil. This should have been a red flag.

In this regard, the IRS, in reviewing the case with the OCC, explained that making payments to a corporate interest that is not a direct party to the transaction is a common, illegal means to circumvent the reporting of income. Interestingly, the payments were not even in the form of checks or expense disbursements; rather, they were made directly from the bank's general ledger income account.

Murtagh discovered this possible illegal fee arrangement and tax evasion on about May 9, 1994, and submitted her written findings to the OCC's District Office in Atlanta, Georgia, on June 3, 1994. Even though all banks are required to submit their criminal referrals within thirty days of determining there is a possible criminal violation or a transaction that is unusual or suspicious, the District Office did not send in a criminal referral on the embezzlement and tax evasion issue until February 24, 1995, almost nine months after getting Murtagh's report.

While this delay was bad enough, OCC headquarters, in a very unusual move, directed that the referrals be recalled five days later. After this happened, a number of discussions ensued as to whether McConnell should be included in the referral pertaining to the appraisal fees—even though he was clearly receiving illegal, under-the-table payments for work he was not involved with and was most likely not paying taxes on. Eventually, on May 5, 1995, over two months later, the OCC submitted all appropriate criminal referrals. The delay was never explained.

When two FBI agents showed up at the bank to discuss the criminal referral on the appraisal fees, McConnell was able to figure out not only that the OCC was the source of the referral, but that Murtagh was the one who had uncovered the problem.[5] He sought to get even.

He wrote a scathing letter, dated December 13, 1995, to the OCC's ombudsman, complaining about a defamation of character, demanding that Murtagh be fired and threatening a lawsuit:

> I am preparing a $120 million lawsuit against the Atlanta Office; the Charleston, West Virginia, Office; and the Charlotte, North Carolina, Office [of the OCC]. I have never sued anyone in my life, but I will not have my character flawed [sic] in any way; nor will I have this institution (which is the best run and the best capitalized bank in the United States) criticized. I think it is imperative that we meet with you and the top people of your Agency—or, we are going into a very tough lawsuit. The attorney who will be handling this lawsuit is the best attorney in the United States, regarding matters of this kind. He says that without a doubt, our case is unbeatable. . . .
>
> I will be demanding that the person who circulated the information about. . . . me not paying income taxes, and having the F.B.I. called in to investigate us, be "fired"—and, that person is: KAREN MURTAGH! Many people will be called in from your Office when this case comes to trail [sic], and it is not going to be good—I can assure you.
>
> (Emphasis in the original.)

Of course, no good attorney—let alone the "best"—would guarantee results in any case. As it turned out, McConnell never brought the lawsuit, but the FBI and the IRS also did not follow up on what should have been a straight-forward case of failure to report income and pay taxes.

* * *

In spite of these issues, the OCC continued to rate the bank as a "2." This was the fourth consecutive examination to rate the bank as a "2" even though there were a myriad of continuing issues. Call report violations and accounting deficiencies had been cited twice. In addition, other violations of law had been cited. Also, there were loan losses that had not been recognized; there was concern about bank management's willingness to operate the bank in a safe and sound manner; and there were two informal administrative actions that had been taken against the bank.

Even though the OCC was treating the bank more gently than it should have and even though there had not been an examination of the bank for almost a year prior to the 1994 examination, McConnell wrote to one of the OCC's senior deputy comptrollers on April 28, 1994, complaining about excessive examinations.

In his letter, McConnell alleged that the examiners were "out to do harm to" the bank. He then went on to tout the bank's fantastic earnings record and the fact that the bank's ratio of capital to assets was "a 'whopping' 16%"—which curiously was the adjective one of the *American Banker's* articles was to later use in describing the bank's return on assets.[6] McConnell also claimed that the bank was the most profitable large community bank in the country. Of course, this was all false.

McConnell asserted that the bank's board of directors had given him one month to find out why the OCC was being so strict. He wrote that if he was not able to satisfactorily answer that question, he was under a directive to switch the bank's charter so that the bank would be supervised by the state of West Virginia and either the FDIC or the Federal Reserve, rather than the OCC.[7] This was, in effect, a threat that, if the OCC did not start treating the bank more kindly, it would get out from under the jurisdiction of the OCC and would switch to potentially more lenient regulators.

McConnell piled on this threat of changing charters with the threat of yet another lawsuit, using his favorite sports metaphor:

> I am not quitting, and I am not going down without "swinging." I am going to find out exactly why we are being treated in this manner. I am not going to put up with it! There will be severe consequences over these examinations that are prescribed by your office. . . .
>
> If we have to go to court, then that will be my next course of action. . . .
>
> I have discussed this matter with two of the top lawyers in the United States. . . .
>
> Believe me, I am not upset with you, nor am I upset with Mr. Ludwig. I am just telling you that something is wrong with the approach your examiners are taking with our institution. I want to put you on notice that this could be a devastating problem for your office and this institution—however, I am not going to back down.

For good measure, McConnell put a "cc" at the end of the letter to the famous criminal defense attorney, F. Lee Bailey. The idea that

F. Lee Bailey would take such a transparently poor civil case is hard to believe.

Ignoring all of McConnell's threats, the OCC sent "supervisory letters"[8] on September 8, 1994 to each member of the board of directors, warning them again that continued call report violations could subject them personally to civil money penalties.

On September 13, 1994, a few days after receiving the supervisory letters, McConnell wrote another letter directly to Comptroller Ludwig. In the letter, McConnell again gave totally unsolicited and unwanted advice as to how the comptroller should run the OCC and contended—with no evidence—that many national banks were leaving the OCC for other regulators. McConnell told Ludwig that the way to stem this tide was to "train examiners on how to get along with people" and that the OCC should have "examiners either psychologically analyzed or have someone discuss with them how to perfect a dialogue with bankers." Dealing with bankers of all backgrounds is what bank examiners do for a living and, actually, are trained to do. The idea that they need, first, to be certified public accountants and, second, psychologically tested in some way is unfounded, but reflective of McConnell's strange approach to these matters.

What is additionally curious is that McConnell claimed in the letter that George H. W. Bush, shortly after he was elected president, personally urged McConnell twice to take "an extremely high position" within the federal government—which McConnell did not specify. McConnell's purported response in declining the offer, though, was that he would not be suitable for the federal government because he would want to fire everyone in whatever agency he was put in charge of. Like the many other stories McConnell told, this reeks of being just another tall tale.

The mercurial McConnell, when subsequently contacted about the letter by an aide to Ludwig, said "that Ludwig was the brightest star in the regulatory heavens." Obviously, McConnell was given not only to hyperbole, but also to random mood swings.

* * *

When McConnell made personal attacks against particular examiners, OCC's initial reaction was to excuse the examiner from further duty at the bank on the belief that "this will help alleviate a great deal of the tension that has built up between the bank and the [OCC] duty station personnel." Of course, the tension never subsided and the OCC began to realize that it had to start ignoring McConnell's harangues.

Specifically, as more complaints and criticisms rolled in from McConnell, the OCC started to react by noting that they must be "just another misrepresentation by Knox" and by responding accordingly.

For instance, when McConnell wrote Ludwig yet again on December 12, 1994, claiming that, deep down, McConnell viewed Ludwig as a friend and as someone who was on "the right course," but—in the same letter—comparing Ludwig's bank examiners to "Hitler's S.S. men," Ludwig finally took the appropriate approach of responding in a bland, four-line letter thanking McConnell and saying that staff was reviewing his letter.

1995

During the course of 1995, McConnell explained to the OCC's EIC that Gaston Caperton (D), the governor of West Virginia; Nick Rahall (D), the U.S. Congressman for the congressional district in which Keystone was located; and U.S. Senator John "Jay" Rockefeller (D-W.Va.) were not only supportive of the bank, but, allegedly, would testify on McConnell's behalf in any court proceeding.

In addition, McConnell said that he had contacted U.S. Senator D'Amato, chairman of the Senate Banking Committee (R-N.Y.); Congressman Leach, chairman of the House Banking Committee (R-Iowa); and even former Attorney General Richard Thornburg (who served under Presidents Ronald Reagan and George H. W. Bush) and reported that they were all "pissed" at the way the OCC handled a Change in Bank Control Act application[9] McConnell had submitted.

McConnell explained the matter in a letter to the OCC's ombudsman, dated December 13, 1995. In the letter, McConnell admitted that the matter went back seven to eight years:

> Now, I would like to go back 7 or 8 years. When I was approaching 10% ownership of our bank, I notified your Atlanta Office. Two weeks after I notified the Atlanta Office, I received a telephone call from Mr. Frank Forrest, and he indicated that before I could seek a 10% interest in this institution, I had to answer some questions. He asked me if I had ever been in jail. I replied that I had never been detained by the police under any conditions. He asked me if my mother or father had ever been in jail. I told him that they had never been in jail. He then asked me if my grandparents (on both sides of the family) had ever been in jail. I relayed that this would be hard to prove, but I was certain they had never been in jail. Mr. Forrest said he would

have to have proof of this. He also said this was not the end of the questions—he wanted to know if my great grandparents (on both sides of the family) had ever been in jail.

This was fantastical. Asking for personal criminal information is common in any background check, but no such investigation would ever go back to parents, grandparents, or great grandparents. This was a conversation that McConnell obviously made up and, purportedly being seven-to-eight years old, tended to indicate McConnell was not only obsessive, but was also becoming unhinged. What makes this incident even stranger is that McConnell's Change in Bank Control Act application was approved. To compound the matter, though, McConnell issued a threat against Forrest that was not at all subtle: "I know where he is . . . I'm not done with that guy."

McConnell further claimed that OCC Field Office Director Cathy Ghiglieri had instructed him to remove a picture of then-President George H. W. Bush that was in McConnell's office. This was not true. What actually happened is that, almost every time the examiners went into McConnell's office to talk to him, he would pretend to be talking to President Bush on the phone, so they complained to Ghiglieri. She called McConnell and told him to stop trying to intimidate the examiners, mentioning the phone calls and the pictures on the wall. She was never actually at the bank and did not tell him to take any pictures down. The conversation between Ghiglieri and McConnell occurred in 1992, and, yet, three years later, McConnell was still complaining about it.

In fact, he ended up threatening her as well, saying that he was going to "take care of her" given that, by that time, she was in Texas—as the banking superintendent for all Texas state banks—and that McConnell had close connections with the then-governor of the state. That, of course, was a reference to the former president's son, George W. Bush.

With regard to Karen Murtagh, the examiner who uncovered the possible tax and kickback fraud, McConnell's specific threat against her was quite graphic: "her ass is in deep, deep, deep trouble. . . . I want her ass dead."

So, not only was examining and otherwise dealing with the First National Bank of Keystone difficult and stressful, it was unsettling and frightening. Why the OCC did not react more strongly to these untoward threats against federal officials is a mystery.

* * *

On May 8, 1995, the OCC started a "safety and soundness" examination of the bank. The examination concluded that the bank's compliance with the outstanding commitment letter was satisfactory (although three articles needed further confirmation) and that the bank's earnings and capital were satisfactory. The bank received an overall rating of "2" again even though the accounting issues from the 1994 examination persisted. Part of the accounting issues was the fact that the bank was out of balance in the amount of $8 million to $12 million, out of an overall Title One loan portfolio of $130 million. As the report of examination noted, there was "an absence of basic accounting controls." In addition, for a second time, deficiencies in connection with liquidity and interest rate risk management were cited. As with all of the examinations since 1991, management of the bank was rated a "3."

In a relatively rare move, based on the May 8, 1995 examination, the FDIC—which was monitoring the bank for purposes of determining the risk the bank posed to the FDIC deposit insurance fund—downgraded all of the OCC's individual ratings of the bank by one notch and, accordingly, downgraded the OCC's overall rating of the bank to a "3." Even more extreme, the FDIC would eventually downgrade OCC's composite ratings two more times before the bank failed. (These downgrades fundamentally reflected a basic disagreement between two federal banking agencies over the rating of the same bank based on the same examination.)

Alongside of the May 8, 1995 examination, the OCC commenced an examination of the bank's Title One loan program on June 5, 1995. This examination found a number of significant weaknesses, including the fact that the Title One loans represented two-thirds of the bank's total assets. The bank's general ledger accounts were not consistent with the reports from the loan servicers (which were monitoring and collecting the monthly payments on the loans in the various securitization deals). Further, the examiners found that the bank records did not always make it clear who owned certain loans.

These two matters—the reconciliation of the bank's records with servicers' reports and the ownership of loans—later proved to be at the center of a massive fraud within the bank. However, it would take another four years for the examiners to figure this out.

* * *

While it would take the examiners that long to uncover the fraud, they were considering steps that would have led to its discovery in 1995. Specifically, on July 6, 1995, the EIC of the bank reported that his team had reviewed all 7,498 Title One loans held by the bank. They had put them all on a spreadsheet and had "double checked them." This was a mammoth undertaking. The problem was that their findings did not agree with the bank's general ledger. In fact, the examiners found $10 million in duplicate loans. Some of the duplicate loans had different outstanding balances and some had identical account numbers, but different borrower names. There was no explanation for this, and the EIC suggested the need to undertake a direct verification of all the loans in order "to see if the loans exist."

Going to the outside loan servicers and doing a direct verification would have been a very unusual step. But the notion got some traction from within the higher echelon of the OCC. In this regard, OCC's chief national bank examiner, Don Coonley, reacted to the EIC's memo by saying, "usually I would make the bank do it and review the results, but this case is different . . . I agree that it appears there is enough info to warrant our direct verification."

Unfortunately, no direct verification was done, as the bank provided some documentation that tended to explain the duplicate loans and the discrepancies between its general ledger and the servicing reports. Had the OCC followed up on the examiner's suggestion and taken the steps to verify the loans, the OCC could have determined early on that the loans, in fact, did not exist. That discovery would have saved the FDIC deposit insurance fund an untold amount of money—because the underlying fraud just kept getting bigger.

* * *

At the end of the June 5, 1995 examination, the individual component for management was again rated a "3." However, this time, capital and liquidity were also rated a "3," tipping the scales to a composite "3" for the bank.

In spite of the OCC's "3" rating for the June 5, 1995 examination and the FDIC's downgrading of the earlier 1995 examination, the OCC allowed the revised commitment letter from 1993 to stay in place. After all of the accounting issues, the call report violations, the weak management, and the unusual growth—and risk—of the bank's securitization program, a more stringent action clearly would have been more appropriate. This was especially the case where two criminal referrals had been filed on the bank—reflecting possible self-dealing and fraud on the part of senior bank management.

In October, 1995, examiners went back into the bank a third time that year for a targeted review of the issue that had arisen with regard to who owned certain loans—Keystone or City National Bank in Charleston,

West Virginia. The two banks had developed an arrangement by this time whereby Keystone would select the loans to be placed into securitizations, but City would actually fund the purchase of the loans. Thus, the loans would be owned—and held—by City. City National Bank was under an agreement to sell the loans back to Keystone when it came time to put them into a securitization deal.

This arrangement was entered into by Keystone primarily for liquidity and capital reasons in that it enabled Keystone to purchase loans for securitization purposes without actually expending the money itself or running the risk of carrying the loans on its books until the next securitization deal was finalized. However, not only did Keystone select and physically purchase the loans on behalf of City, the loans were assigned Keystone's identification number provided by HUD, leading to continued confusion for the examiners and auditors.[10] So, once again, the true state of affairs with regard to who owned the loans eluded the examiners.

1996

On January 22, 1996, McConnell appealed the "3" rating for the June 5, 1995 examination to the OCC's ombudsman. While the appeal was pending, the ombudsman, Sam Golden, and his assistant paid a personal visit to the bank, traveling all the way from Houston, Texas, to the hard-to-get-to tiny town of Keystone. McConnell was delighted with the attention, and thanked the OCC profusely for the visit. Golden followed up the visit with a lengthy phone call about a month later, promising McConnell that the OCC would "handle all ongoing and future dealings with [the bank] in a fair and professional manner, devoid of bias." When relating the discussion in an email to the comptroller, Golden, curiously, did not have to mention McConnell's and Church's last names—referring to them just as "Knox" and "Terry." Apparently, Ludwig and the OCC had become so aware of the bank (out of the several thousand banks that the OCC supervised) no last names were necessary.

To the chagrin of the bank, though, on May 30, 1996, Golden upheld the examiners' "3" rating of the bank and correctly noted that the bank's "controls were not sufficient to fully manage the risk that the FHA program posed to capital, earnings, and liquidity." Unfortunately, the bank did not take to heart Golden's admonition that, with "First National Bank of Keystone being the market maker in FHA Title I securitization, it is imperative that the process works efficiently, safely, and profitably." As noted above, at this time, the bank was losing money and was falsifying its books. By the end of the year, the bank would be insolvent.

On January 24, 1996, just after McConnell appealed the 1995 rating, the OCC terminated the revised commitment letter on the grounds that the bank had adequately complied with it. However, according to one examiner, the commitment letter was just no longer relevant. The OCC did not replace the commitment letter with another administrative action until two years and four months later, when it had the bank enter into a formal agreement.

* * *

On February 15, 1996, the FDIC, beginning to focus even more on this little bank, asked for permission to participate in the upcoming OCC examination, scheduled to start June 17, 1996. (At this time, the FDIC had to either ask for permission to participate in another agency's examination or have the board of directors of the FDIC vote in favor of the request—which was a cumbersome process.) The OCC granted permission, but waited almost four months to do so, making the decision only twelve days before the examination was scheduled to start.

The 1996 examination team included three capital markets experts to focus on the Title One program. The examiners found the bank's financial condition to be satisfactory and noted that there were improvements in "mortgage inventory controls." However, the examiners also found that the audit coverage was unacceptable, that there were legal lending limit violations, call report errors, liquidity deficiencies, and a need for a qualified chief financial officer. In spite of this, the resulting composite rating was a "2," with almost all the individual CAMEL ratings rated a "2"—even management.

The only non-"2" rating was for the "Earnings" component, which was rated a "1." At this time, of course, the *American Banker* newspaper was reporting the bank as being the most profitable large community bank in the entire country for two years running, 1994 and 1995—due to the bank's false financial reporting.

Although the 1996 examination gave the bank very favorable ratings, and noted improvements in the Title One program, the report of examination devoted six pages to detailing ways the bank should further improve the program.

* * *

To close out the year, on November 18, 1996, about eleven months after first raising the issue, McConnell wrote another letter to Ludwig, asking again whether National Bank Examiner Karen Murtagh (whom

McConnell identified in 1995 as having accused him of not paying federal income tax on the appraisal fees he had received) had been disciplined. McConnell claimed that the OCC owed him an apology. The letter purported to "cc" Senator Rockefeller, Senator Byrd, and Representative Rahall.

Senior advisor to the comptroller Mark Jacobsen, in forwarding the letter to Ludwig, categorized the letter as "another ranting from Knox McConnell"—without deeming it necessary to identify the bank. Ludwig, in his response, correctly explained to McConnell that disciplinary actions were confidential, but disingenuously claimed that neither Murtagh nor the OCC had accused McConnell of evading taxes or of any other inappropriate activity. In truth, the OCC specifically set forth this accusation in its referral to the IRS: "As a result of the bank not reporting this income to the IRS, and the funds going into a business account rather than a personal account, we suspect that this income [related to the appraisal fees] was not reported by Mr. McConnell on his 1993 Federal and State income tax returns."

In 1995, in his original letter, McConnell had also complained about the examiners alleging that the bank was "bugging" the room in which they worked in. McConnell took umbrage over this notion and vehemently denied it. In the November, 1996, letter, McConnell dredged up the same issue. In responding to this complaint, Ludwig acknowledged that the allegation was not supported by the facts. This was unfortunate because the allegation would later turn out to have a large degree of validity. As noted above, it was later uncovered that the bank was surreptitiously tape recording all telephone conversations with the OCC, had security cameras monitoring the examiners' workspace, and was downloading the examiners' hard drives when they went to lunch.

1997

This year represented a steep decline for the bank in the eyes of the OCC. Around 1996–97, the bank had started to invest in "high loan-to-value" (HLTV) loans instead of just Title One loans. As noted in the previous chapter, this gave the bank more flexibility in terms of the size and type of loan it could purchase, but, at the same time, the product was even riskier than what the bank had been dealing with.

In order to deal with this risk, the bank had previously sought and received permission from the OCC to establish an "operating subsidiary," known as the Keystone Mortgage Corporation (KMC). It was designed to house and operate the subprime mortgage securitization business that the bank was engaged in. However, being an operating subsidiary meant that KMC was the same as a division of the bank. All of the assets and all of the risk associated with the securitization product remained on the books of the bank.

On June 10, 1997, the bank applied to the Federal Reserve for permission to form a bank holding company. The purpose was primarily to take KMC out from under the bank entirely and to place it into a bank holding company. That would have gotten the risk of the securitization product off the books of the bank. More importantly—from the bank's perspective—it would have placed supervision for KMC with the Federal Reserve instead of the OCC.[11] However, this application was turned down by the Federal Reserve on September 18, 1997 because of the bank's poor condition.

* * *

In preparing for the 1997 examination of the bank, the OCC assembled a comprehensive team, including a securitization expert, a credit expert with fraud experience, a fraud specialist, a certified public accountant, a certified financial analyst, two capital markets experts, a credit expert, a mortgage expert, and an examiner with HUD fraud experience. The OCC also had several capital experts, valuation experts, economists, and attorneys located in Washington, D.C. assigned to provide off-site support.

The examination, conducted as of June 30, 1997, found that the bank's records were inaccurate; that the bank had failed to charge off severely delinquent loans; that the bank's Allowance for Loan and Lease Losses (ALLL) was inadequate; that the bank's reported earnings were "inaccurate and overstated"; that the bank's accounting had serious deficiencies; and that the bank's internal audit was unacceptable—as the OCC reports had indicated for the previous four years. In addition, the volume of past due loans held by KMC had gone from 1.09% of total loans, as of the previous examination, to 5.8%—a fivefold increase.

Further, the OCC was concerned about the adequacy of the controls for the securitization process in light of the bank's continued extreme growth and history of problem loans, and the fact that previously identified concerns had not been effectively addressed. As noted in the report of examination:

> Management's commitment to properly supervise KMC's activities is questionable since many deficiencies cited in this report were identified in previous examinations.

With regard to the bank's Title One program, one OCC examiner noted that the bank's entire volume of "home improvement loans should be considered as 'Substandard' at best," and further noted that the bank's Title One loans represented 35% to 40% of that type of lending nationwide. The examiner was concerned that criticizing such a large number of Title One loans might create a "public policy issue" (due to the popularity of the program which serves low-to-middle income people), but concluded by succinctly saying, "Regardless, a bad loan is a bad loan, and these stink."

The examiner also noted that, if the Federal Home Loan Bank Board cancelled the line of credit it had extended to the bank, the Keystone bank would fail.

Unfortunately, these stark facts—a small bank holding the largest percentage of Title One loans of any bank in the country; the loans themselves being not only fairly risky home improvement second mortgages, but actually "substandard" by bank examination criteria; and the bank being at risk of failing—were not adequately followed up on by the OCC.

In addition, according to the report of examination, the bank's new chief financial officer, Ron Mitchell, "[did] not possess the experience to oversee the financial and accounting operations of KMC." (This was the same person who was an associate of Melgar's and who made up the first part of "Ronhardan," discussed in the previous chapter.)

The report of examination concluded that "Capital is currently exposed to a high level of risk as the bank's mortgage operations represent 327% of capital." It was pointed out that this meant, if the value of the loan portfolio fell by 10%, capital would be reduced by over 30%, which the bank could ill-afford to have happen.[12] This extremely high concentration of Title One loans continued and even increased up until the time the bank failed.

To top it off, the OCC cited the bank for call report violations for the third time, for the March 31, 1997 and the June 30, 1997 call reports. As examples of the accounting discrepancies, examiners "noted significant fluctuations on recent month-end balances on several accounts which call into question the accuracy of reported balances" and noted that a "significant number of inconsistencies still exist in the reported loan balances." Of course, unusual month-end transactions are frequently indicative of "window dressing," which involves making artificial entries at month-end to improperly make a company's financial statement look better.[13]

* * *

According to the 1997 report of examination, the bank's "poor and inaccurate accounting practices render call report and bank performance data meaningless." In other words—by this time at least—the examiners did not believe a word of the *American Banker's* articles touting the bank as the most profitable large community bank in the country.

One of the OCC capital markets specialists who participated in the 1997 examination had recommended that the OCC consider requiring the bank to cease its Title One lending program until the bank could "provide [an] accurate MIS [management information system] and accurate books and records." At around this same time in 1997, Rick Spelsberg, the assistant deputy comptroller for this part of the country, was even more emphatic:

> It appears to me, based on all that has taken place so far, including the early results of the loan sample, that we should immediately prepare a [temporary cease and desist order] that puts a stop to any additional funding or purchase of Title I FHA loans and similar proprietary products until such time as the books and records of this bank can be restored and maintained in a true and accurate fashion. I think we have sufficient evidence that *the program is out of control* and that the records of the bank are unreliable. The only way that we are going to be able to get control of this is to stop production, get the records straight and then *figure out if we still have a bank*. Now is not too soon to start in my opinion.
>
> (Emphasis added.)

So, the examiners at the bank and the assistant deputy comptroller in the field were saying that the records of the bank were totally unreliable and that there was a possibility the bank was insolvent. They were suggesting that, at a minimum, the Title One activity—which was "out of control"—should be suspended for a period of time through the legal process of issuing a temporary cease and desist order.

Unfortunately, this prescient suggestion was not followed up on. Actually, it was specifically rejected by OCC headquarters:

> We are not considering [the option of requiring the bank to cease its Title I lending program] presently. This line of business has been

enormously profitable for the bank and is the bank's principal line of business. To shut off Title I lending would effectively shut down the bank. Granted, there are serious deficiencies the bank must address, but we do not believe it necessary to shut down operations in order for the bank to resolve its problems.

While it was understandably difficult for the regulator to shut off the bank's primary line of business which seemed so profitable and even integral to the bank's survival, the failure to take some strong action was—given the call report violations and the inability to get reliable records from the bank—a failure in supervision on the part of the OCC.

This theme was picked up on by the Office of the Inspector General (OIG) when it did a postfailure review. The OIG was sympathetic to the OCC's situation, but was also critical, noting that the OCC could have done more to stop the bank's reckless growth:

> While the OIG understands the dilemma OCC was facing at the time, the situation raises the question as to when should growth and/ or profitable activities be curbed if fundamental controls to ensure reliable books and records have been historically deficient. . . .

> Given Keystone's historical lack of cooperation with OCC, the OIG believes that it is unlikely OCC would have gotten Keystone to agree to a formal agreement provision curbing growth, or to consent to an equivalent article in a Cease & Desist Order. Therefore, using a Temporary Cease and Desist (TC&D) would have been a means to restrict growth as an interim measure. . . .

> The bank's condition at the time appeared to meet the requirement for a TC&D. Specifically, the bank's books and records were so inaccurate that the OCC was unable to determine the financial condition of the bank.

Not only were the books and records unreliable, the bank, in the words of the OIG report:

> had demonstrated a pattern and practice of noncompliance with other enforcement actions, repeated regulatory violations, potential management integrity issues, and less than satisfactory management. . . .

* * *

There was also a concern over the possibility that borrowers in the bank's Title One program were submitting inaccurate loan applications and were using the loan proceeds for unauthorized purposes. Consequently, the OCC reviewed 425 loans, and found numerous inaccuracies in payment histories and other problems.

OCC examiner John Chopel, a large-bank examiner ordinarily assigned to the examining team reviewing Wells Fargo, was tasked with the job of looking for this potential fraud in the Keystone bank's loan portfolio. His findings were fairly startling, as set forth in an email to his supervisor, Tim Long, deputy comptroller for multinational banks:

> Is there fraud in this place—HELL YES THERE IS and in damn near every loan I looked at today. Should the OCC do anything about it—I DON'T KNOW.
>
> There is obvious fraud in the work that was done to people's homes—$5,000 to plant 5 trees at $500 each and lay 400 square feet of grass sod. $3,000 to put in a water cooler—swamp box—on the roof. People . . . saying they are going to do the $15,000 in repairs themselves—plumbing /electrical work—add a bath and remodel a room on what looks to be a brand new home to start with. People getting $25,000 loans to do future improvements and a year later having only spent $7,000 to $8,000 on actual repairs. The examples go on and on. But all of this is disclosed so what do you do? I wouldn't buy this paper but the issue with the fraud seems to be more of a HUD issue—ours is safety and soundness in that these people pay a little while and then stop because they pissed the money off somewhere else and can't pay anymore. Am I missing something here?
>
> Also, 75% of the files I reviewed today have incomplete collateral assignments in them. . . .
>
> Is this place broke? I doubt it—not from a capital standpoint anyway—but I reserve the right to change that opinion later in the week. . . .
>
> The EIC here is well in control of things—as best anyone could be and deserves an award when this is over—if his [assistant deputy comptroller] doesn't put him in for one I will—but there are so damn many issues to deal with something is going to get missed—count on it. Schneck [the director of the Special Supervision/ Fraud Division] and the [Enforcement and Compliance] attorneys need to tell us what info they need to support a [cease and desist order] so we can get it and get out of here. . . .
>
> P.S. —YOU OWE ME ONE—LOBSTER TOO!
>
> (Emphasis in the original.)

Chopel went on to note in a subsequent memo that:

> [The bank's] failure to properly review applications for such obvious fraud only perpetuates the fraud. Consequently, HUD's program as administered through [the bank] promotes few legitimate interests.

He also noted that the bank's Title One lending program was "little more than loan sharking as it predominately targets minorities and low- and moderate-income families."

Although the examiner's point was well taken that the OCC's focus was on the health and safety and soundness of the bank—not any possible fraud in a HUD-administered program—the OCC eventually arranged for a meeting with HUD to go over these findings in February, 1998.

* * *

In 1997, two years after the issue first arose, various examiners—and even senior officials—started to talk again about the need to get information directly from the servicers for the bank's loans in order to verify the existence and condition of the loans.

This time, one of the OCC's senior deputy comptrollers advocated taking the unusual step of performing direct verifications in this case. In doing so, he harked back to an earlier case:

> This is beginning to sound eerily familiar, i.e., 23 years ago Gary Pannell,[14] Billy Wood[15] and I pulled the string on a small, remotely located bank that was raking it in from [a loan] program involving out-of-area loans that suddenly seemed to go sour. In that case, the collateral files looked well documented, but when I drove around trying to verify it . . . , some of it simply didn't exist and the rest of it was defective—not saleable. Further investigation, including a visit to the state insurance archives, showed relatives of the chairman/ controlling stockholder at the center of the sham. Losses wiped out most of the bank's capital. We were able to force the bank's sale before it failed, but the [chairman]/controlling shareholder's equity was wiped out. My only point here is that we wouldn't have intervened in time to save the FDIC some loss if we had not tried to verify at least some of the collateral supporting the bank's main book of business. The examiners in the [Keystone] bank are best positioned to determine whether such drastic measures as collateral verification seem appropriate in this case, but I really encourage them to think about it.

However, even with this urging from a senior deputy comptroller, nothing happened.

In September of 1997, Examiner Chopel, who had reviewed the bank's Title One loans for fraud, recommended that the OCC undertake direct verification of the loans. He complained about the information the bank was providing the examiners and noted that: "There is a big risk that the bank is sanitizing [information] before they provide it."

In his message to OCC headquarters, he pleaded for assistance, arguing that:

> These people are impeding the examination of a national bank by playing these games—I know we are now a more friendly agency, but putting up with this type of activity is too much. Somebody pass this by legal but get us direct access to the servicers.

But, again, it did not happen. Perhaps the OCC was just too "friendly."

Chopel ended his message to headquarters noting that he was not in charge, but did so with a touch of humor:

> I know I'm not the person to be directing traffic here but after having talked to [the OCC's EIC] last night I just want to make sure our week is as productive as possible. . . . If we don't emerge from the coal fields come Friday afternoon, send in Ranger Walker.[16]

It should be noted, though, that even with the various alarms Chopel was sounding off, he was primarily looking at fraud committed by the borrowers—not by the bank.

However, there had been earlier signs of fraud by the bank itself. In 1994, for instance, the call report violations revealed various indicia of fraud, including treating loans as current that were receiving only partial payments. By the end of 1997, it began to really hit home.

Specifically, at this time, the EIC of the Keystone bank was beginning to point out wholesale discrepancies in the bank's books and records:

- loans that were paying as agreed, but whose principal balance was not being reduced on the bank's books;
- loans that were paid in full, but that were still on the bank's books;
- loans that were in the sample reviewed by examiners, but that were not in the bank's data base;
- loans that had inaccurate payment dates; and
- loans that were missing payments according to the servicers, but not according to the bank.

This was not just fraud by the borrowers. It was a cover-up by the bank. But it still did not raise the specter of a fraud large enough to threaten the viability of the bank.

However, it was enough to, once again, raise the issue of needing to go directly to the loan servicers in order to verify the existence and condition of the loans. On this point, the EIC noted that, with the accounting discrepancies, it was impossible for the bank to reconcile its own books and that the various discrepancies "and high potential for fraud, clearly demonstrated [the] need for [a] 100% audit and verification of [the] data base." But, again, it did not happen—not for another two years.

* * *

As a result of the 1997 examination, the OCC downgraded the bank to a "3" rating. However, the component CAMELS ratings were 3, 4, 4, 4, 3, and 3 (assets, management and earnings all being rated "4"). If anything, this was a "dirty 3" and probably should have resulted in a composite "4," given the history of problems, the recurring call report violations, and the suspect and unreliable management.

The 1996 examination had rated the bank as a "2"—in fact, straight "2s," with a "1" for earnings. Perhaps the OCC did not want to downgrade the bank from a "2" to a "4" all at one time. However, the FDIC had no such compunction and downgraded the bank to a "4" based on this examination. This was the second time in three years that the FDIC disagreed with the OCC and downgraded the OCC's ratings for this bank.

Subsequent to making the downgrade, the FDIC sent a letter to the bank informing it of this decision. The FDIC letter was pretty blunt:

> We have received and reviewed the OCC's July 28, 1997, Report of Examination of your bank. Based on the heightened risk profile of your institution, we have downgraded the composite [CAMELS] Rating from a "3" to a "4" on the FDIC's data base. We believe the lower rating is supported by the serious weaknesses in asset quality, earnings, and management depicted in the report.
>
> Asset quality concerns result from the concentration in the subprime FHA Title 1 loans . . . which were criticized for poor recordkeeping, low quality, and extended holding periods. . . . These subprime loans represented 61 percent of total assets and 382 percent of equity capital and reserves. . . .

> Earnings were characterized as overstated . . . Deficiencies in the loan and lease loss reserve and the FHA reserve were the result of seriously delinquent [FHA] loans cited as loss in the examination report. . . .
>
> Capital was a concern because approximately one-third of the bank's capital base was comprised of deferred taxes, mortgage servicing rights, and loan securitization residuals which lack supporting documentation and periodic evaluation. Funding strategies have also exposed the bank to increased risk.
>
> Risk management and supervision over the bank's affairs, particularly administration of the [FHA] loan program, are inadequate.

There was nothing inaccurate about the FDIC letter—in fact, it was based directly on the OCC's own report of examination. So it had to be confusing to the bank to get two different ratings from the federal government based on the same examination report. Also, it was unclear how the bank could appeal or complain about the rating. The bank would have to appeal to both agencies or, at a minimum, appeal to the harsher agency in order to persuade it to reverse itself after it had already gone to the extreme of contradicting the other agency. This was unlikely to succeed. It would seem that neither agency would want to back down once it had knowingly taken a conflicting position on such an important issue. This was especially true for the OCC, which would not have wanted to reduce its rating and look even weaker than the FDIC had already portrayed it to be.

This was not lost on the bank itself. In complaining in 1999 about the continuing differences in ratings between the two agencies, Owen Carney, who was then the president of the bank and no stranger to interagency rivalries,[17] wrote to the FDIC as follows:

> You must understand how preposterously unfair these split ratings appear from our perspective. More importantly, it is clear that the appeals process can only be entered into after your staff has already made up its mind to overrule the OCC's ratings determination. We are therefore concerned that the appeals process will involve significant elements of interagency rivalry that may contribute to an understandable reluctance on the part of FDIC staff to admit they may have made a mistake in second-guessing the OCC's composite rating.

The dissention was not only between agencies, but within them. Significantly, the OCC's EIC of the bank, Doug Daugherty, and his field supervisor, Rick Spelsberg, agreed with the FDIC and told their Washington, D.C. superiors that they strongly opposed the OCC's "3" rating for the bank. Spelsberg went so far as to tell Washington that the bank should be rated a "5," a rating even harsher than FDIC's:

> I believe the bank should be "5" rated, but could support a "4." I could not support a "3" on this bank.

OCC headquarters was unmoved.

Eventually, the OCC recognized—at least to a large extent—the risk posed by the bank, and, on September 9, 1997, transferred the supervision of the bank to the Special Supervision/Fraud Division in Washington, D.C., which was responsible for the more specialized monitoring reserved for problem banks. When this happened, Church got on the phone with National Bank Examiner Kathy Gerardy, the OCC Washington supervising analyst for the bank. Gerardy told Church straight-out that the transfer was due to the OCC's concerns about the quality of the bank's Title One loan portfolio and the need to monitor the bank more carefully.

Unsatisfied—or displeased—with that explanation, Church called Mark Jacobsen, the senior advisor to the comptroller. He told her that the "best experts were in Washington and that this allowed senior management to stay more closely connected with the bank." While many of the experts were, in fact, in Washington, OCC senior management had no real desire to stay "closely connected" with this bank, and, moreover, that was not the reason for the transfer. So his statement was a bit of a stretch. However, Jacobsen went on to "intimate" to Church that the transfer "may have been in response to concerns generated by Knox's letter and also issues that they are finding in the exam." While the latter was true, the former appears to be beyond a stretch.[18] However, Church ate it up and was very pleased with this explanation. Leann Britton, the senior deputy comptroller for Bank Supervision Operations, was also pleased—but for different reasons—and said that Jacobsen had done a nice job and had put the transfer in the best possible light. Anything to stop the complaining from this one difficult, annoying bank.

At this time, most of the senior officials of the OCC were aware of the bank and were following it closely. Britton was keeping the comptroller personally informed of the condition of the bank. The large bank division of the OCC was releasing some of its senior examiners to help examine and understand this relatively small bank. Meetings were called of the three deputy comptrollers to discuss staffing and to brainstorm on how to handle the upcoming 1998 examination of the bank. This was all very unusual.

Notes

1. Some of the examiners stayed at Cherry's bed and breakfast once and found it cold and creepy. The doors did not lock; there were no curtains in the rooms; the place was empty; and the trains kept the examiners up all night.
2. In a large fraud case involving the U.S. National Bank of San Diego, California, in the early 1970s, the CEO of the bank, C. Arnholt Smith, had his bank employees do the same thing. However, this practice, to say the least, is very unusual.
3. A loan being on "nonaccrual status" means that it is delinquent (usually more than ninety days) and, thus, the bank cannot record—or accrue—interest income from the loan as it might otherwise be allowed to.
4. Criminal referrals are letters sent to the Department of Justice alerting it to possible violations of criminal laws. These reports are now known as suspicious activity reports.
5. McConnell claimed that a bank employee found documents relating to the criminal referral in the examiners' work area "on the floor, under the table, which were almost concealed." It is more likely that the bank got its information by rifling through the examiners' trash and surreptitiously downloading the hard drives of the examiners' laptops.
6. Alan Kline, "New Lineup of Profit Stars—Mostly S Corporations," *American Banker*, June 8, 1999.
7. Chapter Seventeen of this book discusses this regulatory quirk unique to bank supervision—that is, the ability of a bank to choose which banking regulator will charter and supervise it, and the ability of a bank, generally, to change regulators when it wants to.
8. Supervisory letters are letters sent to a bank or its directors informing them that the OCC could have taken an administrative action against them, but had decided not to; warning them, however, that the next time they might not be so lucky.
9. The Change in Bank Control Act requires anyone seeking to obtain more than 10% of the stock of an FDIC-insured bank to first obtain regulatory permission. This Act was an effort to keep people from obtaining secret control over federally-insured banks and using them for money laundering or other illicit purposes.
10. Meredith Hale, as discussed on Chapter Three, was aware of the subsequent, identical arrangement that the bank had with United National Bank. In that situation, Hale, of course, was fired over her refusal to falsify the fact that United owned most of the loans in question, not Keystone.
11. The Federal Reserve supervises all bank holding companies and their non-bank subsidiaries.
12. To put it in real numbers, if the bank's high risk loan portfolio of $370 million were reduced by 10%, or $37 million, then the bank's capital of $113 million would be reduced to $76 million—a reduction of 33%.
13. This is more typically done at the end of each calendar quarter and at the end of a company's fiscal year.
14. Gary Pannell was the OCC's regional counsel in Atlanta, Georgia.
15. Billy Wood was the head of the OCC's Regional Office in Atlanta, Georgia.
16. This, of course, was a reference to the popular TV show, *Walker, Texas Ranger*, which ran from 1993 to 2001, and starred Chuck Norris.

17.   Owen Carney was a former national bank examiner with the OCC who was very briefly the president of the Keystone bank. (This is discussed at greater length in Chapter Eight.)

18.   Five days before the change in supervision from West Virginia to Washington, D.C., McConnell had written a short "personal and confidential" letter to the comptroller, saying simply that items had come to McConnell's attention concerning the 1997 examination team and that it was "very, very, urgent" he speak to Ludwig. The letter, however, did not even explain what the issues were.

This cryptic letter was not going to have triggered a significant change in the way the bank was to be supervised. The bank, though, even after so many ridiculous letters McConnell had sent over the years, apparently believed that its complaints were valid and that its letters were being taken seriously.

7

1998 Examination

In 1998, the FDIC again asked for permission to participate in the upcoming OCC examination of the Keystone bank. In its formal request, dated February 13, 1998, the FDIC noted that the bank's risk profile was high and increasing; that the bank had serious weaknesses in asset quality, earnings, and management; that subprime loans represented over 60% of the bank's total assets and almost 400% of the bank's capital; and that the bank's earnings were overstated.

All of this was accurate and acknowledged by both agencies. However, unlike the previous year, the OCC flat-out denied the FDIC's request. The OCC explained that the FDIC's participation would be "unnecessarily burdensome" for the bank. This was at best a poor excuse. The convenience of the bank should never have been a reason to deny such a request.

The OCC also claimed: "There is no evidence to indicate that capital, which is in excess of 19% of assets, is significantly threatened by these operational and managerial deficiencies." That flew in the face of all that was known by both the OCC and the FDIC.

As the FDIC had indicated in its letter to the OCC:[1]

> Capital is . . . a concern because approximately one-third of the bank's capital base is comprised of deferred taxes, mortgage servicing rights, and loan securitization residuals which lack supporting documentation and periodic evaluation. Management is considered weak and responsible for the problems the bank is encountering. This bank appears to present heightened risk to the deposit insurance fund.

Again, all of this was true.

Furthermore, the OCC recognized these concerns in its own internal emails. Just two months before the FDIC's request, the OCC's lead examiner wrote:

> Numerous critical deficiencies [were] found . . . [A] change in scope [of the previous examination was] warranted by [the] high level of risk posed by [securitization] operations . . . *Bank's condition [is] unsafe and unsound* due to poor supervision and administration by management and the board, and deterioration in asset quality. . . . Risk assessment factors [are at a] high level. . . .
>
> Poor risk supervision and deterioration of asset quality *pose unacceptable risk to capital*; highly leveraged position of [Title One] loans to capital of over 3:1 *puts nearly 50% of capital at risk* for a 15% drop in portfolio value. . . .
>
> [There is a] concentration in loans from California where losses have run [two times] the national average . . . *Errors in call reports prevent identification of true [capital] ratios.* . . .
>
> Net income . . . [is] seriously overstated. . . .
>
> [There is] nearly zero asset liquidity. . . .
>
> (Emphasis added.)

In addition to all of this, the OCC was preparing civil money penalties against the Keystone board of directors and a formal agreement for the bank to enter into—finally upping the ante from the two commitment letters that the OCC had let lapse in 1996 without being replaced.

So, for the OCC to contend that the FDIC did not have a sound basis for wanting to participate in the upcoming 1998 examination was close to spurious.

After receiving the OCC's response, the FDIC staff, on April 22, 1998, took the rare step of preparing a formal memo requesting authorization from the FDIC Board of Directors to participate in the examination. In the memo, the staff set forth the fact that the FDIC had downgraded the OCC's ratings of the bank twice before; that the Title One loans held by the bank represented 327% of its capital; that the bank's capital was materially overstated; and that the OCC itself had noted in its supervisory files that "[m]anagement [of the bank] had demonstrated a willingness to misrepresent the bank's condition." The FDIC staff believed that, given all of these issues, it was unable to accurately assess the risk to the FDIC insurance fund without having an on-site presence at the bank.

On June 22, 1998, the OCC finally said it would allow one FDIC examiner to join the examination. On July 29, 1998, after another month of negotiations, and five months after the FDIC's initial letter, the OCC relented more and said that it would allow two out of the three requested FDIC examiners to participate in the 1998 examination, which was to start on August 31, 1998.

Even though the OCC relented, it still had reservations. Specifically, the assistant deputy comptroller in the field, Rick Spelsberg, noted to his superiors that:

> [H]e thought the FDIC staff was there "just to watch us," and they were not necessarily there to do any work. The FDIC staff sent two office analysts from Atlanta to Keystone, not field examiners. It's disappointing that they were not able or willing to complete some exam work, but probably not worth making a ruckus about. It happens sometimes.

In turn, Spelsberg was reminded that he had to play nice and was directed specifically not to exclude the FDIC from any discussions.

The concern and suspicion went the other way as well. In a memo before the examination was to start, the FDIC guardedly said:

> The OCC would like the FDIC to reconcile accounts and review the accuracy of CALL reports. We did not take exception to this assignment, but expect to assess the risk to the deposit insurance fund and may have to delve into other areas of the bank.[2]

* * *

Prior to these negotiations, as a result of the 1997 examination, the OCC examining staff had recommended civil money penalties against Church and the individual directors of the bank for the repeated violations involving the filing of inaccurate call reports. The OCC viewed the violations as serious and willful, especially because there had been two previous citations of call report violations (in 1991 and 1994), and now the one in 1997 was the third violation. In addition, the OCC had warned the board of directors about the possibility of civil money penalties if the violations continued. The examiners recommended a penalty of $100,000 be assessed against Church and $10,000 against Cherry and the other directors.

Based on the examiners' recommendations, on May 8, 1998, the OCC sent preliminary letters to the board of directors of the bank informing them that the OCC was considering assessing civil money penalties against them individually for the repeat call report violations. On August 6, 1998, the OCC notified the board of its decision to assess a $25,000 penalty against Church[3] and $10,000 against Cherry and the other directors. This matter dragged out a bit, but was finally settled on December 8, 1998, with Church paying a civil money penalty of $13,000 and the five directors each paying $2,000.

Prior to settling with the OCC, Michael Gibson, a member of the bank's board of directors and a local attorney, sought an informal opinion from the West Virginia State Bar to see if the civil money penalty would have any impact on his license to practice law. They advised him that it would not, but, even with that assurance, Gibson viewed the civil money penalty as being "as serious as a heart attack."

On May 28, 1998, the OCC also had the bank enter into a formal agreement to address the issues raised in the 1997 examination. Unlike a commitment letter, a formal agreement is a public document and is enforceable through the issuance of civil money penalties or the issuance of a harsher administrative action, namely a cease and desist order.

One of the problems at this time was the fact that the OCC did not view the bank's local accounting firm as having sufficient expertise to audit the bank's complicated Title One and HLTV securitization program. In fact, the examiners had not even heard of the firm, Herman & Cormany, prior to seeing them at the Keystone bank. Consequently, the agreement required the bank to retain:

> a nationally recognized independent Certified Public Accounting (CPA) firm with extensive securitization auditing and accounting experience . . . to perform an audit of the Bank's mortgage banking operations and determine the appropriateness of the Bank's accounting for purchased loans and all securitizations.

The bank, in order to comply with the agreement, contacted most of the big accounting firms in the country. However, it was turned down by almost all of them. Coopers & Lybrand was not accepting any new engagements with clients involved in the subprime lending industry. Arthur Andersen had adopted the same policy. Deloitte Touche set up a meeting with the bank, but it never took place. Ernst & Young did not return calls. Neither did KPMG. The bank ended up having to ask for two extensions on the deadline of the formal agreement in order to continue to search for a willing accounting firm.

The accounting firm of Grant Thornton—the fifth largest accounting firm in the country at the time—finally stepped forward and agreed to take the assignment.

Of the six specific things Grant Thornton was directed to do pursuant to the formal agreement, one of them was to:

> determine the appropriateness of the Bank's accounting for:
>
> . . .
>
> (d) reconciliations between the Bank's records and loan servicer records.

The OCC had no way of knowing this, but this one item would turn out to be the key to unraveling the widespread fraud at the bank.

However—as later established by the FDIC—Grant Thornton failed to adequately fulfill this requirement. Had it done so, it could have uncovered the fraud at least six to eight months before the examiners finally did.

The agreement also required the bank to do a number of other things, but none so crucial toward uncovering the mystery behind Keystone's uncanny and phenomenal earnings and growth.[4] While the agreement did require the bank to "take all steps necessary to ensure that the Bank's books, records, and management information systems (MIS) are maintained in a complete and accurate condition at all times," the bank was never going to really do this. It was going to take an independent, competent, outside source to straighten out the bank's records. Grant Thornton was supposed to be that entity, but it was not up to the task.

* * *

Prior to the 1998 examination getting underway, Kathy Gerardy, the Washington, D.C. analyst overseeing the bank for the OCC, called the bank about various capital issues and got the full Church and Cherry treatment:

> I called Terry Church to ask her about discrepancies between my [risk-based capital] calculation and hers. Towards the end of the conversation I said that I would send an undercapitalized notification letter and started to relay what that meant. Terry replied that I couldn't send that letter, as although both our calculations showed the bank to be undercapitalized, we had different numbers. I said that our

numbers would be very similar after a few adjustments were made based on our conversation. At that point, Billie Cherry, president of the bank and mayor of Keystone, entered the conversation although prior to that point I was unaware of her presence. She accused the OCC of ulterior motives, said that if it was our intention to close the bank, we should just send them a letter telling them so, wanted to know if this was still the United States of America as last she looked, they still had rights, said they'd been well run for 20 years until the OCC got involved, and wanted to know just what had happened to change that, said that with all the correspondence we were sending they couldn't get anything done, and more along that vein. I let her vent and then did my best to explain the OCC's position and sympathize with her frustration over the vast amount of work that has to be done to comply with the formal agreement. I think she was close to tears she was so angry.

What should have been a relatively simple issue of calculating the capital position of the bank turned into a series of petty accusations against the OCC of bad faith, incompetence, and vindictiveness. Basically, the bank was continuing the belligerent, self-righteous approach that had been carried on by the late Knox McConnell.

It was only going to get worse.

* * *

The 1998 examination, like the one in 1997, was staffed by the OCC with an array of experts. There was a securitization expert; an examiner who was a certified public accountant and a certified financial analyst; an analyst from the Special Supervision/Fraud Division in Washington, D.C.; and a senior level capital expert. In addition, as with the 1997 examination, the OCC designated various capital experts, valuation experts, economists, and attorneys to provide assistance from Washington, D.C. The FDIC, on its part, sent an examiner who was a senior capital markets and securities specialist and an examiner who was a certified public accountant.

* * *

During the course of the 1998 examination, National Bank Examiner Mark Blair tried to simply confirm the past due status of $21.9 million in loans that had been transferred from one of the bank's partners, City National Bank, to Compu-Link, one of the bank's primary loan servicers. When Blair told Church that he was going to contact City Bank, she became very upset and objected, saying it was improper for the examiners to contact City National Bank. Blair went ahead, though, and made the contact.

City Bank indicated that the loans had been transferred, but Blair wanted to confirm the transaction from the other side as well. So he called Dan Pearson at Compu-Link. Pearson, though, could not confirm the transfer and indicated that the report Blair was reading from was not a Compu-Link report—rather, it had been generated by Keystone itself. This set off alarms in Blair's head. But within five minutes of having made the call to Compu-Link, Church came running into the room, very upset that Blair had contacted one of the bank's servicers. Arms flailing, she said, "I need to see Tim and Kathy." (Tim Knaak was the examiner-in-charge of the 1998 examination and Kathy Gerardy was the Washington, D.C. analyst who was on-site at the bank.)

When Knaak and Gerardy came back from the meeting, they asked to speak to Blair outside in the alley—where there were no surveillance cameras or possible listening devices. After Blair explained to them what he had done, the three of them went back in to talk to Church. She was still very upset that Blair had contacted City National Bank and Compu-Link without her permission and claimed that having the examiners take the unusual step of contacting them would raise questions about the books and records of the bank and would, consequently, harm the bank's reputation. She also explained that the report she had given Blair was really from Compu-Link, but had simply been generated by a different department than Pearson's, which is why he did not recognize the form. Church also said that the bank had asked Compu-Link to produce the report on 8½" × 11" paper to make it easier for the examiners to read—another reason why Pearson supposedly did not recognize the form. In addition, Church said that Compu-Link had initially rejected the loans because City National Bank had withheld payment. That is why the loans were not on the July 31, 1998 report—they had not been accepted by Compu-Link until sometime in August.

Other than alerting the bank's external auditors, Grant Thornton, to the issue, the OCC dropped the matter. Once again, the examiners failed to take the crucial step of contacting the loan servicers and verifying the loans on the bank's books. However, even at this point in time, the examiners were not of the impression that there could be millions—let alone hundreds of millions—of dollars' worth of loans that were missing from the bank. Rather, the examiners were only trying to determine the credit quality of the bank's loans—not the actual existence of the loans.

* * *

The 1998 examination produced dire results. The OCC's overall conclusion was that the bank was a "4" rated bank—with management being a "5," the worst rating. The report of examination (ROE) stated that the "bank's current condition severely impact[ed] the viability of the bank" and that "failure [was] a distinct possibility." The specific problems cited by the examiners in the ROE covered each one of the CAMEL components, as set forth below.

Capital

The examiners found that the bank's capital level was insufficient in relation to the high concentrations of the bank's risky assets. Specifically, the bank's mortgage product at this time represented over 500% of the bank's capital—meaning that if 20% of the bank's portfolio went bad, the bank would be insolvent. In addition, mortgage loans from California alone represented 98% of capital. As set forth in the ROE, the bank's subprime HLTV and Title One loans represented an "unsafe and unsound" concentration in relation to the bank's capital.

Another disturbing matter was that senior management of the bank purportedly reviewed a "tape"—or listing—produced by the accounting firm of Arthur Andersen to conclude that most of the bank's Title One and HLTV loans were first mortgages instead of home equity loans (also known as second or junior mortgages). If the loans were actually first mortgages, the bank would have been allowed to reduce by half the amount of capital required to support the loans. This calculation would have meant that the bank was deemed to be "well capitalized," and, thus, able to pay dividends and accept brokered deposits. No such "tape" ever surfaced, though, and a quick sampling of the loans by the examiners established that the overwhelming majority of the loans were home equity loans, not first mortgages.

In fact, it was later determined that, of the $823 million in securitized loans and loans in the bank's portfolio, only $20 million to $50 million—approximately 2.5% to 6%—qualified as first mortgages. That meant that the bank had made a $773 million mistake—assuming for a moment it was even a mistake. In this regard, the OCC had stated in its draft 1998 ROE that the fact that the bank's calculations had placed it "in the well-capitalized category . . . suggests that the bank's capital calculation was manipulated to achieve this capital category." After the bank complained, the OCC agreed to take out the word "manipulated," but the suspicion remained. It had taken the examiners less than two hours to review a sample of loans and come to the realization that the bank's numbers were seriously flawed.

This triggered another call report violation—the fourth one. As the ROE noted, the bank had not filed an accurate call report for the previous seven consecutive quarters—or twenty-one months—even though it had been formally warned a number of times about the possibility of civil money penalties being assessed. The examiners viewed this latest violation as particularly egregious given the fact that the bank could have easily verified whether or not the loans in issue were first mortgages.

The primary constraint that resulted from the bank's undercapitalized position was that it was prohibited from accepting or rolling over brokered deposits—large deposits that are solicited through brokers for a fee. Up to this point, the bank had been relying extensively on brokered deposits to fund the purchase of loans from all over the country to be placed into the securitization deals.

Assets

There had been a downturn in the quality of the bank's assets as of this examination. In the previous examination, in 1997, the amount of classified assets (i.e., assets that the examiners classified as being of poor quality—either substandard, doubtful, or loss) represented only 16% of capital. At the 1998 examination, this jumped to 224% of capital. In addition, the examiners criticized the bank's valuation model which was designed to determine the present market value of the mortgage portfolio. First, the examiners criticized the fact that the model was created by Coast Partners, one of Melgar's related companies, because Coast had a "vested interest in the outcome." The better the valuation results, the better Coast would look and the more fees it could try to charge. Second, the examiners' testing proved that the model was next to worthless. As stated in the ROE:

> We noted numerous instances where small changes to the input data produced unexplained and unreasonable changes in the valuation estimates. . . . In addition, on several occasions the identical inputs were loaded into the model for the same securitization transaction and different valuations were produced.

Management

Management was rated a "5" by the OCC in 1998 for the first time. The basis for this rating, as set forth in the report, was the fact that "Management does not demonstrate the technical knowledge necessary to manage the bank's complex mortgage activities"; that "Management has failed to return the bank to a safe and sound condition"; and that "Management and board supervision continues to be unsatisfactory." In addition, management was criticized for having failed to improve fundamental systems and controls, despite having been told to do so. Further, the many accounting issues and resulting violations were properly laid at management's feet.

The examiners also criticized the fact that Ron Mitchell was being paid $300,000 a year, and yet was no longer acting as a chief financial officer for the bank's mortgage subsidiary and was primarily just a marketing representative for the subsidiary.

A further reflection of the poor management situation was the examiners' determination that Billie Cherry was not qualified to be the president of the bank. She was grossly overpaid (at $368,000 a year); did mostly public relations work; and was not involved in the bank's securitization business—which was the bank's primary business. She did not participate in any discussions about the securitization business and did not understand any of it.

Earnings

The examiners determined that earnings were insufficient to support capital. More importantly, the examiners concluded that "the general unreliability of the bank's books call[ed] into question the profits [the bank] reported."

On this issue, the examiners pointed out that the bank's accounting continued to be deficient, resulting in the numerous call report violations and raising an issue as to the "reliability of the bank's true condition."

Liquidity

Not only was the bank's liquidity inadequate, the examiners' concerns about liquidity dated back to the 1994 examination. The situation was so serious that the examiners stated:

> The bank's *undercapitalized* . . . status as of September 30, 1998 place[s] restrictions on the ability to use brokered deposits or grow

assets. This will likely force the bank to sell loans for *liquidity* needs. The bank's financial condition is such that major sources of funding could diminish rapidly. Management has failed to adequately address potential unplanned changes in funding sources and react to changing market conditions. *Management's* failure to satisfactorily resolve the bank's liquidity in a short time frame could jeopardize the bank's continued viability.

(Emphasis added.)

This comment reflects, of course, the interconnection between capital, assets, management, and liquidity, all of which were bad.

In spite of the harshness of the OCC's ratings and narrative, the FDIC took an even more negative approach and downgraded the OCC's overall rating of the bank for the third time, from a "4" to a "5," the lowest possible score.

As a result of the examination findings, the OCC held a meeting with the bank on December 7, 1998—which turned out to be a day that would live in infamy for the bank.

At the meeting, the OCC followed up on its conclusion that Billie Cherry was a figurehead president and that Terry Church was really running the bank. At the meeting convened in Washington, D.C., the young-looking examiner-in-charge told the seventy-four-year old Cherry, in front of the entire board of directors of the bank, its attorneys and consultants, and numerous attendees from the OCC itself, that she needed to step down as president of the bank. Cherry exploded, incongruously telling the OCC that she knew where the vault in the bank was and yelling at the examiner that he was not in a position to tell her that she was unqualified.

For a long time afterward, the bank complained bitterly about the meeting.

Notes

1. This letter repeated a lot of what was contained in the FDIC's rating downgrade letter to the bank.
2. In a case involving a different bank that failed around the same time as Keystone, the FDIC's Office of Inspector General (OIG) noted that "[T]he OCC would only allow FDIC personnel to input data onto a spreadsheet. No additional examination tasks were assigned to [FDIC] staff and the OCC examiners did not accept [FDIC] comments, conclusions, and suggestions." (It should be noted that Jerry Hawke, the comptroller at this time, formally responded in writing to this FDIC report, saying that it was "gravely flawed" and was "so incomplete that it fails to accurately convey key events." Hawke also noted that the FDIC OIG failed to

"solicit any input from the OCC" in coming up with its report. The follow-up OCC staff response called the report inaccurate, misleading, and completely disingenuous, noting in the case at issue that data entry was the "primary objective of the on-site review" and that it was not, as the FDIC demeaningly called it, "women's work.") So, inaccurate or not, tensions were high between the agencies.

3. The OCC reduced the possible $100,000 CMP to $25,000 before issuing the Notice of Assessment.

4. For instance, the agreement also required the bank to hire a new chief financial officer; improve loan administration; establish an independent loan review system; review the adequacy of its ALLL; implement an adequate internal audit program; implement an effective monitoring system for interest rate and liquidity risk; correct bank information system deficiencies; and correct outstanding violations of law.

8

The Last Year of the Bank

I made a mistake in presuming
that the self-interests of organizations,
specifically banks and others,
were such as that they were best capable of protecting
their own shareholders and their equity in the firms.
—Alan Greenspan, testimony before the U.S.
House Oversight Committee, October 23, 2008

Owen Carney

After the unsettling meeting with the OCC on December 7, 1998, in which the bank was directed to retain a new president, they turned to Owen Carney.

Carney—a well-respected former OCC national bank examiner—specialized in capital markets and securitizations issues. He had worked for the OCC from 1967 to 1995. In 1975, he established the OCC's Investment Securities Division and headed it up until he left the agency. In addition, since June 26, 1998, he had been working for the Keystone bank off and on as a consultant, so he was familiar with the bank.

The bank approached him several times, asking him to be the president of the bank, but each time he turned them down. At one point, he shared with the OCC that he had turned down an offer from the bank. The next day, Terry Church came storming into the room where he was working as a consultant for the bank and started screaming at him—complaining that disclosing the fact he had turned down a job offer was somehow a betrayal. Carney never quite knew how Church found out about his phone call with the OCC, but suspected that Church might have been bugging his phone calls.

Church eventually calmed down and kept putting more money on the table, to the point where Carney could not refuse the offer. The resulting annual salary given to Carney was $500,000 in order to entice him to come run a relatively small bank in the middle of nowhere.

He became the president of the bank on February 1, 1999. However, he viewed it as a short-term matter—probably for one year—and did not even sell his house outside of Washington, D.C.

Carney—extremely bright and capable—was in a unique position to assist the bank in its securitization efforts. However, the bank continued to have problems. For instance, there were restrictions prohibiting the bank from accepting brokered deposits, which were key to its ability to fund the purchase of subprime loans from all over the country. In addition, the OCC was planning to assess civil money penalties against the directors a second time for violations of the call report requirements. In fact, the OCC sent letters to the bank's directors notifying them of the potential civil money penalties (CMPs) on February 1, 1999—the same day Carney became president of the bank.[1]

Carney recognized that the bank staff was close-knit. Most of them had grown up in the area, had worked for the bank for many years, and were distrustful of outsiders. Accordingly, Carney's one condition in heading up the bank was that he be allowed to have his wife, Jane Carney, assist him. She was a former OCC national bank examiner as well and, in addition, a certified public accountant. More importantly, in Owen's words, she was extraordinarily smart and diplomatic, but absolutely relentless when she had to be. Owen wanted at least one such strong and capable person by his side—whom he could trust implicitly.

The bank agreed to bring Jane Carney on as the acting chief financial officer and insisted on paying her a salary as well—$125,000 a year.

Unfortunately, Jane Carney proved to be a little too strong for Terry Church. At one point, Church was proposing to unilaterally amend the minutes of a board meeting after the fact—which was clearly wrong—and Jane blurted out, "You can't do that." Like the old E. F. Hutton commercial, everyone immediately became quiet when she spoke. Very few people were willing to talk back to Church or to correct her in any fashion, and the bank employees were stunned.

Following this event, one of the bank's directors, Michael Gibson, and the bank's outside attorney, Michael Lambert, asked Owen out to dinner by himself. At the dinner, the two men had the temerity to direct Owen to tell his wife that she needed to be "conscious of Terry's feelings" and to ask him to "keep a leash on Jane." Owen was not about to try to control his wife in this fashion—even if he could. He simply replied that they would try to be sensitive to Church's feelings, but that a lot of changes needed to be made at the bank.

In fact, he had already started to focus on ways to improve the bank's situation. He set out to do three things in particular.

First, he was planning to dispose of some of the bank's mortgage-related assets. They were the purported source of great earnings for the bank, but they represented a huge concentration of credit. They also created funding pressures on the bank—in order to support the purchase of the large volume of subprime assets, the bank had to generate a large amount of deposits. Both of these matters were an obvious concern to the OCC. In addition, Carney, himself, wanted to eliminate these issues. He started to accomplish this objective by contacting First Union National Bank, a large, multinational bank which had a great deal of expertise in subprime mortgage and high loan-to-value securitizations, to come up with an independent valuation of the bank's loans and to propose alternative sources of funding for the Keystone bank.

Second, he was reaching out to respected loan servicers that specialized in handling problem loans. His objective was to consolidate all of the bank's loans under one, more efficient loan servicer.

Third, Carney was lining up a highly regarded consulting firm that specialized in securitizations of subprime mortgages to do a complete management review. The firm would provide an independent analysis of the bank's securitization program and would recommend ways to correct problems in the program and ways the bank could diversify into other types of businesses.

Carney shared the first two proposals with Church, but she was not very receptive. Carney did not tell her about the proposed management review for fear that she would view the effort as a threat to her authority. Nonetheless, Carney had an impression that she somehow knew about this third proposal.

Later, in hindsight, Carney said he believed that any one of his three proposals would have uncovered the underlying fraud at the bank. Church could not afford to let that happen.

At one point during this timeframe, Carney was out of town trying to line up a company to take over the servicing of the bank's loans. After returning from the trip, he decided to go into the bank early the following morning, March 21, 1999, to catch up on paperwork. Upon arriving at the bank, he found Church alone in her office—which was unusual because several people shared the large office with Church and were typically present in the office as well.[2] Carney decided to take advantage of the opportunity to talk to her.

He approached her and bluntly said:

> Look, whatever happened in the past is history. What happens going forward is on my watch. If you do anything that violates the law, I'm going to have to turn you in. I can't put up with this. Do you understand me?

Church had to know that, coming from Owen Carney, this was not an idle threat.

Carney was focused on the relatively serious call report violations cited several times by the OCC—he had no way of knowing that Church was most likely thinking of the much more serious underlying fraud in the bank and the fact that the bank had been operating on an insolvent basis for over two years. Perhaps she had initially thought that she could control Carney, but she was coming to the realization that he was too strong and independent for this to occur. She had to do something.

Two days later, on March 23, 1999—one day before the monthly board meeting where Carney was going to present his three proposals, and two days before the bank's annual shareholders' meeting—Church called Carney into a meeting with Director Michael Gibson and bank officer Michael Graham. Church informed Carney that the bank employees had voted their shareholder proxies against him becoming a director of the bank. This meant that Carney could not continue to be the president of the bank because, under the governing law, the president of a national bank also has to be a director.

The decision to not vote in favor of Carney becoming a director was possibly dictated by Church. She controlled a large number of shares in her own right, and had the ability to vote the stock held by McConnell's estate—by virtue of her position as the executrix of the estate. In fact, between Church, Cherry, and McConnell's estate, they controlled approximately 40% of the bank's stock. In addition, the employees held their stock in the bank through an Employee Stock Option Plan which Church supervised and controlled. Consequently, the voting process was not secret and, if an employee voted in a way that displeased Church, she would know and there would be a price to pay.

As a way of explaining the employees' vote, Church informed Carney that a number of women at the bank were unhappy with Carney's supposedly aggressive manner. After the fact, Gibson interviewed many of the bank employees and found this contention to be more or less bogus and that the employees' complaints were "chicken shit."

The meeting itself had been carefully orchestrated. When Carney returned to his desk, he found that both his computer and phone had been disconnected. His ensuing resignation letter was bland—citing family commitments and the like. It did not reveal the true cause of his separation from the bank. Carney's wife, Jane, of course, resigned with him and they left town, happy to get back to the Washington, D.C. area. Their tenure at the bank had lasted only seven weeks and two days, but they escaped unscathed.

Strangely, in the process of firing Carney, Church threatened him with bogus allegations of securities fraud—claiming he had revealed confidential information to an outside party who was interested in buying shares of the bank—and yet also offered him a $250,000 consulting agreement at the same time. The bank made the offer of a consulting agreement two more times over the next two months, but it was unwilling to accede to Carney's demand that he report only to a committee of independent, outside directors. So the consulting arrangement—which, perhaps, was designed to keep tabs on Carney and to entice him not to turn against the bank—went nowhere.

Ellis

To replace Carney, the bank sought out a much more pliable, less experienced individual—Gary Ellis, who was the president of a neighboring bank in West Virginia. That bank had recently undergone a merger with a larger institution, and Ellis was due to lose his position. On April 26, 1999, Ellis accepted the position as Keystone's new president.

One of the reasons why Ellis accepted the position was the fact that, on April 19, 1999, exactly one week before, Grant Thornton had issued a clean audit report for the bank, pronouncing the bank's books and records to be commercially reasonable. Grant Thornton was the nationally recognized accounting firm selected by the bank to do a complete and independent audit of the bank—as required by the May 28, 1998 formal agreement the OCC had imposed upon the bank. Grant Thornton's audit report turned out to be totally wrong and useless, but Ellis had no way of knowing that.[3]

Once Carney was out of the way, Church and other senior bank management could continue cooking the books with regard to the unprofitable securitization deals. Ellis was put in charge of the bank only and had little to nothing to do with the subprime mortgage subsidiary of the bank, the Keystone Mortgage Corporation—which was run by Church and Graham.

Last Examination

With Ellis safely in place and the clean audit by Grant Thornton a matter of record, the bank was prepared for the next OCC examination, which started on June 21, 1999. However, this examination was going to be like no other.

While the OCC had initially denied the FDIC permission to join the 1998 examination, the OCC, due to its mounting concerns about the bank, agreed to the FDIC's request to participate in the examination in 1999, and even moved up the date to accommodate the FDIC. In addition, Leann Britton, the senior deputy comptroller for Bank Supervision Operations, gave Mark Blair, the examiner-in-charge (EIC), permission to hand-pick the examiners he wanted on his team and to indefinitely excuse them from all other duties. One of the examiners he chose was Bryan Heath. Blair had met Heath the year before at a conference and had learned of Heath's experience in dealing with fraud at several Houston, Texas, banks. When it came time to select examiners for the Keystone examination, Blair reached out to Heath and said, "I have the bank for you."

The 1999 examination team was extremely well-staffed. The EIC had considerable experience in asset securitization, had participated in the 1998 examination of the bank, and was also a certified public accountant (CPA) and a chartered financial analyst. He was supported by two securitization experts; a retail credit expert; the lead capital markets expert for the OCC's Southeastern District; another capital markets expert; and a fraud specialist. The FDIC contributed two CPAs; a senior capital markets and securities specialist; and six more examiners with relevant expertise.

The reason the OCC wanted unlimited time for the 1999 examination was explained by Blair as follows: "At the FNB of Keystone, management delayed giving us requested information because, in my opinion, they were aware we were required to complete the onsite work in a certain time frame."

In spite of the fact that the bank had been reported to be the most profitable large community bank in the entire country for three out of five years between 1994 and 1998, the examiners did not believe the bank's numbers. The examiners joked amongst themselves that the only number that was correct at the bank was its telephone number. They had known for a while that something was amiss and, this time, they were determined to find out what it was.

The examiners were certain they were going to find problems at the bank. However, they had no idea they would discover that half of the bank's assets were missing.

Review of Insider Transactions

Due to the fact that insider abuse has historically been one of the more prominent causes of bank failures, examiners typically look at the accounts and transactions of senior bank management. Church was a necessary subject of this type of review, especially given the fact that she was the highest paid person in the bank. In 1997, she made $403,500 (not counting her due diligence fees). This was before any bonus, which, in 1997, amounted to $100,000. In 1998, her base salary had been increased to $460,000.

As the examination got underway, Church took unusual steps to try to shield her accounts from examiner scrutiny. Among other things, she had bank employees pull the signature cards for about eight of her accounts at the bank, remove her name from the accounts, and take new signature cards across the street to the JLT convenience store[4]—where her brother, Larry Fisher, worked—and have him sign them. In order to make the newly signed signature cards look old, the employees threw them on the floor, stepped on them and sprinkled cigarette ashes over them.

Church later denied having orchestrated this and claimed that the bank employees took it entirely upon themselves to disobey her directive to hand all of her signature cards over to the OCC. At her first criminal trial, she claimed that the employees fraudulently altered the signature cards all on their own. This meant that, technically, Church could not gain access to her own accounts. Her testimony was just not credible.

During the 1999 examination, she also claimed that some of the accounts in the bank that the examiners had asked for were really accounts handled solely by her husband.

Examiner Heath had nonetheless started to look at these accounts on July 15, 1999. President Ellis happened to come by and noticed what accounts Heath was looking at. About five minutes later, Church arrived in the room. She immediately picked up the account items and loudly confronted Heath by asking, "Bryan, why are you looking at my husband's account?" He quietly explained to her that he was doing a normal review of insider bank accounts.

Not happy with that explanation, she went to complain to the EIC, Mark Blair, stopping him in the stairwell of the bank and asking him what the examiner team was doing.

She knew that the OCC was considering assessing additional civil money penalties, and so, among other things, she was concerned that the OCC was trying to determine her net worth so it would know how much she could afford to pay in way of a penalty. Church yelled, "I bet you're happy the OCC is assessing me $100,000 in civil money penalties. This is bullshit."

Heath, who came upon the discussion in the stairwell, told her that he was not looking at the accounts for that purpose, but, rather, he was trying to verify the source of funds in the accounts for various transactions tied to her. The explanation was not satisfactory for Church.

A few weeks later, Ellis complained to Blair that the review of insider accounts was very extensive, that the employees were becoming "extremely nervous" and that Heath was being "gruff" with the employees. Ellis went so far as to claim that the bank had brought in a doctor due to concern about the health of some of the employees. Ellis asked the examiners to be "as polite as possible." Blair suggested that it would be easier if the bank examiners could have direct access to the account records, but Ellis rejected this obvious—and normal—procedure, saying that, since the "Knox McConnell days," the bank had always required examiners to ask for records and for bank employees to oversee the examiners when reviewing records. That was not going to change.

The next day, Church announced that she wanted the examiners to review her accounts in her presence in order to relieve the women in the bookkeeping department. The examiners agreed to that arrangement, but Church went on to say she would pull specific transactions by check number, as requested. The examiners, on the other hand, wanted to look at all of the checks at once in order to determine if any were unusual and needed to be examined further. So they could not agree. As an examiner later related, Church blew up:

> Terry Church, once she realized that Heath's intentions were different from hers, exploded with a string of expletives, shouted that she felt this was harassment and started slamming and throwing stacks of checks back into a cardboard filing box. . . . She then threw the box toward Heath and told us to take them into the room where we were working.

While the examiners are entitled to look at any account in a bank, the examiners in this case had a specific reason.

At the beginning of the examination, the examiners had asked for a list of Church's accounts. However, she had not disclosed all of them. Heath discovered this when he noted that Church had paid her $13,000 civil money penalty in 1998 with a check she signed drawn on an account that had not been produced.

In addition, Heath noted that Church had taken out a $500,000 loan from the bank which was collateralized by two other accounts that had not been identified as being connected to her. One account was titled the H&TC Trust Account, which stood for Terry Church and her husband Hermie. The second account was titled "Hog Pen," which was the name of the place where Church's husband stored and worked on his motorcycles (hogs). There were various other accounts—including a second Hog Pen account—in which there were transactions conducted by Church, but which Heath had not been told about.

Some of the transactions in these accounts were very large, including the following:

Date	Type of transaction	Amount
1/2/98	Deposit	$2,836,156.23
1/2/98	Deposit	$1,838,650.89[5]
1/26/98	Withdrawal	$600,000.00
2/9/98	Withdrawal	$296,176.25
6/8/98	Withdrawal	$500,000.00
12/28/98	Deposit	$150,000.00
12/28/98	Deposit	$50,000.00
12/28/98	Deposit	$25,000.00
12/28/98	Deposit	$125,000.00
12/28/98	Deposit	$100,000.00
12/28/98	Deposit	$50,000.00[6]
1/27/99	Deposit	$900,000.00
1/27/99	Deposit	$100,000.00
2/1/99	Withdrawal	$990,000.00

These transactions were unusual and suspicious. They needed to be investigated, especially given the fact that they did not correlate to Church's income from the bank. However, Church persisted in claiming that the transactions were all related to her husband—who was unemployed—and not to her.

Later, at her first criminal trial, she continued with this argument, and her attorneys tried to bolster her story by putting her husband on the stand. This was a big mistake.

Hermie Church's direct testimony added absolutely nothing in support of his wife's case. However, on cross-examination, he actually hurt his wife's case substantially. He freely admitted that his wife handled all banking transactions, that he knew nothing about the Hog Pen accounts and, specifically, that he knew nothing about any large deposits into the Hog Pen accounts. In his words, "I didn't write the checks and things." In addition, he had never even heard of the H&TC Trust and did not seem to be able to even read the monthly bank account statements.

The testimony went as follows:

> Q. [Prosecutor John Michelich:] Well, I was just assuming—and correct me if I'm wrong, but I was just assuming that H&TC would stand for Hermie and Terry Church?
> A. Well, I would assume that it would too, but as far as having knowledge of it, I don't know.
>   . . .
> Q. And is it your testimony that you're unaware of [the H&TC] account?
> A. Sir, I don't know anything about it. I don't even know—are these numbers—are these like money that has been deposited, that's highlighted?
>   . . . .
> Q. Well, with regard to a transaction at the very top on June 8, 1998, that's a transaction—let's just take that one. That's $500,000, sir. Do you see that transaction?
> A. Yes, sir, I do.
>   . . . .
> Q. Are you familiar with the account that that one came from?
> A. No, sir.
> Q. Well, do you know if your Hog Pen Enterprise has a second bank account?
> A. No, sir, I don't.
>   . . . .
> Q. There is a deposit on January 2, 1998, in the amount of $2,836,156.23. Does that help your memory?
> A. No, sir, it don't.
> Q. Now, Hog Pen Enterprise is your business, isn't it, sir?[7]
> A. Yes, sir. I'm the president.

Q. All right. And there is a deposit on the same date, January 2, 1998, in the amount of $1,838,650.89. Do you see that, sir?

A. Yes, sir, I do.

Q. Does that refresh your recollection about this account?

A. No, sir.

Q. When I showed you a few minutes ago . . . a withdrawal from your account in the amount of half a million dollars. Does that help your recollection [in] anyway?

A. No, sir.

Q. Are you telling us, Mr. Church, that you didn't know that your business had almost four and a half million dollars in deposits in your business's bank account, sir?

A. No, sir, I didn't.

Q. This comes as news to you?

A. I—I have never seen this before.

At this point, Michelich simply stopped and let this incredible testimony sink in for the jury.

None of the defense counsel had any more questions for Hermie Church.

Temporary Restraining Order

To prevent the examiners from looking at anything in the bank at all, the bank management and attorneys took an extraordinary step: they sought a restraining order against the examiners from a federal district court.

Pursuant to federal law, the OCC has the authority to review any of the books and records of any national bank. Unlike law enforcement authorities, federal bank examiners do not need probable cause, a warrant, or a subpoena to go into a bank and look at any and all transactions. So, to overcome this unusual legal authority, the bank had to have extreme justification.

The bank found its justification in a series of inflammatory emails from an OCC bank examiner that the bank claimed to have stumbled upon.

It was on a Sunday night, July 18, 1999, when the bank's attorneys appeared before Senior District Court Judge Faber at his home, presenting damning emails written by an OCC examiner, Doug Daugherty. In an affidavit filed under seal with the judge, Michael Graham, a vice president of the bank, claimed that, three days before, on Thursday, July 15, 1999, he was moving some of the examiners' documents into the bank's vault for safekeeping over the long weekend, and in order to

137

clear the examiners' room for a Weight Watchers meeting that evening. According to Graham, one of the boxes fell off his cart exposing a file that said:

> Keystone E-Mails. DDD E-mails. If you want. If not shred.

Graham interpreted these words to mean that the OCC's EIC of the bank at the time, Doug Daugherty (whose initials are DDD), had bank-generated emails (instead of OCC emails about the bank)—and that this conclusion justified reading through the emails and handing them over to Church.

There were two OCC emails that were of concern. The first email, addressed to Kathy Gerardy, was particularly troublesome, and was dated October 27, 1997, the day after former president Knox McConnell died:

> it was too bad about mcconnell—it couldn't happen to a "nicer guy". now i have the pleasure of dealing with church and cherry. maybe we can put them with mcconnell.

> we have got the bank where we want it now—with your help we can finally win and put the number one bank in the country out of our hair for good . . . i know our office will be over joyed.[8]

The second email, addressed to Mark Blair and dated the next day, was equally volatile:

> by now you have heard that our old buddy mcconnell died. we don't have to worry about trying to do him in anymore. i guess i will miss fighting with the sob. . . . i bet church and cherry will want our sympathy but they are not getting any from me. now maybe we can close the number 1 bank in the country i certainly am going to try. with your help and kathy's we can do it.

Doug Daugherty was the EIC for the bank from 1994 to early 1998, but had left the OCC in June, 1998, over one year before the bank purportedly found his emails. He was no longer connected with the OCC or the bank. But, on their face, these two-year old emails were disturbing, if not threatening—talking about putting two remaining senior officials of the bank where McConnell was—in the grave—and trying to close the bank on spurious grounds.

So, on an *ex parte* basis, Judge Faber issued a temporary restraining order (TRO) at 9:45 PM from his home. The order was actually fairly bland—requiring that the documents in issue be personally delivered to Comptroller of the Currency John D. Hawke, Jr., and that no document—generated or modified by OCC representatives—be altered or destroyed without Hawke's written permission.

When the senior management of the OCC found out about the emails and the TRO, they pulled the examiners from the bank, a result the bank must have hoped for from the beginning. It was, naturally, the only safe course of action. In addition, the examiners could not continue their examination without generating and modifying documents and altering those documents. In reviewing the emails, Hawke, only half-jokingly, said he wished that Daugherty were still with the OCC—so he could be fired. Tensions were understandably high. With all this going on, some of the examiners thought that their own careers were on the line.

The examiners were actually called back to Washington, D.C. to explain themselves. The concern was so great that some senior officials wanted to replace Mark Blair, the EIC, and Kathy Gerardy, the Washington, D.C.-based problem bank analyst (who were the purported recipients of the emails). Robert L. Clarke, a former comptroller of the currency assisting the bank at this point, made a personal pitch to the comptroller to replace the entire examination team. One suggestion was that a new crew of examiners from the Office of Thrift Supervision be called in.

Replacing the examination team would have played into the hands of the bank because it would have given the bank that much more time to come up with made-up stories and fraudulent documents. In addition, it would have made it virtually impossible to find any wrongdoing as the new examiners would have had to spend too much time getting up to speed.

There were a series of high-level meetings at the OCC over what to do. Curiously, the TRO was only addressed to the OCC; it did not affect the FDIC, so its examiners had actually stayed in the bank. Accordingly, one of the more compelling comments in one of the meetings came from Rick Spelsberg, the assistant deputy comptroller for West Virginia. He advocated going back into the bank—that day. He told Comptroller Hawke, "I will tell you, Mr. Hawke, I would not want to be in your shoes, sitting in front of Congress trying to explain why FDIC examiners were in a national bank while our examiners were in a hotel." Hawke slammed his fist on the table and said, "Goddamn it, you guys get back in the bank and do your job."

Blair, for his part, never really wanted to be the EIC for this bank and did not relish the thought of going back to Keystone. He was already having bad dreams about the bank and Church. But he went back, and Gerardy continued to oversee the examination from Washington, D.C.

In the end, the examiners were only out of the bank for a week as the incendiary emails were promptly hand-delivered to the comptroller.

The OCC did not know what to make of these emails. They were troublesome, but their validity was very questionable. So the OCC forwarded the emails to the Inspector General's Office (OIG), which started its own investigation. The OIG eventually found—as many people had suspected—that the emails were fraudulent. No OCC examiners could remember having received these emails. There was no record of the emails in the OCC's computer system and, most importantly, the emails proved to be incompatible with the OCC's email software used at that time.

Curiously, Owen Carney, the former president of the bank, later stated that the bank had shown him these, or very similar, emails back in December, 1998 or January, 1999—approximately six to seven months before they purportedly fell off Graham's cart. Carney decided to ignore the emails for fear that they would aggravate an already tense situation and because he had more important matters to deal with in the bank. He had noted to himself, though, that the validity of the emails was questionable:

> They were mildly shocking, particularly one about the death of former bank president McConnell and the examiners' animosity toward Terry Church and Billie Cherry. My reaction was either the emails were forgeries, or the West Virginia examiners were as crazy as the bankers. No right-thinking examiner would have put those kinds of comments in writing. . . .

> They were official OCC documents and discovery of them would have gotten the examiners in a lot of trouble, perhaps fired. . . .

> I had not made up my mind whether the emails were real or not and I was sure the directors would react badly. I did not see any point getting in another confrontation with the regulators or Terry Church at this point in time. The two or three board meetings I attended were focused on more important issues.

While the IG's office eventually came to the right conclusion with regard to the fake emails, one of the IG agents on site at Keystone was initially totally off-base.

The OIG started its investigation on August 26, 1999, one week after being notified of the matter by the OCC. Three IG agents went to Keystone and started by interviewing bank employees, because the examiners were too busy. There were indications of various fraudulent activities swirling around and things were very chaotic for the examiners. The examiners were fearful that the bank would have to be closed. A week later, they were proven right.

Consequently, the IG agents interviewed Church, who claimed that the OCC examiners were conducting a "witch-hunt" and were "after [her] ass." Unfortunately, one of the agents apparently believed Church and decided to take things into his own hands without waiting to explore all of the facts.

While the OIG was conducting its one-sided inquiry, Scott Griffith, the head of the bank's IT department, approached examiner Heath and informed him that he knew what the examiners were looking for, but that he and his wife were resigning from the bank that day due to their fear of Church. They wanted to take advantage of the fact that Church was temporarily out of town.

Heath asked Griffith to hold off resigning until he could get back to him. Heath informed EIC Blair and they together relayed the information to OCC headquarters. OCC executives immediately told the examiners to interview Griffith as soon as possible outside of the bank. So the examiners got Griffith to agree to meet with them that night at the examiners' hotel.

That night, Blair was in his hotel room at the Hampton Inn in Princeton, West Virginia, conferring with the FBI about the bank and the new development of an inside source of information.

The one troublesome IG agent, however, insisted on talking to Blair. He went to Blair's room, and was initially denied entrance by the FBI, but somehow got past them. He confronted Blair and grabbed him by the shoulders and shoved him down onto the bed, yelling, "I ought to arrest you right now." In Blair's view, he was a nutcase.

When the IG agent learned about the confidential source, he said that he was prohibiting Blair and the other examiners from talking to Griffith, claiming that it would be interfering with law enforcement activities. Two other examiners were in the room and the discussion got very heated—primarily because issuing such a prohibition was wholly outside of the IG's authority. The IG agent did not think the OCC was capable of conducting the interview, and wanted the FBI to conduct it instead. However, the FBI overruled the IG agent and told the OCC to go ahead and conduct the interview.

The interview with Griffith later that night went on for two hours and laid out critical information about the bank. Griffith also revealed the fact that the bank had removed truckloads of documents from the bank, but he did not know where they were taken. This information, and Bill Miles' tip, later led the FBI to Church's ranch.

In order to straighten things out going forward and to allow the bank examination to continue unimpeded by the IG's Office, Morris Morgan, a national bank examiner, called OCC headquarters to get the one IG agent removed from the case. Robert Serino, a deputy chief counsel of the OCC, contacted the IG's Office and accomplished this. The remaining two IG agents were reasonable, and the investigations by the OIG and the FBI, as well as the examination by the OCC and the FDIC, were able to continue.

Long after the bank failed, Judge Faber decreed that the $1,000 bond the bank was required to post in obtaining the TRO was to be forfeited to the Department of Treasury. This was small recompense, however, for the anguish that the bank had created for Daugherty, the other examiners and the OCC as a whole.

An additional fallout was visited upon the attorney—who was also a bank director—who had arranged for his firm to appear before Judge Faber to get the TRO. The attorney, Michael Gibson, had unwittingly accepted the story given to him about the emails having fallen off Graham's cart. He said later that it was difficult to face Judge Faber as an attorney after that because he was associated with this false story—even though it was not his doing. He simply was too trusting of the senior management of the bank, with whom he had been working for some time.

Graffiti

Once the examiners returned to the bank after the TRO lapsed, the bank had to realize that the examiners were serious and that they were not going to give up. This fact was reinforced by a meeting the bank had in Washington, D.C. on August 12, 1999, when the OCC told the bank that the examiners were not going to leave until they "determined the true condition of the bank."

So bank management resorted to even more drastic measures.

First, they buried the four truckloads of documents on August 12th and 15th on Church's ranch.

Second, threatening graffiti appeared at the bank, clearly directed at the examiners.

It was on the morning of August 16, 1999, the examiners arrived at the bank, and Church told them that someone had painted "serious" threats on the street in front of the bank. Church said that the threats were aimed at everyone at the bank and that the examiners had to take down the Styrofoam cup that they had placed over the security camera in the room where they worked. The examiners wondered how doing so would assist the bank in monitoring activity outside of the bank, but they nonetheless complied.

Two days later, on August 18, 1999, Church told the examiners as they arrived that, again, there were "serious" threats—this time painted on the back door of the bank. Church indicated that they had painted over the graffiti in both cases so as not to alarm anyone. She also claimed that the local police had told her not to tell anyone what the specific threats were.

Ellis finally told the examiners that the graffiti in both cases said "auditors go hum" and "Fuck you, examiners." Although never proven, it is more than likely that the bankers themselves wrote this graffiti and misspelled the word "home" on purpose, trying to play to a bad stereotypical image of a West Virginian.

Regardless, it was getting scary for the examiners.

OCC headquarters called the local police in Keystone to get more details, but were stonewalled. A sergeant on the Keystone police force denied that the graffiti said "auditors go hum," which, of course, contradicted what Ellis had said. Headquarters then contacted Bob Krasne, the bank's outside counsel at Williams & Connolly, who confirmed that the sergeant had misled the OCC, apparently in an attempt to down play the situation. The sergeant had seen the graffiti, but dismissed it as "just profanity."

Of course, the Keystone police department was answerable to the chairman of the board of the bank, Billie Cherry, because she was also the mayor of Keystone. The bank, in effect, had total control over the small town.

In reaction to this series of exchanges, OCC headquarters noted that the situation "gives new meaning to the term 'Keystone cops.'"

Guards

Following the second graffiti incident, Church explained to the examiners that the bank was hiring two private guards to protect the bank employees. She claimed that the guards were to also protect the bank examiners.

143

The hired "guards," however, seemed to be more designed to monitor the examiners than to protect them. The guards followed the examiners around, even to the restrooms, knocking on the bathroom door to see if they were done. This was all in order to "protect" them, as well as the bank employees. Actually, it was the examiners who were afraid of the bankers. Blair, for instance, was afraid that Church was under such stress that she might do something drastic, and he was afraid that she had guns in her office.

Blair's fears were not unfounded. In fact, Church did have a gun in her desk. The day the bank closed, law enforcement recovered guns both in her office and in her car. Long after the bank failed, Church felt it necessary to approach Blair during a break at one of the ensuing trials and say, "Mark, I want you to know, I would have never hurt you." For the head of a bank to have that on her mind and to feel compelled to defend her actions in that way is incredible.

One of the scarier days with the guards was when one of them told the examiners, "You better watch yourselves driving home; there are some crazy drivers out there." As noted earlier, there was no place for the examiners to stay in Keystone, West Virginia, so each day they had to drive approximately forty-five minutes along Route 52, a winding, mountain road that, in the best of situations, is uncomfortable to drive. There is no other road in or out of Keystone. So the examiners took the guard's comment as a serious threat that they might be run off the road.

By August 5, 1999, even before the two graffiti incidents, the OCC was considering the need to ask the U.S. Marshals Service to come in and protect the examiners. After the graffiti and the encounters with the bank's guards, the examiners got together and, in a close vote, decided to leave the bank. They did not believe that OCC headquarters appreciated the gravity of the situation. However, upon hearing of the vote, Leann Britton, the senior deputy comptroller for Bank Supervision Operations, agreed with the examiners and pulled them out of the bank.

Robert Serino, the OCC's deputy chief counsel, contacted the Marshals Service to arrange for protection for the examiners for the rest of the examination. This took a few days, wrestling with the protocol of such a request and whether Judge Faber had to authorize it. To expedite matters, the OCC considered having the comptroller call either the head of the Marshals Service or senior Treasury officials, like Jim Johnson or Larry Summers. However, the Marshals Service finally agreed to provide protection and showed up at the bank starting Wednesday, August 25, 1999, which turned out to be exactly one week before the OCC closed the bank.

One unfortunate side effect was the lack of subtlety of the Marshals Service, as set forth in an OCC email:

> So much for the low key approach. Bank's counsel Mike Lambert called and told me that sometime this afternoon, the 2 US Marshals went into the bank, walked up to the teller counter and announced themselves as US Marshals while flashing their badges. . . . Obviously, their visit caught the attention of the tellers and word spread rapidly through the bank, and by now, probably the town that the US Marshals were there.

While law enforcement has been called in for protection with regard to some bank closings over the years, this is probably the only time in the annals of bank examinations that examiners had to be protected in the middle of an examination.

Brokered Certificates of Deposit

To support its securitization program, the bank had purchased subprime loans from all over the country, and, in order to do this, the bank needed funding. Ordinarily, a bank's funding comes from local deposits, but the Keystone bank needed a huge amount of money—and the impoverished McDowell County, West Virginia, was not going to be a viable source. So the bank had become highly dependent on using brokered certificates of deposit (CDs). These are large deposits which the bank solicits through a broker and typically pays a higher than average amount of interest for, over a fixed time. They are very attractive for institutional investors who are seeking to obtain additional income, but they can be expensive for a bank. Due to their volatility and the fact they frequently exceed FDIC insured limits, the regulators permit only "well-capitalized" banks to use brokered CDs. If a bank is only "adequately capitalized" or is "undercapitalized," it cannot purchase or roll-over such deposits.

On three different occasions—June 29, 1998, August 5, 1998, and November 24, 1998—the OCC sent formal letters to the bank advising it that it was not allowed to use brokered CDs due to the bank's poor capital levels. However, not only did the bank continue to accept and roll-over brokered CDs, it hid them and even falsified numerous documents to cover up their existence.

As of June 30, 1999, the bank had approximately $514 million in brokered deposits, representing at least 80% of the bank's overall deposits. Due to this volume, and the restrictions the bank was under, it was necessary for the examiners to review the bank's use of CDs.

To avoid having the examiners discover the fact that the bank was continuing to acquire new brokered deposits, Church had her staff identify and remove all expense checks that corresponded to the bank's payment of interest to brokers for CDs.

Deborah Shrader, a bank employee, provided the remaining expense checks to an examiner to review. She knew that a number of the checks were missing from what she was providing him, so she took a bold step. She offered the examiner the monthly statements that corresponded to the expense checks. She knew that, if he compared the checks he received to the monthly statements, he would have been able to see that a number of checks were missing. But he did not understand what she was trying to do and she could not come right out and explain it. She was running a big risk as it was and could not blurt out that the bank was committing fraud.

So the examiner turned her down. She repeated her offer, but he turned her down a second time.

Another examiner, Michael Morgan, from the FDIC, was assigned the task of reviewing the bank's CDs. This ended up requiring the skills of a trained detective.

The bank's CDs were filed upstairs in the bookkeeping section of the bank. Morgan was going through the filing cabinets for the CDs—always under the watchful eyes of the bank employees—when he found, tucked behind the regular hanging files, an envelope. The envelope contained four brokered CDs, all from CEDE and Company (on behalf of Morgan Stanley)[9] and all dated in 1999, a period of time when the bank was clearly not allowed to accept brokered CDs.[10]

As Morgan opened the envelope, he glanced up and his eyes met those of Ellen Turpin, a bank employee, who was sitting off to his side. He noted that she immediately picked up the phone and made a call. Turpin knew right away what Morgan had found:

> Mike Morgan from the FDIC was looking through all of our CD files. I sat at this end of the room. We had cabinets at this end of the room—file cabinets—and they were full of CDs. And we have one envelope that we kept this particular company's in. And he opened it and I just looked . . . back at him and he just dropped his head, and I knew what he seen.

Morgan looked to see whether the CDs were on the list that Church had provided him, but they were not. On that list, however, he found that there were four CDs purchased by CEDE in 1998—in the exact same amounts; CDs that he had already reviewed and had checked off. The only differences between the 1998 and the 1999 CDs were the certificate numbers and the dates:

Morgan Stanley/CEDE Brokered CDs			
Church's 1998 List		1999 List from Envelope	
Date	Amount	Date	Amount
9/19/98	$7,500,000	1/19/99	$7,500,000
9/8/98	$1,000,000	3/8/99	$1,000,000
9/12//98	$2,099,000	3/12/99	$2,099,000
9/17/98	$5,000,000	3/17/99	$5,000,000
Total	$15,599,000	Total	$15,599,000

Because the 1998 CDs were on the list that Morgan had and he had already checked them off, he initially thought that they were the real ones. Accordingly, he asked Patricia Orell, a bank employee, to call up the 1998 CDs to look at the account history. Orell tried, but could not. "That's strange," she said. "I've never seen that before . . . These are dated in September of 1998, but I'm not showing any interest payments being made." At that point, Morgan realized that it was the 1999 CDs that were real and that the 1998 ones were fake.

Orell did not understand why she could not pull up the 1998 CDs. She conferred with Turpin and they realized that they needed to discuss the matter with Church. So they went down to her office to get direction as to what to do. Church's first decision was to keep Orell away from the examiners. Orell was too nervous and upset to be around the examiners, so Church directed Orell and Turpin not to return to the bookkeeping area of the bank.

Orell and Turpin found an empty office to go to and hide in the dark. They repeatedly called Gracie Wooldridge in bookkeeping to find out if the examiners had left and, thus, whether the coast was clear for them to return. They stayed in the darkened office for about an hour, but Orell kept peeking out of the door. At one point, Turpin heard someone coming down the hall and pushed the door shut too fast, slamming Orell's fingers in the door.

The bank had received the CDs in 1999, but Church had internally recorded them on her personal computer as having been received in 1998. It was this internal report that she had given to Morgan. However, the bank's mainframe computers had not been altered. When Church realized that the examiners had discovered that there was no official record of the 1998 CDs on the mainframe, she had to work fast.

Church brought her senior staff together after working hours and told them to create fake CDs dated in 1998. The machine that produced the certificates of deposit, though, could not be easily manipulated. When the staff put in the 1998 dates, the machine came up with an interest rate that corresponded to 1998—not to the actual rates provided to CEDE in 1999. When the staff told Church about this problem, she just said, "Well, whatever you have to do, I don't care what you do."

In order to get the result Church wanted, the staff had to manually manipulate the date format. Lora McKinney, a bank employee, found four CDs from 1998 that had matured. Then, Turpin used those CDs to create four fake CDs with dates from 1998, but which contained the data from the 1999 CDs. To do this, she had to use scissors, Wite-Out and Scotch Tape to cut and paste the information onto the fake CDs and then copy them so they looked genuine. The resulting CDs were dated 1998 and had new certificate numbers, but otherwise had the same information as the 1999 CDs—name, dollar amount, and interest rate. But the documents had one tell-tale mistake: the fake 1998 CDs had the same maturity date as the 1999 CDs—five years from the 1999 dates, but six years from the 1998 dates.

After creating the fake 1998 CDs, the bank staff created corresponding general ledger (GL) tickets reflecting the existence of the CDs. The GL tickets represent the official transactions of the bank, and bank examiner Morgan had asked for them. He wanted the GL tickets for the 1998 CDs and had to be kept at bay—from a Thursday to the following Monday—while the fake 1998 GL tickets were being created. One excuse was that the GL tickets were not in the bank, but in storage. Another delaying tactic was for Vice President Graham to complain that Morgan was bothering the bank employees, thus making it difficult for him to press for the information he had requested.

In creating the GL tickets, the bank had to find two employees to initial them, other than those who had created the underlying CDs. Gracie Wooldridge was one employee called upon to initial the fake GL tickets. The other person whose initials they needed was Connie Evans. The problem, though, was that Evans had left the bank in July,

1999, and it was now August. So Wooldridge signed Evans' initials to the GL tickets, after first practicing. It later came to light that Evans was not even in the bank at the time the fake 1998 CDs were supposedly created. She was on a cruise with her husband and did not return until after the September, 1998 dates for the fake CDs.

Once the fake 1998 GL tickets were created, another problem was they did not look the same as the real GL tickets from 1999. The machine that produced the GL tickets had been repaired in late 1998 or early 1999, and, afterward, the GL tickets had the notation "UDC2" on the lower left corner of the ticket, and the proof stamp on the back of the ticket had a square around the stamp, instead of an arrow under it. McKinney noted these differences. When the doctored tickets were finally provided to Morgan, he noticed them too:

> These tickets looked to be very unusual to me. . . . I had taken the opportunity to go through the entire box of general ledger tickets for September, 98, . . . these four tickets were unusual in particular because they had some identifying marks on them that none of the other tickets had in the whole box. . . . [T]here were probably hundreds of those tickets, and those other tickets didn't have those marks, so it raised some suspicion. . . .

> [T]he four tickets that I was looking for, and I found, had a mark on the lower left-hand corner of each ticket . . . , and that mark [said] UDC2. . . .

> I really don't know what that stands for, but what I do know is that mark was not on any of the other tickets. . . .

> [T]he proof stamp on the back of the general ledger ticket was different than any other GL tickets that I had seen in the box. The stamp on these four general ledger tickets had a square index . . . had a square mark around them. So the stamp was different than any other stamps that I saw on the GL tickets in that box for 1998, and it was only these four tickets that had these identifying marks that were different.

Normally, after the GL tickets are created, they have to be sent through the bank's proof machine, which makes a microfilm recording of all the bank's transactions. Accordingly, Morgan asked for the microfilm as well, and was initially told—as he was for the GL tickets—that there would be no problem. After a number of hours, a flustered McKinney came back and said that the microfilm—like the GL tickets—was across the street in storage. Later that day, the bank informed Morgan that the microfilm no longer existed. The bank claimed that, starting in January, in order to save space, it had started to reuse the microfilm. The examiners did not buy the story. When the bank gave the examiners this explanation, it was all they could do to keep from laughing out loud because they knew it was patently false.

First, microfilm was kept in canisters that took up very little room, so the excuse about storage was clearly bogus. Second, microfilm is like thirty-five-millimeter film—once it is exposed, that is it. It cannot be reused; it can only take one picture. As a result, microfilm is recognized as one of the most reliable forms of documentation.

This was all on a Thursday. On Monday, the story changed once more. Graham said that they had found the microfilm. He told the examiners that they "could look at the microfilm, however . . ." The examiners responded, "However? What does that mean?" Graham said, "We've got the microfilm that you could have looked at, but you can't because the machine is broken."

The microfilm reader was indeed broken. At Church's direction, McKinney and Turpin had disabled it. At first, they only broke the light bulb in the machine. Church explained to them that replacing a bulb was too easy and that they had to do more. So the two bank employees stood on either side of the microfilm reader—so the overhead camera would not see them—and proceeded to dislodge the belt in the machine, yank out wires, and take out screws in the machine. According to Turpin:

> We pulled one screw out, and I was going to put it back, and I stripped it. The only kind of glue we had in the bank was fingernail glue. We used it to get the screw back in, but first I glued it to my fingers, then Lora [McKinney] had to take it from me and put it back in with the fingernail glue.

In spite of their ineptness, they succeeded in their goal. The examiners never got to use the microfilm reader. The microfilm being sought was later found on Church's ranch—in the ditch she had her workmen dig.

Finally, Morgan tried to verify the existence or nonexistence of the 1998 CDs by reviewing the bank's incoming wire log. Because the CDs were so large in dollar amount, it was clear that they would have been paid for by a wire transfer to the bank. Turpin kept a hand-written internal log of all incoming wires in a blue notebook. Morgan had seen

Turpin's log and recalled that he had not seen any CEDE wires from 1998. So he asked to see the notebook again.

In response to this request, Turpin seemed flustered and claimed that her notebook was missing. A few days later, she said she found the book and provided it to Morgan. The incoming wires to pay for the 1998 CDs were indeed in the book.

But Morgan did not believe that the information in the book was accurate.

As it turned out, Turpin had taken out the relevant pages in her book and had painstakingly rewritten them to add each wire that had purportedly come from CEDE in 1998—working late into the night and finally finishing around noon the next day. She had to rewrite three pages altogether, omitting actual wires in order to make room for the fake ones she had to insert. She then shredded the original pages.

When asked about it at a subsequent trial, she said: "Morally, I knew it was wrong, but . . . I thought that was the only way our bank was going to survive."

Following his instincts, Morgan took a very unusual step. With the assistance of the EIC, Mark Blair, he went to the Federal Reserve Bank of Richmond and asked for a copy of the actual wires that corresponded to the unique certificate numbers attributed to the wires for the 1998 CDs. They did not match.

In fact, the numbers were way off. For instance, as set forth in the chart below, the $1 million wire that the bank supposedly received from CEDE on September 8, 1998, was actually for a wire in the amount of only $500 from some other source.

Date	Bank created wires	Actual wires per Federal Reserve Bank
9/8/98	$1,000,000	$500
9/11/98	$2,099,000	$400,000
9/16/98	$5,000,000	$99,000
9/18/98	$7,500,000	$9,784,000

At this point, there was no question that the bank had provided the bank examiners with fraudulent information and false documents with regard to the CDs that supposedly were issued in 1998. There were false CDs, false GL tickets, false wires, false proof tickets, missing microfilm, misrepresentations about illegally purchased CDs, and an extensive cover-up to mislead the federal bank examiners.

The examiners decided to confront Church.

On August 17, 1999, the examiners met with Church to review all of this. To the examiners, she seemed agitated, and said that she would ask "the ladies in bookkeeping" about the issues.

The next day, August 18th, Church met with the examiners and changed her story. This time, she admitted that she had issued the CDs in 1999 to CEDE due to liquidity issues at the bank. Disingenuously, she claimed that she had thought doing so was perfectly legal. But when asked why the bank created the 1998 CDs, she stammered and did not have a good explanation.

However, she again took action to have the bank's books and records match her changing story.

One problem with changing the records back was the fact that McKinney—who had helped put together the false 1998 CDs and other records—was, by this time, on vacation. She had worked until Sunday afternoon, August 15th, altering the CDs, and had delayed her anniversary celebration with her husband by two days. Their vacation site was Church's marina in South Halston Lake, Tennessee, which reflects how beholden she was to Church. McKinney was due to stay there a week. However, when Church admitted that the 1999 CDs were real all along, she had to call McKinney back from vacation that Wednesday, August 18th, to change the 1998 CDs back to 1999 CDs. So, that night, McKinney was back at the bank assisting in recreating the 1999 CDs and recreating corresponding GL and proof tickets.

On Friday, August 20th, Church produced a one-page document which she, Turpin, Orell, and Virginia Burks had signed. She had typed it herself—in her customary capital letters—and had the three employees sign it without reading it. It sought to explain and justify why the bank had accepted the CEDE CDs in 1999. She tried to do it in a way that would specifically exonerate herself, but the explanation ended up being more incredible than the previous explanations she had given.

The document explained that the wires for the CDs had originally arrived in 1998—over the course of eleven days—from CEDE. However, the bank returned them because it had received too many CDs from other sources and did not need the CDs from CEDE.[11] The document went on to say that, when the 1999 CDs came in—this time, over the course of three months—Connie Evans, a bank employee, somehow knew in each case that they were in the same amounts and from the same source as the 1998 CDs, and instructed Burks to use copies of the 1998 CDs she had as templates. It was never explained why Burks would have kept copies of these particular 1998 CDs in her desk out of hundreds of other CDs. Also, it was never explained how Evans knew that Burks had supposedly kept copies of the CDs.

In any event, according to the document, that is what Burks did, but, upon completion, she supposedly sent the wrong CDs to be inputted into the general ledger. She did this four different times between January and March, 1999.

The women creating the GL tickets, based on the wrong CDs, apparently did not notice the four-to-six month discrepancy between the 1998 CDs and the date when they were actually creating the GL tickets. They somehow created GL tickets in 1999, but had them dated 1998. The story was that they did this four different times.

Then the GL tickets were co-signed by someone who also did not notice the incorrect dates—four times. Then someone else inputted the GL tickets into the proof machine four times—each time failing to notice the incorrect dates.

Church enlisted a frightened Orell to explain all of this to the examiners. Orell knew it was not correct and insisted on Church telling her word-for-word what she should tell the examiners. The examiners, after listening to the story, were skeptical.

The story, however, proceeded to get even stranger. After Church explained all of these machinations, the president of the bank, Ellis, told Blair that the former president, Owen Carney, had authorized the purchase of the illegal brokered CDs in 1999 and had hidden them from the board. According to Ellis, when this was discovered, the board fired Carney. When asked why Church admitted to purchasing the CDs herself if Carney were the guilty party, Ellis just shook his head. He said, "Mark, you write the memoirs and I get the bylines." In other words, Ellis was the one telling the story, but Mark Blair would be the one interpreting it.

There were a number of problems with Ellis' story. First, Carney did not become the president of the bank until almost two weeks after the first 1999 CD was issued in January. Second, if the bank's story had been true, the bank should have notified the OCC of the violation in March, 1999, not the following August, after devoting so much time to falsifying so many records and concocting so many conflicting stories. Third, Carney was the one concerned about the bank not violating any laws and had threatened to report Church if he caught her doing so. The history of the bank's violations long predated Carney's involvement with the bank; it had started on Church's watch. Everything pointed to Church and her senior management.

In addition, the bank employees who Church had sign the explanatory statement knew the document was false and were furious that Church had involved them in this fraud. One of those employees, Orell, was particularly upset. Turpin recounted Orell's reaction as follows:

> One morning, I'm not sure when it was, it was during the end of the bank closing, Patricia Orell come upstairs and she said, "I've just signed my life away" or "I've just signed my jail sentence," or something like that. I said, "What are you –" I mean, Patricia is loud, and she come in screaming it.
>
> I told her, I said, "Come here, girl. What are you talking about?" She said, "Terry just made me sign some kind of papers with some kind of lies on it." I said, "No, she didn't." She said, "And don't laugh because she is coming after you."
>
> And when [Church] come to me, she had Patricia's name, Virginia's name [on the document]. She put it to me, she was standing over my desk like this. She said, "Sign this." Ginny [Burks] and Patricia have already signed off on it, where Patricia had done something to the CDs. She went through a long explanation. I signed it, she signed it, and she left. I didn't even get a copy of it. I didn't even read it. I just done as she said.

Burks was so upset when she finally read Church's written explanation about the CDs that she quit her job at the bank. She had worked for Church for twenty years and was very hurt and angry about being wrongly accused of having made so many mistakes relating to the CDs. She felt that it was all too unfair:

> I was a good employee. I had been there 20 years, and I did not cause any trouble at the bank.

Burks quit on Friday, August 27, 1999—five days before the OCC closed the bank.

Loan Servicer Reports

Meanwhile, the examiners noted that there were continuing discrepancies between the reports from the loan servicers and the reports the bank was producing. There were erratic balances; unexplained changes in due dates; charge offs on the bank's books that did not agree with its call reports; and "loans appearing, disappearing, and reappearing" on loan balance reports. It was a mess. But, even with these discrepancies, the examiners still were focused on the performance of the loans—due dates, principal balances and such—not on whether the loans were owned by the bank.

Due to the discrepancies they were noticing, the examiners decided to go to the loan servicers to resolve the confusion and to arrive at correct numbers. As a courtesy, on June 30, 1999, the examiners notified Church that they were going to send letters directly to the servicers seeking appropriate answers. Church was not about to let that happen. She convinced the examiners that it would be better and more efficient to have the written requests go out under the bank's letterhead and to have the responses come back to the bank—rather than to the OCC's duty station in Charleston, West Virginia, approximately three hours away. The examiners hesitated, but reluctantly agreed. They were on the right track, but made a serious error in leaving things in Church's hands.

The examiners mistakenly thought that the servicers were sending the bank hard copies of material—reports that could not be manipulated by the bank. But when the information came in on July 12, 1999 from the two primary servicers, Church handed the examiners three computer disks—one labeled Compu-Link and the other two labeled Advanta—all in the same handwriting.

The examiners were getting suspicious, so they persisted in their inquiry. On July 29th, the examiners met with Church and told her again that they wanted to communicate directly with the servicers. Church agreed, so long as the bank could be present on the call, which was set for August 4th. However, the day before, the bank reneged and asked for another chance to explain the discrepancies in the numbers. A meeting with the bank was set for August 5th.

At that meeting, Church, Graham, and Cherry blamed everything on Meredith Hale, the employee whom Church had fired for having refused to do as Church told her. Church explained that the electronic reports the bank received from the servicers did not contain headings, so Hale was supposed to adjust the reports and insert proper column headings. However, according to Church and Graham, Hale was not a good employee and was going through serious marital problems with an abusive husband who was harassing and stalking her. As a result of her personal problems, Hale allegedly made a series of mistakes on the reports. Of course, it was not true—Hale, whatever personal issues she may or may not have had, was too good to make those types of mistakes.

When they heard this account, light bulbs went off for the examiners. They realized—for the first time—that the bank could manipulate the reports that were being delivered by the servicers. After years of examining the bank, this was a revelation.

The examiners caucused and returned to the meeting to inform the bank that they had decided to go directly to the servicers. The bankers went into a tirade. They said they were concerned that, if the OCC took the unusual step of going to the servicers, the bank's reputation would be ruined and the bank would not be able to sell its loans in the market.

Church was extremely upset and indicated "she [would] not agree to allow [the examiners] to request this information directly from the servicers." She accused the OCC of not trusting them. According to one examiner:

> She blew up. She was very upset. She was screaming and yelling at us. She said, "Just say it. You don't trust us. You don't trust us. . . . You told us you weren't going to go to the servicers. You promised us. You promised us."

Graham was also very upset—angry and red-faced—and kept saying, "You're out to close the bank. You're out to close the bank."

Cherry, though, took the cake. She too was very upset, but started to resurrect a series of old grievances. She was yelling:

> [The examinations] went smoothly until Doug Daugherty started performing examinations. The OCC does not want two women running the bank. The OCC does not have the ability to evaluate management. The OCC is only good at evaluating numbers and figures. I informed . . . Mark Blair two years ago City [National Bank] was not servicing loans properly. You did nothing about it. A 30-year old, Tim Knaak, humiliated me at [the December 7, 1998] meeting in Washington in front of the board of directors. . . . [This] bank was always in good shape until Knox died two years ago and the OCC started criticizing [the bank]. The OCC has been examining the bank for a year and a half now.

The screaming and yelling was so bad the examiners finally had to get up and walk out. As one examiner, Cindy Wilson, recounted:

> I consider myself to be a pretty experienced examiner . . . , but I had never, never, ever been talked to the way these three people talked to me. They were just outraged.

Despite the verbal explosion, the examiners decided to go ahead with their decision to contact the servicers directly. If anything, the reaction of the senior management of the bank caused the examiners "to dig their heels in more." They wondered why the bankers would react "so outrageously to something that seemed pretty simple."

The examiners would soon find out.

The OCC's certified letters to the loan servicers went out on August 6th, but they did not hear back from the servicers for a number of weeks. As it turned out, the bank management was continuing to try to thwart the examiners' efforts.

On August 10th, for instance, Graham contacted one of the servicers, Advanta, and explained to them that the OCC really needed to receive information not only about the loans the Keystone bank held, but also the loans held by United National Bank.

Then, on August 17th, Graham contacted Advanta again via fax and told them the same thing. Fortunately, Advanta contacted the OCC examiners, who were able to countermand Graham's instructions.

On August 23rd, Church called Advanta twice, and, when Advanta told her they understood what the OCC wanted, she said, "Oh no, you must send the data for all [the] files."

When Graham called Advanta again, he reached Dee Romero who told him that Advanta was not going to send any information to the OCC on the loans held by United . . . because they had received a letter from the OCC that clearly indicated that it did not want that information. Graham finally realized that the bank had lost this battle. He got very quiet and just said, "Okay," and hung up the phone.[12]

With the other servicer, Compu-Link, the OCC was not as lucky. Even though the OCC had asked for Keystone-owned loans only and asked for the information to be sent directly to the OCC, the servicer ignored both requests. Rather, they sent information on the loans owned both by Keystone and United directly to the Keystone bank. When asked why they did this, they simply responded it was pursuant to the client request: the bank had gotten to them.

After the OCC received the report from Compu-Link, the OCC tried to print it out, but it was taking several hours just to print the report. Even though the OCC had been expecting thousands of loans to be on the list, this report was still far too long. So the OCC called Compu-Link and determined that the company had sent too much. The OCC had to clarify again that it only wanted loans owned by Keystone.

On August 23rd and 24th, there were a series of calls and letters back and forth between Compu-Link and the OCC, trying to straighten the situation out.[13] But it was not until Compu-Link got a letter on August 24th from Ron Schneck—whose title "Director of Special Supervision/Fraud" surprised and scared them—that the company woke up and sent the correct information.

The OCC finally got Advanta's information late in the afternoon on August 23rd. The information from Compu-Link came in late the next day. The examiners were stunned. They were expecting the servicers to report on thousands of loans and yet were looking at reports setting forth only a fraction of that. Advanta, for instance, was supposed to be servicing 6,445 mortgages for Keystone. In actuality, it was servicing just 162 loans.

In dollar amounts, Advanta reported $6 million in loans versus the $233 million the bank reported on its books. Compu-Link reported $31 million in loans versus the $319 million the bank claimed for Compu-Link-related loans.

There was a discrepancy of $515 million between what the bank was reporting and what the servicers reported. This was no longer simply a matter of a few incorrect due dates and conflicting principal amounts. This far exceeded the bank's capital of $180 million. This was nothing short of a disaster. If the numbers were accurate, it was going to be one of the ten biggest bank failures in the history of the FDIC.[14]

* * *

In order to hide its ever-mounting losses created by the ill-conceived securitization program and the millions of dollars embezzled by bank insiders, the bank had been pretending that the loans sold—first to City National Bank and then to United National Bank—were still owned by the Keystone bank.[15] But they were not. It was all a house of cards and it had finally collapsed.

In order to be sure that the bank was insolvent and that it was not all a big mistake, the examiners decided to explore all possible explanations for the missing loans. As one OCC examiner explained:

> We—our agency—wanted to basically leave no stone unturned. We wanted to make sure that we exhausted all avenues we could in making sure that there was no doubt about the existence of this fraud.

On Wednesday, August 25th, Kathy Gerardy, Mark Blair, and Joey Johnson, another OCC examiner, left their hotel in Princeton, West

Virginia, and drove the twenty-seven miles to the Keystone bank to meet with the bank's senior management and outside auditors, Grant Thornton. Stan Quay, the lead auditor for Grant Thornton, was defensive, if not dismissive. He claimed that Grant Thornton had verified the loans and that they existed. He was flippant, comparing the amount of the potential loss to the size of a small country's gross domestic product. He was in denial. And the examiners were not impressed:

> He made those comical-type remarks about it, rather than showing concern and trying to ask the questions: why is it like this and what is the basis of this? He was pretty much brushing it aside with those remarks.

Church joined the meeting in progress and, when told of the issue, simply "shrugged her shoulders and stated she had no idea why there was a discrepancy and that the bank did indeed own the $500 million of loans in question." Having said her piece, she promptly left the room.

So, faced with the question of a $500 million hole which wiped out all of the bank's capital, neither the nationally renowned, outside accounting firm nor the head of the bank had an adequate answer.

The examiners called for an emergency meeting with the board of directors of the bank for the next day, Thursday, August 26th. In attendance at the meeting were senior representatives from OCC headquarters who flew in specially from Washington, D.C., including Ann Jaedicke, the deputy comptroller for Special Supervision and Fraud. The examiners explained the situation to the directors, and, wanting to be as fair as possible, gave them until the close of business the following Monday to try to come up with answers.

The outside directors were committed to move heaven and earth to find the loans, but the bank's two professional, outside auditors apparently had other ideas.[16] That same day, even though they had just been told they had potentially missed over half a billion dollars in assets in connection with their $1 billion client (despite having been auditing the bank's books since the previous August), they decided to leave town—even before the board meeting was finished—and return home to Cincinnati, Ohio. One of the reasons for this decision was the fact that Quay's son had a football game he wanted to attend. So they drove to Roanoke, Virginia, to get a flight to Cincinnati the next morning. When their flight was canceled due to weather, they decided to drive from Roanoke to Cincinnati. The directors had to call Quay on his cell phone in mid-trip and ask him return to Keystone.

* * *

After the meeting on Thursday, August 26th, the OCC made numerous calls to both loan servicers, Advanta and Compu-Link. They talked to the relevant associates at the loan servicers several times. They talked to the associates' bosses. And then they talked to the bosses' bosses. In the case of Compu-Link, the examiners talked to the president of the company, John LaRose. Nothing in these conversations changed the examiners' view that the bank was insolvent.

To eliminate any doubts whatsoever, though, on Friday, August 27th, OCC and FDIC examiners physically traveled to the servicers—one located in Lansing, Michigan and the other in San Diego, California. The examiners found the records to be in very good order and in keeping with the reports the servicers had sent to the OCC on August 23rd and 24th. The servicers' records clearly reinforced the conclusion that the loans were not there and that the bank was insolvent. As part of this verification process, the examiners obtained affidavits from the two servicers attesting to the small volume of loans they held in the name of the First National Bank of Keystone.

In the meantime, the bank purported to work on finding the missing loans. Quay claimed that it would be easy to determine if the loans existed: he would simply look at the actual interest payments the bank was receiving from the loan servicers to see if they matched the volume of loans the bank claimed it owned. The logic was that, given a certain volume of loans, it would generate a certain amount of monthly principal and interest payments that the loan servicers would remit to the bank. All one had to do is look at the actual income receipts and see if the amount reasonably corresponded to the supposed volume of loans. It would take only a few minutes to do this. When this was explained, more than one director wondered, if it were so simple, why hadn't Grant Thornton done this as part of its audit, and, further, why hadn't Quay done this before leaving town early for a plane that wasn't going to depart until the next morning?

Church claimed she also was looking for the interest income, but, after about forty-five minutes, returned to say she could not find it. When Quay looked for the interest income, he too returned after about forty-five minutes and said he could not find it either. The paltry interest income the bank had received from the servicers did not begin to match what the bank should have been receiving.

Over the weekend, Quay kept pressing Church, "Where is the cash? Where is the cash?" On Monday night, Church finally admitted to him:

> There isn't any cash, and there has never been any cash. I guess my goose is cooked.

Truer words were never spoken.

Quay figured there was nothing more he could say or do at that point. He excused himself as quickly as he could and left the bank with Ellis. Together, they went to a local restaurant, Websters, in the town of Bluewell, West Virginia, a little town about sixteen miles away. From the restaurant, they called Michael Gibson, an outside director of the bank and a local attorney, and asked him to join them. It was about 10 o'clock at night. It was late, but things had gone from bad to worse.

When Gibson arrived at the restaurant, Quay and Ellis told him what had happened, and they decided to hold another emergency board meeting the following morning, Tuesday, August 31st, at 8 AM, at Gibson's law office in Princeton, West Virginia.

At the meeting the following morning, most of the outside board members were in attendance, including Bernard Kaufman by phone from the West Coast, where it was 5 o'clock in the morning. Quay and Susan Buenger from Grant Thornton were there, as well as the bank's outside attorney, Michael Lambert, who called in from Denver. The consensus was that Church and Graham had to go—they needed to be immediately put on administrative leave.

The job of informing them was given to Ellis, but, when he did so, Church became upset, said she did not want to be the scapegoat and claimed that she could find the loans if given more of a chance. Ellis talked to the directors about this, and they decided to relent, thinking that Church knew where all the documents were and that she might be able to assist in sorting things out. So the decisive action by the board was reversed. It did not matter, though; the damage had occurred a long time before and there was not much Church or Graham could do to make it worse.

* * *

The U.S. Marshals had been at the bank since Wednesday, August 25th, and the investigators from the Inspector General's Office had been at Keystone since August 26th. In addition, high level OCC officials from Washington, D.C. had descended on the bank. So word started to get out that something was wrong at the bank. As the week was drawing to a close, a number of depositors became concerned and showed up en masse to withdraw their funds. The bank was not due to get a shipment of cash until Monday, August 29th, and it was running out of money due to the greatly increased withdrawal demand. Meanwhile, the examiners were monitoring the cash flow closely. The cashier for the bank was in tears, crying that there was not enough money. The bank staff was trying to limit the amount of money being withdrawn, trying to convince depositors not to withdraw all of their funds. It was like the scene from the movie, *It's a Wonderful Life*, where Jimmy Stewart is pleading with the townspeople not to withdraw all of their money from the Bailey Building and Loan Association, but only the amount they needed in the short term, until he could find—or replace—the $8,000 that Mr. Potter had stolen from Uncle Billy. But in the case of the First National Bank of Keystone, there was going to be no happy ending.

The bank made it to the end of the week and opened on Monday morning. However, the OCC deadline of Monday, close of business, came and went and still there was no sign of the missing loans.

On Tuesday night, the state police arrived to guard the bank building and to ensure that nothing happened to Cherry's storage building across the street from the bank—it was feared that someone might try to burn the storage building down. The examiners wanted to go to the bank that night, but the U.S. Marshals dissuaded them because the phone coverage in Keystone, which is in a valley, was so poor.

Wednesday morning, hundreds of townspeople were milling around the bank, waiting for it to open so they could withdraw more money. At the same time, OCC officials with the papers to close the bank tried to fly out of Washington, D.C., but their flight was canceled, again due to weather. The papers had to be faxed to the examiners in Keystone, who served the bank with the official notice that, as of 8:05 AM, the OCC was declaring the bank to be insolvent and was handing it over to the FDIC as receiver. That was it.

The only thing left were the clean-up details.

For instance, Ellis had driven to the bank that morning from his hotel—where he had been living since becoming the president of the bank—to be confronted with the news of the bank's failure. The OCC, the FBI, and the state police had surrounded the bank. One state police officer impounded Ellis' car, explaining to him that, because it was owned by the bank, it was now under the control of the FDIC. So Graham drove Ellis back to the Ramada Inn, and then Ellis called his wife, who was visiting her sister in Raleigh, North Carolina, to ask her to drive all the way to West Virginia to pick him up.

Much more substantively, the criminal prosecutions and the myriad of administrative and civil cases that followed would go on for years.

Notes

1. A second round of CMPs in two years against one bank is unusual. For there to be two rounds of CMPs for call report violations is extremely rare. In addition, these CMPs were to be the largest ever for call report violations—$100,000 for Church and $25,000 for the rest of the members of the board of directors.
2. Church's office was 20' × 30,' and she shared it with two to three other people.
3. As set forth in Chapter Thirteen, Ellis sued Grant Thornton for issuing this incorrect audit report that he had relied on.
4. JLT stood for "Junior," which was the nickname for Church's husband; "Larry," who was Church's older brother; and "Tony," who was Church's step-grandson, who was also known as Bubba.
5. These first two deposits turned out to be the proceeds from the certificates of deposit (CDs) the late Knox McConnell held in his company, Marbil—discussed in Chapter Four.
6. The six deposits on December 28, 1998 add up to $500,000 and represent the proceeds of a loan the bank made in the name of Daniel Halsey, who became a director of the bank in March of 1999.
7. Hog Pen was not an actual business. It was only where Hermie Church worked on his motorcycles.
8. The emails were all in lower case as shown here.
9. CEDE & Co. is a company that serves as a clearing house for stock transfers and commercial CDs, along with other things. It is the nominee name for The Depository Trust Company.
10. The bank had professed some confusion in the fall of 1998 as to whether it could accept certain kinds of brokered CDs as an exception to the general prohibition. Also, as set forth in the previous chapter, the bank had improperly counted approximately $800 million worth of second mortgages as first mortgages which succeeded in making the bank look well-capitalized, and, thus, eligible to accept brokered deposits. Regardless, in 1999, the bank was clearly prohibited from accepting brokered deposits.
11. This was not a credible excuse—the wires for the CDs purportedly came in over a period of ten days in 1998. So, for the bank's story to make sense, the bank would have waited ten days before returning the wires—long after the first wire would have been processed.
12. In addition to the above, the bank continued to provide the examiners with false printouts. For instance, the bank gave the examiners a printout from Advanta signed by Alexa Del Pilar reflecting a huge number of loans being serviced by Advanta on behalf of Keystone. However, the report was not

accurate; there was no such report to be found later within the records of Advanta; and, upon further research, it was determined that Del Pilar was on vacation during the week the report was supposedly generated. All of this, though, was not uncovered until after the bank failed.

13. Ironically, because the examiners were out of the bank and were working from their hotel rooms during this time—due to the fact they were waiting for the U.S. Marshals to arrive—the examiners were more comfortable in contacting and talking to the servicers.

14. As noted at the end of Chapter Two, the volume of ultimate losses was not quite at the level the FDIC first estimated, and, consequently, the failure turned out to be "only" the forty-second largest failure at the time it occurred in 1999. (The bank's actual losses were approximately $532 million, which were down from the original estimate of over $800 million in losses.) Looking at the entire history of bank failures from 1933, when the FDIC was created, until December, 2015, Keystone is the sixty-ninth largest failure.

15. The bank, as noted earlier in Chapter Six, was selling the loans for capital and liquidity reasons, with the understanding that the bank would repurchase the loans when it came time to put the loans into a securitization deal.

16. During the audit, there were only two auditors on-site at the bank from Grant Thornton, Stan Quay and Susan Buenger.

9

The Criminal Cases

Well, you know, if you look back at the savings and loan days in Texas, the fraud would have been very pervasive back there, in many institutions, but this [the Keystone fraud] is so pervasive in terms of the effect of the financial statements it almost makes those institutions look like Snow White... because of the amount of the assets that are ... nonexistent.
—Harry J. Potter, FDIC's outside forensic accountant in the Keystone-related cases.

In the waning days of the bank's existence, a number of the women who worked at the bank started to express concerns over the fact that it might fail and they would be out of a job. Terry Church responded by saying that their worries were insignificant compared to her own concern about going to jail. As Patricia Orell, a bank employee, recounted:

> We were talking about whether we needed to get our money out of our ... accounts. And I think I had asked about, you know, were we allowed to tell our family members or anything, and then I made the comment that I needed this job ... Church ... told me all that I had to lose was my job, that she could go to jail.

So Church had to have known, in her own words, that "her goose was cooked." She later denied having said these words, but it is clear she knew that criminal indictments and prosecutions were likely. However, when they came, she—and her partners in crime, Billie Cherry and Michael Graham—decided to fight them, at least initially.

Church I

As recounted at the end of the first chapter of this book, Church and Graham were indicted for obstruction of a federal bank examination on November 10, 1999—less than two and a half months after the bank failed.[1] The indictment contained three counts. Counts Two and Three were for the two separate days they buried bank documents on Church's ranch. Count One was for conspiracy to obstruct the examination and listed a number of "overt acts," including:

- Church and Graham removing documents from the bank and concealing them from examiners;
- Church and Graham burying bank documents in the ground so the examiners could not review them;
- Church directing employees of the bank to disable the microfilm reader at the bank so that the examiners could not view certain bank records;
- Church having employees of the bank sign a document containing false and misleading information and presenting the document to the examiners;
- Church requesting one of her employees to dig a large hole on August 12, 1999 on the C&H Ranch;
- Graham removing records from the bank and from a storage location on August 12, 1999, and personally participating in loading the records on to trucks to be taken to the C&H Ranch;
- Church personally directing one of her employees to dig another hole on August 15, 1999 on her ranch and directing him to bury bank documents in the hole;
- Church, the week prior to the closing of the bank, directing one of her employees to remove boxes of documents from her office at the C&H Ranch; and
- Church, two days before the bank failed, removing records from the bank and concealing them at her home.

The trial lasted thirteen days, going from April 7, 2000 to April 27, 2000. The prosecution was handled by Susan Arnold and Bryan Spann, assistant U.S. attorneys out of Charleston, West Virginia, and John Michelich, a senior trial attorney out of Main Justice in Washington, D.C.

The prosecution called twenty-nine witnesses, including seven C&H Ranch and Keystone Hardware employees and ten bank employees, all of whom cooperated and testified against Church and Graham. They testified at length and in great detail about the removal and burial of bank documents; the creation of false certificates of deposits; the concoction of various stories to explain away the false certificates of deposit; the effort to disable the microfilm machine; the alteration of the signature cards for Church's accounts; and the various misrepresentations made to the examiners.

For the former bank employees, testifying was very difficult. They had been loyal to Church and were obviously upset over the failure of the bank and what that meant to the community as a whole and in terms of their own lost jobs. Most of the employees were scared and had never talked to an FBI agent before. Many initially stuck to the party line of denying any wrongdoing when being interviewed. However, by the time the trial took place, they were all cooperating, even to the extent of incriminating themselves. The following questions and answers between Church's attorney and Ellen Turpin were reflective of what most of the former bank employees were going through:

Mr. Love: Mrs. Turpin, are you now employed?

Ms. Turpin: No. No.

Q. Ms. Turpin, you have testified here that you—today in response to Mr. Michelich's questions that you have committed several crimes. Do you recall that?

A. Yes.

Q. You've also testified that the government can prosecute you for what you have testified about here, that you know that, don't you?

A. Yes.

Q. You have testified that the government has not made you any promises about whether they will prosecute. Isn't that true?

A. Yes.

Q. You hope, do you not, that after today and your testimony here against Terry Church that the government will not prosecute you? Isn't that your hope?

A. Wouldn't that be everybody's?

Q. Is that your hope?

A. That's my hope. It doesn't mean it will happen.

Q. So that by your testimony here today you can avoid being prosecuted, right?

A. Not necessarily.

Q. You believe, do you not, that if you had not changed your story to [FBI Special Agent] Selbe that you would in fact be prosecuted, [don't] you?

A. Not really. I just – the first time I met with him I was very uncomfortable and I didn't want to tell him anything, and it was like that I should be able to pick up the phone and call Terry and say, "What do I do?" That's what I wanted to do. And do you think that I like sitting here talking about her like this? I don't.

Q. Ms. Turpin, just try to answer my questions. I'm sure Mr. Michelich will give you an opportunity to speak. What you're doing here today is attempting to trade your own freedom for that of Terry Church['s], isn't it?

A. No, it's not. It's to tell the truth.

Q. You have sold your soul to escape responsibility for your own acts, haven't you?

A. I have never sold my soul.

Mr. Love: That's all I have of this witness, Your Honor.

The fact that Turpin, and others, were not testifying under a grant of immunity did not help the defense. The fact that they were testifying without the benefit of a plea agreement did not help the defense either. The fact that they hoped not to be prosecuted was hardly surprising. So, having lost the battle, Love stopped. There was no need to make things worse by continuing. Turpin had held her own. Ultimately, the jury looked at what Love was trying to do—sow some doubt as to the motive for Turpin and others to testify against Church—and they did not buy it. Instead, they believed Turpin and the other former bank employees.

Clearly, Turpin and the other former bank employees did not want to be in court; did not want to be testifying against Church; and did not want to be testifying about possible misdeeds they committed. To this day, most of them still do not want to talk. They were put in a horrible situation and are still feeling the effects of it. But, for the trial, they were willing to come forward and testify to the truth.

The prosecution also called five bank examiners who were able to talk about the resistance and obstruction they encountered in trying to complete what should have been a routine examination. Two representatives from the bank's primary loan servicers, Advanta and Compu-Link, testified to Church's and Graham's efforts to convince them to send reports to the examiners that included loans that the Keystone bank did not own. Three FBI agents, called as witnesses, described the hole that they dug up on Terry Church's C&H Ranch and explained what they found. The only things not reviewed in the trial were the graffiti and the forged emails. In the case of the former, there was probably not enough evidence; after all, the graffiti had been quickly painted over. In the case of the latter, the IG's Office did not issue its report until December 12, 2000—over a year after the indictment in Church I was issued and almost eight months after the trial finished. Even without these extras, the case against Church and Graham was extremely strong.

The defendants were represented by private counsel who called fifteen witnesses, including the two defendants themselves. However, most of the defense witnesses did not add much to their case.

The first witness the defense called to testify was Billie Cherry. She ended up admitting on cross that, during the last examination, she sold 3,000 of her shares of bank stock, netting $742,000 and that she withdrew $749,700 of her deposits at the bank the day before it closed. If she had not withdrawn that money, she would have lost approximately

$592,000 in uninsured deposits. This testimony did not help the defense. Cherry's quasi-justification for having sold her stock was that she had to pay $289,000 in taxes. The prosecutor's quick and effective rejoinder was: "Oh, we all have to pay taxes, Mrs. Cherry."

The defense also called Church's husband, Hermie. In his direct examination, he described the layout of the C&H Ranch; where the various buildings and double-wides were located on the ranch; where his sons worked; the fact that his aunt, Dee Hughes, worked for the bank primarily as the person who shredded documents; the fact that the C&H Ranch stood for Church and Hughes; and the fact that they had buried documents once before, about seven to eight years before the bank failed. It was pretty much useless testimony.

However, the cross-examination—quoted in Chapter Eight at length—was devastating for the defense's case, demonstrating that Terry Church—not her husband—handled all of the banking accounts and financial transactions. Why the defense put Church's husband on the stand without determining in advance how crippling his testimony could be is beyond understanding.

The defense also called former outside director, Michael Gibson. On direct, he added little to nothing to the defense's case. On cross, however, he had the opportunity to explain that the outside directors knew nothing about the truckloads of bank documents being buried on Church's ranch; that they knew that the bank was under a directive from the OCC not to destroy any documents; and that he would never have approved the burial or destruction of the bank documents. The prosecution's closing questions for Gibson hit home:

> Q. Mr. Gibson, you're not here to testify that burying four truck-loads in a hole in the ground on Burke Mountain [where Church's ranch was located], truckloads of bank records, recent bank records, is a part of the ordinary course of business of the First National Bank of Keystone, are you?
> A. No.
> ....
> Q. And burying four truckloads of bank records, recent bank records in a hole in the ground in Burke Mountain is anything but ordinary, isn't it?
> A. I would think so, yes.

So, in calling Gibson, the defense counsel succeeded in only bolstering the case against their own clients.

In a similar fashion, the defense called Michael Lambert, the bank's outside counsel, as a witness. Lambert, a partner with the large law firm of Kutak Rock, who is based in Denver, Colorado, had spent a lot of time advising the bank on legal matters, mostly concentrating on the bank's securitization program.

On direct, defense counsel asked Lambert some general questions about document production and document destruction, but there was nothing much of any consequence to assist the case for the defense. On cross-examination, though, Lambert was asked about the issue of document destruction in more depth:

> Q. And Ms. Church indicated to you at that time [summer of 1999] that she had some old bank records that were of no consequence to anything that needed to be disposed of; isn't that true?
> A. Yes, it is.
> Q. And isn't it true, Mr. Lambert, you advised her she needed to retain everything?
> A. I said that, yes.
> . . . .
> Q. Mr. Lambert, when did you first learn that the defendants, Terry Church and Michael Graham, had taken four truckloads of bank records and buried them in a hole in the ground on Burke Mountain during the course of the 1999 federal bank examination?
> A. The first time that I recall hearing anything about that was sometime in October or November, when it was published in the press. That's where I found out about it.
> Q. And wouldn't it be fair to say, Mr. Lambert, that when you read that you were absolutely shocked?
> A. I was shocked. Flabbergasted. I couldn't believe it.

This testimony clearly did not help the defense.

In addition to presenting witnesses who did not help the defense's case, Church's counsel had some unusual legal theories they propounded, which did not help either.

One theory, set forth during the opening statement by Church's attorney, Charles Love, was that the bank documents were removed from the schoolhouse and buried at the ranch during the day—thus, there could not have been any criminal intent:

> First of all, bank records were removed from the schoolhouse and buried on Burke Mountain. That, in fact, happened. There was no effort

made to hide that or conceal it at the time it happened. It happened in the broad daylight, middle of the day, while this bank examination was going on, so there wasn't anything secretive about that. It didn't happen late at night with one person; it happened with a bunch of people driving trucks through downtown Keystone.

Love could not have been more wrong. Church and the others had intentionally waited until the examiners had left town for a long weekend, and—despite the broad daylight—knew that no one in the impoverished town of Keystone was going to say anything. This argument was not going to fly with the jury.

Another theory was that Church believed that the OCC examiners were "out to get her," so she was justified by some notion of "self-defense" in destroying official bank documents. When her counsel tried to go down this path and introduce one of McConnell's many letters to the OCC from 1995, even the judge ridiculed the effort:

> The Court: Well, what's all this got to do with the obstruction of justice? I mean –
>
> Mr. Love: What it has to do, Your Honor, with the obstruction of justice, if I understand the statute correctly, it deals with corrupt intent. And if the intent of the party was not corrupt, but rather was simply one of self-defense because of the past experience and attitude of the OCC, then it seems to me that this is clearly critical as a beginning point as to the reliance of that intent.
>
> The Court: So your theory of the case is that this microfilm the bank examiners wanted in 1999 was buried in the ground by Ms. Church because of trouble between Knox McConnell and the examiners in December of 1995?
>
> Mr. Love: No, that's not correct, Your Honor. . . .
>
> The Court: What have all these complaints that Knox McConnell had against the [examiners] or the OCC back in 1995 got to do with—I don't understand the connection. . . . So what if there had been a bad relationship and bad feelings? The issue in this case is whether the examiners were obstructed in 1999 by the destruction of records and the various other things that we have heard two weeks of testimony about, and I don't see how what Mr. McConnell felt back in 1995 has got anything to do with that.

Rebuffed once, Love nonetheless tried again a little later on the same day to introduce some technical material about allegedly conflicting information the OCC gave the bank. The issue concerned the interest rate that the bank could advertise it would pay for certificates of deposit. Of course, the real issue was not the interest rate, but whether the bank had covered up the existence of the certificates of deposits it had issued when it was clearly prohibited from issuing them. In the ensuing discussion, the judge became as sarcastic as the prosecuting attorney:

> The Court: How's this relevant?
>
> Mr. Love: It shows the inconsistent positions taken by the OCC, and it's a record that reflects that clearly during the critical time period, and it shows the confusion and frustration that was being occasioned by the employees to the bank—its Board of Directors and employees by these actions of the OCC, and I think that's very important to motive in this case.
>
> Mr. Michelich: So that's why they buried the records?
>
> The Court: They buried the records because they were getting inconsistent directions from the OCC about what rates to advertise on the internet?

The court went on to formally reject defense counsel's proffered evidence:

> The Court: You know, if Ms. Church was confused or mad at the OCC or something like that, in the court's view that still doesn't justify the things that are charged in the indictment.[2]

* * *

Church took the stand and was initially a strong witness, blaming most everything on the former employees of the bank. Again and again, according to her testimony, it was the employees who disobeyed her orders or who engaged in misdeeds on their own for no apparent reason. However, if she had claimed this once or twice, it might have played out well, but her insistence on everything—including the burial of recent bank documents on her own ranch—being someone else's fault ceased to be credible after awhile.

For instance, Church claimed that she had ordered Deborah Shrader, a bank employee, to pull the signature cards for her accounts and to give them to Turpin to give to OCC examiner Heath. Of course, this directly conflicted with the testimony of both Shrader and Turpin, who said they altered the signature cards and stepped on them and put cigarette ashes on them to make them look old—at Church's instruction.

Similarly, according to Church, it was Turpin and McKinney who complained to her about the schoolhouse roof leaking and raised the need to move the bank documents that were stored there. Church claimed that it was the employees—not she—who marked the boxes that could be destroyed. Again, this was contrary to all of the other testimony presented at the trial.

Further, Church blamed Melissa Quizenbeury for taking in the illegal certificates of deposit. Church also blamed various other employees— Orell, Burks, and Turpin—for telling her false information that she later incorporated in her written statement to the examiners. Church claimed that the employees said that the examiners had lost the tickets relating to the CDs, so the employees had taken it upon themselves to duplicate—and falsify—entries relating to the CDs. Church even claimed that McKinney had come back early from her anniversary vacation because her husband had to be back at work—rather than admit that she, herself, had ordered McKinney back to the bank to help alter the forged 1998 CDs so they looked like 1999 CDs again.

The prosecutors cross-examined Church for an extended time; the transcript of this part of her testimony took almost two-hundred pages. Again and again, the prosecutors were able to point out the inconsistencies of her testimony and the unlikelihood that the employees would engage in a series of illegal transactions all on their own, behind her back and in a way that hurt the bank.

At the start of the cross-examination, Michelich asked Church the following:

> Well, based on your testimony yesterday . . . the OCC and the FDIC were out to get you, and had been for years; the bank employees who worked for you secretly took in brokered deposits in violation of the OCC order and didn't tell you about it, did it all on their own; bank employees, all on their own, created phony bank documents, without your knowledge; and bank employees made mistakes repeatedly, but of course you didn't make any mistakes; you didn't know that there was recent 1999 microfilm buried in the hole as you stood there throwing boxes in the hole. . . .
>
> And the loan servicers who serviced these hundreds of millions of dollars' worth of loans are lying, and the bank really did own the loans

on its books, it's just that you haven't been able to find them. Have I summarized your testimony fairly?

Church simply responded by saying "No," but the point had been made. Michelich went on:

Q. So all of this problem that the bank was having with the regulators about undercapitalization, less than well capitalized status and all of that, was part of their efforts to get you? They're out to get you; is that right?

A. No, sir.

. . . .

Q. The four CDs that we have talked about throughout this trial . . . the ones that Ellen Turpin testified she made with Wite-Out and scissors and tape and a photocopy machine while you stood over her and watched, those four CDs, is it your testimony that you did not know about them when the bank took them in?

A. No, I did know. I did know that we had taken in CDs in January, March and April [of 1999].[3]

Q. And it's also your testimony that you thought it was okay. . . . You thought it was okay?

A. Yes, sir.

Q. And you were the boss at the bank?

A. Well, I shared the responsibility, but yes, sir.

Q. Right. So if you thought they were okay, and you knew when they came in, what's all this phony paper trail that was created to make them look like they came in in 1998?

A. Well, I've thought about why they would do that. . . . I have no idea. It doesn't make sense to me at all.[4]

. . . .

Q. So all of these loyal employees of yours have made this story up; is that right?

A. Apparently they have.

Q. And they have made this story up for no apparent reason, because you thought the CDs were proper and you knew about them at the time?

A. Yes, sir.

It just was not credible. In fact, Church actually apologized from the witness stand to the three women whom she directed to sign the false written explanation to the examiners. She said she was sorry "for putting them through this." This flummoxed the prosecutor, who asked why Church was apologizing when she continued to claim she had done nothing wrong:

Q. Well, in retrospect, [the written explanation] doesn't seem to be logical, then?

A. No, and I'd like to publicly apologize to Virginia Burks, Connie Evans and Tricia Orell[5] for putting them through this.

Q. Well what have you done, ma'am, to put them through this, if they made the mistake?

A. By me typing that statement up believing that it was true, I have put them through undue process at this court.

. . . .

Q. Well, but if this document you prepared was based on what they told you, then you only wrote down what they told you, and you haven't put them through anything here, have you?

Church was not making sense. She was professing innocence and blaming her employees for misconduct they allegedly engaged in, while, at the same time, apologizing to them.

The prosecution was also able to point out that Church's testimony did not make much sense with regard to the bank documents taken from the schoolhouse. Michelich pretended to play dumb in asking an obviously rhetorical question:

> Well, let me understand. You wanted to protect the records from the rain in the schoolhouse, so you buried them; and you buried them because you couldn't burn them because of the drought. But if there was a drought, there wouldn't have been any water in the schoolhouse. Have I got this—am I confused?

Church's response was that there was water on the plastic tarps covering the boxes' worth of documents. But McKinney and Turpin did not mention anything about there being any water or even any tarps when they testified about going over to the schoolhouse the day they were instructed to mark some boxes.

When it came to the actions of the loan servicers, Church's testimony was equally strange. She claimed that the missing loans really existed and that the two servicers, Advanta and Compu-Link, both made the same mistake:

Q. All right. So, ma'am, so that I can understand your testimony, I believe that you said that this must be a mistake by the servicers, a coding error. Am I right?

A. There is a boarding or coding error, or a loan number mistake . . . I am saying that there is a definite boarding error.

Q. Well, it's quite a mistake, because it's half a billion dollars' worth.

A. Yes, sir.

Q. And is it your testimony that the same mistake was made by both Compu-Link in Lansing, Michigan, and Advanta in San Diego, California?

A. Yes, sir. . . There is a record missing, and that is all that is missing. The loans exist, and I pray to God right now that I have an opportunity to go and find these so I can resurrect the bank.

Of course, neither Church nor anyone else ever found the "missing loans," and the bank remained closed. The idea that two independent loan servicers located in different parts of the country would both make the same or similar "boarding" mistakes totaling half a billion dollars that neither the Keystone bank nor United National Bank (which actually owned the "missing loans") ever caught was not credible.

After this crippling cross-examination, Graham's attorney had no questions; Church's attorney had less than two pages' worth of questions which were ineffectual.

As noted in the previous chapter, if the loans really existed and if the Keystone bank owned the loans, the bank should have been receiving monthly remittances from each of the two loan servicers, representing the bank's income from the principal and interest payments on the loans being serviced. However, no such income was ever received by the bank. And the bank, for some unexplained reason, was never aware of this large shortfall of income, in the amount of $4 to $5 million a month.

Michelich's last few questions for Church were on the issue of where the lost income payments went:

Q. Ma'am, is it your testimony that these missing loans, as you've described them, are still being serviced by Advanta and Compu-Link?

A. Yes, sir.

Q. And the money that is being made in terms of payments on those loans is being sent somewhere, or are the servicers keeping the money?

A. I have no way of knowing that.

Q. So if they're still in existence and they're still being serviced, the money has to go somewhere, right?

A. Yes, sir.

Q. Didn't come to Keystone Bank, did it?

A. No, sir.

According to Church, the loan income from the servicers was either being mysteriously sent to some undeserving third party or was being embezzled by the servicers. She did not know. And, of course, while the bank was alive and was supposed to be receiving millions of dollars of this income from the servicers, it never raised a question.

The only really successful testimony for the defense was from two friends of Michael Graham and from his wife. The friends were able to relate that they went motorcycle riding with Graham on August 15th—the second day of the burial of the bank documents. The friends testified that they went from Bluefield, West Virginia, to Roanoke, Virginia, on that day—about a four-hour round trip—meaning that Graham could not have been at the bank or the schoolhouse disposing of documents to be buried on Church's ranch.

The first friend, David Sexton, knew that they had left Graham's home about 12:30 to 1:00 PM and did not return until 5:30 PM, and had a date book to substantiate his recollection. The second friend, Steven Copolo, recalled the day because, in addition to riding their motorcycles to Roanoke, he picked up a cabinet at Wal-Mart on the way back. Graham's wife could recall that she was with her husband that morning, before she left for church, and was able to prove her attendance at church through a contribution check dated August 15th.

As a result of this testimony, Judge Faber issued a directed verdict dismissing Count Three of the indictment with regard to Graham—meaning that the court took the decision out of the hands of the jury. The jury acquitted Graham on the conspiracy charge (Count One), but convicted him on the second count of the indictment—pertaining to obstructing the examination by disposing of bank documents on August 12, 1999.

The jury convicted Church on all three counts.

Even though Graham was only convicted on one count, Judge Faber sentenced him to four years and three months. With a maximum sentence of five years available, this was pretty stiff, especially for a "white-collar" crime. He was also fined $7,500.

Judge Faber sentenced Church to four years and nine months for each of the three counts she was convicted of. However, the sentences were to run concurrently, meaning that the time she served for one count would satisfy the other two. She also received a criminal fine of $100,000.

Church appealed her conviction, but it was upheld rather easily. The appeal was based primarily on the argument that the statute prohibiting obstruction of a federal bank examination, 18 U.S.C. § 1517, was unconstitutionally vague. This was a very difficult argument to make. In reviewing the issue, the appellate court held as follows:

> During the [examination], Church had directed bank employees to alter records sought by bank investigators, provide some documents while concealing others, and misrepresent to bank investigators certain bank transactions. Church also had ordered employees from her hardware store and her farm to assist bank employees in removing and burying bank records from the bank and . . . the schoolhouse on August 12 and 15, 1999.
>
> . . . .
>
> The record shows that Church enlisted Graham and other employees to lie to the government agents, to falsify documents, and to assist in the transportation and burial of bank records sought in the investigation. Such conduct falls squarely within the common-sense meaning of section 1517.
>
> . . . .
>
> Because Church was fairly on notice that her conduct was prohibited by the statute and evidenced the requisite corrupt intent, this Court finds the statute was not unconstitutionally vague.

Graham appealed his conviction too, but withdrew the appeal as part of an agreement to cooperate with the government. He became the lead witness for the prosecution in the next criminal case.

Church II

The next criminal case, referred to as Church II, was against Church and Cherry for their embezzlement from Knox McConnell's estate, as set forth in Chapter Four. Graham and Barbara Nunn, a former employee of the bank, were both unindicted co-conspirators, meaning that they were not being prosecuted, but that their testimony and actions could be used against the defendants, based on the premise they were all part of the same conspiracy.

The Church II Indictment

The indictment against Church and Cherry was handed down on March 22, 2001. It contained twenty-five counts, the first of which was for conspiracy to, plain and simple, "loot the Estate of J. Knox McConnell." Counts Two to Five were for bank embezzlement and Counts Six to Eight were for mail fraud. In essence, Counts Two to Eight dealt with the creation of the two fake codicils, the seizing of the assets of Marbil and the changing of McConnell's accounts to make them look like they were owned not just by McConnell, but also by Cherry. The charge for "bank embezzlement" was due to the fact that the defendants allegedly misapplied money entrusted to the "custody and care of [the] First National Bank of Keystone by falsifying . . . records of the bank."

Counts Nine to Twenty-five were directed only against Cherry, and were for money laundering. Basically, the charge was that Cherry had taken her ill-gotten gains from McConnell's estate and had tried to hide them by disbursing large amounts of money out of her accounts. The disbursements were used to pay for cars and McConnell's two condominiums, and to transfer money to other accounts held by Cherry, her children and grandchildren, and her new husband's six children, three of whom she had not even met.

The disbursements were as follows:

Date	Amount	Payee or purpose
11/3/97	$30,177.52	To Friendly Honda (to purchase a car for her son, Michael Cherry, which was selected the day of McConnell's wake)
11/3/97	$50,000.00	To Michael Cherry
2/3/98	$175,000.00	To Michael and Roslyn Cherry
2/3/98	$300,000.00	To Michael Cherry
2/3/98	$1,330,000.00	To establish fourteen new accounts in the names of Cherry's relatives, all in the amount of $95,000, just under the FDIC $100,000 insurance limit at the time
2/4/98	$111,934.98	To Cherry (the funds were deposited into an account held by her in Illinois)
6/5/98	$50,000.00	To purchase a cashier's check for Cherry
11/12/97	$600,000.00	To establish six new accounts for her husband's six children
11/18/97	$100,000.00	To purchase two vehicles from McConnell's estate for Cherry
1/27/98	$100,000.00	To purchase a cashier's check for Cherry—deposited into a Florida account

(Continued)

(Continued)

Date	Amount	Payee or purpose
1/27/98	$100,000.00	Same
1/27/98	$100,000.00	Same
1/27/98	$100,000.00	Same
1/27/98	$100,000.00	Same
4/22/98	$67,000.00	To purchase the Pittsburgh condominium from McConnell's estate for Cherry
4/22/98	$117,000.00	To purchase the Orlando condominium from McConnell's estate for Cherry
Total	$3,431,112.50	

The Church II Trial

The trial in the Church II case started on October 2, 2001. However, just five days beforehand, Cherry's attorneys filed a motion to disqualify the presiding judge on the grounds that he had been a close personal friend of McConnell's. Cherry claimed to have just found a letter written by the presiding judge, Judge Faber, to McConnell, dated September 19, 1991, thanking him for his support of Faber's appointment to the bench. The letter was only three paragraphs long and read as follows:

> It was great joining you for dinner in Bluefield on Monday. Debbie and I enjoyed the evening immensely and we appreciate your hospitality.
>
> I also want to thank you for copying me on all of your recent correspondence with officials at the White House and Department of Justice. Your continued support is a source of great comfort and inspiration and I am delighted that you have picked up the ball for Nancy Hill and are championing her cause as well.
>
> You are a most worthy friend of the President [George H. W. Bush] and I know his re-election effort in West Virginia is in good hands for 1992.[6] One of the few regrets I have about becoming a federal judge is that I will miss the fun of helping you. Please keep in touch and do not forget to call me upon your next visit to Charleston.

Judge Faber did not take kindly to this last minute effort to scuttle the trial. On October 1st, the day before the trial was to start, Faber ruled against Cherry, questioning the idea that she had only recently found the letter and pointing out that he had met McConnell fewer than a dozen times; that he had not been a close friend of McConnell's; that the motion was based solely on a single letter written more than ten years before; that, while McConnell had supported Faber's appointment to the bench, many other people had as well; and that McConnell had died more than four years before and was "far beyond any care or concern which involves this litigation." Faber also made the point that the alleged victims in the case were the beneficiaries of McConnell's original will, not McConnell himself.

The trial lasted seven days. The government called thirteen witnesses; the defense for Cherry called only one—Cherry. Church's lawyer called no witnesses—Church herself declined to testify. She also declined a plea agreement, claiming that she did not want to testify against her friend. Unfortunately for her, Cherry had no such concern, and attempted to lay all the blame on Church.

Specifically, Cherry tried to exculpate herself by testifying that Church was the brains behind it all:

> Q. Is it your testimony that you knew you were a joint account holder with McConnell?
> A. I was told that.
> Q. Who told you that?
> A. Terry.
> Q. On that day?
> A. Yes.
> Q. But you didn't know it ahead of time?
> A. No.

What she was saying is that Church orchestrated the creation of the joint accounts and the transfer of money from McConnell's estate to Cherry's banking accounts. Ironically, it was Cherry's attorney who elicited this testimony, not realizing (or having forgotten the lesson from every first-year law school curriculum) that anything a co-conspirator (like Church) does in furtherance of the conspiracy, the other co-conspirator (Cherry) is held equally responsible. So Cherry's attorney's effort to blame Church was, in effect, implicating his own client as well.

The government put on seven former bank employees; two FBI agents; one person from the IRS Criminal Investigations Division; a representative from Waynesburg College; an attorney from the First State Bank and Trust Company of Rainelle, West Virginia; and the attorney appointed by the court to oversee the probate process for McConnell's estate. As with Church I, most of the former bank employees were not happy to have to testify, but they did their best. Nunn, testifying for the government, probably put it best when challenged by defense counsel that she would have testified differently if she were not awaiting sentencing for an earlier guilty plea for income tax evasion:

> My testimony would be the same, because I want to tell the truth and get this off of me. I have to live with this the rest of my life.

The case was relatively straightforward and the jury convicted the two defendants on all counts. However, the defense scored a significant legal victory after the trial. They contended that the guilty verdicts for bank embezzlement under Counts Two to Five were improper due to the fact that the indictment did not charge an "intent to injure or defraud the bank" as an essential element of the statute, 18 U.S.C. § 656. This was a technical, but accurate argument. The statute had historically set out the requirement of "intent to injure or defraud . . . ," but, in 1948, it had been dropped because it was thought to be redundant. However, the courts had continued to require it—both in the indictment and in the proof. It would seem that, in the trial, the prosecution established the requisite intent beyond a reasonable doubt, but the indictment did not contain the magic phrase. So the courts were required to throw out those four counts for both Church and Cherry.

When it came to sentencing, though, it hardly mattered. Judge Faber sentenced Church to twenty-two years and seven months. To make matters worse, this term was ordered to run consecutively with her first sentence, for a total of twenty-seven years and four months.

Along with the term of years, Church was ordered to pay restitution to the FDIC in the amount of $812,670,629.88. The court ordered her to pay this sum off at $25 a month while she is incarcerated, and $300 a month after her release. The judge received some good-natured ribbing as the result of this decree (and the fact that it would take Church a bit of time at that rate to reimburse the FDIC); he countered, though, that his order was pursuant to established guidelines.

Cherry got sixteen years and five months. She was seventy-seven years old at the time, so it was a presumptive death sentence.[7] In the end, she died in prison of a cerebral hemorrhage on December 29, 2006, at the age of eighty-two. She still had nine and a half more years to go in her sentence, counting for time off for good conduct. She was scheduled to be released on August 16, 2016, which would have been her ninety-second birthday.

Appeal of Church II

Cherry duly filed an appeal to her conviction, complaining about ineffective assistance of counsel (due not to conduct before or during the trial, but a supposed failure to ask for a downward adjustment in sentencing); seeking to lay almost all of the blame on Church; and contending that her own role in any misconduct was "minimal, minor, or somewhere in between"—whatever that meant. She also pointed out that she had been the mayor of Keystone and on the advisory board of the Kennedy Center, as if that should sway the court.

However, the court of appeals upheld the conviction easily, paraphrasing Mark Twain by saying:

> Rumors of the Bank's financial success were . . . greatly exaggerated. In truth, Bank employees had doctored the Bank's books to create a false appearance of profitability.

In upholding the conviction, though, the court of appeals agreed with the district court that the bank embezzlement counts had to be dismissed. Due to that, the forfeiture order of $6,121,238.89 had to be reduced by $4,282,588—the amount stolen from McConnell's four bank accounts. The remaining amount—$1,838,650.89—represented the amount of the first CD misappropriated from McConnell's company, Marbil.

Among the other items ordered to be forfeited by Cherry were the two condominiums owned by McConnell, as well as two cars he owned. There was, however, a curious development with regard to one of the two cars Cherry had purchased from McConnell's estate. The car was a classic 1956 Ford Thunderbird. It had been seized by the U.S. Marshals Service and was eventually handed over to the court-appointed trustee for McConnell's estate in 2005. However, on December 6, 2005, apparently after seeing a "Notice of Forfeiture" in the paper, a Joseph Ray Davidson, in a handwritten letter to the court, claimed that he was entitled to the car. Davidson's letter was full of misspellings (e.g., Planitiff, Goverment, Defendents, Plantiff, and Proscutor), but he claimed that he had sold the car to McConnell on July 31, 1993, for $2,000, with the stipulation that:

> if car were to ever be desposed [sic] of, for any reason, seller, Joseph Ray Davidson, would have right to repurchase at same price.

> This agreement was wittness [sic] by, Senator John D. Rockerfeller [sic], Congressman Nick Joe Rahall II, State Senator Odell Huffman . . . when transaction took place.

Unfortunately for Davidson, his claim did not go very far. The U.S. Attorney's Office asked him for a bill of sale for the car which he was unable to produce, claiming his deal was based only on a verbal agreement. Accordingly, the court denied his claim. On August 20, 2005, the trustee sold the car for $36,500.

Church III

Church appealed her conviction in Church II, along with Billie Cherry, but Church withdrew her appeal as part of her agreement with the government to plead guilty to the third criminal case brought against her—pertaining to the cooking of the books of the bank. The case, known as Church III, was based on two counts, one for bank fraud and one for "conspiracy to commit money laundering." In an "information"[8] issued on January 29, 2002, the government charged Church with a "scheme and artifice to defraud" the First National Bank of Keystone. Specifically, she was charged, among other things, with the following:

- concealing the losses sustained in the bank's securitization program;
- falsely inflating the value of the bank's financial interest in the securitization deals;
- falsely recording loans not actually owned by the bank—so the assets of the bank were fraudulently inflated;
- falsely recording interest income it did not receive;
- making "false, fraudulent, and fictitious" entries in the bank's general ledger; and
- embezzling money from the bank.

On the last point, the information alleged that Church had embezzled more than $30 million between 1993 and 1998 and that McConnell had embezzled $5.7 million between 1993 and the time he died in October, 1997. The information also alleged that Graham, an unindicted co-conspirator in the case, had embezzled—with Church and unnamed other individuals—$13.6 million.

At the end of the information, there was a list of 335 separate withdrawals, transfers, or payments Church had allegedly engaged in, all greater than $10,000, which represented "separate monetary transactions in criminally derived property." In layman's terms, this meant that the government was charging Church with money laundering—engaging in all of these transactions in order to distance the funds from their underlying criminal source. In all, the information set forth the allegation that Church had spent $2.7 million on vehicles; $5.1 million on houses; $9.5 million in transfers to third parties; and $9.9 million on business and personal investments. Quite a bit of money. And yet in the Church II and Church III cases, she was reduced to having a federal public defender represent her, instead of high-priced, private counsel.

Church pled guilty in Church III on March 4, 2002. She was sentenced on May 29, 2002 to twenty-seven years and three months for Count One, bank fraud; and ten years for Count Two, conspiracy to commit money laundering. The sentences, however, were to run concurrently with one another and with the remaining imprisonment terms from her first two cases. So, from May 29, 2002, she was looking at an additional twenty-seven years, meaning she would get out of prison sometime in 2029, not counting for time off for good behavior.[9]

Graham II

After Graham was convicted in Church I and decided to cooperate, part of the deal was that he withdraw his appeal, as noted above. He also had to plea to one last criminal case, referred to here as Graham II, which involved two counts: one for bank fraud and the other for money laundering. The case was modeled somewhat along the lines of Church III, and charged Graham and unnamed others with the following:

- making false entries in the bank's books and records;
- receiving $25 million from the bank, without the knowledge or approval of the board of directors;
- fraudulently creating and using two commercial loan accounts at the bank to facilitate the embezzlement of funds, including in connection with investments in gas companies in Florida;
- receiving more than $8.5 million from fraudulent loan accounts to make private investments in bingo businesses in Piedmont, Alabama[10] and a solid waste landfill in Summers County, West Virginia;[11]
- falsely reporting the interest income from the securitization deals;
- falsely inflating the value and ownership of loan securitization transactions; and
- falsely reporting in excess of $515 million in loans as assets of the bank which were actually owned by other banks.

Graham pled guilty to the two counts on November 16, 2000, and was sentenced on December 17, 2001 to twelve years and six months for the first count, involving bank fraud, and ten years for the second count, involving money laundering. The terms, however, were to run concurrently and he was to be given credit for time served from his first sentence. In other words, he was to be imprisoned for a total of twelve and a half years from July 31, 2000—the date of his initial sentencing—to January 31, 2013. As it turned out, Graham was released on June 17,

2011, having presumably received time off for good behavior. In all, he served almost ten full years in prison.

He was also required to pay back the missing $515 million to the FDIC, but, like Church, in paltry amounts. While in prison he was to have paid $50 a month and, after his release, $300 a month. However, the judge decided not to levy a criminal fine against Graham due to the fact that he did not have the assets or income with which to pay a fine and due to the requirement to make restitution. Also, the judge was mindful of the undue burden that a fine would place on his family members who were financially dependent on him. Further, the judge recognized the fact that Graham provided substantial assistance to the government in various cases and had been one of the first to come forward to say that McConnell was already dead when the codicil was prepared and executed. As noted above, he was the lead witness for the government in Church II, the criminal case focused on the looting of McConnell's estate.

Graham's Previous Conviction and Revocation of His CPA License

Graham's convictions in Church I and Graham II were not his first run-in with the criminal justice system.

In 1984, he pled guilty to, of all things for a CPA, failing to pay income taxes. At the time, he had ten employees and was withholding taxes from their pay, but, for a year and a half, failed to pay the required FICA (Federal Insurance Contribution Act) taxes on behalf of the employees.

Three times during the investigation of this matter, Graham claimed to an IRS agent that he had filed the necessary tax returns. According to the agent, this was false. Graham also claimed that he did not file the returns because he did not have the money. According to the IRS agent, this too was false. Graham had a checking account he failed to disclose to the agent and, moreover, by the agent's calculations, Graham had an average of $6,000 to $7,000 in his accounts and, at one time, his balance was $25,000. Graham also offered several other excuses which the IRS concluded were not true.

Accordingly, the court sentenced Graham to three years' probation and ordered him to serve 250 hours in community service, pay a fine of $1,000 (reduced from $10,000) and pay back taxes of $37,000. In delivering the sentence, the judge noted that Graham had abused his position of trust:

> You are advising people and so forth as to tax problems and so forth, then you are not living up to the law, yourself. There is no question

in the Court's mind but what, you know, you have violated the law in this case and that it was an intentional violation on your part.

As a result of the conviction—which occurred in Virginia—the Virginia Board of Accountancy (BOA) suspended Graham's CPA license for three years, from March 6, 1986 to March 4, 1989. The West Virginia BOA did not find out about Graham's conviction and the suspension of his license until almost a year later. Based on the fact that the crime involved dishonesty or fraud and based on the reciprocity that it gives to other states, the West Virginia BOA suspended Graham for the remainder of the three-year period, noting that, after March, 1989, Graham could apply to have his license reinstated.

In March, 1992, and then again in April, 1994, Graham applied to have his West Virginia CPA license reinstated. Both applications were notarized by Church, so she clearly knew of Graham's situation. However, the West Virginia BOA discovered that Graham had been representing himself as a licensed CPA and had even issued a favorable audit opinion for the Keystone bank with respect to its 1992 and 1993 year-end financial statements. Graham unsuccessfully tried to excuse himself by claiming that he thought that his license had been reinstated. In June, 1994, in a continuing effort to get his CPA license back, he submitted five certificates from a correspondence school known as Western Schools as evidence of his satisfaction of the continuing education requirements. Unfortunately, the West Virginia BOA determined that he had forged all five certificates. Western had no record of Graham having completed the courses, and the person who purportedly signed the certificates did not start working for Western until July, 1995, one to three years after the certificates were supposedly issued.

As a result, Graham never got his CPA license back in West Virginia.

The OCC knew that Graham did not have a CPA license and noted it in its 1994 ROE. However, most of the directors—apparently not given much time to read the OCC's ROEs by the senior management of the bank—failed to notice this and were never told explicitly. Director Gibson later found out through other means and went to senior management about the issue, but was assured that Graham had been reinstated as a CPA, which was not true.

Other Criminal and Administrative Cases

In addition to the cases against Church, Cherry, and Graham, there were other assorted former bank employees against whom charges were leveled—as set forth in Appendix A. Also, there was one additional, curious person caught up in the aftermath of the bank's failure, described below.

Norma Faye Canipe

Norma Canipe proved that one felon cannot trust another. Canipe had nothing to do with the First National Bank of Keystone or the town of Keystone, West Virginia. She was convicted of unrelated bank fraud and ended up as a friend or acquaintance of Terry Church's in the Alderson Federal Prison Camp for women, located in Alderson, West Virginia.

Canipe, who also went by various aliases, including Norma Brown, Norma Pritt, and Laura Pritt, was indicted along with her friend or husband, John Francis Tatham (aka Todd Michael Goodrich), on March 12, 1998, in the Western District of Virginia, and charged with three counts. On May 14, 1998, there was a superseding indictment which added one more count, all for bank fraud.

The basis of the first three counts was a series of simplified check kites.[12] According to the court records, Canipe and her associate would each open a checking account at different financial institutions with nominal cash deposits. Then, they would write large checks drawn on one account and deposit the checks into the second account, making it appear that the second account had a sizeable balance. Then they would simply withdraw cash from the second account and spend it. Canipe and her associate allegedly received $2,695 in this fashion.

The fourth count involved a much simpler series of transactions and yet generated much more money. According to this count, Canipe and her associate opened (or attempted to open) accounts at eight different banks, including two banks in Princeton, West Virginia (about an hour away from Keystone), and proceeded to write bad checks drawn on the accounts. According to the indictment, they cashed checks at forty different establishments in amounts ranging from $12.45 at the Princeton Mart to $10,056.81 at a Lowe's hardware store in Christiansburg, Virginia. In all, they allegedly reaped about $46,000 by writing these worthless checks.

Canipe pled guilty to all four counts on June 16, 1998, and was sentenced on December 17, 1998 to two years and six months for each count, all to run concurrently. She was also required to make reimbursement of over $48,000 to the victimized banks and establishments. After her prison term, she was to be on probation for five years.

On January 25, 1999, she was sent to Alderson. She was released from there on August 2, 2001, approximately one year after Church started serving her time at the same prison. Apparently, at some point, they met each other.

Having heard Church's story and knowing that the court-appointed trustee was trying to sell a number of Church's assets, Canipe allegedly came up with a scheme to fraudulently acquire some of the assets. She wrote up an order purporting to be from Judge Faber and presented it to Church's family at the C&H Ranch, convincing them to hand over all sorts of assets. The "order," which was on the fake letterhead of a law firm, instead of the court's letterhead, and had a reference line to the law firm instead of to Terry Church or her case number, was a mishmash of legal gobbledygook and poor grammar:

> Mr. Wolf Puckett and David Faber in conference meeting in the Estate of Church Property Bid was placed for the amount of 1.8 million dollars ($ 1,800,000.00) in the escrow account at Ameribank, account # 05100020 was accepted . Hold was taken off all contents except, Land, Houses unitl Deeds are completed. Dencil Pritt has full control of all vehicles, Motorcycles, contents of buildings and guns (List Included) Ect. And is turned over to him at this time.

> Dencil Pritt has comfirmed infront of me that no property, houses, vehicles, motorcycles, guns or any contents will be turned over or sold to any of the Church's or Church family members.

> David A. Faber, United States District Judge do hereby certified to this, on February 4, 2002 and on this day personal acknowledgement given under my hand.

Some of the obvious misspellings and other mistakes were "unitl" instead of "until"; "Ect." instead of "etc."; "And" instead of "and"; "comfirmed" instead of "confirmed"; "infront" instead of "in front"; and "Church's" instead of "Churches." Some of the more obvious ungrammatical phrases were as follows:

- "Estate of Church Property Bid";
- "was placed for the amount";
- "David A. Faber . . . do hereby certified to this"; and
- "on February 4, 2002 and on this day."

But this "legal document" was enough to fool Church's husband and family. The order itself was faxed to the Church family on March 12, 2002, from a Kinko's in Sterling Heights, Michigan. The Church family apparently failed to appreciate that not too many West Virginia court orders are faxed from a Kinko's in Michigan.

What they handed over to Canipe and her alleged son, Dencil Pritt, reflected Church's lifestyle, and included the following:

- Seventy-seven guns in all—which took up four boxes—including:

  - five .357 Magnums;
  - an AK-47;
  - three 9-mm guns;
  - a Thompson submachine gun;
  - four derringers; and
  - various shotguns;[13]

- Seventy-one vehicles in all, including:

  - two 1967 Pontiac GTOs;
  - numerous motorcycles;
  - three snowmobiles;
  - a motorboat;
  - six tractors;
  - two Jet Skis;
  - a fire truck;
  - a backhoe;
  - a track loader; and
  - a golf cart.

Canipe hauled most of this away. Some of the heavy equipment, vehicles, trailers, and guns were transferred to Roanoke, Virginia, and Warren, Michigan, and sold. What is interesting is that Canipe also allegedly arranged for the person known as Dencil Pritt to start living in one of the houses on the C&H ranch and for the Church family to start paying rent to stay in the other houses and double-wides on the ranch. It was estimated that, in all, Canipe got $170,000 from this enterprise.

Canipe was finally tracked down and indicted on June 5, 2002. The case was initially assigned to Judge Faber, but, due to the fact that his name was on the forged court order, the case was reassigned. Canipe pled guilty on August 5, 2002, and was sentenced on February 21, 2003, to fourteen years and seven months and was ordered to pay reimbursement. Canipe appealed her sentence, but the court of appeals summarily upheld it, without even permitting oral argument in the case.

Conclusion

Ultimately, five people were sent to prison for a variety of misdeeds relating to the failure of the First National Bank of Keystone. And three more people were placed on probation.

While these criminal cases were ongoing, there was a series of civil and administrative cases as well.

Notes

1. This first criminal case is referred to as Church I.
2. Michelich correctly explained the irrelevance of the interest rates as follows: "The evidence with regard to the brokered deposits was that their acceptance of brokered deposits was in violation of a longstanding OCC prohibition, which was never in doubt. The interest rates to be charged, seventy-five basis points over the local or national rates, has nothing whatsoever to do with the brokered CDs that have been at issue in this case."
3. Actually, the CDs at issue were received in January and March, 1999.
4. In addition to professing innocence, Church tried to argue that the bank had purchased seven CDs in 1999, and that it was unclear why the bank employees would have falsified the information about only four of them. This issue, though, appeared to be more of a red herring than anything substantive. It seems that the examiners only found the four CDs in issue.
5. Church was slightly mistaken in her list of employees who signed the paper; it was Orell, Burks and Turpin—not Evans (who had actually resigned from the bank in July, 1999).
6. Actually, Clinton beat George H. W. Bush in West Virginia in 1992 by thirteen percentage points.
7. She was in ill health at this time. After her imprisonment, Cherry complained about having congestive heart failure, backaches, and constant problems with her hip, which would eventually need to be replaced.
8. An information, as opposed to an indictment, is often used when the prosecution and the prospective defendant have agreed to a plea bargain.
9. See Appendix A for additional information on Church's incarceration. As explained there, Church eventually got her sentence reduced and was released on September 20, 2015, having served fifteen years.
10. Graham allegedly was involved through friends in this bingo operation that was supposed to benefit a Keystone charity. However, according to news stories, the charity, the Elkhorn Valley Development, was not registered with the West Virginia Secretary of State and did not file required tax forms. The bingo hall, Frontier Palace, which was more than 400 miles from Keystone, purportedly deposited $5.8 million into an account in the Keystone bank, but the Elkhorn charity only received $500. In 1995, the Alabama Department of Revenue filed a $500,000 lien on Frontier Palace and concluded that Elkhorn was a phony charity. Subsequently, an Alabama state court judge shut down the bingo operation. (Article by Maryclaire Dale, Charleston Gazette, 4/23/95 (No Bingo Bonanza for Small Charity); and articles by Larry Messina, Charleston Gazette, 10/13/99 (Ex-Keystone official subject to past probes) and 10/17/99 (Failed Keystone bank linked to Ala. bingo hall scheme).)
11. The bingo hall and the landfill fraud, as well as the gas company investment, were also the basis of an FDIC action discussed in Appendix B.
12. A check kite is when a person has two or more checking accounts at different banks and writes a check drawn on insufficient funds from one account to

pay for something. When the check comes back to the first bank for payment, the person writes another check (also drawn on insufficient funds) from the second account and deposits it into the first bank to purportedly cover (or pay for) the first check. If the banks give the person immediate credit for checks deposited that have not yet been collected, the check kite can go on indefinitely. It is primarily a method of getting a free loan through the use of the check float—the amount of time it takes a check to clear. Example—a person opens an account at Bank A with a cash deposit of $100. The person then opens a similar account at Bank B. The person writes a check drawn on Bank A for $1,000 to pay for goods. Before the check comes back to Bank A for payment, the person writes a second check for $1,000 drawn on Bank B and deposits it with Bank A to "cover" the first check. When the second check is sent to Bank B for payment, the person writes a check drawn on Bank A to cover the second check, and so on. All of the checks are worthless, but if each bank is willing to give immediate credit to the checks, they do not know that the checks are no good.

13. It is no wonder that the examiners, bank employees, and townspeople were scared of Church. This was more than enough to arm a small militia.

10

The Civil and Administrative Cases

I have known a vast quantity of nonsense talked about
bad men not looking you in the face.
Don't trust that conventional idea.
Dishonesty will stare honesty out of countenance,
any day in the week, if there is anything to be got by it.
—Charles Dickens

In the aftermath of the failure of the bank, in addition to the criminal cases, there were three SEC cases for insider trading (described in Appendix A); two OCC administrative cases; and fourteen civil cases.

The civil cases involved a myriad of different plaintiffs. There was a lawsuit by the two schools that were supposed to have inherited from McConnell's estate. There were several lawsuits brought by uninsured depositors. There were lawsuits from shareholders who lost their investments. There was a lawsuit pertaining to the securitization deals, which started before the bank failed and continued afterward. And there was even a lawsuit brought by one of the entities that had encouraged the bank to get involved in the misbegotten securitization process.

This chapter will focus on the lawsuits brought by the two schools, the depositors, the shareholders, and the regulators—the FDIC and the OCC.[1]

The Two Schools' Lawsuit

Waynesburg College v. Church, et al.

McConnell died on October 26, 1997, and Church officially became the executrix of his estate on November 18, 1997, when she filed the will and the fake codicil with the court. However, she waited over a year, until January 26, 1999, to file the appraisement of the estate.

Waynesburg College knew that it was to be left something from McConnell's estate, but did not know how much. The school had a copy of a 1969 will that provided for the care of an elderly aunt of McConnell's and indicated that, after her death, the remainder of the estate would go to the college. The aunt had passed away by the time McConnell died, and there was a new effective will at that time, dated 1993, but the schools did not have a copy of it.

The college dutifully sent a representative to the funeral, and then waited. The month of November came and went and it heard nothing. So, in December, the college sent someone down to the Mercer County courthouse to obtain a copy of the will and codicil. Upon reviewing the codicil and seeing the inclusion of the Hargrave Military Academy, the college got in touch with the Academy and they started to coordinate the matter.

The schools did not want to appear overly pushy, so they waited through the month of December. The college finally contacted Church in mid-January and arranged for a meeting on February 10, 1998. The meeting did not go well. Matt McConnell (no relation to Knox McConnell) and Roy Barnhart from the college traveled about 250 miles to Keystone. When they got there, they started the meeting with Church. A little later, Cherry came in, explaining that she was late because she had been on the phone with one of West Virginia's U.S. Senators. This was right out of the stale McConnell playbook. The meeting only got worse.

In the meeting, neither Church nor Cherry was cooperative. According to Barnhart:

> It was a little disturbing in that we could not really seem to get past a point where they seemed to feel a little antagonistic toward us. They didn't want to look us in the eye, really, during the whole half-hour or 45 minutes that we were there. We would ask various questions and we wouldn't get very good answers, really.

Barnhart asked Church what she thought the estate was worth, excluding the Keystone stock. She responded, "Well, possibly around a million dollars." This was far from the truth: the estate, even without the purported $11 million in Keystone bank stock, amounted to over $12 million.

Church also said that the Keystone bank stock was selling at $85 a share, when the value was closer to $200 a share. Church discussed the possibility of buying the two schools out at the $85 a share price, but they did not go for it. The following year, the stock hit a high of about $300 a share. However, if the schools had accepted this initial offer, they would have each received approximately $5 million.[2] That amount was much more than what they eventually received.

In spite of her grossly underestimating the value of both the Keystone bank stock and McConnell's overall estate, Church took the opposite tack when she expressed concern about how much the schools would have to pay in taxes due to the fact that the estate was so large. Barnhart tried to explain to Church that the college and Hargrave Military Academy were nonprofit institutions of higher learning and were exempt from paying taxes.

This point is understood by almost everyone. And, in this case, for a person like Church, who was well-versed in financial matters, it should have been a given. However, she would not drop the issue. In fact, she went so far as to sue the college and the prep school to get them to pay what would have been part of the tax burden she and Cherry would otherwise have. The lawsuit did not make sense, but it did succeed in delaying the probating of the will. Due to the fact that Church, as executrix, could exercise total control over McConnell's bank stock in the interim and the fact that she and Cherry had already stolen over eight million dollars from McConnell's estate, getting their fraudulent 20% of McConnell's bank stock did not matter that much. It was more important to keep the two schools at bay and to not allow them any degree of control over the bank.

The schools were getting frustrated trying to talk to Church. Eventually, Church, herself, indicated that she was not comfortable talking to the schools and told them she had retained legal counsel in Washington, D.C. to help her with the estate. However, she refused to even tell the schools who the attorneys were, let alone how to get in touch with them.

The two schools invited themselves to the next two annual shareholders' meetings, held in late February, 1998 and in March, 1999. The bank did not try to stop them from attending, but it issued written instructions to them that they could not ask any questions during the meetings on the grounds that they were not shareholders of record. To quietly enforce this directive, the bank had several large men, who were the husbands of women employed at the bank, sit next to the representatives from the schools.

The two schools eventually brought a suit relating to the McConnell estate. The complaint was filed on January 28, 2000, and was against

Church, Cherry, Graham, Quizenbeury, four directors, and unnamed others. The complaint alleged a series of bad faith encounters and sought treble damages under the Racketeer Influenced and Corrupt Organizations (RICO) Act, as well as punitive damages.

However, on March 3, 2001, the FDIC stepped in and took over the case. This was to reoccur in most of the civil cases. Due to the fact that the FDIC had to pay money out to the insured depositors, it stood first in line—before uninsured depositors, shareholders, and creditors—to collect whatever was left from the demise of the bank and whatever could be obtained from the various defendants. The FDIC's efforts, though, were going to prove to be nowhere near enough to fill the hole left by the fraud at the Keystone bank.

In the eventual settlement of the case, on October 15, 2002, the two schools only got $500,000 from the estate—quite a bit less than even the lowball offer Church made of $10 million.

The schools had encountered legal fees of approximately $300,000. So, all the time and grief expended trying to obtain their bequest from their renowned alumnus was barely worth it. Of course, given the fact that Hargrave Military Academy was not even in the legitimate will, it should not have gotten anything at all.

Depositors' Cases

Anderson v. Church, et al.

This was a case filed by some uninsured depositors who hoped to serve as the representatives in a class action suit of similarly situated people who had more than $100,000 in an account at the bank, and, thus, were not completely insured by the FDIC. The complaint estimated that there were over five hundred such uninsured depositors.

The lawsuit was filed on October 21, 1999 in state court, against Church, Cherry, Graham, Quizenbeury, five directors of the bank, Deborah Watkins, Keystone Mortgage Corporation, McConnell's estate, and the bank's two outside accounting firms—Herman & Cormany and Grant Thornton.

The defendants successfully petitioned for the case to be removed to federal district court on the grounds that the plaintiffs had included federal allegations in their complaint relating to the RICO Act. Subsequently, the FDIC intervened as the sole plaintiff and successfully had the court dismiss the case so that the FDIC could bring its own separate action.

Grand Rapids Teachers Credit Union v. Grant Thornton, et al.

This case was brought by three federally insured credit unions, the Grand Rapids Teachers Credit Union in Michigan, the St. Louis Postal Credit Union in Missouri, and the Chetco Federal Credit Union in Harbor, Oregon, that had each purchased large certificates of deposit from the Keystone bank in excess of the FDIC-insured limits. Why credit unions—especially ones for teachers and postal employees— were investing in jumbo CDs at a high-risk bank engaged in the securitization of subprime mortgages is unknown. They were supposed to be cautious custodians of their members' funds, but, instead, proved to be too greedy for the high interest rates the Keystone bank was offering.

They should have known better. It was already a matter of public record that the bank directors had been assessed civil money penalties for filing incorrect call reports, and that the bank itself was under a formal administrative action requiring it to retain a nationally known accounting firm to properly reconcile its books and records.

Between the three credit unions, they had purchased over $1.4 million in CDs and lost over $900,000 in uninsured deposits. They brought their lawsuit on behalf of all similarly situated individuals and entities that had purchased CDs from the Keystone bank, hoping, like the other depositors' case, to be the class action representatives.

The defendants in the case included Grant Thornton, Herman & Cormany, Church, Cherry, Graham, the bank directors, and McConnell's estate. However, as with the other cases, the FDIC stepped in and took it over. On November 22, 1999, the FDIC moved to dismiss the case, and, on May 26, 2000, the court granted FDIC's request.

The three credit unions did not end up faring very well. The Grand Rapids Teachers Credit Union was merged with some other credit unions in the early 2000s. The St. Louis Postal Credit Union became the Neighbors Credit Union. And the Chetco Federal Credit Union, after a decade of poor operations, was put into conservatorship in September, 2011, and then closed in December, 2012.

Shareholders' Lawsuits

Shareholders, because they stand last in line behind all other creditors, are always at the most risk when there is a bankruptcy or bank failure, but that did not keep the lawsuits from being filed when the First National Bank of Keystone went under.

Gariety I

On November 8, 1999, just a little more than two months after the bank failed, the first of the shareholder class actions was filed. It was titled *Gariety v. Grant Thornton,* and was known as "Gariety I." This case was premised on alleged violations of federal and state securities laws, breach of fiduciary duty, fraud, negligent misrepresentation and civil conspiracy. The case sought compensating damages as well as punitive damages.

The defendants in the case included Grant Thornton, Herman & Cormany, Church, Cherry, Graham, Ellis, McConnell's estate, the directors of the bank, and various professional broker dealers that had sold the bank stock. The plaintiffs were an unfortunate group—numerous people who had bought the stock of the bank and had lost a lot of money. Some of them included the following:

- Horst Bischoff, who lost over $280,000, which was described as "virtually all of his life savings";
- John Cline, who lost $97,000, termed "a substantial portion of his life savings";
- Thomas Shannon, who lost $429,000;
- Elizabeth and Michael Sponseller, who lost over $100,000;
- Terry Overholser, who lost $60,000;
- Charles Thornton, who lost almost $60,000;
- SMV Holding Company, which lost $52,600; and
- Fred Millner, who lost $26,000.

Curiously, the name plaintiff, Debra Gariety, lost only $5,130.

Gariety filed an amended complaint on August 16, 2000, which added bank employees Turpin, McKinney, and Vorono as defendants. The first two were later charged with insider trading by the SEC, but Vorono was not and the case against her was eventually thrown out.

On July 27, 2000, the court granted the FDIC's motion to intervene in the case, and, subsequently, the FDIC filed its own complaint.

Gariety II

On April 15, 2002, Gariety filed another class action, titled *Gariety v. Church* and known as Gariety II. With one small exception, the plaintiffs were the same as in Gariety I. The substantive difference between the two cases was that Gariety I was a class action for damages—primarily under the securities laws—against a number of different people, while Gariety II was a lawsuit against the insiders of the bank who allegedly sold—or "dumped"—their bank stock between 1998 and 1999 with the benefit of insider knowledge. The suit was seeking a judgment requiring the defendants to turn over the proceeds of the stock sales to the plaintiffs, as well as to pay treble damages. The defendants in Gariety II ended up being Church, Cherry, one director, and sixteen employees of the bank. Unfortunately, the lawsuit was fairly indiscriminate in its breadth and included people who had not sold their bank stock based on insider information.

Specifically, the lawsuit brought charges against four bank employees without any basis. The first two were Jeanie Wimmer and Evelyn Herron, who together ran the bank's branch office in Bradshaw, West Virginia, which was about eighty miles—and two hours through mountainous roads—away from Keystone. So they were physically removed from the machinations and intrigue going on at the bank.

They each sold 1,000 shares of bank stock to McConnell in 1994 to 1995. In November, 1998, they each sold an additional 500 shares. In May, 1999, they again each sold another 500 shares. However, at this time, they both refused offers to sell additional shares. Ironically, they both deposited the proceeds of their sales into accounts at the Keystone bank. When the bank failed, Wimmer had more in her deposit account at the bank than the FDIC insurance limit, so she lost a lot of money. Similarly, Herron lost money from her IRA account at the bank. In addition, at the time the bank failed, they each still owned a sizeable amount of worthless bank stock: Wimmer owned 2,906 shares and Herron owned 3,571 shares. So, rather than "dumping their stock" and benefiting from their supposed insider knowledge, Wimmer and Herron lost a lot of money.

The third employee wrongly accused was Vida Headrick, who was a lifelong friend of Billie Cherry's and who worked at the bank, first during the 1980s and then a second time for seven months in 1998, as Cherry's secretary. She had also worked for Graham in the early 1990s, outside of the bank.

Judge Faber, the presiding district court judge in the case, found the factual allegations against Headrick—how she bought her stock originally; and that she somehow gained inside information about the bank while working for Graham—"to be sheer speculation unsupported by any evidence of record." In addition, Judge Faber accused the plaintiffs of distorting deposition testimony as "a last ditch effort to create a disputed issue of material fact. . . ." He was not pleased. But he saved his real ire for the plaintiffs' charges against Vorono, McConnell's long-suffering secretary.

Judge Faber started out his comments by saying, "Suffice it to say that plaintiffs have taken great liberty in their recitation of the 'facts' concerning Vorono." Vorono performed only clerical duties, including:

> Taking dictation for, and typing letters; initiating telephone calls at the direction of Mr. McConnell; making some bank deposits for Mr. McConnell; providing coffee and other refreshment for Mr. McConnell and his guests or visitors; maintaining the ledger which recorded the ownership and transfer of shares of stock in Keystone; and other miscellaneous duties.

At one point, Church had alluded to the fact that Vorono might be made a vice president of the bank, but that never materialized. Vorono retired in December, 1997, two years before the bank failed, still—in her words—"punching the time clock."

Since that time, she had not been involved in the bank's business in any way except to attend the annual shareholders' meeting in March, 1999, where she was told the bank was doing great. In April, 1999, she sold 1,000 shares of her bank stock (which was a small amount relative to her overall holdings) to a broker. The next day, the broker approached her and asked her to sell all of her bank stock, which she did, with the exception of 300 shares. According to her testimony, she had "no knowledge or belief that the bank was in financial or regulatory difficulty." And the plaintiffs in the case had no evidence to the contrary. Consequently, Judge Faber dismissed the case against her—as he had done with regard to the other three employees.

The plaintiffs appealed this decision, but got nowhere. In dismissing their appeal, the U.S. Court of Appeals for the Fourth Circuit agreed with the district court, and, further, noted that Vorono had more than the FDIC-insured limit in her checking account at the time the bank failed, losing a lot of money.[3]

On September 26, 2003, Gariety I and Gariety II were consolidated. Subsequently, the FDIC was designated as the sole plaintiff in the case, having a superior claim over the shareholders of the bank.

So, all of the cases brought by the uninsured depositors and the deceived shareholders were eventually placed under the sole control of the FDIC.

The FDIC Cases

The FDIC, by intervening in lawsuits and by filing its own lawsuits as the receiver for the First National Bank of Keystone, sued the directors of the bank, as well as the bank's outside attorneys and accountants. The FDIC also sued some of the individuals and entities that encouraged the bank to get involved in the securitization process to begin with.

With regard to the actions against the directors, the FDIC argued that they failed to adequately oversee the bank:

> Keystone's Board of Directors completely abdicated their fiduciary duties in connection with the sub-prime lending and securitization program. The Keystone Board of Directors had no experience or knowledge to enable them to properly evaluate the sub-prime lending and securitization program; nor did they ever learn enough about the effect that the program was having on the financial condition of the institution. Despite this, the board failed to investigate properly the merits of the sub-prime lending and securitization program, failed to enact adequate policies and procedures to govern the program, and failed to hire or train adequate or qualified personnel to operate, manage, and monitor the program.

While this was all generally true, it neglected to point out that the board had tried to hire Owen Carney—albeit pursuant to the OCC's mandate to obtain a new president. The complaint also neglected to point out that the board had hired two very prominent law firms, Williams & Connolly and Kutak Rock, and had retained former Comptroller of the Currency Robert L. Clarke to assist the bank. Further, the complaint neglected to point out that the board had hired the nationally recognized accounting firm of Grant Thornton—again, at the insistence of the OCC. So, it is not as if the directors had taken no action at all.

It is correct, though, that the directors knew nothing about buying subprime mortgages from all over the country, and knew nothing about the securitization business. In addition, it is correct that the directors did not—or probably could not—properly manage the likes of McConnell, Church, or Graham. However, it is also true that the board never suspected that there was a massive fraud going on at the bank.

Ironically, when the FDIC filed its lawsuit in the Mitchell case discussed immediately below—against some of the people and entities that had encouraged the bank to get involved in the securitization process—the FDIC specifically absolved the outside directors from any active wrongdoing, as set forth in its complaint:

> At all relevant times, Keystone's outside directors (those directors who were not officers or employees of Keystone). . . . were unaware

of the conspiracy to defraud Keystone, and Keystone's corrupt management, the Coast parties and defendants herein [i.e., the defendants in the Mitchell case] actively and fraudulently concealed the conspiracy from them.

The directors ended up settling with the FDIC and Gariety plaintiffs for amounts that were covered by the directors' liability insurance policy. The FDIC got $900,000 and the class action plaintiffs got $300,000. In all, that was a fair result. The directors were not out of pocket and the FDIC and Gariety plaintiffs got some recovery.

FDIC v. Mitchell

This was one of two very complicated civil cases that actually went to trial.[4] It was the case that the FDIC brought against some of the individuals and entities that had assisted and guided the bank through the process of securitizing subprime mortgages.

In describing the case, the private counsel representing the FDIC noted that it was "a case about deception, lying, cheating, [and] stealing." The allegations were basically that the twenty-two defendants in the case had engaged in a civil conspiracy to commit fraud against the bank. Among the things that the defendants were alleged to have done included:

- concealing losses from the bank and its regulators;
- creating sham entities;
- engaging in sham transactions;
- making fraudulent payments on loans to make them look current;
- charging "unreasonable, unfair and often undocumented fees, bonuses and commissions, including fees for no services";
- taking out loans from the bank with no intention of repaying them;
- selling Bakkebo's company, Prime, to the bank for far more than it was worth;
- arranging to have the bank buy "virtually worthless residuals" from Conti; and
- receiving kickbacks.

The name defendant was Ron Mitchell. However, by the time the case went to trial, Mitchell and all of the other defendants—with one exception—had either settled, defaulted, or were in bankruptcy, leaving the FDIC with mostly hollow victories.

The one defendant who did not settle or default was Harald Bakkebo, who had fled to Norway. He was represented in absentia by legal counsel at the ensuing six-day trial. The case focused on recovering the losses from six securitizations that Bakkebo and the other defendants were involved with, plus the losses emanating from the over-priced sale of Bakkebo's company, Prime, to the bank.

According to the FDIC's evidence, the six securitizations at issue created the following losses:

Securitization	Loss incurred by the securitizations
1995–2	$11,958,365.17
1995–3	$6,306,219.98
1995–4	$5,652,666.22
1996-6	$47,273,024.77
1996–2	$51,247,045.93
1996–3	$24,463,527.24
Total losses	$146,900,849.31

The losses on the Prime transaction amounted to $14,565,889.67, bringing the total damages to $161 million. While this was a huge amount, it was dwarfed by the estimated total damages of approximately $532 million stemming from all nineteen securitizations and the various embezzlements.

The evidence that the FDIC put on in the case was quite strong, but, at the same time, it was virtually unopposed. Bakkebo's attorney had never even met his client and had no witnesses to call. As he explained to the court, "I'm putting on essentially no case. All I'm doing is arguing against theirs." With no effective rebuttal, the FDIC's evidence was more than enough.

One of the twelve witnesses the FDIC's private counsel called was Terry Church, who was incarcerated at this time in Danbury, Connecticut. She was transported back to West Virginia in handcuffs and chains and the defense counsel could hear her shackles outside of the courtroom, reminding him of the ghost of Jacob Marley in Charles Dickens' *A Christmas Carol*.

The FDIC's private counsel—the law firm of Mullin Hoard Brown, LLP in Amarillo, Texas—put on an effective case, but, unfortunately, decided it was necessary to supplement some of the testimony with their own. Specifically, numerous times, they used leading questions in examining their own witnesses in order to ensure that the right things were said. This was especially egregious in connection with their

examination of one of their expert witnesses—a damages "wizard"—
Harry J. Potter, who testified in one section mostly by just saying "yes":

> Q. Mr. Dorrell [the defense counsel] asked you your opinion as to
> whether these damages related to Harald Bakkebo. And you
> gave him your opinion; right?
>
> A. Yes.
>
> Q. All of those damages relate to the activities of Mr. Harald
> Bakkebo, don't they?
>
> A. In my opinion, they do.
>
> Q. That's right. And we showed a bunch—and we showed you a
> bunch of stuff. . . . Do you remember that?
>
> A. Yes.
>
> Q. Well, is your opinion also perhaps based on the fact, in addition
> to the loans being bad, could it be based upon the fact of the
> misrepresentations that this jury has heard so much about?
>
> A. Yes.
>
> Q. And the fact that Mr. Melgar and Mr. Bakkebo were in a
> conspiracy? Could that be part of the thing that you base your
> opinion on?
>
> A. Yes, it is.
>
> Q. Could it be the fact that Mr. Bakkebo was paying kickbacks to
> Mr. Melgar? Would that be a fact you relied upon to support
> that opinion?
>
> A. Yes.
>
> Q. What about the cross-ownership this jury has heard so much
> about?
>
> A. Yes.
>
> Q. Did you consider that in formulating that opinion?
>
> A. Yes.
>
> Q. So it wasn't just the 68 percent of the loans, or 40 percent of
> the loans [that Bakkebo's company supplied to Keystone for the
> securitization deals]? It was all of that, and it was the conspiracy,
> correct?
>
> A. Yes.
>
> Q. And that is what you concluded?
>
> A. Yes.

This was a key part of Potter's testimony, who was the FDIC's most
important expert witness, who arrived at and supported the dollar
amount of the damages. Yet, in this instance, it was the attorney
testifying through the guise of asking questions—rather than the actual
witness providing his own testimony.

In addition to the leading questions, the FDIC's counsel presented
some of the most complicated testimony possible—dealing with default

rates; over-collateralizations; cross-collateralizations; residuals; master service certificates; negative cash flows; premiums; weighted average coupons; bondholders; trustees; and on and on for six days. For the average jury, it was nearly impossible to follow.

The following testimony represents just some examples of how ridiculous the testimony got for the jury.

Scott Mannes, from Conti—the company that was the co-sponsor for the first four securitization deals—testified on the FHA Title One program:

> Q. Explain just briefly—I know there's probably volumes derived, but explain briefly what is the FHA Title I program.
> A. Well, the program allows, in effect, a—a mortgage lender to originate a—in effect—what is effectively a high-LTV loan to a subprime borrower for the purpose of making a home improvement.
> And so what happens is that the FHA comes in, and they guarantee on a stop-loss basis 10 percent—the first 10 percent losses on a pool of mortgage loans.
> So it increases, in effect, the—the salability of those loans, at—at a later date because there's loss—there's an insurance policy or there's loss protection on those loans.
> Now, the thing about the FHA policy is, is it's not an ironclad guarantee.
> It's subject to—to claims denial on a loan-specific basis.
> It's subject to a stop loss of 10 percent on a portfolio basis.
> And so it wasn't—it was a form of credit support; it wasn't a form of credit support that entirely lent itself to the secondary mortgage markets.

This was too much for any jury to absorb. In addition, it was not at all clear. The ten percent FHA insurance restriction—that he was unsuccessfully trying to explain—understandably meant that the FHA would only insure 10% of a loan portfolio. But what is complicated—and was not explained—is that the insurance would initially cover up to 90% of any one loan in the portfolio, but, once the insurance payments reached 10% of the entire portfolio, there would be no more insurance coverage on any of the loans.

Another example, this time with the attorney for the FDIC partially "testifying" while questioning the representative of Conti:

> Q. Mr. Mannes, are you familiar with a term called "cross-collateralization"?

A.   Yes.

Q.   And could you explain what cross-collateralization is?

A.   Well, cross-collateralization in this case was the—was basically the pooling of the four transactions we did into one master trust.

And what—what that effectively did is that it—it allowed FSA and, for that matter, the residual holders—primarily, it was for FSA's benefit—allowed FSA to use collateralization and/or credit support in one transaction toward another transaction to the extent another transaction wasn't performing . . .

Q.   And in that sense, from a—a residual interest holder who—a party who owns the residual—residual interest, the fact that payments from one securitization has to go to secure payments under another one negatively impacts their ability to collect a residual stream?

A.   Yes.

Even assuming that the jury understood what a "residual interest holder" and "residual stream" were, this was difficult to follow.[5]

Another example, this time coupled with an ironic effort to make the testimony of the representative from CapMac (which replaced FSA) understandable for the jury:

Q.   Can you tell me what or describe for me what the business of CapMac was?

A.   CapMac was a monoline financial guarantee insurance company that provided credit enhancement to structured finance markets, such as short term asset backed commercial paper financing and also term financing through the public and private bond markets.

Q.   *If you were going to describe that to a lay person* what would you say CapMac was in the business of doing?

A.   CapMac was in the business of guaranteeing to investors to a triple-A rated level of probability repayment of principal and interest on bonds that they acquired that were guaranteed by CapMac.

(Emphasis added.)

If anything, the second answer was more indecipherable than the first.

In spite of—or, perhaps, because of—the complicated subject material and testimony over the course of six days by twelve witnesses reviewing charts, graphs, formal agreements, contracts, deals, and letters explaining the securitizations in great detail, the jury seemed to just accept the FDIC's unopposed evidence, and after two hours and fifty-nine minutes—from 10:11 AM to 1:10 PM—returned with a unanimous verdict against Bakkebo. This quality time spent deciding a $161 million case included the jurors' lunch break.

The case is still touted by the law firm that handled the litigation for the FDIC as the eleventh largest jury verdict in the United States in 2004 and the largest verdict against an individual in the history of West Virginia. However, it was all for naught.

As the attorneys for the FDIC themselves indicated in their summation in the case:

> [Bakkebo] is in Norway. He is not coming back. He can't be extradited. He knows that.

Bakkebo knew that. The FDIC knew that. The attorneys for the FDIC knew that. Yet the FDIC spent hundreds of thousands of dollars for private counsel to put on a six-day trial in West Virginia with twelve witnesses from various parts of the country. And the FDIC never checked in advance as to whether—if it were to "win"—it could ever collect. The simple answer was no. When Bakkebo was killed a little over one year later, in March, 2006, the FDIC tried to collect from his estate, but the Norwegian courts ruled that, under Norwegian law, his entire estate went to his son, who was allegedly also involved in the sham transactions involving the sale of Prime. The FDIC should have figured this out in advance.

The FDIC and the OCC Cases Against the Bank's Law Firm and Accounting Firm

The FDIC and the OCC each brought actions against the bank's law firm, Kutak Rock, as well as Michael Lambert, the primary Kutak Rock lawyer representing Keystone. In addition, the FDIC and the OCC each brought actions against the bank's accounting firm, Grant Thornton. These cases are discussed in the next two chapters.

Notes

1. The rest of the civil cases are set forth in Appendix B.
2. The math is as follows: 146,619 shares × $85 = $12,462,615 × 40% = $4,985,046. When Church filed the Appraisement for the Estate, she valued McConnell's Keystone bank stock at $109 a share.

3. During the summer of 1999, Director Gibson, who owned 8,900 shares of bank stock, purchased $10,000 to $20,000 worth of additional shares. Obviously, he incurred a significant loss when the bank failed, but his attorney jokingly noted that it was the best bad investment Gibson ever made—it succeeded in preventing a lawsuit being filed against him for insider trading.

4. The other civil case that went to trial was the one the FDIC brought against Grant Thornton, covered in Chapter Twelve.

5. In Keystone's first five securitizations, the income for each deal also served as collateral for the other four deals. So until all five securitizations were resolved, it was impossible to determine what the profit or loss was regarding any of them. This is known as "cross-collateralization."

11

The Case Against the Attorneys

*There are other unanswered questions presented by this case.[1]
[Charles] Keating testified that he was so bent on doing the "right
thing" that he surrounded himself with literally scores of accountants
and lawyers to make sure all the transactions were legal. The questions
that must be asked are:*

*Where were these professionals, a number of whom are now asserting
their rights under the Fifth Amendment, when these clearly improper
transactions were being consummated?*

*Why didn't any of them speak up or disassociate themselves
from the transactions?*

*Where also were the outside accountants and attorneys when these
transactions were effectuated?*

*What is difficult to understand is that with all the professional talent
involved (both accounting and legal), why at least one professional
would not have blown the whistle to stop the overreaching that took
place in this case.*
—District Court Judge Stanley Sporkin, in the case of Lincoln S&L
Assn. v. Wall

Introduction

In addition to all the criminal, administrative, and civil actions set
forth in the two previous chapters, there were legal actions brought
by the OCC and the FDIC against the law firm, Kutak Rock, which
represented the First National Bank of Keystone from 1993 until its
failure on September 1, 1999.[2]

In 1993, Kutak Rock, which is headquartered in Omaha, Nebraska,
was a national firm with more than 325 lawyers.[3] Starting at that time,

the firm provided legal services to the bank related to the design and execution of its securitization program.

The firm had about nine attorneys working on Keystone-related matters. Michael Lambert was the lead partner representing Keystone and he devoted a great deal—if not most—of his time to the bank. Starting in 1993, Lambert billed 700 hours to the Keystone bank. By 1998, he was billing 1,600 hours and, in 1999, he was on his way to billing 1,875 hours.[4] That is roughly thirty to thirty-six hours a week of billable time devoted to one client. From 1998 through 1999 alone, the firm as a whole billed the bank approximately $1.5 million in legal fees.

Lambert was an accomplished attorney, having graduated with a B.S. in economics from the University of California, Riverside in 1973, and having received a J.D. in 1978 from the University of California, Los Angeles (UCLA), where he was on the law review. In between, he got an MBA in 1975 from the Stanford Graduate School of Business.[5]

Oddly, one summer job he had during this time was driving the train around Disneyland. At the time, he could have had no idea how much more of a fantasyland working for the Keystone bank would turn out to be.

During the course of his representation of the bank, Lambert was seemingly unaware of and uninvolved in the massive fraud, but he did adopt McConnell's negative view of the examiners and the OCC. He also bought into the notion that the OCC was "out to get" the bank.

In addition, he was aware of the bank's undisclosed taping of phone conversations with the OCC—which was legally permissible because both Washington, D.C. and West Virginia were "one-party consent states," meaning that only one side of a phone conversation had to agree to the taping for it to be legal. While legal, there is some degree of unseemliness to be surreptitiously taping phone conversations with one's federal banking regulator. The Kutak firm also actually typed up transcripts for some of these conversations. When the OCC finally found out about these taped conversations, they ordered the bank to stop the practice, calling the behavior unacceptable.

Even more questionable, Lambert was aware of the fact that the bank was retrieving examiner notes and work papers from the trash and piecing them back together during the night. The Kutak firm did nothing to halt the practice.

Further, the Kutak firm conducted research for the bank about whether the bank could "sue to enjoin [a supposedly] abusive [OCC] examination." This work was undertaken starting on Thursday, August 5,

1999, just a week and a half after the examiners had returned from being forced out of the bank by the temporary restraining order—based on the forged emails purportedly authored by examiner Daugherty.

The bank knew by this time that the examiners were not going to leave until they determined the true condition of the bank—meaning until they uncovered the fraud; and the bank wanted to prevent that from happening. The law firm assigned four attorneys to work through the weekend on this issue for Keystone. As it turned out, the firm was prepared to advise the bank against bringing such a lawsuit.

While the law firm's adoption of the bank's negative view toward the examiners and the OCC was problematic given the extreme nature of the bank's attitude, the real problem was that the firm, and Lambert, allegedly lost sight of the fact that their real client was not McConnell or Church or the rest of the senior management of the bank, but, rather, the board of directors of the bank. According to the FDIC's eventual action against the firm and Lambert, there were major red flags which Kutak Rock failed to bring to the attention of the board.

Red Flags

According to the FDIC, the firm and Lambert failed to identify and report nine major red flags. McConnell, Church, and Graham were aware of the issues, but the board was not. Lambert and Kutak Rock should have reported these red flags to the board, but, as alleged by the FDIC, they did not.

First Red Flag—HUD's Case Against Master Financial

As set forth in Chapter Five, the first co-sponsor with the bank for the securitization deals was to have been a company called Master Financial, which was also providing nearly a third of the loans for the first securitization deal. However, at around the same time of the first deal, HUD leveled fraud charges against Master Financial with regard to lying about the quality of loans they were providing and the creditworthiness of the borrowers. Lambert was allegedly aware of these charges.

The HUD charges indicated, of course, that the loans and entities that the bank was getting involved with were, at best, suspect. As set forth by the court summarizing the FDIC's evidence:

> The first red flag reflects that the loans going into Keystone's securitizations were of poor quality, that Master Financial was dishonest, and that the residual valuations were overstated.

However, Lambert allegedly did not report these facts to the Keystone board.

Second Red Flag—Loans to Ronhardan

As set forth in Chapter Five, ContiTrade Services Corporation replaced Master Financial as a co-sponsor of the securitization deals. However, after four deals, Conti realized that the deals were losing propositions and alleged that Melgar, the guru behind Keystone's securitization program, had misrepresented the deals. In order to buy Conti out—and, perhaps, pay for its silence—the bank made a series of loans to Melgar, his compatriots and the shell company they formed, Ronhardan, to fund the payments to Conti.

However, the loans were very questionable—some of the loans went to Ronhardan; and some of the loans went to the individuals who formed Ronhardan. Church apparently explained to Lambert that the personal loans were really not loans, but a means for the individuals to guarantee the loan to Ronhardan. But this did not make sense. First, all of the loans to the individuals were actually disbursed; the notes were not held as some kind of collateral or guarantee for the Ronhardan loan. Second, the loan to Ronhardan was not large enough by itself to buy out Conti (the loan to Ronhardan was only $4 million, while the amount necessary to buy out Conti was $6 million). Third, making separate additional loans is not a normal way of obtaining guarantees; if a bank wanted a guarantee, it would simply have the individual or individuals sign on the original loan as guarantor(s). (Lambert, himself, apparently acknowledged that what the bank did was not a "standard banking practice.") Fourth, the loans were in the form of "consumer" loans instead of business or investment loans. On top of all this, the whole transaction underscored the fact that the securitization deals were not performing well.

These were all red flags that indicated something was amiss. In addition, Lambert allegedly knew many if not most of these underlying facts, given the fact that, according to the court, he was representing Ronhardan in the matter—which alone may have been a conflict of interest, given his simultaneous representation of the bank.[6] Yet he allegedly never informed the board of these issues.

Third Red Flag—Bakkebo's Indictment

Also in Chapter Five, the indictment against Bakkebo was explored at length. Lambert was allegedly not only aware of the indictment, but also aware of the fact that the United States Attorney's Office in Louisiana, in connection with this criminal case, was seeking the forfeiture of Bakkebo's company, Prime Financial Corp., which was a primary servicer of the loans Keystone was acquiring and securitizing. Lambert allegedly recognized that the Keystone bank's interests were in jeopardy as a result of this pending criminal case, but failed to inform the board of the threat.

Lambert was fully engaged in the Prime matter: according to Church, he was the one who wrote letters on behalf of the bank demanding that Prime allow the bank to transfer the servicing rights to another company after Bakkebo's indictment. In addition, he was allegedly involved in negotiating the sale of Prime to Keystone—which ended up occurring at a grossly inflated price, after a series of crazy machinations involving a variety of known and unknown parties in foreign countries.

Fourth Red Flag—Filing of a SAR on Clearview

Clearview was the company that Bakkebo formed in order to hide the conflict of interest he had in both providing loans to Keystone and servicing the same loans. When it became apparent that Bakkebo and two Clearview officers were fronting loan payments to Prime (in other words, making loan payments out of their own pockets in order to make it fraudulently appear that delinquent loans were really paying as scheduled), Kutak Rock partner Alan Strasser prepared a suspicious activity report (SAR) for the bank to file with federal law enforcement agencies. According to the reviewing court summarizing the FDIC's evidence, this original draft SAR was fairly accurate. However, Lambert allegedly reviewed and redrafted the SAR. As a result, according to the court's summary, the SAR became so sanitized that it did not even disclose the fact that Bakkebo owned both Prime and Clearview.

This would have hidden Bakkebo's involvement and the fact that the bank was working with a person engaged in a conflict of interest and various alleged wrongdoings.

Again, Lambert allegedly failed to bring this whole matter to the board's attention.

Fifth Red Flag—Withdrawal of CapMac

After Conti withdrew from Keystone's securitization program after the fourth deal, another company, Financial Securities Assurance Company (FSA)—the entity that was providing insurance above and beyond the HUD insurance—withdrew after the fifth deal. A company by the name of CapMac (Capital Markets Assurance Corporation, a large Wall Street insurance entity) replaced FSA. However, CapMac also withdrew shortly thereafter.

Clifton Lewis, an assistant vice president of CapMac, allegedly told Lambert that CapMac withdrew because the Keystone "deals were blowing up" and that the "Bank's performance [was] awful, [and] everyone knows it." This, of course, went to the heart of the bank's securitization deals and its supposed fantastic profits.

Again, Lambert allegedly failed to report CapMac's devastating verdict to the board.

Sixth Red Flag—OCC's Criminal Referral

As set forth in Chapter Six, the OCC filed a criminal referral against McConnell and Church for their alleged involvement in extracting and splitting improper appraisal fees and for failing to pay taxes on the income.

Lambert allegedly learned of the criminal referral—perhaps from McConnell who, in turn, probably found out by going through the examiners' work papers and hard drives. Regardless, Lambert allegedly failed to inform the board of the referral or of the underlying improper activity involving the most senior management of the bank.

Seventh Red Flag—CFO Mitchell

One of Melgar's associates was Ron Mitchell—who made up the "Ron" of Ronhardan. At some point, Mitchell came to work directly for the bank as its chief financial officer (CFO) at an annual salary of $300,000, plus bonuses, with a five-year contract. Subsequent to his coming to the bank, Mitchell allegedly confided in Lambert that he was not qualified to be the bank's CFO and that the arrangement was all a sham. Mitchell allegedly explained that he had no duties and lacked the necessary qualifications.[7]

Curiously, according to the court's summary of the evidence, Lambert was the one who drafted Mitchell's employment contract with the bank. However, even armed with all this information, Lambert allegedly did not disclose this untenable situation to the board.

Eighth Red Flag—Spin-off of KMC

The Keystone bank's operating subsidiary, Keystone Mortgage Corp. (KMC), housed and ran the bank's securitization program. However, as an operating subsidiary, its assets, income, and losses were treated as a part of the bank—just like any department or division of the bank. In order to avoid the OCC's continuing scrutiny of the program, the bank wanted to "spin-off" KMC as a separate entity so that it would stand on its own and be separate from the bank.

In order to accomplish this, however, the bank needed $200 million in financing. The bank approached BancOne to try to obtain the necessary loan and offered, as collateral, the bank's interest in the securitized loans—known as the residuals. Unfortunately for the Keystone bank, BancOne had the sense to review the residuals before committing itself.

BancOne found that the residuals were only worth approximately $26 million—not the $200 million the Keystone bank claimed they were worth. Keystone was off by almost a factor of ten. BancOne concluded that the value of the loans making up the residuals was marginal and that the loans had little to no resale value. So it declined to make the requested loan.

Lambert, according to the court, was involved in the effort to secure this financing and was allegedly aware of this outcome, which, again, served to totally undermine the notion that the bank's securitization program was extremely profitable. But he allegedly never advised the board of this bleak news. According to the reviewing court summarizing the charges:

> Lambert and Kutak were intimately involved in the efforts to secure financing for the proposed spin-off as evidenced by Kutak's billing records which indicated that the firm, and especially Lambert, spent substantial time on the matter. Although these problems should have been disclosed to the Board, neither the inability to find a buyer for the loans nor the BancOne devaluation of Keystone's residuals was ever disclosed to Keystone's Board by Lambert or anyone else at Kutak.

Ninth Red Flag—Lehman Brothers

The ninth and last red flag involved disclosures Lehman Brothers made to Keystone. In a meeting with the bank that Lambert attended, Lehman Brothers—which was the underwriter of fourteen of the securitization deals—allegedly told the attendees that the bank was not making any money from the securitization of subprime mortgages.

If this were news to the attendees, it would have been a shock—given that the bank was supposed to be the most profitable large community bank in the entire country—out of over 5,000 such banks. To be informed that the bank's primary source of income did not exist would have—or should have—caused everyone to realize that all of the bank's recorded earnings over the years had to be reversed. This was horrible news.

And yet, Lambert again allegedly failed to inform the board. In fact, Kutak Rock subsequently drafted a proxy statement for the public saying that "a significant portion of the Bank's profit resulted from its securitization business."

Of course, it would seem that Lehman Brothers itself had an obligation to alert the public that the securitization deals it was underwriting were so poor that the bank was losing money on them. Lehman, however, did nothing of the kind.

The notion that Lambert and Kutak may have known of these red flags and allegedly did not inform the Keystone board—which was paying the firm $1.5 million in fees over the course of less than two years—is astounding. These matters were of grave concern and went to the very heart of the securitization program that the bank had bet everything on. The board should have been told as early on in the process as possible. Because this allegedly did not happen, the losses kept mounting.

Damages

The losses, or damages, that Kutak Rock was allegedly responsible for were in the millions of dollars. In fact, the FDIC claimed that Kutak Rock was responsible for approximately $300 million in damages. The FDIC calculated that, if Kutak Rock had brought its concerns to the attention of the board in early 1996—the time by which the FDIC determined Kutak Rock should have gone to the board—the securitization program would likely have been terminated and the bank would have avoided $261 million in losses from the securitization process, $15 million from the sale of Prime, and another $17 million from operating losses.

Settlement

Unlike the senior management of the bank and its outside accountants, Kutak Rock and Lambert had the good sense to settle the various cases brought against them.

FDIC's Action Against Kutak Rock and Lambert

The FDIC negotiated with Kutak Rock and Lambert for over a year, from March, 2002 to May 23, 2003. Finally, they reached a resolution.

216

The law firm and Lambert denied "any and all liability" in the settlement document, but acknowledged that the "terms and conditions of [the] Agreement [were] fair, reasonable, adequate, and in the best interests of the Settling Parties."

The substantive terms of the settlement were that Kutak Rock would pay $4 million, over a period of four years; that the firm's primary professional liability insurer would pay out $8 million, constituting what was left of the firm's policy coverage; and that Kutak Rock and the FDIC would pursue claims of another $10 million against the firm's secondary professional liability insurance carrier. Depending on how much the FDIC recovered from the second insurance carrier, Kutak Rock would pay up to an additional $2.75 million.

In all, the FDIC set the value of the settlement at approximately $22 million.

OCC's Action Against Kutak Rock and Lambert

The OCC, in pursuing the law firm and Lambert, focused on equitable— or nonmonetary—relief. On May 21, 2003, the OCC settled with the firm and, separately, with Lambert, in actions that complemented each other.

The action against the law firm—in which the firm neither admitted nor denied wrongdoing or liability—required the firm, among other things, to "supervise Lambert to ensure that he does not participate in the representation of any Insured Depository Institution." If Lambert were to leave the firm for another law firm or a financial institution, Kutak Rock was required to provide the prospective employer with a copy of the OCC agreement with Lambert if the employer asked for a written evaluation or recommendation.

The agreement with the firm was to last for a period of three years. Consequently, on August 1, 2006, slightly more than three years after it was signed, the OCC terminated the agreement.

With regard to Lambert himself, the OCC entered into an agreement with him—in which Lambert neither admitted nor denied wrongdoing or liability. Pursuant to the agreement, Lambert agreed not to provide legal services or serve as counsel for any financial institution. This prohibition has no time limit. If Lambert left the firm within five years of the effective date of the agreement, he was to give a copy of the agreement to his prospective employer if it was a law firm or a financial institution. The action against Lambert is still outstanding.

Notes

1. This case involved Charles Keating of the "Keating Five" fame, who was the poster child of the savings and loan crisis of the 1980s.
2. The FDIC and the OCC also brought actions against the bank's primary outside accounting firm, Grant Thornton, as set forth in the next chapter.
3. Currently, the firm has over 500 attorneys and seventeen nationwide offices.
4. This is on an annualized basis, using the figures from 1/1/99 to when the bank failed, 9/1/99.
5. Stanford, of course, was McConnell's supposed alma mater for graduate studies.
6. The conflict could have been waived, but there is nothing in the court record one way or the other.
7. Eventually, the OCC criticized the situation and the bank let Mitchell go.

12

The Case Against the Bank's Accounting Firm—Grant Thornton

Grant Thornton . . . missed the fact that half the bank did not exist.
—Opening statement of attorneys for
the FDIC in the lawsuit against Grant Thornton

Introduction

Pursuant to the OCC's formal agreement imposed on the First National Bank of Keystone on May 28, 1998, the bank was required to retain a nationally prominent accounting firm to review the bank's books and records. After some searching, the bank retained the firm of Grant Thornton.

One of the specific requirements of the formal agreement was that Grant Thornton had to "determine the appropriateness of the Bank's accounting for . . . reconciliations between the Bank's records and loan servicer records. . . ."

This was the hidden key to resolving the mystery of the bank's inexplicable growth and earnings. If there had been a valid, independent and competent effort to reconcile the bank's records with those of the two main loan servicers,[1] the bank's fraud would have been uncovered and Church's house of cards would have collapsed.

The bank's previous auditors, the firm of Herman & Cormany, a very small firm out of Charleston, West Virginia, had not been up to the task. The bank's business and the accounting related to the securitization of subprime mortgages was simply too complicated. A prominent, nationally recognized firm was deemed to be the appropriate answer. However, Grant Thornton was not up to the task either. It failed miserably.

219

Basis for Requiring Grant Thornton's Assistance

For years, the OCC had been criticizing the bank's accounting. There were deficiencies, mistakes, and worse throughout the 1990s. The OCC had even assessed civil money penalties against the directors for poor accounting practices and for submitting inaccurate quarterly financial reports.

Grant Thornton knew this background. In taking on this assignment, it reviewed the OCC's reports of examination (ROEs), which included such statements as the following:

> [P]oor and inaccurate accounting practices render call report and bank performance data meaningless.[2]

> Accounting systems and controls are seriously deficient and do not ensure accurate reporting of the bank's condition and results of operations. Numerous instances of noncompliance were noted with call report instructions, generally accepted accounting principles [GAAP], and fundamental bank accounting controls and practices.[3]

Grant Thornton's own summaries of the ROEs acknowledged and spelled out the bank's overall deficiencies:

> The First National Bank of Keystone was assigned a CAMELS rating of "4" which means the institution generally exhibits unsafe and unsound practices. Additionally, serious financial or managerial deficiencies which result in unsatisfactory performance were noted. The weaknesses and problems are not being adequately addressed and resolved by [management] and the board of directors.[4]

In addition, the OCC's ROEs focused on the specific need to perform direct verification of the loan servicer reports to see if they agreed with the bank's records:

> **Incorrect database information.**
>
> Our review of a sample of purchased loans revealed numerous inaccuracies in the bank's database. Because of these inaccuracies, a 100% verification of information contained in the database must be done. Inaccuracies pertained to past due status, application of loan payments, paid-off loans still on the books, servicer records differing from the bank's records on basic items, such as borrower name or address, and inaccurate loan payment dates.[5]

So, Grant Thornton knew exactly what the situation was.

Background of Grant Thornton

Grant Thornton was founded in Chicago in 1924 and had offices in forty-five cities across the country. It also had five hundred offices worldwide and had over 2,700 employees, including over 700 partners and managers. It was a huge outfit—especially compared to Herman & Cormany, which was a small outfit in Charleston with only six accountants.

The lead Grant Thornton partner for the Keystone bank assignment was Stan Quay, who had an undergraduate degree in accounting (summa cum laude) from the University of Cincinnati and a masters of business administration (with a 4.0 grade average) from Xavier University in Cincinnati, with a concentration in finance. He had been a certified public accountant (CPA) since 1979, became a partner with Grant Thornton in 1987, and was the director of Grant Thornton's financial services practice for the Midwestern region.

His assistant, Susan Buenger, had an undergraduate degree in accounting from the University of Dayton and had been a CPA since 1992. She joined Grant Thornton in 1994 and, at the time of the Keystone audit, was a senior auditor.

Bank's Fear of Grant Thornton

Over the years, the bank had been able to fool and confuse Herman & Cormany. Now, however, the bank was faced with one of the big five accounting firms. There was no fooling this firm—or so the bank thought.

Church, for one, was scared to death. She did not expect Grant Thornton to be supportive of the bank. She thought that the jig was up:

> Q. Now, when Mr. Quay was initially hired, you didn't expect him to be your champion, did you?
> A. No. . . .
> Q. What were you expecting when you learned that the bank was going to hire Grant Thornton as your . . . auditing firm?
> A. That my ass was in a jam and that I would be found out very shortly . . . Well, with a big five [accounting firm] coming in, I mean, we've had auditors that knew what they were doing and some that you could bluff your way through, but working with a big five firm, Mike [Graham] and I both knew that our butts were in a jam.
> Q. Did you expect that Grant Thornton was going to find all your frauds?
> A. Yes.
> Q. The fraud—the bingo/landfill fraud, the due-diligence fraud, the inventory fraud, the interest income fraud, all those frauds. . . .[6]

Instead of being "in a jam," though, Church—and Graham—were able to feed Grant Thornton false and questionable information and get away with it. Grant Thornton looked right at the misleading information and did not even blink.

Obligation of Grant Thornton

The primary responsibility of Grant Thornton was to follow Generally Accepted Auditing Standards (GAAS) and, specifically, the auditing standard which dictates that:

> The auditor has a responsibility to plan and perform the audit to obtain reasonable assurance about whether the financial statements are free of material misstatement, *whether caused by error or fraud.*
> (Emphasis added.)

The responsibility of an auditor is, basically, to act as a "public watchdog" in order to ensure that the books and records of publicly held companies are reasonably accurate and can be relied on by the investing public. As Chief Justice Warren Burger wrote in a decision in 1984:

> An independent certified public accountant performs a different role. By certifying the public reports that collectively depict a corporation's financial status, the independent auditor assumes a public responsibility transcending any employment relationship with the client. The independent public accountant performing this special function owes ultimate allegiance to the corporation's creditors and stockholders, as well as to the investing public. This "public watchdog" function demands that the accountant maintain total independence from the client at all times and requires complete fidelity to the public trust.[7]

The FDIC alleged that Grant Thornton became more of a watchdog for Church than for the bank, let alone the public.

Grant Thornton's Review and Understanding of the High Overall Risk Profile of the Keystone Bank

As part of its duties, Grant Thornton was required to take into consideration the overall risk profile of the Keystone bank, as well as the specific risks associated with auditing the bank. The risks were numerous.

Overall Risk

As set forth earlier, the CAMELS ratings for the bank, at the time, were uniformly poor. When Grant Thornton started auditing the bank, the

OCC's composite CAMELS rating for the bank, based on the 1997 ROE, was a "3"; and the FDIC's was even worse—a "4." Further, the OCC's rating for management was a "4." The OCC's 1998 ROE gave the bank an overall "4" CAMELS rating, while the FDIC gave it a "5." So things were bad and getting worse.

Then there were the risks specifically connected with the bank's subprime mortgage securitization business. Grant Thornton knew that many competitors in this business had gone into bankruptcy or were otherwise forced out of business. As it was, the bank's involvement in this area was excessive—only a small portion of its business involved normal, retail banking; and the bank's interest in the residuals (the riskiest part of the securitizations) represented 40% of its total assets.

Because of the securitization deals, the bank had become overly reliant on the use of brokered deposits and, accordingly, the bank's liquidity was unduly stressed. In addition, the bank's capital levels were strained. The 1998 ROE specifically stated that "Failure [of the bank] is a distinct possibility if the problems and weaknesses are not satisfactorily addressed and resolved."[8]

Furthermore, the OCC had issued a number of public administrative actions against the bank, one of which—the formal agreement of May 1998—was the reason Grant Thornton had been hired.

Accounting Risks

In addition to the general overall risk profile of the bank, there were severe accounting issues that greatly increased the risks for Grant Thornton in reviewing the bank's books and records.

The OCC had criticized the bank's accounting incessantly since 1993 and, most recently, had made such comments as the following:

> Management also demonstrates an unwillingness or inability to follow accounting guidelines and comply with laws and regulations.[9]

> Accounting systems and controls continue to be deficient. These deficient systems continue to result in questionable reliability of the bank's true condition.[10]

> A wide range of questionable transactions have passed through a number of accounts making it extremely difficult to ascertain the true condition of the general ledger and income expense accounts on an ongoing basis. Records appear to be disorganized, incomplete, unavailable, poorly documented, and do not provide a reasonably reviewable audit trail.[11]

As noted, the OCC had issued civil money penalties for inaccurate financial reporting, and, during the course of Grant Thornton's audit, the OCC was preparing additional civil money penalties for the very same issues.

Integrity Risks

On top of the general risks posed by the bank's securitization process and its abysmal accounting practices, there were integrity issues that Grant Thornton needed to take into consideration.

For one, there was the fact that Church controlled almost everything in the bank: she was responsible for the bank's operations and she approved most of the transactions. Quay himself recognized this from the very first day. It was an obvious risk issue—having control of the bank centralized in one person.

Also, Grant Thornton was aware of the OCC's accusation in its 1998 draft ROE that Church was potentially manipulating the capital numbers of the bank; the fact that the FBI had investigated Church and McConnell for a kickback scheme involving the splitting of appraisal fees; the fact the bank was recording its phone conversations with the OCC; and the fact that the bank was even going through the examiners' trash at night.

With regard to the manipulation of the capital numbers, which was the result of the bank purportedly relying on a tape—or report—from Arthur Andersen, Quay said that, if the tape did not exist or did not say what Church claimed it said, he would be "out of here"; that he was "going to quit" the assignment. However, when he did find out, he failed to quit as promised. Instead, he wrote:

> It was subsequently discovered that the tapes used by Arthur Anderson were flawed. We do not believe there is an integrity issue with the client, but will include this in our fraud risk factors.[12]

This was a $770 million "mistake" in a $1 billion bank—which the OCC never thought was a mistake. Yet Quay stayed on, defending the bank until the very end. The fact that Grant Thornton did not consider this to be an integrity issue and decided to only "include [the matter in its] fraud risk factors" is amazing.

With regard to another issue, the examiners told Church that she could not rebook over $1 million worth of loans that had been previously charged off. She claimed that Quay had told her she could do it. When asked, though, he denied ever having told her anything like that.

This alone should have alerted him to her untrustworthiness. However, his overall conclusion was as follows:

> Even though FNBK management received a "5" rating, our dealings with management have **proved** that they are upstanding, honest people. . . .[13]
>
> [Emphasis added.]

With all of the bank's history, it is incredible that Grant Thornton would say this, especially as the supposedly independent watchdog.

As acknowledged later by Quay and Buenger, Church and others in the bank lied to them every day and fed them false information, but neither of them ever caught on.

As related by Buenger:

> Q. Throughout the course of your audit, bank management lied to you every single day, did they not? . . .
> A. Yes.
> Q. There wasn't a day that you worked on that audit in West Virginia where bank management didn't lie to you to your face, true?
> A. That is pretty much true, yes.
> Q. You didn't catch them one time, did you? Not even one time; am I right?
> A. I don't recall catching them. . . .

And then, similarly, Quay's testimony:

> Q. Every single day that you were in West Virginia . . . bank management was giving you phony documents, true?
> A. True. . . .
> Q. There wasn't a day that didn't go by they didn't give you phony, fraudulent documents.
> A. Yes, sir.
> Q. And you never once detected that any one of those documents was a fraud, correct?
> A. Correct.

Even though Grant Thornton trusted Church and the rest of the bank's management and concluded from the outset that management had been "proved" to be "upstanding, honest people," Grant Thornton did, in fact, rate the risk of the bank as high as it could. According to Quay:

> [The risk] was not just maximum. It was maximum/maximum . . . maximum on internal controls, maximum on the environmental

> assessment and it has the impact of placing the preponderance of the audit reliance on performance of substantive tests versus any reliance on the [bank's] system of internal controls.

As it turned out, this was an accurate synopsis. In addition, Quay claimed again and again that his "fraud antenna was up as high as it could get." However, it is questionable whether Grant Thornton really ever adhered to this risk rating or whether it was ever sufficiently skeptical of the integrity of the bank's management.

Skepticism

Skepticism is, actually, one of the necessary attributes of a proper audit function. According to the audit guidelines:

> Due professional care requires the auditor to exercise *professional skepticism*. Professional skepticism is an attitude that includes a questioning mind and a critical assessment of audit evidence.
> (Emphasis in the original.)

This industry standard was reflected in Grant Thornton's own audit manual:

> We must maintain an attitude of appropriate skepticism in obtaining audit evidence. Accordingly, when applying procedures to the client's records, schedules and supporting data, we should be on guard to avoid accepting documents and explanations at face value.

Skepticism should also have been extremely high in this case due to the "maximum/maximum" risk involved. As one of the FDIC's experts explained:

> In this case, Mr. Quay rated this audit as a maximum risk audit. And in that kind of circumstance, you would expect an even higher, a heightened degree of professional skepticism beyond the ordinary, show-me attitude here.

Yet, time and again, Grant Thornton accepted documents from the bank only to verify the information against other bank-generated documents. Grant Thornton, thus, never found the underlying fraud.

Grant Thornton's Level of Independence

One of the other basic tenets for an auditor is being independent of the institution undergoing the audit. Without independence, and without a required level of skepticism, the audit is going to be unreliable. Further, the level of independence should be extremely high and above reproach in a high-risk audit.

The examiners, though, felt from the outset that Quay seemed to side with the bank, no matter what the issue. As one examiner said:

> I felt there was a compromise of independence on [the part of] Mr. Quay based on his actions, . . . when there was a question or a problem, he tended to side with the bank . . . in every instance.

He was viewed by another examiner as defensive and uncooperative. Further, he and Buenger worked right in Church's office—which presented a very strange appearance. As one examiner noted:

> Q. Where did Mr. Quay work while you were in the bank . . . ?
> A. That was unusual. He worked in [Church's] office. And what I'm accustomed to seeing in my other prior experience is that usually the auditors work in a separate room where they can confer privately, have confidential discussions and phone calls, but he worked in her office when he was at the bank. . . . It should be independence in fact and in appearance.

Grant Thornton was also supportive of making Church the chief financial officer (CFO) of the bank, which some directors thought was a bad idea, primarily because the CFO is supposed to be—like the auditor—independent. The CFO needs to independently review and approve the transactions in the bank. And, in this case, it was Church, herself, who instigated or approved most of the transactions to begin with. So, as CFO, she would be reviewing her own transactions. As one of the experts in the ensuing litigation against Grant Thornton explained:

> She was totally controlling the organization . . . So making her CFO in effect took the person [who] was really operating and controlling the whole operation of the bank and also gave that person accounting responsibility. . . . So it's really an incredible recommendation for an independent auditor to be making. . . .

Grant Thornton went so far as to criticize the OCC for having assessed civil money penalties for the bank's failure to file accurate financial reports—even though call report issues had persisted for seven straight quarters and in spite of constant criticisms of this area by the OCC from 1993 onward. Ironically, Grant Thornton itself recognized that there were hundreds of millions of dollars' worth of adjustments that needed to be made to the bank's financial records. Also, Grant Thornton was aware that Church tried to improperly rebook the $1 million in charged-off loans, mentioned above.

The examiners noted that Quay was involved in not just auditing the bank, but was involved in inputting data for the bank; as EIC Blair said: he "was really inputting the information in the model for the residual assets and, since that was a major asset of the bank, he was serving more of a role as management versus an auditor." According to Blair, Quay was not just an auditor, but also a consultant and an advisor for the bank, a de facto member of the bank's management.

Even Ellis, the bank's titular president, acknowledged numerous times that Quay was effectively a "critical member of the management team of the bank." Others noted that Quay was performing the functions of a CFO at the bank. For a supposed outside, independent auditor from a big accounting firm, this was an incredible situation. Quay got so wrapped up in working for the bank that he even threatened to resign if the OCC disagreed with him on his valuation of the bank's residual assets.

Not only did Quay seemingly defer to the bank on almost all issues, he was openly hostile to the OCC. At one board meeting, on June 24, 1999, Quay pointed to examiner-in-charge Blair and told the board, "There is your problem." Quay later tried to assert that he meant that the bank's problem was the goal of pleasing the OCC, but that was not how it was received and Quay's after-the-fact explanation seems strained at best. In addition, Church herself took Quay's statement at face value:

> Q. Did Mr. Quay make any criticism of Mr. Blair at the [board of directors] meeting?
> A. He wasn't too nice to him, if that's what you mean.
> Q. Okay. Did Mr. Quay ever state in your presence that Mr. Blair was the problem?
> A. . . . He said something to that effect. . . .

When Mike Shiery, the interim CFO, resigned because of the issuance of the civil money penalties and the other problems in the bank, Quay approached him and asked him to sign a statement that said he was resigning, at least in part, due to intimidation by the examiners. Shiery said that that was not the case and refused to sign any such statement:

> Quay asked me at that point if I would include in my resignation a statement that I was leaving because I was concerned with the

> pressure that the regulators were putting on the bank or me. I don't remember exactly the phraseology, but that I was leaving in response to regulatory pressure. And I told him that I most certainly would not do that because that was not the reason I was leaving.
>
> . . . .
>
> In all my career, I've never been asked by an auditor anything about my resignation letter, let alone to include any specific provisions in a resignation letter, so that part was unusual.

The FDIC's expert noted that this demonstrated a lack of objectivity on Quay's part.

One explanation for all this strange behavior, according to the complaint filed by the FDIC against Grant Thornton, was that Quay was simply seeking more fees:

> Instead of performing the independent role for which he was hired, Quay became just another "yes man" for Keystone's corrupt management, particularly Terry Church. Quay was more interested in gaining Church's personal confidence (forgetting that Keystone, not Church, was his client) in order to ingratiate himself with her for the ultimate purpose of landing much more lucrative consulting work [with] Keystone.

With regard to fee income, it should be noted that the First National Bank of Keystone was one of Quay's biggest client during this time frame. Also, Quay's income, as a partner with Grant Thornton, was based in part on how much fee income he generated. So it was in his personal interest to generate as much fee income as possible.

At the outset, the fee income from the Keystone assignment was projected to be approximately $200,000. As it turned out, Grant Thornton billed the bank just shy of $600,000. The fees grew in large part due to the nonauditing services Grant Thornton provided for the bank.

As set forth by the FDIC in its opening statement in the case against Grant Thornton:

> [Church gave Grant Thornton] work to help her as executrix of McConnell's estate, . . . work on regulatory matters, battling with the OCC. He became her advisor on trying to spin off the mortgage company. He became the bank's advisor on selling the residuals. He became the bank's advisor on strategic planning [thus, generating] more and more fees. . . .

> At the same time that all that additional work is coming [in], you have Mr. Quay starting to become the advocate for Mrs. Church. Instead of the independent neutral, he starts telling the board of directors that Mrs. Church is right, she's honest, she's good, she's a valuable employee; the OCC's wrong. They don't know what they're talking about; don't believe them. And the board accepted Mr. Quay's word over that of the OCC. He had more credibility with them. And so Mr. Quay abandoned his independence.

It would appear that all of this extra work—performed primarily by the two people from Grant Thornton tasked with doing the audit—may have distracted Grant Thornton to some extent from its primary task of auditing the bank. If so, this was probably by design on Church's part.

Quay's apparent lack of independence was also reflected by the fact that he let Church "fix" a speeding ticket for him. The road to Keystone is a winding, mountainous road and is treacherous at best, especially for nonlocals; however, Quay was caught speeding.[14] Church was gracious enough to help him out. According to Quay's sanitized version, the policeman—after the fact—"reconsidered." With Church asking a favor of the policeman and with Cherry being the mayor of Keystone and, thus, the policeman's boss, it is little wonder that he "reconsidered."

Experience of the Grant Thornton Auditors

An additional, fundamental problem facing Grant Thornton was the fact that neither of the two auditors it sent to the Keystone bank had ever encountered a high-risk financial institution. Even Quay, who had audited over five hundred financial institutions, had never handled a "maximum risk" audit. In addition, Buenger was unfamiliar with securitizations, which represented a big problem in that the OCC's formal agreement specifically required that the firm selected by the bank have "extensive securitization auditing and accounting experience." While the firm as a whole might have had that background, at least half of the two-person team the firm sent to the bank did not.

In addition to her lack of experience, Buenger had never audited a bank where the management had been subjected to civil money penalties; had never audited a bank subjected to a formal agreement; and had never audited a bank whose president resigned at the insistence of the supervisory agency. Further, Buenger was personally uncomfortable with the "cultural differences" she identified at the bank—the fact that the top person in the bank had a gun in her desk drawer, and that many of the female employees had tattoos.

On top of all this, Grant Thornton did not seem to even understand how the First National Bank of Keystone was supervised. In this regard, in its "Environmental Assessment," Grant Thornton claimed that the bank was regulated by the OCC, the FDIC, and the state of West Virginia. While this is a bit of an esoteric area for a layman, anyone auditing financial institutions should know that this is wrong. National banks are chartered and supervised by the OCC. The FDIC has a certain degree of "back-up" examination authority, but it is not in a position to directly supervise or regulate national banks. And the states have nothing whatsoever to do with national banks. States only charter and regulate state banks.

Risks and Problems Noted During the Audit

As set forth above, there were various risk components associated with auditing the Keystone bank. Once the audit commenced, it became even more complicated. Numerous discrepancies and anomalies associated with the books and records of the bank cropped up that should have further concerned Grant Thornton. Further, these discrepancies should have also called into question the integrity of the bank's management in creating the questionable figures and transactions to begin with.

For one, there was a $31 million "input error" made by Michael Graham, the head of the bank's mortgage securitization subsidiary. When the mistake was uncovered, Owen Carney, the bank's very short-term president, remembers Graham simply saying, "Golly, I made a mistake." Carney could not remember any other explanation. To him, it was like dealing with Gomer Pyle, the hapless, simple-minded marine played by Jim Nabors in the 1960s TV comedy.

The presiding judge in the FDIC's case against Grant Thornton concluded that Buenger violated auditing standards by failing to investigate how and why Graham made—in the court's words—this $31 million "input error."

There was also the instance of the bank's portfolio of local loans[15] going from $17 million to $33 million in one month and, later, over a two-month period, from $18 million to $1.9 million and, then, back up to $12.9 million. According to the FDIC, this latter event represented wild swings that were as if the local, impoverished community of Keystone paid off all of its loans one month and, then, the following month, took out new loans. This, of course, was illogical, but went unexplained by Grant Thornton.

Further, Grant Thornton, in its reconciliation of loans, reviewed a chart Graham had generated showing loans held by Keystone in the amount of $566 million. However, Grant Thornton was only able to validate an inventory of $402 million, representing a substantial discrepancy. In addition, neither of these numbers corresponded to the bank's public call report numbers for this period of time of $462 million in loans.

Even though Buenger realized that these numbers in Graham's chart "were not reasonable" and made "no sense," she continued to use other numbers from this chart and failed to investigate the material discrepancies. The presiding judge ruled that this, again, reflected a violation of GAAS.

* * *

Even more curious was the fact that, at one point, the bank recorded interest income received of approximately $20 million. Instead of it being offset by a debit to cash, though, the bank offset the interest payment by an increase in loans of approximately the same amount. Technically, this meant that the borrowers were taking out additional loans to pay the interest on their existing loans. This was particularly strange because it involved low income, subprime borrowers who were taking out small loans of around $30,000. When confronted with this data, the auditors simply responded, "You know, on its face, it does appear to be of [a] questionable nature."

This involved $20 million, yet Grant Thornton's objective was to scan, or review, all transactions in the general ledger greater than $20,000 and to identify all unexplained differences. However, Grant Thornton never did this. It never even started doing this. Had it done this review, the underlying fraud would have been uncovered much earlier, according to expert testimony at the ensuing trial.

Grant Thornton's Reports to the Bank

Shortly after Grant Thornton started its work at the bank—which was on August 12, 1998—Quay reported to the bank's board of directors that the books of the bank were the "cleanest and most accurate" they had been in years. This was recorded in the minutes of the board of directors' meeting held on October 29, 1998. The directors took it at face value. The examiners believed that Quay meant it.

Buenger, however, was horrified. The bank's books and records were beginning to look better only because Grant Thornton had just directed the bank to make approximately $160 million in adjustments.

Due to all the needed adjustments, Buenger viewed Quay's statement as ludicrous and preposterous. As she, herself, testified:

> I believe the whole phrase was "After making a hundred million dollars' worth of adjustments, the balance sheet was the cleanest it had ever been," or something. But he quantified a preposterous amount of adjustments that we had booked to [correct] the balance sheet.
>
> . . . .
>
> You asked about the ludicrousness of this. What I was referring to is making $100 million worth of adjustments, in my world, [that] just doesn't happen. That is so farfetched and so absurd, it's ludicrous. That's all I can say about it. It's just the magnitude of that. The most adjustments I've ever made, prior to Keystone, was probably two million or something. So, you know, this is 50 times greater than anything I had ever done in terms of mere dollars before.

She wanted to pull him down by the back of his pants and make him shut up, but he was the partner; she was not. She even had a term for Stan Quay's propensity to be dramatic—she called it a "Stanism." This, apparently, was a "Stanism."

To make things worse, Grant Thornton had a long ways to go before completing its audit. It had not verified the bank's interest income. And the firm had not yet verified the bank's primary assets—the huge volume of loans purportedly held on its behalf by the two loan servicers. So any statement about the soundness or integrity of the bank's books was very premature.

Long after the fact—when he was trying to explain why he had told the board that "the balance sheet was the cleanest it had ever been"—Quay tried to make light of his statement as a "facetious comment." However, as noted, the board did not take it that way and the examiners did not hear it that way. Even Buenger, apparently, did not get the joke.

Quay and Buenger also tried to explain away the comment by contending that they were called into the board meeting unexpectedly and that Quay was dressed informally. Quay, in fact, was wearing "Dockers." As recounted by Buenger:

> As I recall, Mr. Quay being dressed, he had on a pair of, for lack of [a] better term, Dockers and a long sleeve golf shirt and his leather jacket on. We were in no way dressed in a manner that would indicate that we were going to a formal board meeting, or had intended to go to a board meeting.

According to Quay, "I made a brief entrance . . . prior to leaving for Cincinnati. . . [I was dressed] extremely casually. I think actually I had jeans on."

So if your high-priced auditor comes to a meeting dressed in Dockers, or other casual attire, you apparently should not believe anything they say. Unfortunately, the board of directors of the Keystone bank learned of this Grant Thornton rule too late.

* * *

Grant Thornton's final report was not issued until April 19, 1999. However, several weeks before that, at the March 24, 1999 board of directors' meeting, Quay told the bank that it was going to get a "clean audit" report. The next day, at the bank's annual shareholders' meeting, Quay repeated the news and passed around copies of the report. He later claimed that the report was only in draft form, but the report was not marked draft, per the policy and requirements of Grant Thornton. As it turned out, the "final" report did not materially change in the intervening few weeks.

The report declared the bank hale and hearty, with no significant discrepancies in the bank's books and records.

Grant Thornton's Confirmation Process

The most crucial aspect of Grant Thornton's assignment at the bank was to confirm, or verify, the bank's loan portfolio and to reconcile it to the reports from the loan servicers which held the Keystone loans and collected and disbursed the interest from the loans. In fact, as noted above, this was clearly set out in the OCC's formal agreement requiring the bank to hire a firm like Grant Thornton.

At the time, the bank had two primary loan servicers, Compu-Link and Advanta, which held most of the loans Keystone owned. This should have made verification of the loans very easy, but it apparently did not help.

Compu-Link, as noted in Chapter Eight, unwittingly provided Grant Thornton with incorrect numbers—as directed by the bank. Very simply, Compu-Link sent the auditors not only the information pertaining to the loans Keystone owned, but also the loans that Keystone's partner, United National Bank, held. One of the confusing factors here was the fact that these two banks had previously instructed Compu-Link to carry the loans on one trial balance—under Keystone's name—with the loans attributable to each bank being under subsidiary trial balances, instead of being in two totally separate accounts. In addition, the Keystone bank had had a standing request for years that Compu-Link report "all loans" to Keystone, whether currently owned or just previously owned by Keystone.

So Grant Thornton received incorrect information from Compu-Link that was not discovered until the very end.

However, with regard to Advanta, Grant Thornton received the correct loan data—twice—and failed to properly act upon this information.

In January, 1999, Grant Thornton sent a vague, poorly worded confirmation request to Advanta. Instead of saying, "Provide me with the loans serviced by you and owned by the First National Bank of Keystone," or words to that effect, Grant Thornton's letter simply said "please provide [Grant Thornton] with the balance as of December 31, 1998 of the loans being serviced by you."[16] Nonetheless, Advanta sent back a correct response, reflecting that it was servicing slightly over $6 million in loans for Keystone. However, neither Buenger nor Quay ever looked at the response. It sat untouched in Grant Thornton's offices in Cincinnati.

Buenger waited two months, from January 17th to March 16th, before getting back to Advanta to inquire about the confirmation response. This was now eight days before the Keystone board of directors' meeting and nine days before the bank's shareholders' meeting at which time Quay was planning to tell everyone that the bank was going to get a clean bill of health. The only problem was that Grant Thornton had still not verified the loans purportedly held by Advanta—which represented one quarter of the bank's assets and exceeded the bank's capital.

So Buenger asked Advanta to resend the confirmation response, which it did on March 17th. This time, Buenger received it, but did not look at it—let alone examine it carefully. In her words, she put it on the "back-burner," even though confirming these numbers was crucial to the audit and even though Buenger had plenty of time to review Advanta's response. As it was, Buenger spent ninety-one billable hours at the bank in the last two weeks of March pursuing less important matters. So Quay proceeded to give the bank a clean bill of health and communicated that to the bank's management, directors, and shareholders.

Finally realizing that she had not looked at Advanta's confirmation response, Buenger pulled it out around April 7th. Upon reading it, she should have had something close to a heart attack. She was expecting the confirmation response to say that Advanta held $242 million in loans on Keystone's behalf. However, it reported only $6 million. It was a difference of $236 million and enough to render the bank insolvent. Even so, Buenger thought that it was nothing major—she thought that it was just a "boo-boo."

Buenger claimed she talked to bank management about it, but it was apparently so inconsequential to her that she could not remember whom she talked to or what they said:

> Q. Then what did you do, noticing that there was a 236 million dollar difference? What was the next thing you did?
> A. I believe I talked to the client to see why they thought there was a discrepancy.
> Q. What did the client say? Who did you speak with?
> A. Probably Mr. Graham or Ms. Church.
> Q. And what did they offer?
> A. I don't recall a direct conversation, but that would normally be the first step we would take. . . .[17]

That same day, she called Patricia Ramirez at Advanta to ask what was going on. According to Buenger, Ramirez said that the "United National Bank loans were actually Keystone loans." According to Ramirez, she never said any such thing.

Nonetheless, Buenger wrote out a handwritten note that said, "Per discussion with Patricia Ramirez at (619) ___, the loans coded under the 'United' name actually belonged to Keystone as of December 31, 1998." What is strange here is the idea loans coded "under the 'United' name" would actually belong to Keystone, and, second, how Buenger could have learned that from the phone conversation when she later testified that the name "United" was never mentioned during the call.

In addition, Buenger later admitted that Ramirez never instructed her to combine the United loans with the Keystone loans. Buenger also admitted that she never asked Ramirez why both written confirmations attributed only $6 million to Keystone if the real number was $242 million. And Buenger never asked Ramirez why United's name was even in issue when trying to verify only the loans held by Keystone.

One minute after the short telephone call, Ramirez sent Buenger an email which set forth the numbers for United:

> Investor Number: 406[18]
> Investor Name: UNITED NATIONAL BANK
> Balance: $236,221,923.07

> If you have any questions, please call me at (619) _____.
> Patricia Ramirez

Instead of calling Ramirez, Buenger printed out Ramirez's email and, on the page, wrote out by hand the dollar amount for Keystone—$6,342,110.34—and added it to the number for United—$236,221,923.07—and came up with the sought-after number of $242,564,033.41. Buenger initialed this paper—signifying that she had read it—but backdated her initials to March 17, 1999, or three weeks before the email existed. Quay initialed the document and backdated his initials as well, to March 23, 1999—both dates being before the bank's board of directors' meeting and the shareholders' meeting. Whether this was just continued sloppiness on the part of Grant Thornton or worse is unclear.

After the fact, Buenger reported in her work papers that "Nothing unusual was noted during the confirmation process." This, obviously, was not correct. Even if Grant Thornton had properly resolved the discrepancy in the numbers, the discrepancy did actually exist and should have been noted. According to audit standards, any large discrepancy, even if resolved, should be noted in the work papers.

In addition, the resolution of any large discrepancy should have been confirmed in writing. Buenger could have easily pressed the reply button to Ramirez's email of April 7th, and asked for such a confirmation. She could have called Ramirez and asked for a written follow-up. She did neither.

Besides saying nothing in the work papers and failing to ask Ramirez for a written confirmation, Buenger never reported the discrepancy to Quay, the bank, or the examiners. Quay himself later acknowledged that he saw the name "United" on the papers in big block letters, but admitted that he did not talk to anyone about it.

Curiously, both Buenger and Quay claimed that the conversation with Ramirez was not an oral confirmation. They both swore that it was something else. According to Quay, it was a "clarification of a written confirmation." According to Buenger, it was an "oral clearance of a written confirmation." Both contentions are nonsensical.

Buenger's conversation with Ramirez was oral; the supposed explanation from Ramirez was oral; and the supposed resolution was premised on what Ramirez told Buenger orally over the phone. There was nothing in writing—as required by audit standards. The only thing in writing were the two identical confirmation responses Advanta sent in January and again in March, stating that the volume of loans held for Keystone was only $6 million and the email setting forth what United—not Keystone—owned.

To compound the absurdity, Quay thought that the confirmation was "persuasive" because the number Buenger came up with "fit exactly into the [bank's] General Ledger balance." Specifically, Quay was impressed by the fact that the sum Buenger arrived at "agreed to the penny to what Keystone was carrying on its books." However, he acknowledged that "the name did not."

In other words, the forced addition of two numbers to arrive at an artificial number that the bank management was just barely clever enough to match to the number they put in the bank's records was enough for Quay—even though the crucial number was attributed to the wrong entity, not the bank he was performing the audit for. He tried to explain his reasoning as follows:

> What I'm saying is that we received written information back with respect to these specific loans and clarified the one item on that confirmation that differed from Keystone's records, and that being the name.

For a seasoned CPA doing a high-risk audit of a bank at the direction of the federal banking supervisor to ignore this "small detail" of the name being totally wrong in confirming one quarter of a bank's assets is amazing.

To top it off, presiding District Court Judge Faber, in ruling on the case the FDIC brought against Grant Thornton, specifically found that Buenger's story was not credible:

> [T]he court does not believe Buenger's testimony about the telephone call with Ramirez for the following reasons. First and most importantly, the physical evidence, *i.e.*, the email, contradicts Buenger's account of the phone call. According to Buenger, Ramirez told her "[t]hese belonged to Keystone at 12/31/98." However, one minute later, Ramirez sent Buenger an email which stated:
>
> > Below is the information requested from investor 406 as of 12/31/98. Investor number 406, investor name United National Bank, . . . month end balances $236,221,923.07.
>
> Ramirez's email is completely at odds with the statements Buenger attributes to her. For his reason alone, Buenger's testimony on this point is not credible.
>
> . . .

Finally, the demeanor of Buenger on the witness stand, when taken together with her interests in the case, leads the court to believe she was not entirely truthful.

* * *

One thing that made Grant Thornton's confirmation process almost inevitably flawed was the firm's failure to understand Keystone's business. Grant Thornton, of course, knew that the bank was involved in the securitization of subprime mortgages it was buying from all over the country. And Grant Thornton knew that the bank had capital issues and poor liquidity and was overly reliant on the use of brokered deposits. But Grant Thornton did not put these things together—and did not ask the bank.

For some time, in order to avoid further aggravating its capital, liquidity, and funding issues, the bank had partnered first with City National Bank and then with United National Bank. These banks had agreed to fund—and hold as owners—the subprime mortgages Keystone selected for securitization deals.[19] But Grant Thornton did not know about this arrangement, in spite of the fact that there were references to it in the bank's board minutes and the OCC's ROEs, which Grant Thornton reviewed, and in spite of the fact that United had financed $960 million in loans for Keystone in 1998 to eventually put into securitization deals. This represented almost the entire amount of the Keystone bank's total assets, but Grant Thornton apparently did not notice this huge amount of money flowing through an account at the Keystone bank in United's name.

Quay himself acknowledged that, had he known about the relationship between Keystone and United, it "would have changed a lot of things" and it was fair to say that they would have been able to uncover the fraud sooner. For one, Grant Thornton could have better tailored the confirmation requests and clearly would have understood what it meant when Advanta's response said that the bulk of the loans were owned by United.

Ironically, Grant Thornton prided itself in being "unique" among auditors in stressing the need to understand its clients' business:

> [A]s stated in the [Grant Thornton] manuals and marketing literature, a *unique* feature of the Grant Thornton audit approach is that it tries to understand the business of the client.

. . . .

> [Grant Thornton's] audit approach is business oriented. It focuses on an understanding of the client's business *much deeper than* the knowledge of the accounting system and records on which *auditors have traditionally concentrated.* . . . Our audit focuses on the substance of the underlying business rather than just the financial statements.
>
> (Emphasis added.)

Of course, as much as Grant Thornton liked to think it was special and even "unique," knowing your customer's business is a basic tenet of auditing, especially with regard to the confirmation process, as set forth by the industry's guidelines:

> The auditor's *understanding of the client's arrangements and transactions* with third parties *is key to determining the information to be confirmed.* The auditor should obtain an understanding of the substance of such arrangements and transactions to determine the appropriate information to be included on the confirmation request.
>
> (Emphasis added.)

So, not only was "knowing your client" not a "unique" facet of Grant Thornton's approach to auditing, it was—at least in this case—one that Grant Thornton did not adequately follow through on.

Grant Thornton's Reaction to the News that $515 Million Was Missing

When the examiners started to finally unravel the true condition of the bank, Grant Thornton was still in the bank. The examiners sat down with the board and Quay on August 25, 1999 to tell them that $515 million in loans were missing. Quay's reaction was one of denial. He repeatedly stated that he and Buenger had confirmed the bank's loan balances as of year-end 1998. He stood by his findings.

If Quay were wrong, it meant that all the work he had been performing at the bank for the previous twelve months was completely flawed. It meant that his largest client was insolvent. It meant that Grant Thornton had issued a "clean audit" report for a bank that was hopelessly under water. It was terrible news.

So he asked Buenger to explain how she had performed the confirmations. When he learned that there had, in fact, been a problem with the Advanta confirmation, he started yelling at her: "You did what? . . . Didn't you follow-up in writing? . . . Didn't you obtain more information?" It was turning ugly.

Buenger went running frantically upstairs and came back with some papers to confirm what she had done. But the papers did not support the bank's contentions that the loans were there. Instead, the papers merely showed the forced, handwritten reconciliation by Buenger.

* * *

During the course of the audit of the bank, Buenger was responsible for verifying the bank's income from the loans held by the servicers. It should have been relatively easy because 80% of the interest income in 1998 was coming from only one of the two primary servicers—Compu-Link. So, if Grant Thornton had looked at just twelve remittances, or incoming wires, from Compu-Link during 1998, the auditors could have determined that the bank was not receiving anywhere near the interest income it was supposed to be getting.

According to Grant Thornton's policies and manuals, due to the high-risk nature of the Keystone audit, the auditors were required to perform a "test of details," as opposed to an "analytical review." The former required looking at actual receipts, wires, remittances, and so forth, and not relying on the bank's self-generated reports. The latter— the "analytical review"—entailed comparing the given numbers to the norm or to what would be expected.

But instead of performing the "test of details" and reviewing the twelve remittance checks or wires from Compu-Link for 1998, Buenger engaged in a much more cumbersome and time-consuming analytical analysis.[20] She compared the volume of the bank's reported loans to the bank's reported income and determined that the percentage of interest income as compared to the volume of loans was reasonable. In fact, it was. But it merely represented a comparison of one set of bank's records to another.

Specifically, Buenger had looked at three documents. The first document was the bank's call report for year-end 1998. However, Grant Thornton knew that the OCC had complained that the bank had not filed an accurate call report in seven quarters, up to and including September 30, 1998. To assume that the year-end 1998 call report was going to be better was wishful thinking. In addition, Grant Thornton knew that the OCC had assessed civil money penalties against the entire board of directors for failing to file accurate call reports and that, in

January, 1999, the OCC had notified the board that an unprecedented second round of civil money penalties for call report violations was pending.

The second document Buenger looked at was a chart of month-end loan inventories for 1998 that was provided to her by Graham. While Buenger may not have known that Graham was an untrustworthy source of information, it was a bank-generated document that was improperly being used in a high-risk audit to verify the bank's own numbers. In addition, the chart only showed the month-end loan figures. In order to conduct a proper review of interest earned during a month, one needed the *average* monthly volume of loans. The end-of-month figures would not take into consideration the fluctuation of the loan volumes during the month.

The third document was a "remittance report," that reflected $10 million in income from Compu-Link during the month of December, 1998. However, this report only set forth the income for that one month, and did not take into consideration the fact that the volume of the bank's loans should have fluctuated greatly due to the occurrence of two very large securitization deals during 1998.[21] Second, the report came from the bank, so it was inherently unreliable. Third, the report was described as a "trial balance," but it was not. It was a "remittance report."[22] Fourth, although the cover page for the report was on Compu-Link letterhead, signed by an employee of that company, Forrest Krumm, the report itself had no markings on it indicating that it came from Compu-Link. It was just a plain piece of paper that could have been created by the bank instead of Compu-Link. The questioning of Quay on this point was as follows:

> Q. The third source [Buenger used was] the Forrest Krumm letter [that said on the front page,] "Enclosed please find the detailed trial balance." Correct?
> A. Correct.
> Q. And the document attached to it . . . is what you've called a remittance statement, correct?
> A. Correct. . . .
> Q. You do not refer to it as a trial balance, correct?
> A. No.
> Q. And this document that's the remittance statement does not contain any markings to identify it as a document generated by Compu-Link, correct?
> A. Yes.
>   . . . .

Q. And is there any identifying mark on here reflecting that it is a Compu-Link record?

A. No. . . .

Q. So whatever was given to you as a Compu-Link remittance report at the end of March, 1999, would be something that was provided to you by managers of the bank, correct?

A. Correct.

As noted by Judge Faber in his decision, "The analytical test that Buenger did to test interest income only considered information provided by management."[23]

* * *

Days before the bank failed, Quay noted that the easiest way to check the interest income was to look at the actual remittance wires or checks, and said that it would only take forty-five minutes or so. Blair offered to provide Quay with the interest remittance reports he had in his own work papers, but, when he went to retrieve them, he discovered that someone had stolen them. Even Quay started to think "something is very, very strange."

Buenger then asked Lora McKinney for a printout of the general ledger showing the bank's interest income. McKinney said there would be no problem and went upstairs to get it. However, she did not come back for some time, so Buenger went in search of her. McKinney explained the delay was due to the fact that the computer system was being backed up. In the middle of this crisis, this sounded like a bogus excuse. Then McKinney said that she had already given the printout to Graham. He claimed he never received it. To Buenger, it was a "cat and mouse game" designed to keep information away from them.

Quay later contended that, at this time, on the 26th, his "suspicions were very, very high, very, very great," and that he began to "smell a rat." However, even with all of that—the missing $515 million, the rising suspicions, the inability to get to the bank's general ledger—Quay was certain that there was some boarding error at one or both of the loan servicers. He was confident that there was some simple mistake and that everything would be easily rectified. So, even though he had begun to "smell a rat," he continued to give the management of the bank the benefit of the doubt. Consequently, he and Buenger decided to leave town and return to Cincinnati and let the bank staff try to find and sort out the mistake.

As noted in Chapter Eight, they left Keystone on that Thursday afternoon and drove to Roanoke for a flight to Cincinnati the next morning. However, the bank directors called Quay and insisted he return to the bank.

Quay and Buenger did return to Keystone, getting there around noon on Friday. They were still not able to verify the interest income for the bank that would correspond to the $515 million in loans, but, after giving further instructions to the bank staff as to what to look for, Quay and Buenger left Keystone again, not to return until Sunday, August 29th.

As it was, the bank was falsely reporting $98 million in interest income for 1998, when, in fact, it had received less than $2 million.

* * *

On Sunday, after Quay and Buenger returned, Scott Griffith, the head of IT for the bank, told them that he did not know why management was going through the "farce of looking for the loans." He explained that his wife, who was also an employee at the bank, had been asked by Graham to create a report for HUD—for FHA insurance purposes—that did not include the loans held by the loans servicers. As Quay explained:

> Griffith, who is the information technology manager for the bank, pulled Ms. Buenger aside and . . . said, "You guys shouldn't take the rap for this. Management knows that those loans aren't there, and they have known for at least four months that they are not there, because my wife does the FHA reserve and she hasn't been putting those loans in the computation for at least four months."

Griffith, understandably, would not repeat this statement in front of Church and so, mysteriously, Grant Thornton let the matter drop. In essence, two employees of the bank (Scott Griffith and his wife) were telling Grant Thornton that the loans did not exist, that it was all a big fraud and that the bank was insolvent, but Grant Thornton let it go. The auditors apparently did not tell the outside directors[24] or the OCC. They just dropped it.[25]

Throughout this time, Grant Thornton persisted in contending that Compu-Link must have made a $500 million boarding error. This did not seem to be based on anything concrete and the examiners kept trying to explain that there was a large discrepancy at both loan servicers. The bank was reporting $233 million held by Advanta instead of $6 million—a difference of $227 million. And the bank was reporting $319 million held by Compu-Link instead of $31 million—a

$288 million discrepancy.[26] It was not a case where the entire missing amount could be attributable to only one servicer.

* * *

When Quay talked to the Advanta representatives, he became quite agitated, even angry, insisting that Advanta's numbers were wrong. Dee Romero from Advanta, along with Ramirez, thought it was ridiculous. They knew their numbers. They had checked them several times and had never wavered in their conclusions. They repeatedly tried to straighten Quay out, but, in the words of the presiding judge, "Quay . . . resisted straightening."

On Monday, August 30, there was a conference call with the other servicer, Compu-Link. On the line were Quay, Church, the OCC, John LaRose (the president of Compu-Link) and numerous others. Quay was still contending that the loans existed and belonged to Keystone—even though he could not even verify the bank's interest income. LaRose, on his part, acknowledged that Compu-Link's response to the initial, vaguely worded, confirmation request was incorrect—that it was off by $288 million—more than half of the missing $515 million.[27] When Quay heard this, he turned white.

Later that day, Quay started yelling at Buenger again to the point where she was reduced to tears. Ellis, the president of the bank, had to take her into a side room so she could calm down and recover her composure.

It was that evening when Church admitted to Quay that:

> There isn't any cash, and there has never been any cash. I guess my goose is cooked.

The next day, Tuesday the 31st, there was a meeting with the examiners. Blair, the examiner-in-charge, asked Quay and the others at the meeting whether the missing loans were due to a massive fraud or due to ignorance. There was silence in the room. Then, according to Blair, Quay said that they could not determine what the answer was to that question—that they needed to do more investigating.

Quay had been told by Griffith, the head of IT for the bank, that the books were cooked. Quay had not been able to verify the existence of the interest income. Quay knew that the bank's numbers did not agree with those of the servicers. And Church had admitted to Quay that there was no money—that her goose was cooked. In spite of all of that, he let it stand that he needed to do more investigating. He did not tell the examiners about Griffith's comment on Sunday night or Church's admission just the night before.

FDIC's Action Against Grant Thornton

On October 16, 2001, about two years after the failure of the bank, the FDIC brought an action against Grant Thornton, seeking to recover millions of dollars. The FDIC accused Grant Thornton of numerous acts of negligence, including the following:

- Having failed to plan and perform the 1997 and 1998 Keystone audits to obtain reasonable assurance that Keystone's financial statements were free of material misstatements;
- Having failed to conduct its audits as reasonably prudent auditors and in accordance with GAAS and GAAP;
- Having misrepresented that there were no problems with Keystone's financial statements;
- Having misrepresented that regulatory criticisms of Keystone and its management were wrong and/or unfounded;
- Having become an active advocate for Keystone's corrupt management;
- Having failed to maintain its independence;
- Having misrepresented to Keystone's board that the OCC had wrongfully imposed civil money penalties on the Keystone's board;
- Having assumed a defacto position as a member of Keystone's management team; and
- Having ignored suspicious entries in the interest receivable account.

The FDIC, in very strong terms, also claimed:

> Grant Thornton's actions in committing the acts described above demonstrated a complete absence of care, a conscious disregard and indifference to the rights of Keystone and its depositors and an utter disregard for the prudence amounting to gross negligence and recklessness.

However, Grant Thornton refused to accept any blame. Unlike Kutak Rock, Grant Thornton refused to settle the case and insisted on going to trial. This turned out to be a mistake.

What is strange is the fact that Grant Thornton—being accused of having engaged in sixty-four separate acts of negligence; of having lost its independence; of having failed to uncover the fact that its client was insolvent; of having, thus, failed to prevent extensive losses associated with one of the largest bank failures in the history of the FDIC—filed a claim itself against the FDIC, as receiver, for $40,000 for unpaid bills from the bank.

The trial went from May 17, 2004 to June 10, 2004.[28] Grant Thornton blamed everyone but itself. It even claimed that the OCC knew of the missing $515 million for months, but did not tell anyone:

> In late August 1999, after having conducted eight on-site examinations of the Bank between 1993 and 1999, the OCC disclosed for the first time that Keystone falsely carried on its books approximately $500 million in loans that it did not own. While the OCC disclosed this fact for the first time, *at least* months before this the OCC had concluded that Keystone was insolvent and [there] was going to be at least a $100 million loss for the Insurance Fund.
> (Emphasis in the original.)

But the idea that a federal banking regulator could be aware of a massive fraud in a bank that rendered the bank insolvent and would not do anything—would not close the bank and would not tell the FDIC—is preposterous.

Grant Thornton also claimed that all of the fraud and misdeeds of the bank should be attributable to the FDIC—as receiver for the bank—arguing that the FDIC took over for the bank and stood in the shoes of the bank as if the FDIC itself had engaged in the misconduct. The presiding judge rejected this argument out of hand, quoting from an earlier order he had issued in the case, which held, "Grant Thornton may not impute to the FDIC the knowledge or conduct of the Keystone Bank's officers."

Further, Grant Thornton blamed Kutak Rock and tried to make the law firm pay for all of Grant Thornton's liability, on top of the law firm's own liability. However, this was rejected on the grounds that the two firms were performing different roles. As set forth by one reviewing court:

> [The] law firm's alleged acts of misconduct did not run parallel to the auditing responsibilities of the Grant Thornton accounting firm. The legal representation provided to Keystone and the independent audit served different functions.

Grant Thornton even blamed Gary Ellis, the unfortunate president whom the bank hired to replace Owen Carney. What makes this claim particularly absurd is that Ellis came to the bank after Grant Thornton had issued its audit report giving the bank a clean bill of health. So Ellis could not possibly have been in a position to influence Grant Thornton's report. In fact, just the opposite occurred, as discussed in the next chapter.

Finally, Grant Thornton blamed the management of the bank:

> In fact, Keystone had defrauded Grant Thornton throughout the audit process. Its management and directors . . . had provided Grant Thornton with false and/or forged documents and data and had concealed genuine documents from Grant Thornton.
>
> . . . .
>
> Had Grant Thornton known the true facts, Grant Thornton would not have accepted any engagement at Keystone and would not have issued its audit opinion.

This is likely the most absurd statement in the entire case. In essence, it was saying, "If the wrongdoers had confessed their wrongdoing in advance to us, we, the independent, professional auditors, could have found the fraud or, alternatively, would not have taken the assignment to begin with."

Grant Thornton also hid behind the fact that the auditing standards state that "The financial statements are management's responsibility." Taken out of context like this, it would mean that there is nothing for an auditor to do.

What Grant Thornton omitted was the very next line of the auditing standards: "The auditor's responsibility is to express an opinion on the financial statements." In addition, the paragraph preceding this commentary sets forth the overarching requirement for auditors, quoted earlier: "The auditor has a responsibility to plan and perform the audit to obtain reasonable assurance about whether the financial statements are free of material misstatement, *whether caused by error or fraud.*" (Emphasis added.)

Grant Thornton's effort to blame everyone but itself was, perhaps, best summed up by Kutak Rock's statement:

> Over the last decade, Grant Thornton has sought to excuse its conduct by attempting to blame many others for its own negligence, including Kutak, the FDIC, the Office of the Comptroller of the Currency ("OCC"), the outside directors of the Bank, and other third parties.

And Grant Thornton's arrogance and utter unwillingness to accept any responsibility was reaffirmed at length by Quay himself under the following questioning:

> Q. Your audit failed, Mr. Quay, didn't it?
> A. Absolutely.

Q. And you don't take one percent responsibility, your company? I don't mean you, personally. Your company.
A. No, sir.
Q. Your company did everything right?
A. We did everything required under the literature.
Q. Made no mistakes?
A. No, sir.

. . . .

Q. You take no responsibility?
A. That's correct.
Q. And there is nothing you would do differently, right?
A. Nothing.

In spite of all of these denials of responsibility, the district court found against Grant Thornton and ordered it to pay the FDIC $25 million.[29]

After all of this, Grant Thornton did not challenge on appeal the district court's finding that it was negligent in the conduct of the Keystone audit. Even so, the reviewing court felt obliged to note: "the record fully supports the numerous factual findings by the district court regarding Grant Thornton's negligence."

On appeal, Grant Thornton argued some technical issues that the reviewing court found meritless, with the exception of reducing slightly the damages owed to the FDIC by virtue of the Kutak Rock settlement.

Previous Action Against Grant Thornton by the OTS

Grant Thornton's run in with the FDIC was not its first mishap with federal banking regulators. In October, 1996, less than two years before it took on the Keystone assignment, Grant Thornton was the subject of another formal administrative action, brought by the Office of Thrift Supervision. The action required Grant Thornton to pay $9.75 million in restitution to the Resolution Trust Corporation[30] and required the firm to ensure that "Each partner, senior manager, and manager assigned to [audits of an FDIC-insured financial institution] . . . possess the requisite background and experience with respect to insured depository institutions to perform their duties competently and professionally." The OTS Order was in effect for five years, so it was outstanding during the time of the Keystone audit.

In light of the fact that neither Quay nor Buenger had ever been involved in a high-risk audit, and that Buenger was not familiar with securitizations, the provision quoted above dealing with ensuring the "requisite background and experience" of Grant Thornton's auditors does not appear to have been satisfied with regard to the Keystone audit.

Another provision of the OTS order dictated that Grant Thornton perform:

> [A]n assessment of the risk that errors and irregularities may cause the financial statements to contain a material misstatement and, based on that assessment, Grant Thornton shall design the audit to provide reasonable assurance of detecting errors and irregularities....

While Grant Thornton did perform a risk assessment of the Keystone audit and concluded that it was a high-risk audit (maximum/maximum risk, in Quay's words), it does not appear that Grant Thornton undertook sufficient efforts in detecting "errors and irregularities." As the Supreme Court of Appeals of West Virginia noted with regard to Grant Thornton's audit of Keystone:

> It is undisputed that the accounting firm was negligent in performing the audit. Its conduct has been described as "strikingly incompetent."[31]

To rub it in, the Supreme Court of Appeals of West Virginia cited Judge Faber's comment that Meredith Hale, with a high school equivalency diploma, "smoked out" the fraud in minutes while Grant Thornton, with all of its highly educated and trained personnel and its supposed expertise in accounting and auditing, spent a year in the bank and came up with nothing:

> In an instance described by the District Court, a Keystone employee with no previous work experience in the banking industry testified that where United Bank . . . paid the principal balance, the accrued interest and the premium on the loan, it seemed that United Bank owned the loan. The District Court noted that the testimony illustrated the ease with which the fraud could have been discovered had the accounting firm made a proper inquiry of the servicers, United Bank and even [Hale].

The OCC Case Against Grant Thornton

In March, 2004, the OCC brought its own case against Grant Thornton.[32] It was, in effect, a companion case to the FDIC's. However, instead of being in district court seeking to recover damages for the FDIC insurance fund, the OCC's case was an administrative one, seeking civil money penalties and a cease and desist order against Grant Thornton.

The legal basis for the case was that Grant Thornton was an "institution-affiliated party" (IAP) that, in "conducting the business" of the bank, "recklessly" participated in an unsafe or unsound practice which caused a loss to the bank. The practical basis for the case consisted of the various mistakes and missteps set forth in this chapter.

The case was heard before an administrative law judge (ALJ), who determined that Grant Thornton was not an IAP by virtue of not having acted recklessly. However, in administrative cases like these, the ALJ's decision is not final; it is only a recommended one. And the comptroller disagreed with the ALJ in this case and issued a cease and desist order and a $300,000 civil money penalty against Grant Thornton.

The comptroller, in his ruling, held that Grant Thornton was reckless in conducting its audit of the Keystone bank and, further, met the technical terms of being an IAP. His overall conclusion was that this was a particularly bleak case:

> Auditors do not function as insurers and their reports do not constitute a guarantee. Accordingly, an auditor does not become liable to sanctions . . . merely by failing to detect fraud or misstatement. It is only when the conduct of an audit for an insured depository institution departs so far from the standards required by GAAS that it becomes evident that the audit was conducted in disregard of, or with conscious indifference to, the risk of harm to those who might rely on the auditor's opinion regarding the absence of material misstatements in the financial statements, that an auditor or auditing firm may become liable for sanctions under the federal banking laws. This is such a case.

But, after reviewing the comptroller's decision, the Court of Appeals for the District of Columbia reversed. The majority of the court found that Grant Thornton did not meet the definition of an IAP under the statute. The court held that an external auditor, whose audit is aimed solely at verifying the accuracy of a bank's books, does not "participate" or "engage" in a banking practice or in "the affairs" of the bank.

This decision, however, seems to conflict with the legislative history of the governing law. In 1989, Congress passed a piece of legislation—known as the Financial Institutions Reform, Recovery and Enforcement Act of 1989 (FIRREA)—specifically to provide the federal banking agencies with authority over auditors whose negligent audits delay regulatory action or increase the cost of failed bank resolution. Specifically, FIRREA was passed in order to address the fact that the public accounting industry played a major role in masking the insolvency of many failed thrifts during the savings and loan crisis of the 1980s:

> Independent audits are an integral part of the system of controls designed to identify and report problems in thrifts when they arise. A lack of professionalism and poor quality audit work by CPAs helped mask the presence of fraud at a number of failed thrifts. In many instances auditors did not notify regulators about poor management practices at failing thrifts, which ultimately delayed regulatory action against many unscrupulous thrift managements. This delay has significantly raised the FSLIC's cost of resolving thrift failures.

The nub of the majority opinion, though, was that other "IAPs," such as attorneys, advise a bank "in a forward-looking capacity on how to conduct the bank's own business . . . ," but that auditors are merely backward-looking and, thus, do not "participate in the conduct of the affairs of the bank" or "engage in a banking practice." The court's decision effectively nullified the authority of the federal banking agencies under FIRREA because, ordinarily, there is no way for an external auditor to typically "participate in the affairs" of a bank. Although, ironically, Grant Thornton came pretty close to doing that, according to the testimony cited above.

The majority's opinion was short-sighted. Attorneys frequently examine what a bank has done and advise it as to what it should do in the future. Similarly, auditors examine how a bank has put together its books and records and advise it as to what it should do going forward with respect to those books and records. And they can each be severely negligent.

The majority opinion, in closing, pointed to another statutory provision—which was enacted after FIRREA—which requires banks to file an annual report with the FDIC pertaining to accounting and internal control issues—and which grants the banking agencies the authority, "for good cause,"[33] to preclude auditing firms from issuing such reports. However, this is a very limited "removal" authority and does not address normal auditing services performed for financial institutions; just the issuance of this annual, statutorily required, report.

The upshot of the court's reasoning is that an agency can "remove" an entire auditing firm in this one narrow area, but cannot assess a civil money penalty against it or issue a restricting cease and desist order, no matter how egregiously reckless and negligent the auditing firm has been in, say, missing a half-billion dollars' worth of fraud.

The concurring opinion of the third judge held that the majority was wrong in deciding that an accounting firm that performs an external audit cannot be held accountable under FIRREA. The concurring opinion, however, stated that the banking agencies only have authority over individual accountants, and not over an entire accounting firm, unless "most or many of the managing partners or senior officers of the entity have participated in some way in the egregious misconduct"—quoting only a part of the legislative history.

A more expanded part of the legislative history, though, reads as follows:

> Concern was also expressed that a banking agency could obtain enforcement orders against a corporation, firm, or partnership, such as a large accounting, appraisal, or law firm, since the term "person" includes entities as well as individuals, and that therefore enforcement orders would not be limited to those individuals who may have been responsible for a wrongful action.[34] Accordingly, *the Committee expects* banking agencies to limit enforcement actions *in the usual case* to individuals who have participated in the wrongful action . . .
>
> However, the Committee strongly believes that the agencies should have the power to proceed against such entities *if most or many of the managing partners or senior officers* of the entity have participated in some way in the egregious misconduct. *For example, a removal and prohibition order might be justified against the local office of a national accounting firm if it could be shown that a majority of the managing partners or senior supervisory staff participated* directly or indirectly in the serious misconduct to an extent sufficient to give rise to an order. Such an order might well be inappropriate if it was taken against the entire national firm or other geographic units of the firm, unless the headquarters or these units were shown to have also participated, even if only in a reviewing capacity.
>
> (Emphasis added.)

Reading this expanded section of the legislative history tends to indicate that it is focused primarily on removal actions, that is, prohibiting an entire firm from doing any auditing for financial institutions—not civil money penalties or cease and desist orders. Further, the passage talks about "the usual case"—which the Keystone case clearly was anything but.

In addition, the language in the legislative history was not meant to be prescriptive. There is no requirement in the actual statute pertaining to such an overwhelming limitation. Actually, under this reasoning, for a federal banking agency to have jurisdiction over a large accounting firm such as Grant Thornton, a majority of its seven hundred partners would have had to have been involved in the particular audit. This is a practical impossibility. That cannot be what Congress envisioned in passing the legislation.

Interestingly, the concurring opinion itself focused on the importance of holding reckless accounting firms accountable:

> Accountants and auditors perform a critical role in [en]suring the integrity of financial institutions. . . Although I recognize that "[a]uditors do not function as insurers and their reports do not constitute a guarantee," OCC Dec. 2, nonetheless "bank regulators, the bank's shareholders and the public," id., expect to rely on an auditor's professional competence and deserve better than what happened here.

Clearly, the Keystone bank, its regulators, its depositors, its shareholders, and the public at large deserved better than what Grant Thornton provided.

Notes

1. As set forth earlier, two loan servicers held loans that were purchased by other banks in order to be placed into a Keystone securitization deal.
2. OCC's 1997 Report of Examination, 17.
3. Id. at 5.
4. FDIC Exh. 183, Grant Thornton summary, August 31, 1998.
5. OCC's 1997 Report of Examination, 12.
6. The bingo/landfill fraud, discussed in Chapter Nine and in Appendix B, had to do with two business endeavors that Graham was allegedly involved with. The other alleged frauds are discussed throughout this book. (The interest income fraud dealt with the fact that the bank was overstating its income to make it comport with the large volume of loans it supposedly owned.)
7. *United States v. Arthur Young & Co.*, 465 U.S. 805 (1984).
8. OCC's 1998 Report of Examination, 4.
9. Id. at 3.
10. Id. at 41.
11. FDIC Exh. 142, OCC letter to the bank, November 25, 1998.
12. Grant Thornton Planning Memorandum, December 31, 1998.
13. Grant Thornton Environmental Assessment, December 31, 1998.
14. While it is not clear, the speeding ticket was probably given out on Route 52, the road into Keystone from the east.
15. That is, loans to the local community instead of loans purchased from across the country for securitization purposes.

16. An identical letter was sent to Compu-Link and the vague language may well have added to the confusion encountered by that firm. Also, the language used was markedly different from the other confirmation requests Grant Thornton sent out around this time and which Buenger was supposedly using as a model. Up until this time, though, Buenger had never sent out a confirmation request to a loan servicer.

17. Later, Buenger would claim that she did not talk to anyone at the bank—which is more likely. Her repetition of what she might ordinarily do appears to be an after-the-fact explanation.

18. Advanta recorded everything by investor number—Keystone was Investor # 405 and United was Investor # 406—and Ramirez testified about this system as follows:

    Q. Is there any possibility that you told Susan Buenger that the United loans were actually Keystone loans?

    A. No... Because I know who owned the loans. 405 did not belong to 406.

    Q. Is there any conceivable way, in your mind, that you could have represented to her that loans that were owned by United were actually owned by Keystone?

    A. No....

    Q. Have you ever made a mistake concerning investor numbers?

    A. No.

19. As noted in Chapter Six, the Keystone bank selected the loans, but the other banks actually purchased and held the loans until Keystone was ready to buy the loans back and put them into a securitization deal. In this way, Keystone avoided the capital and liquidity issues associated with buying and holding the loans itself.

20. Typically, the analytical review is much simpler than the test of details, but it was not so in this particular case.

21. Due to the securitization deals, a large volume of bank-held loans would have gone into the deals, thus markedly decreasing the volume of loans held directly by the bank.

22. The report handed to the auditors was a remittance report, or a general summary, as opposed to a detailed trial balance showing income from each borrower by name and by date.

23. What is interesting here is that Quay, who had the responsibility of verifying the interest income from the bank's residuals (as opposed to the income from loans held by the loan servicers), used a "test of details"—requiring him to look at the underlying, third-party, independent documents. This income, though, only added up to $11 million. The interest income that Buenger had the responsibility of verifying was supposed to amount to $98 million—making it much more important to verify it completely and properly.

24. Buenger thinks that they "may have" told Director Gibson the following night when they revealed that Church had admitted there was no money, however, her recollection is very vague.

25. As noted in Chapter Eight, Griffith also came to the OCC examiners, who followed up on what he said and closed the bank less than a week later.

26. This made up the $515 million discrepancy; it is slightly different from the confirmation numbers in January—March due to the passage of time.

27. LaRose contended that his firm had sent a corrected confirmation the following month, but that no one from Grant Thornton had contacted them about the amended report.

28. The closing arguments were not held until August 20, 2004.

29. Upon review, the district court lowered the judgment slightly to $23.7 million, providing Grant Thornton a credit for the overlapping liability between Grant Thornton and Kutak Rock. The amount was further reduced to $23.2 million by the Fourth Circuit pursuant to an order issued on June 17, 2011.

30. This was the government-owned "asset management company" in the late 1980s to the mid-1990s responsible for resolving savings and loan associations that failed during the savings and loan crisis of the 1980s.

31. It was the concurring opinion in the D.C. Circuit Court of Appeals that noted, "The conduct of the two Grant Thornton auditors can only be described as strikingly incompetent."

32. The author was involved in this case at the hearing level as a supervising assistant director. He was not involved in the appeal of the case.

33. The term "for good cause" has been defined by agency regulation.

34. It should be noted that this "concern" was raised primarily by the targets themselves of this legislation—the American Institute of Certified Public Accountants and the American Bar Association.

13

The Sad Story of Gary Ellis

We have unmistakable proof that throughout all past time, there has been a ceaseless devouring of the weak by the strong.
—Herbert Spencer, *First Principles*

Even before Owen Carney resigned on March 23, 1999, from the First National Bank of Keystone, after only seven weeks as its president, the bank was searching for a new president. The senior management of the bank knew it was going to fire Carney and they needed to find a replacement. Billie Cherry had been told by the OCC she wasn't qualified, and Terry Church, for some reason, wanted to stay in the background and control things from there.

So the bank reached out to Gary Ellis.

In 1984, Ellis had become the president of the Bank of Dunbar, West Virginia. Dunbar was later merged into United National Bank and Ellis eventually became the president of the merged institutions. However, in 1998, United merged with George Mason Bankshares of Virginia, under United's name. Ellis was welcomed to stay on at the bank, but someone else was selected to be the president. So at the beginning of 1999, Ellis started to look for alternative positions.

At some point in February or March, Cherry called Ellis and invited him to visit the Keystone bank. Over a period of several months, Ellis went to Keystone multiple times. During this process, he met with Stan Quay, the lead partner for Grant Thornton, at least six different times to review the financial statements of the Keystone bank. These meetings were specifically authorized by a motion of the board of directors of the bank.

The first meeting was on March 20th, and, during that meeting, Ellis reviewed Grant Thornton's draft audit report with Quay, examining the assets and liabilities of the bank as set forth in the report and even delving into the footnotes to the report. As Ellis stated:

> I had the opportunity to sit down and talk to many of the number crunchers about the bank's numbers, and how it worked, and had spent some time on high loan to value research too, so I talked to Stan [Quay] and basically went through—basically went through asking him questions about balance sheet accounts, asset and liability side, about footnotes in Stan's report. In other words, I just sort of took the reported part and tried to analyze for my use all the entries on the report. . . .

> [Quay] said that he was finalizing the Grant Thornton annual report and that—and I borrowed a couple pages—draft kind of pages—and quizzed him about the assets that were on the books, quizzed him about the liabilities on the books, to get a feel for what I could at that time. Feel for the numbers. . . .

> He said the books and records were in the best shape ever . . .

Ellis then came back to Keystone on March 24th and sat in on part of the bank's board of directors' meeting, at which Quay presented the draft audit report giving the bank a clean bill of health.[1] After the board meeting, Quay went out to dinner at the Fincastle Country Club with Ellis and two prospective bank directors, Budnick and Kaufman.[2] At this meeting, Quay discussed with Ellis for the third time the fact that the bank's books and records were in good shape. Quay specifically acknowledged that he knew, at this time, Ellis was considering an offer to become the president of the Keystone bank and was relying on Grant Thornton's audit report and Quay's assurances. Quay testified on this point as follows:

> Q. And they—you would have known that they—they were relying on what you would say; right?
> A. What I would ultimately say, yes.
> Q. I take it you recall, then, that Mr. Ellis as well was considering whether to become president of Keystone?
> A. That's correct.

The fourth meeting was the next day, March 25th, at the bank's annual shareholders' meeting. Quay again passed out draft copies of the Grant Thornton audit report and again praised the health of the bank. Of course, at that time, neither he nor Buenger had resolved the little "boo-boo" involving $236 million missing from the loans supposedly held for the bank by Advanta.

The fifth meeting was on March 30th. At that time, Ellis met individually with Quay to once more go over the financials of the bank.

The sixth time was when Quay presented the final audit report at the meeting of the board of directors on April 19th.[3] Ellis was in attendance and once more was assured by Grant Thornton that the books and records of the bank were fine. By this time, even the $236 million discrepancy with the Advanta records had supposedly been resolved by Buenger, although, of course, Quay did not even know about the issue.

* * *

Ellis did not resign from United National Bank until April 20th, the day after being told by Quay and Grant Thornton for the sixth time that everything was fine at the First National Bank of Keystone and the day after Grant Thornton's clean audit report was formally issued. On April 26th, Ellis signed an employment contract with Keystone, making him the president of the bank. In addition to signing on with the most profitable large community bank in the entire country—according to the *American Banker* and as supported by Grant Thornton—Ellis' salary package went from $319,000 a year to $460,000. So he was happy.

By all accounts, Ellis had nothing to do with the fraud perpetrated at the bank by Church, Cherry, Graham, and others. According to Judge Faber, who presided over the numerous criminal and civil cases:

> There is no evidence whatsoever that Ellis had any role in perpetrating the fraud that led to the closure of Keystone, was aware of any of the fraudulent acts of McConnell, Cherry, Graham, Church, and others, or was in possession of any information or knowledge that would have made him suspect that such misconduct was going on.

Ellis' contract with the bank specifically spelled out that his duties as president were limited to only running the bank. Running the bank's mortgage subsidiary, the Keystone Mortgage Company (KMC), was left to Church and Graham.

After the bank failed, Ellis, who was in his late fifties, developed some serious health problems. He began to suffer from atrial fibrillation (a heart disorder involving irregular heart rhythms) and had two arrhythmias (instances of irregular heartbeats). In addition, his efforts to find other bank-related employment were unsuccessful. Even though he had been in banking for twenty years and had been the president of several banks, the taint of Keystone made gainful employment in the area impossible. He searched for sixteen months, talking to more than twenty-four banks, and found nothing. All of the interviews devolved into one inquiry: "Tell me more about Keystone." No one was going to hire him and take on the stigma of the "Scarlet K" that went with anyone associated with Keystone.

Finally, a friend of his at West Virginia State College gave him a job as the assistant for West Virginia State Economic Development, at a salary of $40,000. His salary was later increased to $52,600, but it was still a far cry from what he had been making.

He was also the subject of various lawsuits involving the failure of the bank. Most ironically, Grant Thornton filed claims against him, alleging, among other things, that he should have disclosed to Grant Thornton the public securities reports filed by United National Bank with the SEC. Of course, these reports were public by definition so Grant Thornton already had full access to them. The fact that Grant Thornton knew nothing about the relationship between Keystone and United (and, thus, did not know to look for these reports) appears to be Grant Thornton's shortcoming, not Ellis.' In addition, as stated earlier, Ellis came to the bank after Grant Thornton issued its clean audit report, so how Ellis could have affected the report is a bit of a mystery.

Grant Thornton also claimed that Ellis should not have praised the quality and integrity of Keystone's senior management and should have disclosed that "Keystone's general ledger and financial statements . . . materially misstated Keystone's financial position; . . . that Grant Thornton could not rely on Church, Cherry, Graham, and other Keystone employees to tell it the truth about Keystone's financial condition; and that the above-identified information, documents and data . . . which Church, Cherry, Graham, and other Keystone employees provided to Grant Thornton [were] false or fraudulent. . . ." Of course, Ellis did not know any of this. More importantly, all of this was what Grant Thornton should have found out on its own.

Ellis, in turn, sued Grant Thornton and his claims were litigated along with FDIC's claims against the accounting firm. On the sixth day of the trial, Grant Thornton withdrew its claims against Ellis, providing no reason or explanation.

As noted above, the district court found in favor of the FDIC, concluding that Grant Thornton owed the government over $25 million.[4]

In the same case, the district court held that Ellis had proven his claims and that Grant Thornton owed him another $2.4 million.

Grant Thornton appealed both cases, but, curiously, did not in either case contest the court's finding that the audit was performed negligently. Rather, in the case against the FDIC, Grant Thornton claimed unsuccessfully that the law firm Kutak Rock should be responsible for all of Grant Thornton's liability.

In the case against Ellis, Grant Thornton claimed that it did not owe any duty whatsoever to Ellis. The U.S. Court of Appeals for the Fourth Circuit agreed.

The court of appeals explained that there were four possible legal theories by which Grant Thornton could be held liable, but determined that the third approach, based on something called the "Restatement of Torts," was the most applicable. The court of appeals indicated that this approach required satisfaction of a complicated, six-part test:

1. That the accounting firm supplied inaccurate information;
2. That the information was negligently supplied;
3. That the accounting firm was acting in its professional capacity;
4. That the person bringing the lawsuit was part of "a limited group of third persons for whose benefit and guidance the accountant actually intend[ed] or [knew would] receive the information";
5. That the accountant actually intended to influence or knew that the recipient would be influenced; and
6. That the person bringing the lawsuit was injured as a result of justifiably relying on the accountant's negligently supplied misinformation.

All parties involved acknowledged that elements 1 to 3 were clearly satisfied. The court of appeals, however, held that Ellis failed to satisfy elements 4, 5, and 6.

With regard to element 4, the court held that Ellis was not entitled to rely on Grant Thornton's report because Ellis was not the client—the Keystone bank was. In addition, the court said that Ellis was not a "third party" whom Grant Thornton intended to receive the audit report or whom Grant Thornton knew would receive the report.

With regard to element 5, the court held that Grant Thornton did not intend to influence Ellis and did not know that Ellis would be influenced by Grant Thornton's report.

With regard to the last element, the court held that Ellis was not justified in relying on Grant Thornton's audit report.

Upon analysis, though, the court's reasoning was seriously flawed.

Fourth Element

First, as set forth above, Grant Thornton met with Ellis six different times. During those meetings, the firm knew that Ellis was considering becoming the president of the Keystone bank. Half the meetings were either private, one-on-one meetings or, as in the third case, a small dinner meeting. At these meetings, Quay went over the financials of the bank and Ellis asked specific questions, even about the footnotes in the report. Also, the board of the bank authorized these meetings for the obvious and specific purpose of convincing Ellis to take the proffered position of president of the bank.

Yet the court of appeals said:

> With regard to the fourth element, it is clear that Ellis failed to show that Grant Thornton knew (or intended) that potential employees, like Ellis, were intended to receive the audit report for their benefit and guidance.

How the court could say this is not at all clear. There is no question that Grant Thornton knew—and even intended—that Ellis would be receiving "the audit report for [his] benefit and guidance." Why else was Ellis there? Why else was Grant Thornton meeting with Ellis? What else could Grant Thornton be thinking but that Ellis was relying on the audit report?

The court of appeals went on to point out that:

> Indeed, throughout most of the course of the audit report's preparation, Ellis was an unknown, unidentified potential employee of Keystone. Grant Thornton was not aware of the existence of the potential employment transaction between Ellis and Keystone until after Grant Thornton reached its decision to give Keystone a clean audit opinion.

While these statements are true, they are also irrelevant. The fact is that Grant Thornton was sufficiently comfortable with its findings to share them directly and personally with Ellis multiple times, knowing that, at the time of the sharing, Ellis did in fact have a "potential employment transaction" with the bank, as the court so quaintly put it. The question is not why or when Grant Thornton did the audit; the question is what did Grant Thornton know and intend at the time it shared the audit report with Ellis.

Nonetheless, the court of appeals persisted by claiming:

> There is no evidence in the record to support the conclusion that Ellis was a member of any limited group of persons for whose benefit Quay's statements were made. . . .
>
> Indeed, Grant Thornton was not aware that any potential employee of Keystone was going to base their decision to seek employment with Keystone on the outcome of the audit.

The court claimed that Grant Thornton only had a "tenuous awareness" of Ellis' employment focus. This is not true and it turns all of the evidence in the case on its head. Ellis was relying directly and specifically on the outcome of Grant Thornton's audit and Grant Thornton knew it.

Fifth Element

The court of appeals similarly misconstrued the fifth element of its test. In this instance, the court held that Grant Thornton could not have perceived the risk of Ellis' reliance on the report at the time the report was delivered. Along these lines, the court stated that:

> Here, Grant Thornton was hired to conduct an audit of Keystone. It was aware at the time it was hired and during the auditing process that the audit was being done for the benefit of Keystone and the OCC. It was not aware during this process that its audit was being performed for the benefit of potential employees of Keystone. Indeed, there simply is no evidence in the record that Grant Thornton cared one way or the other who Keystone hired or whether Ellis became president of Keystone. In fact, Ellis was not even on the radar screen until after Grant Thornton concluded that it was going to issue Keystone a clean audit opinion. Moreover, any release of information to Ellis was done at the behest of Keystone, not Grant Thornton. This fact further suggests that Grant Thornton never intended to deviate from its standard auditing functions. In short, to find the fifth element satisfied, we would have to materially change the transaction from an audit undertaken to benefit Keystone and the OCC to one intended to benefit potential employees of Keystone.

The court's reasoning is clouded on a number of fronts. First, the test, as articulated by the court itself, is not who ordered the audit or who was paying for it, but, rather, who it was intended to influence or who Grant Thornton knew it would influence. As set forth above, Ellis was clearly in this latter class and there is no way to exclude him.

Second, the issue of whether Grant Thornton did or did not have a stake with regard to whom the bank hired as president is a red herring. It is not a relevant part of any test. The issue—or test—is whether Grant Thornton knew Ellis received the audit report and was relying on it for guidance and would be influenced by it. The answer to that question is unmistakably yes.

Third, when Ellis came into the picture, it did not represent a "material change"—as the court professed. Ellis came "on the radar screen" while Grant Thornton was conducting its audit and, then, as it was presenting the draft and final audit report. It is that point in time that is key. And it is that point in time Quay personally and individually met with Ellis a number of times to go over the financial condition of the bank—specifically so that Ellis could decide whether or not to become the president of the bank.

Last, the fact that the bank authorized the release of the audit is not a negative factor—it goes right to the test of whether Ellis was an intended recipient of the audit; and he definitely was. The bank specifically authorized the disclosure to Ellis and dictated that it should occur. Clearly, Grant Thornton, in reviewing a pending—and then final—audit report with Ellis, knowing that he was trying to determine whether to become the president of the bank, had to understand that if the report were terribly wrong—due to Grant Thornton's negligence— the repercussion would be that Grant Thornton could face liability for negligently misleading Ellis into thinking that the bank was solvent and that its books and records were sound.

Sixth Element

The court of appeals stated that "Ellis fares no better on the sixth element."

Unfortunately, it is the court that fares poorly, not Ellis.

The sixth element requires, in this case, that Ellis was justified in relying on Grant Thornton's audit report stating that the bank's books and records were sound. First, Ellis knew that Grant Thornton was a prominent, nationally recognized auditing firm—one of the five largest in the country. Second, Grant Thornton had spent months in the bank scouring the accounts and was prepared to issue—and did issue—a clean audit report.

The court, in deciding against Ellis on this element, relied solely on boilerplate language in the report to the effect that the audit report "was not intended for use by third parties." However, this boilerplate language is totally undermined by the satisfaction of the six-part test that the court laid out.

* * *

Not only is the reasoning of the court of appeals flawed, as reflected by the foregoing analysis, the district court itself disagreed with it. In reviewing the opinion of the court of appeals—but being compelled to accept it—the district court voiced its serious concern and disagreement with the decision. Specifically, the district court said:

> [H]ad the case been remanded [to the district court for further consideration], rather than reversed, it is very likely that Ellis would have been able to prove that he could meet all six elements of the test. While the court cannot say with certainty that the result would have been the same on remand, what is certain is that, on remand, the district court would have had the benefit of the Fourth Circuit's decision and the guidance provided therein.[5]

One can feel the forced deference—yet forceful disagreement—in the district court's language. So, based on a decision to reverse, rather than remand, Ellis lost his $2.4 million judgment.[6]

Not content to win—based on legal technicalities that were misconstrued by the court of appeals—and not content with having avoided paying a judgment of $2.4 million, Grant Thornton decided to pursue Ellis for court fees. The so-called fees consisted of the following:

•	Docketing fee	$450.00
•	Printing of the Joint Appendix	$6,285.00
•	Printing of Grant Thornton's opening brief	$244.00
•	Printing of Grant Thornton's reply brief	$47.25
•	Trial transcripts	$1,957.45
•	Premium for appeal bond	$30,000.00
•	Premium for appeal bond	$30,000.00[7]
•	Total	$68,983.70

This represented more that Ellis was making in an entire year. So a company that had thousands of employees and was making untold millions in profits, went after a broken, former president who had done nothing wrong except believe in Grant Thornton's own negligent report.

The district court was not going to let it happen.

Judge Faber rejected Grant Thornton's request for the various fees—which primarily represented Grant Thornton's cost of defending itself—on the grounds that the legal issues were "close and difficult" and that payment of the fees would represent a substantial financial hardship on Ellis. Not happy with that, Grant Thornton appealed Judge Faber's decision.

The court of appeals also understood that Ellis' annual salary was less than the amount being sought by Grant Thornton and recognized that the legal issues were "close and difficult":

> The legal issues in the case were not as clear-cut as Grant Thornton would have us believe. And although the judgment in favor of Ellis was vacated on the basis of a lack of proof to support Ellis' negligent misrepresentation claim, such conclusion was reached with difficulty and only after a thorough and careful evaluation of West Virginia law.

This conciliatory language represented a far different tone from the original court of appeals' decision in which it said such things as: "it is difficult to discern how an individual as sophisticated and experienced as Ellis would justifiably rely on this information [from Grant Thornton] in accepting a job at Keystone."

But the court of appeals seemed to take a personal affront at Judge Faber's decision to protect Ellis from the overreaching of Grant Thornton:

> We begin our analysis by noting that the district court abused its discretion when it refused to award the $7,026.25[8] in costs that were ordered by this court as part of our mandate to the district court.

So the court of appeals allowed the $60,000, representing the cost of Grant Thornton's appeal bond, to be struck, but required Ellis to pay more than $7,000 in extraneous fees, which Ellis could still ill afford to pay.[9]

Notes

1. With regard to the concept of Quay handing out and reviewing a draft report, especially to Ellis, Grant Thornton's own manuals cautioned against doing that for fear of creating the very legal liability that Grant Thornton later faced in the lawsuit by Ellis:

> Unauthorized distribution of a report represents a violation of the confidential relationship between our firm and the client. Frequently we are asked by the client to mail copies of their report directly to third parties. The client should be discouraged from making such requests,

since distribution of reports to third parties *increases our legal exposure to such party (as we are then on notice that specific outside interests will use the reports and will rely on the representations therein).*

(Emphasis added.)

In this fashion, Grant Thornton is acknowledging from the outset that disclosure of an audit report to third parties could result in legal liability, including paying monetary damages, if the report proved to be inaccurate due to Grant Thornton's negligence. As one of the FDIC's experts explained:

Q.   And so Grant Thornton's concerned about this going anywhere—about such reports going to anyone other than the client, because they know people will rely on them and because it increases Grant Thornton's legal exposure, right?

A.   That's correct.

2.   Owen and Jane Carney had not even left town by this time—they were waiting for their dry cleaning to be ready—so they themselves went to the country club that night for dinner. The restaurant was empty, but, strangely, the two parties were seated next to each other.

3.   The Grant Thornton audit report was signed and dated April 19, 1999, and was presented to the board on that day. Grant Thornton later argued that no one could rely on the report at that time because it was not mailed from Cincinnati until April 30th, but this is a dubious argument at best.

4.   As set forth earlier, this amount was subsequently adjusted downward to a little over $23 million.

5.   In the case, Grant Thornton articulated a test similar to the one the court of appeals tried to apply: "In the absence of privity of contract, Grant Thornton owes a duty of care only to those it 'knows will be receiving and relying' on its audit report." Of course, that is exactly what happened.

6.   Ellis petitioned the U.S. Supreme Court to review the court of appeals' decision on October 20, 2008, but the Supreme Court denied the petition on December 1, 2008, less than two months after it was filed.

7.   Grant Thornton filed its initial request for fees approximately two weeks after the thirty-day time limit. It then realized that it had made a further mistake in that it had failed to include $30,000 of the fees, so it filed an amended claim over one month after the due date. Why this did not cause the claim to be dismissed is not clear. However, Ellis, on his part, was late in objecting to Grant Thornton's request for fees.

8.   This represents the sum of the first four items of Grant Thornton's list of expenses.

9.   The court of appeals magnanimously disallowed the $1,900 in costs for the trial transcripts.

14

Aftermath of the Failure of the Bank

Men at some time are masters of their fates;
The fault, dear Brutus, is not in our stars,
But in ourselves, that we are underlings.
—Cassius, *Julius Caesar*

As noted, the failure of the First National Bank of Keystone on September 1, 1999, was initially viewed by the FDIC as one of the ten largest bank failures since the Great Depression. That alone made it significant. More importantly, but almost totally overlooked, was the fact that the bank had been among the first to get involved in the overly risky securitization of subprime mortgages. This product was inherently fraught with problems that needed to be thoroughly studied and guarded against going forward. This did not happen.

It is true that there were some studies and reviews and even a congressional hearing focused on the failure of the Keystone bank, but nothing significant happened as a result, and what little did occur was not followed up on. The last examiner-in-charge (EIC) of the bank, Mark Blair, suggested to OCC headquarters after the bank failed, "Perhaps the OCC should take a stronger stance against banks involved in subprime lending from a broader perspective." Unfortunately, this prescient suggestion was virtually ignored.

The large, multinational banks—such as Citibank, JPMorgan Chase, and Bank of America—are examined on a year-round basis by a large crew of highly trained examiners who effectively reside in the banks; so there is no lack of staff or skill when it comes to monitoring these banks. However, many of these banks became unduly involved in the business of securitizing subprime mortgages after the Keystone bank failed, and they—and the public—paid the price. The latter due to the ensuing financial crisis; the former due to lawsuits and fines. Citibank paid $7 billion to the Department of Justice and others to settle various issues related to its involvement in the securitization of subprime mortgages; JPMorgan Chase paid $13 billion; and Bank of America paid just shy of $17 billion.

In addition to the issues pertaining to the securitization of risky assets, there were many other problems stemming from the Keystone bank failure that should have been studied and addressed, including its high-risk growth; its lack of internal controls; the accounting and auditing failures; the threats made by the bank against the examiners; the deference and support not given to the examiners by their banking agencies; and the poor coordination between these federal regulatory agencies. Some of these issues were touched on or mentioned in studies and hearings, but too little was done to make a difference.

Actions Taken Before the Keystone Bank Failure

Before the Keystone bank failed in 1999, the OCC had started to address the area of subprime lending and asset securitization. Specifically, the OCC had inserted an "Asset Securitization" section into the 1997 Comptroller's Handbook to instruct examiners on how to identify and examine securitization issues.

In 1998, the OCC also undertook a series of examinations focused on subprime lending and found "a number of serious weaknesses" at the banks it examined.[1] The same year, the OCC rated the Keystone bank a "4" under the CAMELS rating system, while the FDIC rated the bank a "5," the most negative rating. These ratings were due primarily to Keystone's unsafe and unsound concentration in subprime mortgages, which threatened the capital of the bank. So the OCC, along with the FDIC, were beginning to focus on the issue.

On March 3, 1999, the federal banking agencies issued a paper entitled "Interagency Guidance on Subprime Lending."[2] The guidance mentioned the "recent turmoil in the equity and asset-backed securities market"—a reference to the Russian debt crisis and the bailout of Long-Term Capital Management, both in the fall of 1998.[3] The guidance spelled out a number of issues, including the fact that:

- subprime lending requires specialized knowledge and skills that many financial institutions may not possess;
- subprime lending and securitization activities can present a greater than normal risk; and

- if the risks associated with subprime lending activity are not properly controlled, the agencies will consider the activity as high-risk and unsafe and unsound.[4]

Of course, Keystone's involvement in this area was not properly managed by qualified staff and was cited by the OCC as being unsafe and unsound. However, in spite of that fact and the existence of this guidance, the OCC did not do enough to curb the activity at the Keystone bank. Further, the OCC and the other banking agencies did not sufficiently address subprime issues pertaining to the whole industry.

Also prior to the failure of the Keystone bank, the OCC, by itself, issued additional guidance on subprime lending.[5] This issuance noted that subprime lending "can offer attractive returns," but also said that "it involves elevated levels of credit and other risks."[6] In closing, the issuance stated the following:

> Subprime lending can be a viable means of enhancing bank income and meeting the credit needs of underserved and unserved markets. However, it requires specialized expertise, sound planning, and comprehensive analysis and systems to control the elevated risks associated with these activities. The absence of such safeguards in a bank that is materially engaged in subprime lending may constitute an unsafe and unsound banking practice.[7]

This was very clear and sound advice, but it was still just advice—guidance; it had no teeth; no weight of law. While it made mention of "unsafe and unsound banking practices," which can serve as a basis for taking formal administrative action against a bank—in this case, to curb or stop the securitization activity—the OCC did not employ this approach with regard to the Keystone bank. The OCC and the other agencies were going to prove equally weak going forward.

Actions Taken After the Keystone Bank Failure

Slightly more than one month after the Keystone bank failed, the federal banking agencies issued an "Interagency Guidance on High Loan-to-Value (LTV) Residential Real Estate Lending" on October 8, 1999.[8] Unfortunately, this issuance said very little of any substance—other than calling for caution.

In December, 1999, the banking agencies issued another paper entitled "Interagency Guidance on Asset Securitization Activities."[9] The

OCC, in its release of this issuance, made the following introductory comment:

> During recent examinations, our examiners have noted an unaccept-able number of national banks with risk management systems or internal control infrastructures insufficient to support the institution's securitization activities.[10]

The body of the actual issuance reinforced this statement:

> While the Agencies continue to view the use of securitization as an efficient means of financial intermediation, we are concerned about events and trends uncovered at recent examinations. Of particular concern are institutions that are relatively new users of securitization techniques and institutions whose senior management and directors do not have the requisite knowledge of the effect of securitization on the risk profile of the institution or are not fully aware of the accounting, legal and risk-based capital nuances of this activity.[11]

This was all clearly the case with regard to the Keystone bank. The question going forward was whether the agencies were going to learn a lesson from the Keystone bank and apply stricter constraints against other banks involved in this area of originating and securitizing sub-prime mortgages. To that effect, the agencies—in the closing words of this issuance—claimed they were studying the issue:

> Moreover, as mentioned earlier in this statement, the Agencies are studying various issues relating to securitization practices, including whether restrictions should be imposed that would limit or eliminate the amount of retained interests that qualify as regulatory capital. In the interim, the Agencies will review affected institutions on a case-by-case basis and may require, in appropriate circumstances, that institutions hold additional capital commensurate with their risk exposure.[12]

In December, 1999, the OCC also formed a special oversight commit-tee, which included several securitization experts, to "help deal with banks that have gotten or may get into trouble because of securitization activities."[13]

This was all very good. But, in light of the resulting financial crisis of 2008, which—according to the official Financial Crisis Inquiry Report—was "sparked" by the securitization of subprime mortgages,[14] query as to whether the agencies studied this area sufficiently or reacted strongly enough, as they promised they would.

Last, on another topic, the OCC issued guidance to examiners on how to identify and react to obstruction of an examination[15]—such as was seen in the Keystone bank examinations.

The guidance set forth a good balance of the OCC's need to obtain bank information and a bank's need to protect privileged documents. It also presented for examiners a series of red flags they should look for—warning signs that seemingly were taken directly from the Keystone examinations: delaying tactics; limiting access to bank documents and staff; destroying or removing documents; and attacking examiners' credibility in order to undermine their effectiveness. In addition, the guidance set forth remedial actions that could be taken to combat such obstruction, including holding meetings to explain the OCC's legal authority; sending letters setting forth requirements for the bank to comply with; issuing administrative subpoenas for the necessary documents; issuing a temporary cease and desist order against the bank to require compliance; filing a suspicious activity report with law enforcement; and even seeking a conservatorship or receivership of the bank. The issuance also emphasized the importance of examiners seeking advice from the OCC's legal staff and senior management. It was a very comprehensive litany of things to look for, examine and react to. It ended with a firm admonition to the banking industry and expression of support to the examiners: "The OCC will not tolerate the abuse of its employees."[16]

This was good, but, for the Keystone examiners, it was way too late.

Congressional Hearing

In February, 2000, just five months after the Keystone bank failed, the House Financial Services Committee held a hearing with respect to the bank—as well as two other banks that failed around the same time. Bank failures were relatively rare at the time, so Keystone was a big deal—even though very few people remember its name now. Chairman Leach issued a clarion call to action—"Clearly, the risks illuminated by Keystone and several of the other recent failures demand the full, coordinated, and timely attention of the federal bank and thrift regulators, particularly before the industry faces any future economic downturn"[17]—but nothing happened. Mostly, the federal banking agencies used the hearing simply as an opportunity to justify themselves and to promise they would coordinate better with one another in the future.

Jerry Hawke, the comptroller of the currency, noted at the hearing that, while there had been three failures of national banks in 1999, there had not been any for the preceding three years.[18] He then made an unfortunate prediction:

> The three national bank failures that occurred during 1999 do not, in any way, foreshadow a much larger number of failures in 2000, nor do they present systemic implications.[19]

He was right that there was not a large number of failures in 2000, but, with the benefit of hindsight at least, it appears—as set forth in the next chapter—that the Keystone bank failure and its involvement in the securitization of subprime mortgages was a harbinger of the financial crisis Chairman Leach feared.[20] Not to be too harsh on Comptroller Hawke, but there were warning signs and, as noted above, the last EIC of the Keystone bank suggested that more scrutiny of this area was probably necessary. In spite of the issuances, guidances, and committees, this flurry of activity did not seem to take sufficient hold. There was no concerted effort to study, let alone limit, the securitization of subprime mortgages.

Worse, statements from some of the other regulators at the hearing bordered on the absurd. Laurence Meyer, a member of the Federal Reserve Board, cautioned, "We must, of course, be careful not to over-react and become any more aggressive or intrusive than is required."[21] This is a bank regulator talking—worrying about the feelings of the banks involved in the high-risk area of securitization.

Three banks had failed in 1998 and 1999 due to securitizations—the Keystone bank; BestBank, Boulder, Colorado; and Pacific Thrift and Loan Company, Woodland Hills, California.[22] BestBank had failed in 1998 due to securitizations related to predatory credit card lending.[23] Pacific Thrift had failed in 1999 with $50 million in worthless securitized subprime mortgage residuals on its books, out of total assets of only $118 million.[24] This was an area that needed attention, not light-handed regulation.

Perhaps the worst statement in the hearing was from Ellen Seidman, the head of the Office of Thrift Supervision:

> We have to understand how to supervise in a manner that both mitigates risk and is respectful of the fact that the institutions we regulate are privately-owned, profit-making entities.[25]

This is like saying that the government should tread lightly with regard to inspections of meat packing plants and pharmaceutical companies because they have shareholders. In this case, the banking agencies are charged with protecting the financial industry of the country and the federally insured deposits of individuals. This is not to be taken casually. In addition, it should be noted that the OTS replaced its precursor, the Federal Home Loan Bank Board, in part, due to the board's improper kowtowing to the "Keating Five"—the five U.S. senators who succeeded in intimidating the agency into treating Charles Keating (the poster child of the savings and loan crisis of the 1980s) more gingerly than it should have.

Seidman went on to try to justify her remarks by noting that: "Thrifts are currently enjoying their best period of sustained health and profitability in over 35 years."[26] Of course, that did not last: eleven years after her testimony, the OTS itself ceased to exist—due in no small part to its weak supervision of Washington Mutual Bank's involvement in the securitization of subprime mortgages.[27]

During the course of the hearing, Chairman Leach, in commenting on the poor coordination with regard to the three small bank failures at issue, asked a very telling question—which went virtually unanswered by the regulatory panel:

> So we have a billion dollars in failures in good times with very, very small banks, and so the question that seems to me particularly relevant is, in terms of coordination, do we not only have adequate coordination with small banks, but what about larger banks and what about situations where instruments at issue may be much more sophisticated?[28]

Seven to eight years later, the marketplace provided the answer—with a financial meltdown.

Material Loss Review of Keystone

Pursuant to law, whenever there is a bank failure that generates a loss to the FDIC insurance fund over a certain amount, there must be an independent review of the causes of the failure, and the lessons to be learned. In the case of the Keystone bank failure, the "material loss review" (MLR), issued on March 10, 2000,[29] touched on all of the following:

- the problems at the bank;
- the time limitations placed on the examinations;
- the "perceived threats" against the examiners;
- the congressional letters sent on behalf of the bank;

- the complaints from the bank to the OCC; and
- the bank's appeals of the examination ratings.[30]

However, the MLR missed a lot. For instance, it only referred in passing to the "perceived threats." It failed to adequately address or study the actual threats and harassment, which included verbal threats ("I want her ass dead"); false accusations against examiners; the graffiti; the temporary restraining order; the fake bodyguards; and the display of firearms. In addition, the MLR failed to address the weak response by the OCC to these threats and related actions, or the resulting difficulty in getting examiners to go to this tiny bank in the backwoods of West Virginia.

Further, the MLR did not address the turf wars between the OCC and the FDIC; the risk for the entire financial market posed by subprime mortgages and the securitization process; the regulatory arbitrage that existed (i.e., the Keystone bank threatening to switch charters); the auditors allegedly performing a negligent audit while pursuing other fee income from the bank; and the failure to give examiners proper deference and support. These broader, more significant issues warranted extensive review, but the MLR did not provide it.

In spite of its shortcomings, the MLR did set forth some criticisms—albeit quite measured and circumspect—making references to the fact that "indicators existed throughout the period that may have dictated [the need for] a more aggressive supervisory response from OCC,"[31] and the fact that "high profitability and capitalization appeared to mitigate OCC's supervisory response."[32] These "criticisms" could have been articulated more forcefully, with more detail. However, the MLR did specifically note that, when the bank failed to comply with various informal administrative actions, "a progressively severe action seemed warranted"[33]—but that did not occur for years.

In its introductory statement, the MLR started to get to the heart of the securitization issue and the weak regulatory response:

> Finally, the OIG recommends that OCC evaluate whether a different supervisory approach is needed to address growth in high-risk activities, accompanied by high profitability and adequate capitalization, without sufficient management systems and controls.[34]

But this issue was not adequately explored or spelled out and, apparently, not sufficiently taken to heart or followed up on. This was a serious missed opportunity because the Keystone bank's high-risk activity—the securitization of subprime mortgages—was also one of the primary causes of the 2008 financial crisis.[35]

Notes

1. OCC Bulletin 1999–15, April 5, 1999, 1.
2. Interagency Guidance of Subprime Lending, March 3, 1999.
3. Id. at 6.
4. Id. at 2–3.
5. OCC Bulletin 1999–15, April 5, 1999.
6. Id. at 1.
7. Id. at 7.
8. OCC Bulletin 1999–38, October 8, 1999.
9. OCC Bulletin 1999–46, December 13, 1999.
10. Id.
11. Id.; Interagency Guidance on Asset Securitization Activities, December 13, 1999, 2.
12. Id. at 11.
13. Office of Inspector General, U.S. Dept. of the Treasury, "Material Loss Review of the First National Bank of Keystone," OIG-00-067, March 10, 2000, 30.
14. Financial Crisis Inquiry Report, "Final Report of the National Commission on the Causes of the Financial and Economic Crisis in the United States," January, 2011 (The Financial Crisis Report), xvi.
15. OCC Policies & Procedures Manual 5310-10, Guidance to Examiners in Securing Access to Bank Books and Records, January, 7, 2000.
16. Id. at 8.
17. Opening Statement of Rep. James A. Leach, Chairman, House Banking and Financial Services Committee, Hearing on Recent Bank Failures, February 8, 2000.
18. Testimony of John D. Hawke, Jr. before the House Banking and Financial Services Committee, Hearing on Recent Bank Failures, February 8, 2000, 12.
19. Id.
20. Eight banks (national and state) failed in 1999; and only seven banks failed in 2000. However, twenty-five banks failed in 2008; 140 in 2009; and 157 in 2010.
21. Opening Statement of Laurence H. Meyer, Member, Board of Governors of the Federal Reserve System, before the House Banking and Financial Services Committee, Hearing on Recent Bank Failures, February 8, 2000, 3.
22. Opening Statement of Donna Tanoue, Chairman of the FDIC, before the House Banking and Financial Services Committee, Hearing on Recent Bank Failures, February 8, 2000, 2.
23. Id. at Appendix to Opening Statement.
24. Id.
25. Opening Statement of Ellen Seidman, Director, Office of Thrift Supervision, before the House Banking and Financial Services Committee, Hearing on Recent Bank Failures, February 8, 2000, 1.
26. Id.
27. The OTS was merged into the OCC as of October 19, 2011.

28. Statement of Rep. James A. Leach, Chairman, House Banking and Financial Services Committee, Hearing on Recent Bank Failures, February 8, 2000, 26.
29. Office of Inspector General, U.S. Dept. of the Treasury, Material Loss Review of the First National Bank of Keystone, OIG-00-067, March 10, 2000.
30. Id. at 4–7.
31. Id., cover letter to Comptroller John D. Hawke, Jr.
32. Id. at 28.
33. Id. at 17.
34. Id., cover letter to Comptroller John D. Hawke, Jr.
35. Financial Crisis Inquiry Report, "The Financial Crisis Report," xvi.

15

Harbinger of the 2008 Financial Crisis

Seldom is a wake-up call as loud and clear
as the one emanating from
the tiny town of Keystone, West Virginia.
—Rep. James Leach (R-Iowa), Chairman of the House
Committee on Banking and Financial Services,
Hearing on Recent Bank Failures, February 8, 2000

The 2008 Financial Crisis

As set forth in a law review article written in 2009, the financial crisis "was triggered by the subprime meltdown that started in late 2006 . . ."[1] The article went on to explain that the meltdown, itself, was caused—or accelerated—by the securitization process:

> The subprime meltdown, in turn, was caused in large part by the financial mechanism that had caused it to surge since the late 1990s, securitization.[2]

> . . . .

> While other factors also played a role in the meltdown, subprime securitization may represent one of the greatest structurally caused financial implosions of the modern world.[3]

Further, echoing this conclusion, the official study of the 2008 financial crisis concluded that the housing bubble of 1997–2007,[4] created by the making and securitizing of subprime mortgages, was the "spark" that "lit . . . the flame":

> While the vulnerabilities that created the potential for crisis were years in the making, it was the collapse of the housing bubble . . . that was the *spark* that ignited a string of events, which led to a full-blown

crisis in the fall of 2008. Trillions of dollars in risky mortgages had become embedded throughout the financial system, as *mortgage-related securities* were packaged, repackaged, and sold to investors around the world.[5]

(Emphasis added.)

We conclude collapsing mortgage-lending standards and the mortgage securitization pipeline lit and spread the flame of contagion and crisis.[6]

(Emphasis in the original.)

These conclusions were further reiterated by a congressional study of the crisis completed by the U.S. Senate Permanent Subcommittee on Investigations:

> In April 2010, the Subcommittee held four hearings examining four root causes of the financial crisis. Using case studies detailed in thousands of pages of documents released at the hearings, the Subcommittee presented and examined *evidence showing how high risk lending* by U.S. financial institutions; regulatory failures; inflated credit ratings; *and high risk, poor quality financial products* designed and sold by some investment banks, *contributed to the financial crisis. . . .*
>
> The first chapter focuses on *how high risk mortgage lending contributed to the financial crisis,* using as a case study Washington Mutual Bank (WaMu). . . .
>
> This case study focuses on how one bank's search for increased growth and profit led to *the origination and securitization of hundreds of billions of dollars in high risk, poor quality mortgages* that ultimately plummeted in value, *hurting* investors, the bank, and *the U.S. financial system.*[7]

(Emphasis added.)

The law review article, of course, was written after the financial crisis. Similarly, the Financial Crisis Inquiry and the Congressional study, both conducted in 2011, were long after the fact. But if the riskiness of the securitization process had been thoroughly studied earlier, perhaps the warning signs could have been uncovered in time to stave off or reduce the impact of the financial crisis.

There were, in fact, clear warning signs stemming from the Keystone bank failure. Back in February, 2000, Chairman Leach had expressed the concern that "the risks illuminated by Keystone" could lead to a "future economic downturn." He identified the Keystone bank failure as a "loud and clear" "wake up call," but, apparently, the marketplace and the federal banking agencies slept through it.

* * *

In addition to these warning signs, it was already apparent during the 1990s that the volume of mortgage loans and subprime mortgage loans and their securitization were growing exponentially. A number of things conspired to bring this about.

First, legislation was passed in 1980 and 1982 to preempt state interest rate caps[8] and to allow variable interest rates and balloon payments.[9] This meant that banks had an enhanced comfort level in making subprime loans by being able to charge high interest rates and being able to adjust the interest rates.

Second, another piece of legislation was passed in 1986 that eliminated the tax deduction for interest paid on consumer loans, but maintained the tax deduction for interest paid on mortgages.[10] Barred from being able to deduct interest payments for consumer loans, borrowers gravitated to mortgage lending, including home equity loans, thus increasing the demand for such lending.[11]

Third, legislation in 1992 set forth several housing goals for two "Government Sponsored Entities" (GSEs) known as Federal National Mortgage Association (Fannie Mae) and the Federal Home Loan Mortgage Corporation (Freddie Mac).[12] Commonly referred to as the GSE Act, it was signed into law by President George H. W. Bush. However, it was greatly enhanced by President Clinton as a result of his National Homeownership Strategy, which was issued in 1994 and espoused the goal of creating eight million new homeowners by 2000.[13]

Pursuant to the legislation, there were three specific goals and several general goals for Fannie Mae and Freddie Mac. The three specific goals were as follows:

- First, 30% of the total number of housing units they financed were to be for low- and moderate-income mortgages.[14]
- Second, Fannie Mae and Freddie Mac were to provide $2 trillion and $1.5 trillion, respectively, to meet the unaddressed needs of low-income families in low-income areas, as well as very low-income families.[15]

- Third, the GSEs were to establish an annual goal for the total number of housing units the GSEs would finance for central cities, rural areas, and other underserved areas, with an interim goal of 30% for mortgages in underserved central cities.[16]

One of the general goals was to "take affirmative steps to assist primary lenders to make housing credit available in areas with concentrations of low-income and minority families."[17] As a result of this general goal, the effort to reach out to underserved families went beyond the GSEs to the individual banks themselves.

In addition, under the Act, HUD was given the authority to increase these goals. Consequently, the first goal—of providing mortgage loans to low- and moderate-income families—was increased from 30% in 1992 to 40% in 1996.[18] Then it was increased to 42% in 1997 and to 50% in 2001,[19] just two years after the Keystone bank failed. In 2008, the year of the financial crisis, it was increased to 56%.[20]

These aggressive goals, formulated under President Clinton, and then continued under President George W. Bush, were noble, but they increased the pressure on the banking industry to make mortgages in general and subprime mortgages specifically, stretching the market beyond its capacity to make sound loans and to monitor them. As a result, a housing bubble started in 1997 and burst in 2007, helping to cause the 2008 financial crisis.

In order to meet the mandated goals, Fannie Mae and Freddie Mac relaxed the credit standards for mortgage loans eligible for purchase by the GSEs.[21] This led to a general expansion of lending, but also a deterioration of credit quality in the mortgage sector. Namely, the overly aggressive, goal-generated growth of subprime lending inevitably led to a deterioration of credit quality, as more institutions chased fewer subprime lending opportunities.

The growth of subprime mortgage lending was extensive. Specifically, new subprime mortgages went from $40 billion in 1994 to $160 billion by 1999.[22] By 2003, it was up to $332 billion.[23] Outstanding mortgage-backed securitizations went from $2.3 trillion in 1995 to $3.4 trillion in 1999.[24] By 2001, the figure reached $4.2 trillion.[25] New mortgage-backed securitizations issued annually went from less than $300 billion in 1995 to more than $700 billion by 1999.[26] By 2001, the figure reached $1.2 trillion.[27] The Financial Crisis Inquiry Commission's report (FCIC Report) noted that the increase in subprime mortgage securitizations resulted not just in greater numbers, but also in a lack of concern about the quality of the loans sold into the securitizations—because that process removed the loans (and the risk) from the books of the banks:

> The record of our examination is replete with evidence of other failures: financial institutions made, bought, and sold mortgage securities they never examined, did not care to examine, or knew to be defective . . .[28]

As a result, mortgage fraud—as seen in the Keystone bank case—greatly increased:

> The number of suspicious activity reports—reports of possible financial crimes filed by depository banks and their affiliates—related to mortgage fraud grew 20-fold between 1996 and 2005 and then more than doubled again between 2005 and 2009.[29]

Between 1993 and 1998, subprime lending increased 760%.[30] By 2008, over half of all mortgages were subprime or its equivalent.[31]

The federal banking agencies and the marketplace were aware of this exponential growth and the corresponding increased risk, but failed to react appropriately. Basically, they stayed on the sidelines and allowed financial institutions to get deeper and deeper involved in riskier and riskier subprime mortgage lending and securitizations.

* * *

In addition to this growth, the profitability of securitizations was ebbing. Due to the "flight to quality" that resulted from the Russian debt crisis and the bailout of Long-Term Capital Management in 1998, interest rates being charged to the originators of subprime loans increased, thus, limiting the attractiveness of subprime securitizations. Even Grant Thornton knew—before starting its work at Keystone—that many subprime lenders had gone into bankruptcy or had been otherwise forced out of business. This unusual growth and the various subprime failures were warning signs that should have been monitored carefully to ensure that small—and large—banks did not overinvest in this area.

There were even warning signs issued by the regulators themselves. For instance, as set forth by The Washington Post:

> In 2004, as regulators warned that subprime lenders were saddling borrowers with mortgages they could not afford, the U.S. Department

of Housing and Urban Development helped fuel more of that risky lending. . . .

Today, 3 million to 4 million families are expected to lose their homes to foreclosure because they cannot afford their high-interest subprime loans.[32]

The FCIC Report also stressed that there were warning signs:

> Despite the expressed view of many on Wall Street and in Washington that the crisis could not have been foreseen or avoided, there were warning signs. The tragedy was that they were ignored or discounted. There was an explosion in risky subprime lending and securitization, an unsustainable rise in housing prices, widespread reports of egregious and predatory lending practices [and] dramatic increases in household mortgage debt. . . .[33]

The FCIC Report, which specifically referenced the failure of the Keystone bank twice,[34] was very harsh in its condemnation of the federal banking agencies. The report criticized the OCC and the OTS specifically for being "caught up in turf wars [and] preempt[ing] state regulators from reining in abuses."[35] However, the report directed its real criticism toward the Federal Reserve and its then-chairman, Alan Greenspan:[36]

> **We conclude widespread failures in financial regulation and supervision proved devastating to the stability of the nation's financial markets.** The sentries were not at their posts, in no small part due to the widely accepted faith in the self-correcting nature of the markets and the ability of financial institutions to effectively police themselves. More than 30 years of deregulation and reliance on self-regulation by financial institutions, championed by former Federal Reserve Chairman Alan Greenspan and others, supported by successive administrations and Congresses, and actively pushed by the powerful financial industry at every turn, had stripped away key safeguards, which could have helped avoid catastrophe. This approach had opened up gaps in oversight of critical areas with trillions of dollars at risk, such as the shadow banking system and over-the-counter derivatives markets. In addition, the government permitted financial firms to pick their preferred regulators in what became a race to the weakest supervisor.[37]
>
> (Emphasis in the original.)

The reference to Greenspan underscored the ironic fact that the most important bank regulator in the world from 1987 to 2006 did not believe in bank regulation—he mistakenly relied on the marketplace to govern the conduct of financial institutions, with all of their risky and hard-to-monitor financial products. As he admitted later in 2008:

> I made a mistake in presuming that the self-interests of organizations, specifically banks and others, were such as that they were best capable of protecting their own shareholders and their equity in the firms.[38]

The FCIC's overall conclusion was picked up on and reiterated by the 2011 congressional report:

> Federal banking regulators failed to ensure safe and sound lending practices and risk management, and stood on the sidelines as large financial institutions active in U.S. financial markets purchased billions of dollars in mortgage related securities containing high risk, poor quality mortgages.[39]

A thorough study of how and why the Keystone bank got involved in the subprime securitization business; the risks presented by the product; and the staffing, expertise, internal controls, liquidity, and capitalization needed could have informed the federal banking agencies and the marketplace as to how to identify and, perhaps, control the risks and issues pertaining to the world of securitization. Such a study might well have reduced the impact of the 2008 financial crisis.

However, that did not occur.

* * *

The crisis started to manifest itself when two Bear Stearns' hedge funds filed for bankruptcy on July 31, 2007.[40] They had over-invested in subprime mortgage securitizations[41] and the chickens had come home to roost. If Bear Stearns' earlier involvement in the obviously disastrous securitization program of Keystone's had been adequately studied, one has to wonder whether Bear Stearns' propensity to get involved in overly risky ventures could have been identified and somehow curtailed. The risk should have been an easy matter to identify as Bear Stearns turned out to be the most heavily invested of all investment houses in subprime mortgage securitizations.[42]

It is noteworthy along these lines that Lehman Brothers, the other poster child of the 2008 financial crisis, had acquired, by the end of 2007, $111 billion in commercial and residential real estate holdings and securities, which was almost twice what it held just two years before, and more than four times its total equity.[43] Lehman Brothers, of course, handled fourteen of the Keystone bank's securitization deals.

A month after Bear Stearns' fateful move, a large French bank, BNP Paribas, suspended redemptions on August 9, 2007 on three of its funds which were overly invested in U.S. subprime mortgage securitizations.[44]

As it turned out, other large financial institutions, like Wachovia National Bank and Washington Mutual Bank, failed or had to be acquired by other institutions during the 2008 financial crisis due primarily to their overinvestment in low-quality mortgages and their securitizations.[45] As set forth by one commentator:

> The banks, investment banks, and others that failed or came near to failing in the financial crisis were all heavy investors in [subprime mortgage securitizations].[46]

* * *

Glass–Steagall Act

The Glass–Steagall Act was passed in 1933 in order to stave off some of the effects of the Great Depression and to prevent the continuation of identified abuses in the financial sector. The times were not dissimilar to the 2008 financial crisis. As one author noted:

> Like in the 2008 crisis, the financial system was weighed down by defaults on mortgages obtained in an easy-money environment based on values inflated by a housing bubble.[47]

There had been repeated warnings of the abuse and conflicts of interest between banks and their unregulated securities affiliates.[48] The Pecora hearings in 1932 delved into such abuses and its findings alarmed the country.[49] Similarly, the Pujo hearings before it, in 1912, had identified securities-related abuses and had recommended the separation of commercial banking and securities operations.[50] As set forth in the report emanating from the Pujo hearings:

> The success and usefulness of a bank that holds the people's deposits are so dependent on public confidence that it cannot be

safely linked by identity of stock interest and management with a private investment corporation of unlimited powers with no public duties or responsibilities and not dependent on public confidence.[51]

In 1932, President Roosevelt, in addressing the issues of the Great Depression, made a series of recommendations, including separating commercial banking from investment banking:

> Sixth, investment banking is a legitimate business. Commercial banking is another wholly separate and distinct business. Their consolidation and mingling are contrary to public policy. I propose their separation.[52]

In 1933, in his first fireside chat, Roosevelt reiterated his concerns in this area by saying:

> We had a bad banking situation. Some of our bankers had shown themselves either incompetent or dishonest in their handling of the people's funds. They had used the money entrusted to them in speculation and unwise loans.[53]

In supporting the Glass–Steagall Act which would implement Roosevelt's recommendations, Senator Glass, one of the primary drafters of the Act, said:

> These [securities] affiliates were the most unscrupulous contributors, next after the debauch of the New York Stock Exchange, to the financial catastrophe which visited this country, and were mainly responsible for the depression under which we have been suffering since, and they ought to be speedily separated from the parent banks, and in this bill we have done that.[54]

Even though the Glass–Steagall Act was in effect for over fifty years, it was chipped away at between 1986 and 1996.[55] It was finally repealed in 1999 by the Financial Services Modernization Act of 1999 after Travelers Insurance Company merged with Citicorp in 1998, setting up the issue for Congress to address.[56]

Dodd-Frank Act

Just as some blamed the Great Depression on the lack of separation between commercial and investment banking, some have pointed to the repeal of the Glass–Steagall Act as one of the causes of the

2008 financial crisis.[57] Hence, one of the remedies was the passage of the Dodd-Frank Wall Street Reform and Consumer Protection Act, signed into law by President Obama in 2010.[58] Contained in the Act is the so-called Volcker Rule that resurrects the spirit of Glass–Steagall Act.[59]

Some claim that the Dodd-Frank Act was an overreaction and unnecessary.[60] However, it accomplished a number of things which many believe are important and useful, including:

- The creation of the Financial Stability Oversight Council, to oversee the risks affecting the entire financial industry.
- The creation of the Orderly Liquidation Authority to oversee the liquidation of institutions that pose a systemic risk.
- Establishment of the Volcker Rule, mentioned above.
- The creation of the Consumer Financial Protection Bureau, which consolidates the functions of the banking agencies to better protect consumers.
- Placing supervision of credit default swaps and other risky derivatives under the SEC or the Commodity Futures Trading Commission.
- Creation of the Office of Credit Ratings to regulate credit rating agencies, which contributed to the 2008 financial crisis by providing unreliable ratings for the subprime mortgage securitizations.
- Placing the regulation of hedge funds under the SEC.
- Creation of the Federal Insurance Office within the Treasury Department to oversee insurance companies like AIG that created risk for the entire financial system.[61]

* * *

According to the Financial Crisis Inquiry Commission, the regulators had the opportunity to stop the level of mortgage securitizations that lead to the 2008 financial crisis:

> Policy makers and regulators could have stopped the runaway mortgage securitization train. They did not.[62]

If the regulators– and the marketplace—had studied the demise of the First National Bank of Keystone sufficiently, especially the effect of the subprime mortgage securitizations and the involvement of Lehman Brothers and Bear Stearns, perhaps some extent of the 2008 financial crisis could have been avoided. It was a serious missed opportunity to learn a lesson and respond appropriately.

Max Blinder of Princeton University and former vice-chairman of the Federal Reserve Board, in his book, *After the Music Stopped*, noted "seven villains," of the 2008 financial crisis. Third on the list was "lax financial regulation."[63] For reasons addressed in Chapter Seventeen, this is a reality that needs to be changed.

If there had been more stringent regulation of the Keystone bank and the large banks that followed suit in the overly risky securitization of subprime mortgages, the financial world perhaps would not have gone through all the turmoil it endured.

As concluded by the Financial Crisis Inquiry Commission, "The greatest tragedy would be to accept the refrain that no one could have seen [the financial crisis] coming and thus nothing could have been done."[64]

Notes

1. Kurt Eggert, "The Great Collapse: How Securitization Caused the Subprime Meltdown," *Connecticut Law Review* 41 no. 4 (May 2009): 1259.
2. Id.
3. Id. at 1260.
4. Peter J. Wallison, "Hidden in Plain Sight," 13.
5. The Financial Crisis Inquiry Commission's Report (FCIC Report), xvi.
6. Id. at xxiii.
7. "Wall Street and the Financial Crisis: Anatomy of a Financial Collapse," U.S. Senate Permanent Subcommittee on Investigations, April 13, 2011 (PSI Report), 2.
8. Depository Institutions Deregulation and Monetary Control Act (DIDMCA) of 1980; Souphala Chomsisengphet, and Anthony Pennington-Cross, "The Evolution of the Subprime Mortgage Market," *Federal Reserve Bank of St. Louis Review*, January/February 2006, 38.
9. The Alternative Mortgage Transaction Parity Act (AMPTA) of 1982; Chomsisengphet and Pennington-Cross, "Federal Reserve Review," 38.
10. Tax Reform Act of 1986 (TRA); Chomsisengphet and Pennington-Cross, "Federal Reserve Review," 38.
11. Chomsisengphet and Pennington-Cross, "Federal Reserve Review," 38.
12. The Federal Housing Enterprises Financial Safety and Soundness Act of 1992, which is Chapter XIII of the Housing and Community Development Act of 1992 (GSE Act).
13. Scott B. MacDonald, and Jane E. Hughes, "Separating Fools from Their Money," 233; Gretchen Morgenson, and Joshua Rosner, "Reckless Endangerment," 11.
14. GSE Act, § 1332.
15. Id. § 1333.
16. Id. § 1334.
17. Id. § 1335.
18. Wallison, "Hidden in Plain Sight," 129.
19. Id.
20. Id. The other goals were similarly increased.

21. MacDonald and Hughes "Separating Fools," 233.
22. Morgenson and Rosner, "Reckless Endangerment," 51.
23. Id. at 117.
24. Andrew Davidson, Anthony Sanders, Lan-Ling Wolff, and Anne Ching, "Securitization—Structuring and Investment Analysis," 4.
25. Id.
26. Id. at 6.
27. Id.
28. FCIC Report, xvii.
29. Id. at xxii.
30. Wallison, "Hidden in Plain Sight," 163–64.
31. Id. at 10 and 29.
32. Carol D. Leonnig, "How HUD Mortgage Policy Fed the Crisis," *Washington Post*, June 10, 2008.
33. FCIC Report, xvii.
34. Id. at 75 and 99.
35. Id. at xxiii. The issue of preemption will be discussed in Chapter Seventeen.
36. Alan Greenspan was the Chairman of the Federal Reserve Board from 1987 to 2006, during the rise and fall of the Keystone bank and its aftermath.
37. Id. at xviii. The issue of regulatory arbitrage will be discussed at length in Chapter Seventeen.
38. Greenspan testimony before the U.S. House Oversight Committee, October 23, 2008.
39. PSI Report, 12.
40. Wallison, "Hidden in Plain Sight," 318.
41. Id.; Andrew Ross Sorkin, "Too Big To Fail," 66–7.
42. Wallison, "Hidden in Plain Sight," 308.
43. FCIC Report, xx.
44. Wallison, "Hidden in Plain Sight," 248.
45. Wallison, "Hidden in Plain Sight," 315–16.
46. Id. at 315.
47. Richard E. Farley, "Wall Street Wars," 15.
48. Id. at 34.
49. Id. at 24–42.
50. Id. at 34–5.
51. Id. at 35.
52. Id. at 6–8.
53. Id. at 61.
54. Id. at 81.
55. Id. at 241.
56. Id.
57. Kimberly Amadeo, "Dodd-Frank Wall Street Reform Act; A Summary of its 8 Regulations," September 26, 2014. http://useconomy.about.com/od/criticalssues/p/Dodd-Frank-Wall-Street-Reform-Act.htm?utm_term=summary%20of%20the%20dodd%20frank%20act&utm_content=p1-main-2-title&utm_medium=sem&utm_source=msn&utm_campaign=adid-12728696-96b2-4805-9409-189dae050190-0-ab_msb_ocode-22879&ad=sem-D&an=msn_s&am=broad&q=summary%20of%20the%20dodd%20frank%20

act&dqi=&o=22879&l=sem&qsrc=999&askid=12728696-96b2-4805-9409-189dae050190-0-ab_msb.
58. Wall Street Wars, 242.
59. MacDonald and Hughes, "Separating Fools," 268.
60. Wallison, "Hidden in Plain Sight."
61. MacDonald and Hughes, "Separating Fools," 268; Amadeo, "Summary of Dodd-Frank Act."
62. FCIC Report, xviii.
63. Wallison, "Hidden in Plain Sight," 98.
64. FCIC Report, xxviii.

16

Lessons Learned

Why has government been instituted at all?
Because the passions of men will not conform
to the dictates of reason and justice,
without constraint.
—Alexander Hamilton, *The Federalist Papers, No. 15*

In addition to the issues pertaining to the 2008 financial crisis, there are a number of other lessons to learn from the failure of the First National Bank of Keystone. Some of the more important ones include the following:

Risk

Banking, of course, is all about risk—primarily credit and investment risk. Banks need to know how to identify all types of risk, how to monitor the risk and how to control or mitigate the risk. Bankers and bank examiners are well aware of all this. However, something was missed with regard to gauging the risk related to the purchase and securitization of subprime mortgages. Perhaps the lack of care was due to the ability of banks to book prospective gain up front—due to "gain-on-sale" accounting. Perhaps it was due to the ability of banks to quickly sell the subprime loans into securitizations and not keep a large interest of residuals. Perhaps it was just due to the greed of banks seeing the large interest rates that could be charged. Whatever it was, the risks of subprime lending and securitization were not sufficiently focused on leading up to the financial crisis. The simple lesson to be learned is that, going forward, all significant risks should be focused on early and directly by the banks and by the regulators.

Some of these risks include poor internal controls; overly risky products; inadequate staffing and expertise; poor and inaccurate accounting; weak audits; concentrations of credit; overreliance on brokered certificates of deposit; and out-of-area lending. In light of the

Keystone failure, the agencies and banks should re-double their efforts in identifying and addressing these risks.

Red Flags

As part of examining for risk, the agencies should stress much more the need to look for, identify, and react to a variety of "red flags." In the Keystone bank case, the examiners were well aware of various red flags, including:

- involvement by the bank in a high-risk product without the necessary background or expertise of bank staff;
- four outside third parties withdrawing from the bank's securitization process—Conti, FSA, CapMac, and, eventually, Lehman Brothers;
- apparent fraud noted in the loan files;
- delays in producing documents;
- threats—both physical and legal;
- harassment;
- concentrations of credit, particularly in subprime residuals;
- out-of-area lending;
- violations of law, primarily related to the filing of inaccurate call reports;
- overall poor accounting and financial records that could not be relied on;
- the need to file criminal referrals;
- an in-house accountant who lost his CPA license in two states;
- excessive growth; and
- exponential earnings (to the point where the bank went from not being on the list of the top 100 banks to being the most profitable large community bank in the country).

The marketplace was aware of this last red flag, given that the bank was prominently featured over a number of years in the *American Banker*. Yet no one was screaming from the rooftops that this was crazy—not to be believed—a tiny bank in the middle of nowhere with no qualified staff and no established infrastructure getting involved in the securitization of subprime mortgages and earning more than any other similarly sized bank in the entire country. To say the least, more could have been done.

These red flags should all have been investigated and addressed forcefully and head-on. But this was not done, even though these issues were set forth in the reports of examination or were otherwise relayed by the examiners to OCC headquarters.

With the accounting issues alone, the line examiners and their direct supervisors were recommending that the bank's securitization process be halted until the books and records could be straightened out, but this suggestion was rejected. The agency was too fearful to address this obvious red flag and to take strong action—that tendency needs to change.

Intimidation

Clearly, the Keystone bank tried all kinds of intimidation, even resorting to having U.S. senators write letters to the OCC and invoking George H. W. Bush's name. Unfortunately, the use of intimidation is not unique to this tiny bank in West Virginia. Even behemoths like J.P. Morgan Chase have resorted to yelling at examiners, as recounted by *The Washington Post*:

> When bank regulators wanted daily profit and loss statements from J.P. Morgan Chase's investment division, the bank initially refused.
>
> When examiners issued recommendations the bank didn't like, executives yelled and called the federal officials "stupid."
>
> At one point, the top brass at the prestigious bank ambushed a junior bank examiner, becoming "loud and combative" when he disclosed disputed results of an exam.[1]

This was from a white-shoe, "prestigious" bank, in an examination involving some of the OCC's best national bank examiners. Imagine what it can be like at less respected or restrained banks that are not newsworthy enough to end up in the press for engaging in such conduct.

Along the same lines, many banks threaten to switch charters, even when they get a "2" CAMELS rating—the next-to-highest rating there is.[2] So, examiners—and the agencies—are always looking over their shoulders to make sure that they do not push too hard for fear of losing banks, which, for the OCC, means a loss of revenue.

The banking agencies have to do much more to protect and support their examiners and to insulate them as much as possible from threats, intimidation and unwarranted criticism.

Deference

It is clear from the Keystone case that more deference is owed to examiners, who are on-site and have the best understanding of what is going on at a bank. Certainly, bank examiners will make mistakes, but they are well-trained, experienced, and skilled. Their review of a bank is a carefully orchestrated one—planned out in advance and reviewed by senior management afterward—before a final report of examination is delivered to the bank. They should not have to constantly defend their actions or conclusions.

As Mark Blair, the last EIC of the Keystone bank, noted:

> There needs to be more faith shown in field examiners and OCC senior management should support the examiners first rather than respond as if the bank is always in the right. Senior management support is critical, particularly when the real problems [start] to surface.

Firm Regulation

One thing that the Keystone bank case should have taught is that weak, or soft-touch, regulation can be a big problem. If a bank is strong, well-capitalized, has adequate staff, uses good internal controls, and can identify and mitigate the risks pertaining to its products, clients, and geographies, then there is no need for any action on the part of the regulators. However, when there are weaknesses or deficiencies, the regulators cannot be afraid of taking appropriate action.

The congressional study of the Keystone bank noted the need for firmer regulatory action:

> **Strengthen Enforcement.** Federal banking regulators should conduct a review of their major financial institutions to identify those with ongoing, serious deficiencies, and review their enforcement approach to those institutions to eliminate any policy of deference to bank management, inflated CAMELS ratings, or use of short-term profits to excuse high-risk activities.

In the Keystone bank case, the OCC issued stern reports of examination that cited violations of law, unsafe and unsound banking practices, and even discussed the possibility of the bank failing. Yet the OCC issued an informal administrative action and—even though the problems persisted—followed it with another informal action and then nothing at all. After the second commitment letter was terminated on January 24, 1996, it was more than two years before the OCC issued the May 28, 1998, formal agreement.

It is not too soon to try to guard against future crises brought on by overly risky banking practices and the lack of sufficient constraints by the regulators.

Direct Verification

In the Keystone bank case, there was a running debate as to whether to perform direct verifications of the loans serviced for the bank by third-party vendors. Doing direct verifications is normally a function of the auditors. However, due to the apparent or possible lack of independence of the auditors and the lack of reliable financial figures from the bank, doing direct verification should have been done much earlier than it was. As Blair suggested after the failure, "During examinations where the OCC finds ineffective audit, weak internal controls, and poor loan review, we should be routinely performing verification procedures to verify the accuracy of records."

Remedies

The obvious remedies to the above-mentioned "lessons learned" are ensuring a continued and more rigorous focus on risk; monitoring and following up on all substantial red flags; protecting examiners from intimidation by banks; giving more deference and support to the line examiners in the bank; not being afraid to take firm regulatory action; and being more willing to perform direct verifications when appropriate.

However, there are three additional suggested actions that should be taken—set forth at greater length below and in the next chapter—first, a relatively small legislative amendment to enhance the agencies' ability to take actions against auditors; second, a change to improve the independence of outside auditors; and last, a reorganization and consolidation of the federal banking agencies—an issue that has been debated since before the Federal Reserve was created in 1913.[3]

Institution-Affiliated Party Definition

As set forth in Chapter Twelve, the case brought by the OCC against the accounting firm, Grant Thornton, was overturned by the U.S. Court of Appeals for the D.C. Circuit due to a narrow reading of the term "institution-affiliated party" (IAP). The court's ruling was not consistent with the legislative history of the statute. Regardless, though, of whether the court was correct, its ruling effectively prevents the banking agencies from bringing an administrative action against an accounting firm, even for an audit that is recklessly conducted and that fails to uncover a half billion dollar fraud. This should be changed.

The relevant statute currently reads as follows:

> The term "institution-affiliated party" means—
>
> . . . .

(4) any independent contractor (including any attorney, appraiser, or accountant) who knowingly or recklessly participates in —

(A) any violation of any law or regulation;

(B) any breach of fiduciary duty; or

(C) any unsafe or unsound practice,

which caused or is likely to cause more than a minimal financial loss to, or a significant adverse effect on, the insured depository institution.[4]

It was alleged that Grant Thornton was reckless in conducting its audit of the Keystone bank and that the audit, had it been conducted properly, would have uncovered the bank's various violations, breaches of fiduciary duty, and unsafe and unsound banking practices. Furthermore, the experts concluded that, had that happened, the regulatory agencies would have been able to stop the bank's ever-increasing losses months before the OCC actually closed the bank.

However, the court of appeals objected to the OCC's lawsuit on the grounds that Grant Thornton was not participating in any alleged violation, breach, or practice engaged in by the bank. Grant Thornton, in the view of the court, was merely reviewing the actions of the bank after the fact and that the statute required "forward-looking" action on the part of the IAP.

The concurring opinion, as a nonbinding part of the court's decision, held that an agency could not pursue a firm as an IAP unless "most or many of the managing partners or senior officers of the entity have participated in some way in the egregious misconduct." For the reasons set forth in Chapter Twelve, this is not correct. Regardless, though, if adopted as a precedent, it would unduly constrict the banking agencies and would prevent any action against a large firm for acts conducted by individual partners, no matter how reckless.

A simple way to overcome the court's decision (both the majority and the concurring opinions) and to enable the federal banking agencies to pursue appropriately egregious cases against accountants—as individuals or as a firm—is to amend the definition of an IAP set forth above to read as follows:

The term "institution-affiliated party" means—

. . . .

(4) any independent contractor (including any attorney, appraiser, or accountant—**whether as an individual, or as a firm acting through any of its partners, principals or senior officials**) who knowingly or recklessly participates in **or, by its knowing or reckless conduct, allows to occur or continue** —

(A) any violation of any law or regulation;

(B) any breach of fiduciary duty; or

(C) any unsafe or unsound practice,

which caused or is likely to cause more than a minimal financial loss to, or a significant adverse effect on, the insured depository institution.

This amendment would preserve the very high bar necessary for bringing an action against an IAP. It would still require that the federal banking agencies prove that the IAP was engaging in knowing or reckless misconduct to the significant detriment of a federally insured bank. However, at the same time, it would permit the agencies to take appropriate disciplinary action against an IAP (either as an individual or as a firm) that chooses to work for such a federally insured bank and does so recklessly or with knowingly bad conduct.[5]

Independence of Outside Auditors

There is not much that can be done with regard to the inherent conflict of an accounting firm performing a supposedly independent audit of a company that is paying for the audit and will be deciding whether to retain the firm in future years. However, consideration should be given to prohibiting or restricting what additional or nonaudit work such an accounting firm should be allowed to do for that particular company. As noted in Chapter Twelve, with regard to Grant Thornton, its projected fee income from the Keystone audit assignment was approximately $200,000. As it turned out, Grant Thornton billed the bank just shy of $600,000, due primarily to nonauditing services Grant Thornton provided for the bank.

Notes

1. Danielle Douglas, "JP Morgan Bullied Federal Regulators, Testimony Shows," *The Washington Post*, March 16, 2013.
2. This issue of regulatory arbitrage will be discussed extensively in the next chapter.

3. The basis for this last recommendation is set forth in the next chapter.
4. 12 U.S.C. § 1813(u).
5. In addition to this change, a further amendment would be necessary to 12 U.S.C. §§ 1818(b)(1) and (i)(2)(B)(i)(II) to delete the phrases "in conducting the business of such depository institution" and "in conducting the affairs of such insured depository institution," respectively. This verbiage is unnecessary and confusingly implies that the IAP must, in essence, be a member of the bank's staff. The whole idea of including IAPs within the scope of the statute is that they do not have to be an employee of the bank.

17

Consolidation of the Federal Banking Agencies

*Federal regulation of commercial banks . . .
is a jurisdictional tangle that boggles the mind. . . .
The bank regulatory structure . . . is duplicative, overlapping and
wasteful of public resources . . . [and]
the principal problem with bank regulation is
the hydra-headed bank regulatory structure
at the Federal level which moves
in three separate directions.*
—Senator Proxmire's description of the U.S. bank
regulatory system in introducing the
"Federal Bank Commission Act" in 1979.[1]

The immediate cause of the demise of the First National Bank of Keystone was, of course, the losses stemming from the securitization of subprime mortgages—an overly risky endeavor that the bank was not capable of handling.

However, a more fundamental problem was the existence of multiple financial regulatory agencies that were in competition with one another. Had there been just one banking agency, the jurisdictional overlap, interagency bickering, turf wars, and concern about being second-guessed would have been eliminated and the sole banking agency would have been able to direct its unfettered resources and attention to investigating and resolving the red flags and deficiencies apparent at the Keystone bank. Such an agency would not have had to exist under the threat of a bank switching charters—which would reduce the agency's income and/or prestige. Accordingly, it would not have been reluctant to take appropriately strong action early on to address the harassment from the bank, the violations of law, the concentrations of credit, the lack of staffing and expertise, and the myriad of other unsafe and unsound banking practices that abounded at the Keystone bank.

Short History of U.S. Banking Regulation

The system of federal bank regulation in the United States is one of the most complex in the world. It started with the creation of the Office of the Comptroller of the Currency (OCC) in 1863 to help fund the Civil War. After a series of financial panics, in particular the Panic of 1907, the Federal Reserve System was created in 1913. To deal with the Great Depression and resulting bank failures, the Federal Deposit Insurance Corporation (FDIC) was established in 1933.[2] At the time these agencies were created, there was much discussion as to where they should be placed or whether they should be separate entities, but expediency won out and it was determined that it was simpler to create each of the agencies separate and apart from one another.

The OCC charters and supervises all national banks—very simply, all banks that have the word "national" in their name, or the initials, N.A., standing for "national association." State banks are no different from national banks, except for the fact that they are chartered and supervised by the individual states. State banks are divided into two categories—state member banks and state nonmember banks. No one outside of the small world of banking has any idea what this means, but, very simply, state member banks are "members" of the Federal Reserve System and are regulated by the states and by the Fed. State nonmember banks are, accordingly, not members of the Federal Reserve System and are regulated by the states and by the FDIC. There used to be some small differences and privileges attributable to being a "member" of the Federal Reserve System, but that is no longer the case. All banks have FDIC federal deposit insurance and all banks have access to the Fed discount window (to obtain emergency lending).

The FDIC insures deposits and supervises—with the states—some state banks. The Fed directs the monetary policy of the country (and has various other tasks) and supervises—again with the states—the state banks not otherwise supervised by the FDIC. The Fed also supervises bank holding companies, regardless of whether they own national banks, state banks, savings and loan institutions, or a combination of the three.

Primarily as the result of the existence of bank holding companies and the cross-jurisdictional scope they represent, almost 60% of financial institutions are supervised by two or more federal banking supervisors.[3] This is not even taking into account that all state banks, by definition, have both a state and a federal regulator or that the FDIC has back-up examination authority over all banks. It is a system that is inefficient, duplicative, and defies understanding.

Some have called it a "tangled web of regulation"; a "crazy quilt pattern"; and a "hydra-headed bank regulatory structure at the federal level which moves in three separate directions." Former Treasury Secretary Lloyd Bentsen called it "a spider's web of overlapping jurisdictions"; former Senator William Proxmire called it "bizarre"; former Fed Vice Chairman J. L. Robertson called it "unnecessarily complex, confusing"; Representative Henry Gonzalez, Senator Alfonse D'Amato, and Senator Donald Riegle, in a letter to President Clinton, called it "costly, burdensome, inefficient [and] archaic"[4]; and Senator Riegle separately noted that "no thoughtful person would ever design such a system from scratch."[5] Few would disagree with him. As Secretary Bentsen noted in 1993, "The United States has a bank regulatory system cobbled together over the past 130 years into a device even Rube Goldberg would marvel at."[6]

It is broken and needs to be fixed.

Effect of the U.S. Banking System

As a consequence of the banking regulatory system, there have been turf wars and friction between the agencies for over a hundred years. In the Keystone case, for example, there were the overlapping examinations and rating differences that occurred in the OCC's and FDIC's effort to jointly supervise the bank. In addition, right after the creation of the Federal Reserve in 1913, there were disagreements and fights. In 1914, the comptroller of the currency refused to send reports of examination to the Fed and directed banks not to send call reports to the Fed.[7] Between 1919 and 1921, the Fed, in turn, supported four separate legislative bills to investigate the comptroller—based on trumped-up allegations of misconduct—and to abolish the OCC, transferring all of its responsibilities to the Fed.[8]

In 1938, in its annual report, the Fed set forth a chart demonstrating the overlapping jurisdictions of the banking agencies in a bald effort to convince Congress that the Fed should be the sole banking agency. It its report, the Fed said:

> ... the development of the mechanism of the supervision has been piecemeal in character and not in accordance with comprehensive plans made with reference to the country's banking needs ... From this process the banking picture emerges as a crazy quilt of conflicting powers and jurisdictions, of overlapping authorities and

303

gaps in authority, of restrictions making it difficult for banks to serve their communities . . .[9]

While all of this was correct (and remains so today), it was merely an effort to wrest complete control over bank regulation. Ever since, the Fed has vociferously opposed all consolidation proposals that do not result in it being the primary or sole banking agency.

In terms of more recent strife, in the 1960s, the comptroller attempted to charge both the Fed and the FDIC between $300 and $5,000 per report of examination sent to them, as opposed to the historical price of $5 to $10.[10] This issue persisted for a number of years. In the 1980s, the agencies publicly disagreed with each other over the issue of what reserves large banks should maintain, leading the then-chairman of the FDIC to remark, "The Fed wears a monetary hat that may not be in the best interest of banks' safety and soundness."[11] This was a very telling remark, reflecting the potential conflict between the Fed's conduct of monetary policy and bank supervision. When the OCC changed the structure of its reports of examination, the Fed threatened to examine national banks itself.[12] The Fed and the OCC have even been on opposite sides of federal court of appeals cases and, significantly, a Supreme Court case.[13]

The fights have continued to today. One recent comptroller, Eugene Ludwig, said he was amazed at the constant bickering between the agencies:

> And then you have, sitting around a table, 20 people. And the bickering that goes on is unbelievable because everybody has a historic position and, God forbid, you should take a position against your own staff. And then when you leave the room, the bickering grinds on and on and on.[14]

Along these lines, former Comptroller Ludwig noted that it took ten years and more for the agencies to agree on uniform capital standards; sixteen years to come up with a uniform report of examination format; and twenty-four years to create a uniform call report.[15] Getting three independent agencies to agree on anything, let alone something important, takes too much time.

Given all of this, it is amazing that the agencies coordinate as well as they do. But it is a constant struggle. The day after the Keystone bank failed, for instance, there was a large interagency meeting in Washington, D. C. at which the regulators spent most of the time pointing fingers at each other as to who was responsible.

As recently as April, 2015, Paul Volcker, former chairman of the Federal Reserve Board, issued a report recommending the merger of the regulatory functions of the federal banking agencies, stating:

> The system for regulating financial institutions in the United States is highly fragmented, outdated, and ineffective. A multitude of federal agencies . . . share oversight of the financial system under a framework riddled with regulatory gaps, loopholes, and inefficiencies.[16]

The historical compromises in creating the U.S. banking regulatory system do not justify the continuation of the needless overlap and turf fighting between the agencies and the resulting inefficiencies.

Regulatory Arbitrage

Aside from all of the interagency fighting and bickering, perhaps the most pernicious effect of the current federal banking regulatory scheme is that it promotes regulatory arbitrage which inevitably weakens and undermines the effectiveness of the regulatory regime.

Quite simply, a bank has the ability to select its regulator by choosing which agency is going to charter it—the state banking agency or the OCC. If the bank selects the state, then it has the further ability to choose whether it wants the Federal Reserve or the FDIC to supervise it at the federal level. There is no other system like this in the world and it supports and encourages a concerted effort on the part of many banks to find what they perceive to be the weakest—or most lenient—regulator.

Not only does the bank make the initial selection of which agency will supervise it, if things do not go well, the bank can "convert," or change its charter, so that it will get out from under an "unfriendly" regulator and try a different agency. This is what Knox McConnell threatened to do numerous times. This is what many banks threaten to do all of the time. It is an absurd situation.

When one deals with the IRS, the Department of Justice, the FBI, the SEC, or any of the other agencies throughout the federal government, one does not have the ability to select an alternative agency—a different IRS, FBI, and so forth—if things do not go well. But banks are treated differently. If they get into trouble, they can try to convert charters in order to obtain more lenient treatment. It does not always work and sometimes the conversion application gets turned down. But the option and possibility are there. And it happens frequently enough. In that regard, *The Washington Post* recounted that, between 2000 and 2009, about 240 banks converted from a federal charter to a state charter (meaning that they converted from the OCC to either the FDIC or the Fed) and at least thirty of those banks converted specifically in order to get out from under regulatory enforcement actions.[17]

As specific examples, Continental Illinois National Bank and Trust Company, the large Chicago bank that eventually collapsed in 1984, changed its charter to the state regulator after it clashed with the OCC over how much it should set aside in reserves.[18] Washington Mutual (WaMu) and Countrywide both converted to the OTS before failing — and, in part, triggering the 2008 financial crisis. In the case of WaMu, the OTS allegedly promised more lenient treatment than the OCC with regard to the thrift's subprime mortgage securitization business.[19]

As former Fed Chairman Ben Bernanke said in his recent book:

> Institutions were able to change regulators by changing their charters which created an incentive for regulators to be less strict so as not to lose their regulatory "clients"—and the exam fees they paid. For example, in March 2007, the subprime lender Countrywide Financial, by switching the charter of the depository institution it owned, replaced the Fed as its principal supervisor with the OTS, after the OTS promised to be "less antagonistic." The OCC at times actively sought to induce banks to switch to a national bank charter. Both the OCC and the OTS benefited the institutions they regulated by asserting that the institutions were exempt from most state and local laws and regulations.[20]

Apparently, the OTS actively solicited WaMu and Countrywide to change charters, and not without reason—the OTS was dependent on fees from the institutions it supervised. WaMu ended up representing 15% of the OTS's budget and Countrywide another 5%.[21] It is clear that, if 20% of your budget is going to be paid for by two entities, you are going to be solicitous of them. Not surprisingly, the OTS was later accused of being a "feeble" regulator vis à vis these two entities and of having fights with the FDIC over how to supervise them.[22]

Similarly, the OCC survives based on the fees it charges national banks, so the more banks it supervises, the better. And the more large banks, like HSBC, Citibank, JPMorgan Chase and Bank of America, the better. With regard to HSBC, it should be noted that, between 1980 and 2004, it switched charters three times.[23] In 1993, the bank switched charters to get away from the OCC, after receiving three years of poor CAMELS ratings.[24] In 2004, HSBC switched back again to get out from under a formal agreement, which the OCC lifted about one and half years later.[25] The OCC failed to take any action of its own against the bank—in spite of numerous anti-money laundering (AML) examinations of the bank in which the examiners uncovered serious AML problems.[26] In fact, the examiners cited a third more AML deficiencies at HSBC that needed the attention of the bank's board of directors than at any other large bank.[27] Twice, the examiners recommended that formal enforcement action be taken against the bank, but those recommendations went unheeded[28]—shades of the Keystone bank. As the Congressional review of the HSBC case determined:

> For more than six years, from July 2004 until April 2010, despite compiling a litany of AML deficiencies, the OCC never cited [HSBC] for a violation of law, never took a formal or informal enforcement action, and turned down recommendations to issue Cease and Desist Orders targeting particularly egregious AML problems, even though the same problems surfaced again and again.[29]

And it is little wonder why the OCC acted in this way. Ninety-five percent of OCC's budget is made up from assessments against banks and the twenty largest banks pay nearly 60% of the assessments.[30] As noted in a scholarly review:

> The OCC's ability to attract large banks to the national banking system results in a significant financial gain. During 2004-2005, the charter conversions of three large, national banks—JPMorgan Chase, HSBC, and Bank of Montreal—resulted in the transfer of $1 trillion of banking assets into the OCC's jurisdiction. This transfer alone raised OCC's assessment revenues by 15%.[31]

So it is in the OCC's financial interest to keep these banks happy. In OTS's case, once it lost the revenue from WaMu, it ceased to be a financially viable agency. This is not a system conducive to protecting the public and the marketplace from potential overreaching by banks or from their engaging in undue risky behavior, such as getting overly involved in the securitization of subprime mortgages.[32]

Rather, in the words of Arthur Burns, the renowned former chairman of the Federal Reserve Board, the system represents a "competition in laxity." That should end.

Conflicts of Interest

Due to the need on the part of the OCC to maintain its funding and in order for the Fed and the FDIC to maintain their professed need to keep their hand in bank regulation, there is an inherent conflict of interest whenever they do anything—issue a charter; allow a conversion; grant an application; interpret a statute or a regulation; take an informal rather than an formal administrative action; and so forth. There will always be an underlying question as to the motivation for the action or inaction on the part of the particular agency, especially when it involves a large bank.

In this regard, some of the licensing decisions of the OCC have been very questionable. Following the doctrine that says activity closely related to banking is permissible, the OCC has approved applications from large banks to construct and operate a highway toll plaza; to run a system to track delinquent fathers; to bring together people who wish to enroll in certain health insurance plans; to manage the processing of motor vehicle title applications; to invest in wind turbines; and to invest in gas leases. Further, under the guise of allowing a bank to invest in property for bank purposes and to "lease out excess space," the OCC authorized a large bank to build an office/hotel/condominium complex which was to have twenty-two floors, even though the bank was going to only use 17% of the building. (In its decision, the OCC disingenuously calculated the percentage to be used by the bank as being a whopping 22% by conveniently ignoring five floors of condominium space.) The OCC justified its approval, in part, by the fact that, in a previous case, the OCC allowed a bank to retain only 11% of the building. In neither of these cases, however, does this seem to represent an investment primarily for banking purposes. While the OCC may have supported each of these decisions with lengthy legal analysis and citations, they tend not to pass the "smell test." In addition, at a minimum, they tend to raise the appearance of an agency making decisions based on ulterior motives.

Similarly, the OCC has been accused of fomenting regulatory arbitrage by virtue of its preemption of state laws. In one of the most controversial cases, the OCC preempted a Georgia state law that would have imposed liability in connection with the securitization of subprime and predatory loans. This type of law was designed to protect investors and the public from shenanigans similar to what the Keystone bank was involved in. However, in August, 2003, four years after the Keystone bank failed, the OCC preempted this law, making it inapplicable to all national banks. Sheila Bair, the chairman of the FDIC, opposed the OCC's policy of preemption and publicly called it an effort to support regulatory arbitrage. The OCC continues to be unrepentant in this area.

In fact, the Financial Crisis Inquiry Commission Report noted that Comptroller Hawke believed that preemption was "an inducement to use a national bank charter" and that it was "a significant benefit of the national charter . . . that the OCC has fought hard over the years to preserve."[33] In the next sentence, the report noted that Hawke explained that the potential loss of regulatory market share for the OCC "was a matter of concern."[34] In other words, supporting preemption is an essential part of the attractiveness of the national banking charter. The report concludes by noting that the three large banks mentioned above announced their decision to convert to a national bank charter shortly after the OCC preempted the Georgia fair lending statute.[35]

Arguments For and Against Consolidation

There have been years of debate, starting from before the Fed was created, as to whether to have one, consolidated banking regulatory agency at the federal level. Of the twenty-two major studies of the issue up until 1989, eight were in favor of the total consolidation of the federal banking regulatory agencies and another seven recommended no more than two agencies. Of the twenty-one major legislative proposals up until 1989, all but five called for complete consolidation. Since then, there were two major efforts to seek the consolidation of the banking regulatory agencies—one in 1993–94 under President Clinton and another in 2004 in the form of the first draft of the Dodd-Frank bill. However, both efforts were defeated by opposition from the Fed and, understandably, a lack of support from the American Bankers Association (ABA) and bankers in general.[36] As one representative of the ABA said, "If the Comptroller is giving me a hard time, it's nice to know that I can go to the state bank department and they will welcome me with open arms."[37] Unfortunately, this represents regulatory arbitrage at its worst. If a banking agency is exercising its supervisory powers in good faith, it should not expect to be defeated by the political expediency of the bank switching charters. It should be up to the judicial system to review administrative actions and to decide whether or not the agency has sufficient legal grounds to proceed. Similarly, the Fed itself, in the form of former Governor John P. LaWare, argued in an article published in the *American Banker* that it is important to maintain more than one regulator so banks can "get out from under an examiner who has become too rigid and inflexible."[38] This is coming from a supposed regulator. Again, though, it should be up to the courts to decide this issue—not the bank that is itself the subject of the administrative action.

In addition, as seen in the Keystone case, there are a number of informal and formal internal means of discussing—and even appealing—the decisions of a line bank examiner.

Arguments Against Consolidation

The various arguments against consolidation—put forth by the Fed, the industry, the ABA, and related interested critics—boil down to several main ones: it would eliminate checks and balances; it would give one agency too much power; it would diminish innovation; the Fed needs supervisory powers to carry out monetary policy; and the FDIC needs supervisory powers to be an insurer of deposits. Each of these arguments is a shibboleth.

Checks and Balances Would Be Lost

The age-old notion is that multiple banking agencies provide a "check and balance" on one another. This sounds great, but it could not be further from the truth in practice. This country is based, of course, on well-thought-out checks and balances between the three parts of government. There is no such thing with regard to the banking agencies; they are simply three different agencies doing the same thing. No banking agency can force another banking agency to do anything or prevent it from doing something.

As the former chairman of the FDIC, William Seidman, correctly noted:

> Today, as a result of historical accident, [the banking agencies] each have a piece of the federal regulatory action. This bureaucratic gang warfare creates a high-cost system rife with duplication and delay, and can from time to time come close to destroying effective and efficient bank supervision.
>
> When these agencies disagree, not the president or the pope can force them to agree. There is no place to get a final decision on important issues—like how much capital banks must have to be safe and sound.[39]

Similarly, former Fed Vice Chairman J. L. Robertson said:

> There are no checks and there is no balance. The Federal Reserve cannot "veto" a decision of the FDIC. The Comptroller needn't seek the advice and consent of the Federal Reserve. The three regulate and supervise in complete independence of one another.[40]

As many have pointed out, if there were effective checks and balances from such a structure, then it would make sense to have two Treasury

Departments, two FBIs, two State Departments, and so forth. As Secretary Bentsen mockingly said:

> The federal government is not Noah's Ark. We don't need two Securities and Exchange Commissions. Or two Food and Drug Administrations. Or two central banks. We don't need two sets of rules and interpreters, or two sets of examinations.[41]

One Agency Would Have Too Much Power

Another argument always put forth by the opponents of consolidation is that it would give the one banking agency too much power. As if, in comparison, the Department of Justice, the IRS, or Homeland Security do not have a lot of power. Further, it should be pointed out that the Fed, with supervisory authority over all bank holding companies, and the FDIC, with back-up examination authority over all banks, both have an extremely large amount of power already.

Contrary to this contention about too much power, it is arguable, as demonstrated by the Keystone bank case and the frequent examples of regulatory arbitrage, that the banking agencies do not have enough power; do not have enough independence; and do not have the ability to supervise without looking over their shoulders and being second-guessed by the other agencies and by the very banks they are supposed to regulate. In addition, it must be remembered that the banking agencies operate by statute and, if they were to overstep their powers, the judiciary is fully capable of reining them in. That would be equally true if there were just one banking regulatory agency.

Innovation Would Be Diminished

Another common argument against consolidation is that it would diminish the innovation of the agencies. Assuming that a solitary agency could be responsible for diminishing innovation in the marketplace, it may be a small price to pay to avoid overly liberal statutory interpretations; weak supervision; applications being approved in order to woo constituent banks; conversions approved to defeat sound regulatory actions; and so on. However, the argument itself does not hold up.

Almost all "innovation" comes from the industry itself, often with the assistance of the legislatures. Examples of this would include the repeal of the Glass–Steagall Act, interstate banking, derivatives, mortgage-backed securities, and so forth. To the extent that an agency would be able to assist in the process, it would mean providing a more liberal interpretation of a statute or a regulation than the other banking agencies, thus setting up even more turf wars and dissention. The role of a banking agency is to supervise and regulate, not to come up with new banking products or services.

The Federal Reserve Should Be a Bank Regulator Because of Its Broad Experience and Knowledge and in Order to Conduct Monetary Policy

The Federal Reserve says two things in opposition to consolidation. One is, basically, that they know more than anyone else. In the words of former Fed Chairman Ben Bernanke, "It's hard for me to understand why, in the face of [the 2008] crisis that was so complex and covered so many markets and institutions, you would want to take out of the regulatory system the one institution that has the full breadth and range of those skills to address those issues," referring to the Fed's "expertise in monetary policy, payment systems and macroeconomics."[42] Along the same lines, Tim Geithner, the former secretary of the Treasury and the former president of the New York Federal Reserve Bank, said, "only the central bank is qualified to oversee the core of the system."[43]

The second point that the Fed asserts is that bank supervision is essential to the Fed's ability to conduct monetary policy. Without hands-on involvement in regulating individual banks, the argument goes, the Fed would not be able to do a good job.

With regard to the first argument, the Federal Reserve only supervises 2,412 state banks, as opposed to 4,177 state banks the FDIC supervises and the 1,621 national banks and federal thrifts the OCC supervises. In addition, many of the state banks the Fed supervises are small, as compared to the banks the OCC supervises. So the Fed's self-professed brilliance and ability are not even currently being used to full advantage. Second, the underlying premise, of course, that it takes the "economic and financial expertise" of the Fed to properly regulate banks is questionable, in light of the OCC's and FDIC's combined 234 years of experience. Third, no one is asserting that the Fed should not have been involved—as it was—in dealing with the recent financial crisis.

With regard to the second argument, it has been pointed out that the Fed needs economic information from many sectors, not just banking. In addition, the banking information it needs is in the aggregate, not from individual banks that it might happen to supervise. Also, academics have noted that "virtually no one argues in favor of using bank supervision as a tool of macroeconomic policy."[44] While accepting the fact that the Fed needs access to bank examination material in order to establish monetary policy, former Federal Reserve Vice Chairman J. L. Robertson explained, "it would be absurd to believe that examiners in the employ of the Federal Reserve would be able to provide information that would be more valuable to the formulation of monetary policy than examiners employed by [other banking agencies]."[45] In terms of implementing monetary policy through bank supervision, Robertson expressed the following thought:

> The overriding reason, however, for seeking to have the supervisory powers vested elsewhere than in the Federal Reserve is my deep-seated conviction that bank examiners should always be free to call the pitches as they see them. They should be insulated from any possible temptation of the monetary authority to use supervisory powers to implement monetary policy by appraising loans with a more critical eye in periods of easy money, when the aim of monetary policy is to expand the money supply.[46]

> . . . in appraising the soundness of loans or investments, bank examiners should never be obliged to switch from rose-colored glasses to black ones, and back and forth again, in an effort to implement the monetary policy of the moment . . .[47]

The Fed also contends that, without its supervisory powers, it would have been unable to handle the 1970 bankruptcy of Penn Central Railroad; the silver market collapse of 1980; the Ohio state thrift crisis of 1985; the 500 point stock market drop on October 19, 1987[48]; or the 2008 financial crisis. Indeed, the Fed handled these matters remarkably well, but did not have any jurisdiction over railroads, the silver market, thrifts or the stock market. In addition, it did not have any direct supervisory authority over the main players leading up to the 2008 financial crisis—Lehman Brothers, Bear Stearns, AIG, Citibank, Bank of America, and so forth. Further, it is hard to see how supervision over a portion of state banks assists in dealing with these national and international economic crises.

As former Fed Chairman Bernanke explained, the Fed believes that it is important for it to supervise not only the very large banks—which it currently does not—but also small community banks:

> Examining banks of all sizes, from all over the country, allowed us to better understand the industry as a whole and to detect potential problems earlier. Examining smaller banks also strengthened our connections with local communities and improved our ability to monitor economic developments at the grass-roots level, leading to

better monetary policy. After all, who knows more about the local economy than a community banker?[49]

However, talking to small-town bankers is not the same as examining the banks and determining their level of safety and soundness and compliance with the law. In addition, with the hundreds of economists and analysts at the Fed, it is hard to see how networking with people in small banks can greatly assist in creating monetary policy based on macro-trends in the national and world economy.

In conclusion, it is noteworthy that even several former members of the Fed have argued that "the supervision and regulation of commercial banks is too important a function in itself to be the Federal Reserve's part-time job."[50] Clearly, the Fed has the far more important task of conducting the monetary policy of the country, as opposed to dealing with relatively mundane supervisory issues, such as deciding which bank should receive a cease and desist order and the scope of the order. Bothering the chairman of the board of the Federal Reserve System with this type of issue is not efficient.

Furthermore, it is important to note that former Chairman Bernanke—aside from his desire to support the Fed's role of creating monetary policy—is worried about the twelve Federal Reserve banks not having enough to do if bank supervision were taken away from them:

> The Reserve Bank presidents were particularly alarmed at the prospect of losing bank supervision duties—one of the Reserve Banks' primary functions. The banks have already endured rounds of staff layoffs over the previous decade. . . . In part I was responding to the concerns of the Reserve Bank presidents, who saw the loss of supervision as an existential threat.[51]

So, self-preservation ultimately is at the root of everything. Hardly a persuasive argument for leaving the bank regulatory structure in a mess.

The FDIC Needs to Be a Bank Regulator in Order to Insure Deposits

The FDIC has historically claimed (similarly to the Fed) that, without direct, hands-on supervisory authority, it cannot carry out its duties— namely, insuring deposits. If that were the case, it is unclear how any private insurance company functions. That aside, it has been noted that, in order to be an insurer, the entity must be relatively cautious and conservative. Ironically, this is the flip side of the argument set forth above in support of innovative regulators.

As Comptroller Robert Clarke testified before Congress in 1989, following the savings and loan crisis:

> A deposit insurer's most immediate objective is to preserve the insurance fund. In an insurer's ideal world, there would be no bank failures, and the insurance fund balance would never decline. Consequently, an insurer can be expected . . . to take an aggressively conservative approach to bank supervision. Promising but unproven activities are likely to be resisted because of their uncertain effects on the volume of insurance claims. . . .

> The [bank] supervisor is more likely to be receptive to measures that will increase competition. Similarly, the bank supervisor is more likely to look favorably upon innovations that, although they entail some risks, will enable banks to adapt to changing demands for financial services.[52]

Moreover, the FDIC does not have direct supervisory responsibility over all the institutions it insures, suggesting that examination authority is not essential for properly executing the duties of an insurer. Furthermore, a little known fact should be pointed out—the original legislation establishing the FDIC did not contemplate that the agency would have supervisory powers.[53]

Arguments for Consolidation

The obvious arguments in favor of consolidation would include:

- absence of divisiveness and turf fights between the banking agencies;
- efficiency of having one federal banking supervisory agency instead of three;
- increased savings due to having one agency versus three;
- lack of regulatory arbitrage;
- uniform supervision over all commercial financial institutions[54];
- consolidated supervision of all bank holding company structures;
- lack of duplication of staffing;
- ability to develop examiner expertise within one agency; and
- enhanced accountability of having only one agency.

If there had been only one federal banking agency supervising the First National Bank of Keystone, it is likely that the ability of the bank to harass and intimidate the examiners—and the agency—would have been greatly diminished and that the supervision of the bank would not have been as cautious as it was.

If there were just one federal banking agency, supervision of banks in the future could be greatly improved.

Notes

1. 125 Cong. Rec. 1782, 1784 (1979). Statements by Senator Proxmire, (D-Wis). Needless to say, this and many similar bills were never enacted into law.
2. In 1932, the Federal Home Loan Bank System was also established, which eventually evolved into the Office of Thrift Supervision and then was merged into the OCC in 2011, but getting into that history just complicates the issues even more. There are also the Federal Farm Credit System and the credit unions, however, that too is beyond this discussion.
3. As of 1994, 15% of banks had three to four federal supervisors.
4. Letter to President Clinton from Rep. Henry B. Gonzalez (D-Tx.), Chairman, House Banking Committee, Sen. Alfonse M. D'Amato (D-NY), Ranking Member, Senate Banking Committee and Donald W. Riegle, Jr. (D-Mich.), Chairman, Senate Banking Committee, November 8, 1993.
5. Consolidating the Federal Bank Regulatory Agencies, Proposal Requested by the Committee on Banking, Housing, and Urban Affairs, United States Senate, November 23, 1993, 3.
6. Lloyd Bentsen, "The Bank Regulation Jumble," *The Washington Post*, November 23, 1993.
7. Ross Robertson, "The Comptroller and Bank Supervision," *A Historical Appraisal*, April, 1968, 446; testimony of Ross Robertson, "Hearings on the Federal Bank Commission Act—1976," Committee on Banking, Housing and Urban Affairs, U.S. Senate, 94th Cong., 2d Sess., February–March, 1976, 56.
8. Robertson, "The Comptroller and Bank Supervision," 116.
9. Twenty-Fifth Annual Report of the Board of Governors of the Federal Reserve System for the year 1938 (Washington, D.C., December 31, 1938), 2–3.
10. Howard Hackley, "Our Baffling Banking System—Part I," 52 *Virginia Law Review*, 565, 630–32.
11. Kathleen Day, "As Banking Crisis Grows, Regulators Collide," *The Washington Post*, June 27, 1988.
12. Minutes of the October 24, 1985 Federal Financial Institutions Examination Council, Washington, D.C.
13. *Board of Governors of the Federal Reserve System v. Dimension Financial Corp.*, 474 U.S. 361 (1986).
14. The American Banker, *Recalling "Unbelievable" Bickering, Ludwig Backs Clinton Regulatory Plan*, quoting Comptroller Eugene Ludwig, February 7, 1994.
15. Testimony of Eugene Ludwig, "Comptroller of the Currency, before the Senate Committee on Banking, Housing, and Urban Affairs," March 2, 1994, 5, 10.
16. "Reshaping the Financial Regulatory System," *The Volcker Alliance*, April, 2015. President Obama, when he was a candidate in 2008, said, in reaction to the financial crisis, that "we need to streamline a framework of overlapping and competing regulatory agencies" in his first speech at Cooper Union in New York on March 27, 2008.
17. Binyamin Appelbaum, "By Switching Their Charters, Banks Skirt Supervision," *The Washington Post*, January 22, 2009. In 2009, the federal banking agencies took some action to alleviate this situation. Specifically, the agencies issued a joint statement saying that applications for bank charters conversions "should not" be approved if they "undermine the supervisory process."

(FFIEC Statement on Regulatory Conversion, July 1, 2009.) However, it is full of precatory language, so it has no teeth, and its coverage is extremely non-specific.

In 2010, Congress passed § 612 of the Dodd-Frank Act which at least specifically recognized that some bank conversions "'are motivated by a hope of escaping current or prospective supervisory actions by [an] institution's existing supervisor . . .'" (Senate Report 111-176, 111th Cong., 2d Session, April 30, 2010, 88; quoting Federal Reserve Board Governor Daniel K. Tarullo.) However, it, too, is not as extensive or forceful as it could be. The Act only prohibits conversions by banks that are under an actual formal enforcement action or a Memorandum of Understanding that involves an—unspecified—"significant supervisory matter." In addition, the section provides for an exception if the post-conversion agency comes up with a plan (that the existing agency agrees with) to "address the significant supervisory matter"—with no explanation as to what that means and with no assurance as to how long the "plan" would stay in place. Section 612 of the Act also requires the existing agency to inform the post-conversion agency of any pending supervisory or investigative proceeding that is likely to result in an administrative action against the bank in the "near term." However, even with that, it does not preclude the receiving agency from approving the charter application and does not require it to continue the "supervisory or investigative proceeding." So the possibility of conversions to seek a more lenient regulator (or a regulator that will be more permissive) still exists and, accordingly, the Dodd-Frank Act does not stop the overall effort of banking agencies to attract banks to their supervisory fold. In that regard, the agencies acknowledged in a statement that "[m]ost conversion proposals are not subject to the prohibitions in section 612." (Interagency Statement on Section 612 of the Dodd-Frank Act—Restriction of Conversions of Troubled Banks, November 26, 2012.)

18.   Steve Klinkerman, "Continental Files to Do U.S.-State Charter Flip," *The American Banker*, November 22, 1993.

19.   Binyamin Appelbaum and Ellen Nakashima, "Banking Regulator Played Advocate Over Enforcer," *The Washington Post*, November 23, 2008.

20.   Ben Bernanke, "The Courage to Act," 97–98.

21.   John McKinnon, "Regulatory Rift Weighted on WaMu," *Wall Street Journal*, April 16, 2010; Appelbaum and Nakashima, "Banking Regulator Played Advocate Over Enforcer."

22.   Stephanie Kirchgaessner, "Regulator's Response to WaMu was 'Feeble,' says Levin," *Financial Times*, April 16, 2010.

23.   U.S. Vulnerabilities to Money Laundering, Drugs, and Terrorist Financing: HSBC Case History, U.S. Senate Permanent Subcommittee on Investigations, Majority and Minority Staff Report, July 17, 2012, 299.

24.   Id.

25.   Id. at 302.

26.   Id. at 302–04.

27.   Id. at 315.

28.   Id. at 310, 316–18 and 328–29.

29.   Id. at 316.

30.   Oren Bar-Gill and Elizabeth Warren, "Making Credit Safer," 157 *Pennsylvania Law Review*, 2008, 93.

31. Id. at 94.
32. While the Fed and the FDIC are, in essence, self-funding and do not charge the banks they supervise, they are constantly seeking new banks to supervise or are trying to keep the banks they already supervise due to the prestige and due to their desire to be banking regulators in order to support their monetary policy function and their deposit insurance function, respectively.
33. The Financial Crisis Inquiry Report, Final Report of the National Commission on the Causes of the Financial and Economic Crisis in the United States, January 2011, 112.
34. Id.
35. Id.
36. Then-Secretary of the Treasury, Hank Paulson, issued a "Blueprint for the Modernized Financial Regulatory Structure" in March, 2008, which propounded the creation of a single prudential regulator. However, it also suggested the creation of a myriad of other financial regulatory agencies.
37. Robert Garsson, "Small Banks in ABA Skeptical About Superregulator Proposal," *The American Banker*, January 12, 1994.
38. Robert Garsson, "Treasury Won't Bargain on Superregulator With Bankers or the Fed, Top Aide Vows," *The American Banker*, January 5, 1994.
39. L. William Seidman, "A New Way to Govern Banks," *The Wall Street Journal*, February 3, 1994.
40. The Federal Bank Commission Act Hearings on S. 2298 Before the Senate Comm. On Banking, Housing and Urban Affairs, 94th Cong., 1st Sess., 6 (1975).
41. Barbara Rehm, "Bentsen Offers Concessions To Superregulator Opponents," *The American Banker*, March 2, 1994.
42. Sewell Chan, "Bernanke Defends Fed's Ability to Supervise Banks," *The New York Time*, February 15, 2010.
43. Tom Braithwaite, "Big Bank Oversight to stay with Fed," *Financial Times*, March 8, 2010.
44. Paul M. Horvitz, "Reorganization of the Financial Regulatory Agencies," *Journal of Bank Research* (Winter, 1983), 259.
45. J. L. Robertson, Federal Regulation of Banking: A Plea for Unification, 31 *Law and Contemporary Problems* 673, 693 (Autumn, 1966).
46. Id. at 692.
47. The Federal Bank Commission Act Hearings on S. 2298 Before the Senate Comm. On Banking, Housing and Urban Affairs, 94th Cong., 1st Sess., 20 (1975).
48. Robert Garrson, "Treasury Chief Blasts Fed for Fighting Single Regulator," *The American Banker*, December 17, 1993; Saul Hansell, "Fed Rebutted by Bentsen On Bank Regulatory Plan," *The New York Times*, December 17, 1993.
49. Bernanke, "The Courage to Act," 395.
50. Testimony of Eugene Ludwig, Comptroller of the Currency, before the Senate Committee on Banking, Housing, and Urban Affairs, March 2, 1994, Appendix, quoting Jeffrey Bucher, former member of the Federal Reserve Board. *See also*, statement by J. L. Robertson, former vice-chairman of the Federal Reserve Board—"supervision is too important a function in itself to be the Federal Reserve's part-time job." Hearings

on Financial Institutions and the Nation's Economy (FINE) "Discussion Principles," Volumes 1–4, House of Representatives, 94th Cong. 1st Sess., November, 1975, 551.

51. Bernanke, "The Courage to Act," 413–14.
52. Statement of Robert L. Clarke, "Comptroller of the Currency, Hearings on the Resolution of the Problems of the Savings and Loan Insurance Corporation," Committee on Banking, Housing, and Urban Affairs, U.S. Senate, 101st Cong., 1st Sess., February 28, 1989.
53. Federal Deposit Insurance Corporation. The First Fifty Years, A History of the FDIC 19331983 (Washington, D.C., FDIC, 1984), 44, 51.
54. Along these lines, it is important to note that former Fed Chairman Bernanke acknowledged that "A perennial problem at the Fed was the difficulty of maintaining consistent, tough supervisory practices across the twelve Federal Reserve districts." (Bernanke, The Courage to Act, 96.) So, according to the Fed itself, its ability to alone exercise sound, uniform supervision of banks is questionable. It should be noted that maintaining uniformity across agency lines is that much more difficult.

18

Conclusion

Why should there not be a patient confidence
in the ultimate justice of the people?
Is there any better or equal hope in the world?
—Abraham Lincoln, *First Inaugural Address*

In this case, there was fraud, deceit, greed, and collusion. As set forth by the FDIC in one of its pleadings in the many civil cases that resulted from the bank's failure:

> Keystone's corrupt management falsified general ledger entries and call reports, hid, destroyed and buried bank documents, intentionally damaged the bank's microfilm reader so that examiners could not read the records, forged certificates of deposit, ordered employees to hide in darkened rooms so they couldn't be found or questioned by examiners, melted microfilm containing bank data in a microwave oven, buried bank records in a ditch in Church's back yard, stole documents from examiners, eavesdropped on examiner conversations, forged "incriminating" examiner email, forged loan servicer loan lists, and routinely lied to examiners, auditors and outside directors.

However, it is clear that justice prevailed. The runaway, corrupt bank was closed. Ultimately, five people were sent to prison and three more people were placed on probation. Those sent to prison included Terry Church, Billie Cherry, and Michael Graham. Graham and Church have now been released from prison, but Cherry died in jail. The only person who really escaped justice was Knox McConnell, who died two years before the bank failed.

In addition, the bank's prestigious accounting firm, Grant Thornton, and the bank's prominent law firm, Kutak Rock, were successfully sued by the FDIC for more than $20 million each.

The only really disgraceful result from all of the legal cases was the failure of the Court of Appeals for the Fourth Circuit to hold Grant

Thornton responsible for its having negligently misled Gary Ellis by providing him incorrect information. As a result of receiving and reviewing this incorrect information, Ellis agreed to become the president of the bank and could not find another banking job after the bank failed in the midst of a scandal.

In the annals of bank examinations there has never been anything like the First National Bank of Keystone. Not only was it one of the largest bank failures of all times, the antics it engaged in were unheard of—recording phone calls with its primary federal banking regulator; scotch-taping the examiners' work papers back together during the evenings; stealing and downloading the examiners' computer hard drives while they were at lunch; filming the use of the copying machine; screaming and yelling; and threatening the OCC and individual examiners with law suits—and worse. But the kicker was burying four large truckloads of bank documents in a 100' × 30' ditch on Terry Church's ranch. Few criminal cases—let alone bank examinations—have ever been assisted with the use of a backhoe.

The banking agencies could have been stronger in its dealings with the bank and definitely could have gotten along better—especially at the Washington, D.C. level. In spite of that, the line examiners in the bank ultimately did an outstanding job—working together very well and overcoming the bullying; the threats; the fake graffiti; the temporary restraining order; the screaming; and the fake body guards. They eventually uncovered one of the most massive frauds of all times—that had eluded the private, outside attorneys and auditors.

Further, the FBI and the Department of Justice are to be commended for their fast and thorough work. Within a month and a half after the bank failed, they had dug up Church's ranch and had arrested Church and Graham for the obstruction of a federal bank examination. And a special accolade needs be given to Senior District Court Judge Faber who presided over all but one of the criminal and civil trials ensuing from the bank's failure.

There were and are many lessons to be learned from the Keystone bank case, but, perhaps the most important one is that the federal banking agencies should not shy away from backing their examiners and taking strong action to ensure that federally insured financial institutions do not engage in overly risky activity.

Appendix A

Additional Information Concerning the Criminal and SEC Cases Brought Against the Insiders of the Bank

Church

As part of her guilty plea, Church agreed to assist the government in a series of cases, and her assistance was viewed as "substantial." The government specifically acknowledged that she was "forthcoming with complete, credible, and reliable testimony about complex fraud claims." At the same time, though, the government noted that:

> Ms. Church's cooperation . . . could have occurred much earlier and could have been of more benefit had it occurred earlier. In fact, in FDIC depositions prior to her guilty plea, Ms. Church gave testimony that was not only useless but false in many respects.

Nonetheless, the government greatly appreciated Church's belated assistance, and joined in her request to the court to reduce her sentence. In further support of her request, Church cited to the fact that she had been helping fellow inmates, teaching them courses on "Basic Money Management" (which some might view as ironic), as well as Adult Basic Education and General Education Development so the women could earn their high school Graduate Equivalence Diplomas (GEDs). In her motion to the court, Church attached some letters of tribute and support written by other inmates.

Some excerpts of the letters, which were addressed to the court, were as follows:

- "She motivates me at times when I want to give up on getting my GED. She is the most caring individual I know in this prison. She doesn't look down or act like she is better than anyone."

- "She takes time to explain things to us, and she's very patient. She also takes time out of her own schedule at night if we need more tutoring.... I hope just writing this one letter can give her hope and courage, the same as she has given me."
- "Those students who want to quit the GED classes or the college classes, she will give them a firm positive lecture. She will then spend more time with that person giving words of encouragement."
- "She is my tutor and she does an excellent job at tutoring inmates here. She has a lot of patience. She always has a positive outlook and a warm smile to greet other inmates. She is definitely what I consider a positive role model."
- "She is an excellent teacher, she shows herself well in her classes, she is very happy, she worries about people, and in her hands there is help for whoever needs it, she is very spiritual and maintains a good relationship with all of the people. She is a lady with very good principles and a huge heart filled with kindness."

Excerpts of other letters, which were addressed to Church, were as follows:

- "I also want to thank you for all your help. Very seldom do we meet someone that cares about other people improving or doing better in their lives."
- "A note ... to tell you how much I have appreciated all of your assistance. Your classes have opened new doors in my mind and given me information that I shall use for the rest of my life.... I shall sorely miss you my friend."
- "You are a great teacher and exhibit concern for everyone you teach."
- "Even though our understanding was limited your patience wasn't. No matter how many times we had to go over the same problems, you endured to the end ☺ and made sure we knew it inside out and upside down. And for that we say thank you!"
- "I also want to thank you for giving me the pep talk. I would have quit school if it wasn't for you talking to me. You helped me to realize that I have to work at something if I really want it bad enough. You are a real friend and an excellent teacher."
- "Thank you so much for helping me get my education. Even when I wanted to quit and walk away you stood by me and kept me going."

According to her attorney, Church decided to cooperate and testify for the government in order to begin to atone—to the extent she could—for all of the harm she had caused:

> While testifying in [the] *Mitchell* [case],[1] ... Ms. Church described herself at the time of her first trial in 2000 as "an arrogant asshole." By the time of her *Mitchell* testimony, Ms. Church had reflected upon

the impact of her conduct upon her victims. She also testified that part of the reason she was testifying on behalf of the Government was to alleviate some of the guilt she feels for her role in this matter and to acknowledge the emotional scars she caused many people.

Based on all of this, as well as some very complex mathematical calculations dealing with concurrent terms and when each began, the court, on December 19, 2005, reduced her sentence to "time served," plus twelve years from that point in time. Accordingly, and factoring for time off for good behavior, she was released on September 20, 2015. In all, Church served over fifteen years in prison.

Graham

Graham, like Church, did some very good work while in prison. He tutored other inmates, helping them to get their GEDs. He completed a course in Braille so he could type books for the blind. He also worked as a hospice volunteer assisting inmates who were dying of complications from AIDS, liver disease, cancer, heart problems, and hepatitis. For a while, Graham also worked in the prison heating and air conditioning area (and was exposed to mold and asbestos in the process).

Melissa Quizenbeury

Melissa Quizenbeury was one of the more senior level employees of the bank. She started at the bank in 1985 as the proof machine operator and became the assistant cashier in 1989. She became the executive vice president and cashier of the bank in 1997. In addition, in October, 1997, she became a member of the board of directors due to the need to fill the vacancy left by McConnell's death. Unfortunately, during the summer before the bank failed, she allegedly engaged in insider trading with regard to selling her bank stock.

According to the information filed against her on April 10, 2001, she "possessed material nonpublic, confidential information" concerning the true financial condition of the bank, including the following:

- Keystone Bank was not adequately capitalized and did not maintain sufficient liquidity;
- Keystone Bank disguised its insufficient liquidity from the OCC by continuing to accept brokered CDs, in violation of a directive from the OCC; and
- Keystone Bank falsely reported and overstated the value of its assets.

On June 16, 1999, with this alleged inside, confidential information, she sold 1,850 shares of bank stock at $220 a share, for a total of $407,000.

On July 6, 1999, after the examination started, she sold an additional 150 shares of bank stock, again at $220 a share, for a total of $33,000.

In a parallel case brought on the same day as the criminal information was filed, the SEC alleged that, by selling her stock, Quizenbeury avoided $440,000 in losses when the bank failed.

The SEC also claimed that, at the time she sold her stock, she knew that it "was essentially worthless." Interestingly, Quizenbeury's first and largest sale of bank stock occurred before the OCC examination started. So, while she may have had damaging inside information about the poor financial condition of the bank, she probably could not have predicted what would happen to the bank.

Quizenbeury pled guilty on May 21, 2001 to the criminal charges and was sentenced on December 17, 2001 to eight months' imprisonment, was fined $5,000 and was required to pay reimbursement of $440,000. She paid the fine and reimbursement in full. She settled the SEC case without admitting or denying any wrongdoing. The SEC enjoined her from engaging in future violations of securities laws, but did not assess her any additional penalties.

Lorene Ellen Turpin and Lora McKinney

Ellen Turpin and Lora McKinney were also charged with insider trading by the SEC. Turpin started working at the bank as a switchboard operator in 1988. Three years later, she was promoted to the bookkeeping department and, in 1992, became the head bookkeeper of the bank. She was appointed a vice president in March of 1999.

McKinney started at the bank in 1985 as a switchboard operator and eventually became the proof operator at the bank.

On July 8, 1999, they each sold 650 shares of bank stock for $220 a share and, on July 14th, they each sold an additional 400 shares at the same price. One day later, on July 15th, Turpin tried to sell 1,000 shares of her remaining 1,022 shares, but it was too late—she could not find a buyer for the stock. That same day, McKinney unsuccessfully tried to sell 1,500 shares of her remaining 2,900 shares of bank stock—a slightly larger number of shares than Turpin had.

Turpin later testified that, just prior to selling her stock (which was slightly more than two weeks after the examiners arrived on June 21, 1999), Church advised her and Quizenbeury to sell their bank stock:

> She told me and Melissa Quizenbeury that the best thing we could do would be to sell some stock, because they were going to have someone

take over the bank and she could no longer guarantee our jobs or our wages, and that that was not to leave that room.[2]

The SEC complaint against Turpin and McKinney alleged that they engaged in acts intended to conceal the true financial condition of the bank and knew that the bank was accepting brokered CDs in violation of an OCC directive. The complaint also alleged that they believed that Church was embezzling from the bank and was falsifying the books and records of the bank. Further, the SEC alleged that, at the time they sold their stock, Turpin and McKinney knew that the bank "was at risk of collapsing."

On September 18, 2002, without admitting or denying the SEC's allegations, Turpin and McKinney consented, in essence, to not violate securities laws. Based on their sworn financial statements, the SEC did not impose any fine or require them to disgorge any profits.

According to the SEC press release, by selling their bank stock, they each avoided $231,000 in losses.

* * *

Turpin and McKinney were also charged with obstructing a federal bank examination.

On April 10, 2001, criminal informations were filed against them, alleging that they each helped obstruct the last OCC examination of the bank by, among other things, disabling the bank's microfilm reader.

On May 21, 2001, they both pled guilty. Turpin was sentenced on December 17, 2001 to three years' probation and was fined $5,000. On July 9, 2004, with about five more months to go in her probation, she wrote Judge Faber asking for an early release from her probation. She promised him "you never have to worry about seeing me in court, or near a court house after my time is up." She also said, "I am not a bad person, and I promise to be even better in the future." Based on this letter, but first confirming that there were no additional criminal cases against her and that she had paid her fine in full, Judge Faber released her.

McKinney was sentenced on December 17, 2001, to three years' probation and was fined $3,000, which she paid.

Barbara Nunn

Barbara Nunn started to work for Michael Graham in 1995 at his CPA firm. In April, 1997, she went on the payroll of KMC, the bank subsidiary that operated the bank's subprime mortgage securitization process.

After the failure of the bank, Nunn pled guilty to charges of income tax evasion for taxable years 1996 and 1997. She was not charged with any crime relating to the operations or failure of the bank. But, as part of her plea agreement, she agreed to testify fully and truthfully in the Church II case.

According to the information filed against her, she reported income of $28,724 for 1996 when, in reality, her income was $110,724. For 1997, as set forth in the information, she reported income of $76,571, when her actual income was $217,241.

She pled guilty on July 16, 2001, and was sentenced on December 17, 2001 (the same day Graham, Quizenbeury, Turpin, and McKinney were sentenced) to five years' probation and was fined $4,000, which she paid.

Notes

1. This is one of the civil cases discussed in Chapter Ten.
2. This damaging evidence against Church actually came out through Church's own attorney's poor questioning:

> Q. And did you talk – you did talk with Ms. Church before you sold your stock, didn't you?
> A. Yes, I did.
> Q. And she told you that she didn't think you ought to sell it, didn't she?
> A. No, she did not.

The answer to his leading question not having gone the way he wanted, but not willing to leave it alone and avoid making it worse, Mr. Love proceeded to ask an open-ended question to which he didn't know the answer – a cardinal sin in cross-examination:

> Q. What did she tell you?
> A. She told me and Melissa Quizenbeury that the best thing we could do would be to sell some stock . . . (as quoted above).

Appendix B

Additional Information Concerning the Civil Cases Brought in Connection with the Bank

Prefailure Case

City National Bank v. First National Bank of Keystone

City National Bank, the bank located near Keystone that had been working with the Keystone bank on the securitization deals, filed suit against Keystone on June 17, 1998, over a year before the bank failed. City had been purchasing and servicing loans for Keystone, but complained about the fact that Keystone had not sent it all the appropriate loan documentation, including the necessary assignments for the loans, the promissory notes, and the deeds of trust.

The lawsuit involved over $21 million worth of loans, and City was seeking damages of more than $700,000, plus equitable relief of $3.5 million.

The case was filed in state court in West Virginia, but, on September 29, 1999, the FDIC—as receiver for the First National Bank of Keystone—filed a successful motion to replace City National Bank as the plaintiff in the case. On October 1, 1999, the FDIC filed another successful motion to remove the case from state court to federal district court.

What this meant was that City National Bank was out of the case and the FDIC, by operation of law, took over the case.

Postfailure Case Relating to Michael Graham

As set forth in Chapter Nine, Graham pled guilty to a series of fraudulent activities in the case referred to as Graham II. The allegations in that criminal case pertained, in part, to investments in a landfill in West Virginia, a bingo hall in Alabama, and gas companies in Florida with a Michael McGlothlin. The allegations also became the basis of a civil lawsuit by the FDIC against McGlothlin and others.

The FDIC case was filed on June 27, 2003, and alleged that McGlothlin and others, with Graham's assistance, obtained three loans totaling $700,000 from the Keystone bank for the investment in the landfill. According to the complaint, there was no evidence that the board of directors of the bank approved two of the loans. Worse, according to the FDIC, the bank paid out more than $5.4 million for this venture, through "hot" checks[1] and transfers from fictitious accounts. The landfill was eventually sold in June, 1993, for $11.3 million, but the bank got only a fraction of this amount—$851,606—which was nowhere near what it was owed.

According to the FDIC complaint, Graham had an active hand in devising the cashier's checks disbursing the settlement dollars from the sale of the landfill:

> Graham . . . and McGlothlin "made up" fictitious amounts for each of the checks. Church did not want to show money directly owed to Keystone because she had removed evidence of any loan relating to the landfill in order to deceive banking examiners and [the] Keystone [directors].

According to the FDIC complaint, instead of going to the bank, $5.2 million of the proceeds from the sale of the West Virginia landfill went to the profitless Florida gas company investment Graham and McGlothlin were involved in. The two ventures—the gas companies in Florida and the landfill in West Virginia—were supposed to be separate ventures. Consequently, there was no reason for any of the landfill proceeds going to cover losses from the gas companies.

With regard to the bingo hall in Alabama, the FDIC complaint noted that the judge overseeing the case had determined that the operation of the bingo hall was illegal. The FDIC also noted that the bank had paid over $8 million to construct and operate the hall and even paid out over $170,000 in bingo prize money.

This case—involving alleged fraud prior to and aside from the securitization-related fraud—was settled on August 30, 2005.

Postfailure Cases Brought by Entities Involved
in the Securitization Program

Coast Case

On June 16, 2000, Melgar and related individuals and companies filed a suit in Washington, D.C. against the FDIC as receiver of the First National Bank of Keystone. This suit was seeking ownership of 10% of the residuals pertaining to seven of the securitization deals and, further, requesting that notes signed by Melgar and Sleight for two $1 million loans from the bank be declared null and void. Melgar and company, of course, were the individuals and entities that encouraged the bank to get involved in the securitization program that was allegedly replete with problems.

The FDIC successfully got the case transferred to the district court in West Virginia, and had it merged with the Mitchell case discussed in Chapter Ten. Melgar's part of the case was eventually settled before the case went to trial.

U.S. Bank, N.A. v. First National Bank of Keystone

Subsequent to the failure of the bank, U.S. Bank, N.A., a national bank in Minneapolis, Minnesota, which served as the trustee for the Keystone bank's nineteen securitization deals,[2] brought three lawsuits.

The first case was the most curious of the three. It was filed on April 27, 2000, by the U.S. Bank against Keystone Mortgage Corporation (KMC), United National Bank, and Compu-Link. The case did not involve any of the nineteen securitization deals the Keystone bank was involved in. Rather, the basis of the case was Deal 1999-2, which was a deal handled exclusively by United National Bank. However, KMC had provided the underlying loans for the securitization and U.S. Bank, as trustee, alleged that a number of the loans failed to meet certain standards, including that the documentation for the loans is properly recorded; that the documents consist of originals; that no relevant documents are missing; that the loans are fixed-interest rate loans; that the loans are for residential mortgages; and that the loans are current. According to the complaint, Keystone agreed to repurchase the loans in question, and cut a check dated August 17, 1999, for $363,479. The check, made out to United National Bank, contained a notation indicating that it was for the "repurchase of loans."

United endorsed the check over to Compu-Link, which, in turn, endorsed it over to U.S. Bank, as trustee. U.S. Bank dutifully deposited the check for collection, but it was too late. Just over two weeks after the check was issued, the bank failed. Consequently, the check was dishonored and sent back with the notation: "Bank Closed."

The case never went to trial; it was settled by the parties on August 23, 2000.

The second case, filed three months later, on November 28, 2000, was against the First National Bank of Keystone, KMC and its successor in interest, the FDIC. The basis for the case was that, in placing loans into the securitization process, Keystone had failed to adhere to the standards set forth above. However, on September 30, 2003, the case was settled.

The third case, filed on December 14, 2000, in essence, was against the FDIC for fees and services U.S. Bank claimed it was owed for providing assistance directly to the FDIC in figuring out the value of the Keystone bank's interest in the residuals remaining from the various securitizations. Most of the claims were decided by Judge Faber based on competing motions for summary judgment, with the remaining factual disputes left for trial. However, the case settled three months later, on July 15, 2005, before any trial took place.

Shareholders' Lawsuits

Allen v. Grant Thornton

An additional shareholder lawsuit was brought by a Thomas Allen, who hoped, like many of the plaintiffs in the other cases described in Chapter Ten, to serve as the class action representative for similarly situated shareholders. Allen had purchased fifty shares of the bank's shares on April 22, 1999, and another ten shares on August 27, 1999, five days before the bank failed. Curiously, according to his complaint, he was able to sell four shares on September 1, 1999, even though the bank had been closed early that morning.

Allen's suit was filed on December 10, 1999, and it named Grant Thornton, Herman & Cormany, Church, Cherry, Graham, Ellis, McConnell's estate, and four directors as defendants. The lawsuit claimed that Allen had paid artificially inflated prices (which was true) and that the acts of the defendants were (in overwrought language) "fraudulent, oppressive, and malicious."

As with the other cases discussed in Chapter Ten, the FDIC intervened as a plaintiff in this case. The case was eventually merged with Gariety I and II.

Notes

1. These are checks drawn against insufficient funds.
2. Very simply, a trustee for a securitization deal takes the money collected by the loan servicers, distributes the funds to the investors, and prepares and distributes reports on the securitization deal to the investors.

Bibliography

Bernanke, Ben S. 2015. *The Courage to Act.* New York: W.W. Norton.

Bitner, Richard. 2008. *Confessions of a Subprime Lender.* Hoboken: John Wiley & Sons.

Cohan, William D. 2009. *House of Cards.* New York: Doubleday.

Cohan, William D. 2012. *Money and Power.* New York: Anchor Books.

Davidson, Andrew, Anthony Sanders, Lan-Ling Wolff, and Anne Ching. 2003. *Securitization: Structuring and Investment Analysis.* Hoboken: John Wiley & Sons.

Farley, Richard E. 2015. *Wall Street Wars.* New York: Regan Arts.

Grind, Kirsten. 2012. *The Lost Bank.* New York: Simon & Schuster.

Lewis, Michael. 2011. *The Big Short.* New York: W.W. Norton & Company.

Lewis, Michael. 2014. *Flash Boys.* New York: W.W. Norton & Company.

McConnell, J. Knox. 1984. *The Boxer and the Banker.* New York: Vantage Press.

MacDonald, Scott B., and Jane E. Hughes. 2015. *Separating Fools from Their Money.* New Brunswick: Transaction Publishers.

Morgenson, Gretchen, and Joshua Rosner. 2011. *Reckless Endangerment.* New York: Times Books, Henry Holt Company.

Shiller, Robert J. 2008. *The Subprime Solution.* Princeton, NJ: Princeton University Press.

Sorkin, Andrew Ross. 2010. *Too Big To Fail.* New York: Penguin Books.

Stewart, James B. 1991. *Den of Thieves.* New York: Simon & Schuster.

Wallison, Peter J. 2015. *Hidden in Plain Sight.* New York: Encounter Books.

Index

18 U.S.C. § 656, 182
18 U.S.C. § 1517, 177–78
2008 financial crisis, 19, 57, 277, 279–89, 293, 306, 313
A Christmas Carol, 203
Advanta, 155, 157–58, 160, 168, 175–76, 234–37, 239–40, 244–45, 259
AIG, 313
Alderson Federal Prison Camp, 188
Allen, Thomas, 332
American Banker, 17, 93, 100, 104, 259, 294, 309
American Bankers Association (ABA), 309–10
America's Most Wanted, 72
appraisal fees, 39, 47, 91–92, 101, 214, 224
Arnold, Susan, 166
Arthur Andersen, 118
    tape, 122, 224

backhoe, 6, 322
Bailey, Diane, 67–68
Bailey, F. Lee, 93–94
Bair, Sheila, 308
Bakkebo, Brian, 73, 207
Bakkebo, Harald, 52–54, 58, 62–65, 68–76, 202–4, 207, 212–13
    death, 71, 207
    FDIC lawsuit, 202–7, 331
    fled to Norway, 202
    girlfriend, 72–73, 75
    indictment, 68–70, 212–13
BancOne, 215
Bank of America, 269–70, 306, 313
Bank of Montreal, 307
Barnhart, Roy, 194–95
Bays, Justin, 67–68

Bear Stearns, 57, 285–86, 288, 313
Bell, Bert, 11
Bell, John C., Jr., 11
Bentsen, Lloyd, 303, 311
Bernanke, Ben, 306, 312–14
BestBank, Boulder, Colorado, 274
Bischoff, Horst, 198
Blair, Mark, 85, 120–21, 132, 134, 138–41, 144, 151, 153, 156, 158, 228, 243, 245, 269, 274, 296–97
Blinder, Max, 289
Bluefield, West Virginia, 6, 49, 81, 177, 180
Bluewell, West Virginia, 161
BNP Paribas, 286
Britton, Leann, 111, 132, 144
Budnick, Victor, 18, 258
    father, 18
Buenger, Susan, 161, 221, 225, 227, 230–33, 235–45, 249, 258–59
Burke Mountain, 2, 26, 169–70
Burks, Virginia, 152–54, 173, 175
Burns, Arthur, 307
burying bank documents, 1–7, 142, 150, 166, 169, 172, 177–78, 321–22
Bush, George H. W., 12, 23–24, 81–82, 94–96, 180, 281, 295
Bush, George W., 96, 282
Byrd, Robert, 84, 101

call reports,
    errors and violations, 86–87, 89, 92, 94, 98, 100, 103, 105, 108–9, 117–18, 123–24, 128, 130, 197, 220, 224, 227, 232, 242, 294
camera
    over copier, 84, 322
    over microfilm reader, 150

Canipe, Norma Faye, 188–90
  Pritt, Dencil, 190
  Tatham, John Francis, 188
Caperton, Gaston, 95
Capital Markets Assurance Corporation (CapMac), 59, 64, 77, 206, 213–14, 294
Carney, Jane, 128, 131
Carney, Owen, 18, 110, 127–31, 140, 153, 201, 231, 247, 257
C&H Ranch, 2, 4, 166, 168–70, 189–90
CEDE and Company, 146–48, 151–52
certificates of deposit for Cadillacs, 14, 82
certificates of deposit held by bank, 89, 123–25, 128, 145–54, 166, 172–74, 223, 239, 321, 325, 327
  OCC restriction on use of brokered certificates of deposit, 128, 145
certificates of deposit owned by Marbil, 37–40, 42, 183
Chadwick, Felipa, 72–73, 75
Cherry, Billie, 2, 11, 14, 23–25, 33–44, 51, 81–83, 117–20, 124–25, 130, 138, 140, 143, 155–56, 162, 165, 168–69, 178–84, 187, 194–99, 230, 257, 259–60, 321, 332
  Cherry Key Inn, 23, 27, 44, 81
  Cherry, Michael, 36, 179
  Cherry, Roslyn, 179
  deemed by the OCC as unqualified to be president of bank, 125
  died in prison, 182
  Jones Mansion, 23–24, 31
  mayor of Keystone, 23, 183
  second criminal trial (Church II), 178–84
  secret marriage, 33, 45, 179
  sentencing, 182
Chetco Federal Credit Union, Harbor, Oregon, 197
Chopel, John, 106–8
Church, Jeff, 4–5
Church, Hermie (Junior), 4–5, 50, 72, 91, 133, 169, 189
  Hog Pen, 38–39
  testimony on Hog Pen and H&TC accounts, 135–37
Church, Terry Lee, passim
  blaming Meredith Hale, 155
  boat marina, Bristol, Tennessee, 3, 17, 152
  education, 49
  firing Meredith Hale, 27–28

first criminal trial (Church I), 136–37, 165–78
  guns, 17, 144, 190, 230
  indictment, first, 7, 165–66
  second criminal trial (Church II), 178–84, 328
  signature cards for her accounts, 133, 166, 172–73
  suspended from bank, 161
  third criminal case (Church III), 184–85
Church, T. G., 1–3, 25
Ciccarelli, Joe, 6
Cincinnati, Ohio, 159, 234–35, 243
Citibank, 269–70, 306, 313
City Holdings, Inc., 75
City National Bank, Charleston, West Virginia, 98–99, 120–21, 156, 158, 239, 329
Clarke, Robert L., 84, 139, 201, 315
Clearview Capital Corporation, 52–54, 62–65, 72–73, 76, 213
Cline, John, 198
Clinton, William, 281–82, 303, 309
  National Homeownership Strategy, 281
coal mining, 28–30
Coast Partners Securities, Inc., 61–63, 65, 123, 202, 331
Compu-Link, 120–21, 155, 157–58, 160, 168, 175–76, 234–35, 241–45, 331
Conemaugh Valley Bank, Blairsville, Pennsylvania, 10
Conn, Billy, 11–12
  boxing history, 13–14
consolidation of the federal banking agencies, 297, 301–15
Continental Illinois National Bank and Trust Company, 306
ContiTrade Services Corporation, 52, 55–58, 77, 202, 205, 212–13, 294
Coonley, Don, 98
Coopers & Lybrand, 118
Copolo, Steven, 177
Countrywide Financial, 306
Court of Appeals decisions
  Church I, 178
  Church II, 183
  Gariety II, 200
  Grant Thornton, 247, 249–50
  Melgar, 64
credit unions' lawsuit, 197

Dalton, Sandy, 67–68
D'Amato, Alfonse, 95, 303
Daugherty, Doug, 110, 137–39, 142, 156, 211
Davidson, Joseph Ray, 183–84
Deloitte Touche, 118
Department of Housing and Urban Development, (HUD), 52, 54, 99, 102, 106–7, 211, 213, 244, 282–84
Department of Justice, 180, 270, 305, 311, 322
depositors' lawsuits, 196–97
direct verification of loans, 98, 107–9, 121, 155–57, 160, 220, 234–35, 296–97
Dodd-Frank Act, 287–88, 309
Dorrell, Jeffrey, 203–4
Doyle, Shannon, 53–54
Drageset, Milton, 53
due diligence fees, 39, 47, 59–61, 64, 91, 133, 221

Ellis, Gary, 84, 131–34, 143, 153, 161–63, 198, 228, 245, 247, 257–66, 322, 332
    Bank of Dunbar, Dunbar, West Virginia, 257
    George Mason Bankshares of Virginia, 257
    West Virginia State College, 260
Ernst & Young, 118
Euro-Play, B.V., 74
Evans, Connie, 148–49, 152–53, 175

Faber, David A., Senior U.S. District Court Judge, 43, 74–75, 137–38, 142, 144, 171–72, 177, 180–82, 185–86, 189–90, 199–200, 231–32, 238–39, 243, 245, 247, 249–50, 322, 325, 327, 332
    decision against Grant Thornton in FDIC case, 249
    decision in case brought by Ellis against Grant Thornton, 259–61, 265–66
    denied Cherry's motion to disqualify, 180–81
    directed verdict for Graham on one count in Church I, 177
    sentencing of Church and Cherry in Church II, 182
    sentencing of Church and Graham in Church I, 177
    sentencing of Graham in Graham II, 185–86

Federal Bureau of Investigation (FBI), 4–6, 92, 141–42, 162, 167–68, 181, 224, 305, 311, 322
Federal Deposit Insurance Corporation (FDIC), passim
    case against Bakkebo, 201–7, 331
    case against directors, 200–202
    case against Grant Thornton, 201, 207, 246–49, 321
    case against Kutak Rock and Michael Lambert, 200, 207, 209–17, 321
    downgrading of OCC examination ratings, 97, 109–11, 125, 223
    permission asked to join OCC examination, 100, 115–17, 132
Federal Home Loan Bank Board, 103, 275
Federal Home Loan Mortgage Corporation (Freddie Mac), 281–82
Federal Housing Administration (FHA), 15, 59, 99, 104, 109–10, 205, 244
Federal National Mortgage Association (Fannie Mae), 281–82
Federal Reserve Bank of Richmond, 151
Federal Reserve System (Fed), passim
Fickins, Dr., 2
Financial Crisis Inquiry Commission/ Report, 272, 279–80, 282–85, 288–89, 309
Financial Institutions Reform, Recovery and Enforcement Act of 1989 (FIRREA), 251–54
Financial Securities Assurance Company (FSA), 58–59, 77, 206, 213–14, 294
Fincastle Country Club, 258
First National Bank of Keystone, Keystone, West Virginia, passim
    branch office – Bradshaw, West Virginia, 199
    closed by OCC and given to the FDIC as receiver, 4, 162
    one of the largest failures in FDIC history, 19, 21, 158, 164
    second largest employer in the county, 19
First State Bank and Trust Company, Rainelle, West Virginia, 37–39, 181
First Union National Bank, 129
Fisher, Larry, 4–5, 133
Forrest, Frank, 95–96
Friendly Honda, 179
F.S. Holdings, S.A., 73–76

gain-on-sale accounting, 17, 58, 90, 293
Gariety, Debra, 198
Gearheart, Rodney, 82
Geithner, Tim, 312
Generally Accepted Accounting Principles (GAAP), 220, 246
Generally Accepted Auditing Standards (GAAS), 222, 226, 231–32, 237, 240, 246, 248, 251
Gerardy, Kathy, 111, 119, 121, 138–40, 158
Ghiglieri, Kathy, 96
Gibson, Michael, 18, 118, 128, 130, 142, 161, 169, 187
Glass, Carter, 287
Glass-Steagall Act, 286–88, 311
    Financial Services Modernization Act of 1999, 287
Goldberg, Rube, 303
Gomer Pyle, 231
Gonzalez, Henry, 303
Government Sponsored Entities (GSE) Act, 281–82
Graffiti (directed against the OCC), 142–44, 168, 276, 322
Graham, Gail, 7, 177
Graham, Michael, 2–3, 7, 24, 37–38, 42–45, 78–79, 83, 130–31, 137–38, 140, 142, 148, 150, 155–57, 163, 165–66, 168, 170, 177–78, 184–87, 196–99, 201, 211, 221–22, 231–32, 236, 242–44, 259–60, 321–22, 325, 327–28, 330, 332
    bingo hall in Alabama, 221, 330
    first criminal trial (Church I), 136, 165–78
    gas company investment in Florida, 330
    indictment in Graham II, 185
    landfill project in West Virginia, 221, 330
    loss of CPA license, 186–87
    suspended from bank, 161
    unindicted co-conspirator in Church II, 178
Grand Rapids Teachers Credit Union, 197
Grant Thornton, 18, 25, 88, 119, 121, 131–32, 159–61, 196–98, 201, 207, 219–27, 229–35, 237–41, 244, 246–52, 254, 257–66, 283, 297–99, 321–22, 332
    analytical review, 241, 243
    fee income, 229
    manuals, 226, 239–41
    test of details, 241

Greenspan, Alan, 284–85
Griffith, Scott, 141–42, 244–46
ground-penetrating radar device, 6
guards, 143–44, 276, 322

Hale, Meredith, 27–28, 155, 250
Hampton Inn, Princeton, West Virginia, 141
Hargrave Military Academy, 41, 46, 193–96
    lawsuit against Church, et al, 193–96
Hawke, John D., Jr. (Jerry), 139–40, 144, 251, 273–74, 309
Haynes, Jerry, 5
Headrick, Vida, 199
Heath, Bryan, 132–35, 141, 172
Herman & Cormany, 118, 196–98, 219, 221, 332
Herron, Evelyn, 199
high loan-to-value loans (HLTV), 77–78, 101, 118, 122, 129, 205, 258, 271
Hill, Nancy, 180
HSBC, 306–7
Hughes, Dee (Mama Dee), 4–5, 50, 169

institution-affiliated party (IAP), 251–52, 297–99
interest income, 160–61, 184–85, 221, 232–33, 241–46
It's a Wonderful Life, 162

Jackson, Gary, 69–70, 74, 76
Jacobsen, Mark, 101, 111
J.D.'s Bar and Grill, 53
Jaedicke, Ann, 159
JLT convenience store, 133, 163
Johnson, Jim, 144
Johnson, Joey, 158
Johnson, Warren, 2
JPMorgan Chase, 269–70, 295, 306–7

Kaufman, Bernard, 161, 258
Keating, Charles, 275
Keystone, West Virginia, passim
    Cinder Bottom, 29
    poverty, 19, 29–30, 171, 231
Keystone Hardware Store, 26, 50, 91, 166, 178
Keystone Mortgage Corporation (KMC), 102–3, 131, 196, 214–15, 229, 259, 327, 331–32
Keystone police, 143, 230

Keystone schoolhouse, 1–2, 25, 170, 173, 175, 177–78
Kimball, West Virginia, 2, 81
Knaak, Tim, 121, 156
Kosa, Penny, 25, 83
KPMG, 118
Krasne, Robert, 84, 143
Krumm, Forrest, 242
Kutak Rock, 74, 170, 201, 207, 209–11, 213, 215–17, 246–49, 261, 321

Lambert, Michael, 65, 74, 128, 145, 161, 170, 207, 210–17
Lansing, Michigan, 160, 176
laptops,
    downloading of hard drives, 84, 101, 214, 321–22
LaRose, John, 160, 245
LaWare, John P., 309
Leach, James, 95, 273–75, 280–81
Lehman Brothers, 56–57, 64, 77, 215–16, 285–86, 288, 294, 313
Lewis, Clifton, 214
limit on loans to one borrower, 15, 87, 100
loan servicers/ loan servicer reports, 15–16, 51–52, 97–98, 109, 119–21, 129, 168, 154–61, 173, 175–77, 219–20, 233–34, 243–44, 250, 321
Long-Term Capital Management, 79, 270, 283
Long, Tim, 106
Love, Charles, 167–68, 170–72, 328
Ludwig, Eugene, 88, 93–95, 99–101, 111, 304

Mackarness, David, 74, 76
Mannes, Scott, 205–6
Master Financial, 15, 52, 211–12
Master Service Certificates, 55, 205
Material Loss Review (MLR), 275–77
McConnell, J. Knox, passim
    arrival at Keystone, 9
    Change in Bank Control Act application, 95–96, 112
    death, 33
    due diligence fees, 59–61, 64
    examination results appealed, 82, 99–100
    first codicil, 40–43, 179
    lawsuits threatened, 82, 92–93, 95, 322
    letters to the OCC, 82, 84–85, 88–89, 92–95, 100–1, 111, 113, 171
    looting of his estate, 33–47, 178–184

Marbil, 37–40, 42, 91, 183
Micronesia Development Bank, Saipan, 11
    obituary, 9–10
    second codicil, 44–45, 179
    Thunderbird car (1956), 183–84
    will, 34
McConnell, Matt, 194
McDowell County, 29–30, 145
McGee, Patrick, 74, 76
McGlothlin, 330
McKinney, Lora, 2, 25, 28, 45, 148–50, 152, 173, 175, 198, 243, 326–28
Melgar, Dan, 15, 50–53, 55–56, 58, 61–66, 70–73, 75–76, 78, 103, 123, 204, 212, 214, 331
Mercer County Courthouse, 194
Meyer, Laurence, 274
Michelich, John, 136–37, 166–67, 169, 172–76
Mickles, Vickie, 43, 45–47, 67
microfilm, 3–4, 6–7, 149–51, 171, 173, 321
    found in ditch with buried documents, 6–7, 150, 173
microfilm reader, 150, 166, 321, 327
microwave, 3, 321
Miles, Bill, 1–5, 142
Millner, Fred, 198
Mitchell, Ron, 58, 103, 124, 202, 214
money laundering, 179, 184–85
Morgan, Michael, 146–51
Morgan, Morris, 142
Morgantown, West Virginia, 33
Mullin Hoard Brown, LLP, 203, 207
Murtagh, Karen, 90–92, 96, 100–1

Neighbors Credit Union, 197
N.Y. Giants, 13
Nunn, Barbara, 24–25, 35, 38, 43–45, 178, 182, 327–28

Obama, Barack, 288
Office of the Comptroller of the Currency (OCC), passim
    case against Grant Thornton, 250–54, 297–98
    case against Kutak Rock and Michael Lambert, 209, 217
    cease and desist order, 250–53
    civil money penalties, 87, 94, 116–18, 123, 128, 134–35, 197, 220, 224, 227–28, 230, 241–42, 246, 250–53

criminal referrals, 90–92, 98, 214
first commitment letter, 85, 87, 92, 116, 296
formal agreement, 85, 100, 116, 118–19, 131, 197, 219, 223, 230, 234, 296
inflammatory emails, 137–42, 168, 211, 321
review of insider transactions, 133–37
second commitment letter, 85, 89, 92, 97–98, 100, 116, 296
temporary cease and desist order, 104–5
Office of the Comptroller of the Currency examinations, 220
1989 examination, 85
1991 examination, 86–87
1993 examination, 87–89
1994 examination, 89–95
1995 examination, 96–99
1996 examination, 100, 109
1997 examination, 101–4, 109, 223
1998 examination, 115–25, 223–24
1999 examination, 132–63
Office of the Inspector General (OIG), 105, 140–42, 161–62, 168, 275–77
Office of Thrift Supervision (OTS), 139, 249–50, 275, 284, 306–7
case against Grant Thornton, 249–50
ombudsman, OCC's (Sam Golden), 82, 85–92, 95, 99
Oosthuizen, Pieter, 74, 76
Orell, Patricia, 27–28, 147, 152–54, 165, 173, 175
out-of-area loans, 14, 56, 58, 60, 72, 107, 293–94
overcollateralization, 66–67, 80, 205
Overholser, Terry, 198

Pacific Thrift and Loan Company, Woodland Hills, California, 274
Pack, Wendy Sue, 50, 53, 65, 67–68
Pais, Louis, 18
brother, 18
family, 18
Pannell, Gary, 107
Pearson, Dan, 121
Pecora hearings, 286
Pennsylvania State Department of Banking, 10
Penny, Doug, 3, 4
Pittsburgh Pirates, 13–14

Potter, Harry J., 204
preemption, 308–9
Prime Financial Corp., 52–54, 61–65, 70, 73–76, 202–3, 207, 213, 216
Sale of, 73–76
Princeton, West Virginia, 6, 43, 81, 141, 158, 161, 188
Proxmire, William, 303
Pujo hearings, 286–87

Quay, Stan, 159–61, 221, 224–30, 232–35, 237–40, 242–45, 248–50, 257–59, 262–64
Quizenbeury, Melissa, 35–36, 45–47, 67, 173, 196, 325–26, 328

Rahall, Nick, 95, 101
Ramada Inn, 163
Ramirez, Patricia, 236–38, 245
Reagan, Ronald, 95
regulatory arbitrage, 93, 276, 305–9, 311, 315
residuals, 57–58, 66–67, 78–79, 110, 115, 202, 205–6, 211, 215, 223, 228–29, 274, 293–94, 331–32
Riegle, Donald, 303
Roanoke, Virginia, 159, 177, 190, 243
Robertson, J. L., 303, 310, 313
Rockefeller, John D. "Jay," 84, 95, 101
Romero, Dee, 157, 245
Ronhardan, 58, 75, 103, 212, 214
Rooney, Art, 11
Roosevelt, Franklin D., 287
Royal Consulting Group. 62–63, 65
Russian debt crisis, 79, 270, 283

St. Louis Postal Credit Union, 197
San Diego, California, 160, 176
Schneck, Ron, 106, 158
Search warrants, 4–7
SEC cases, 193, 198, 323, 325–27
securitization of loans, 15–16, 49, 87, 89, 99
Seidman, Ellen, 274–75
Seidman, William, 310
Selbe, Robert, 167
Serino, Robert, 142, 144
Sexton, David. 177
Shamburger, Bobby, 69–70, 72
Shannon, Thomas, 198
Shareholders' lawsuits, 197–200, 332
Gariety I, 198, 332
Gariety II, 198–200, 202, 332

Shiery, Mike, 228–29
Shrader, Deborah, 25, 83, 146, 172
Sizemore, Scott, 2–3
Sleight, Rick, 331
SMV Holding Company, 198
Spann, Bryan, 166
Spelsberg, Rick, 82–83, 104, 110–11, 117, 139
Sponseller, Elizabeth and Michael, 198
state police, 6, 162–63
Sterling Heights, Michigan, 189
Strasser, Alan, 213
Summers, Larry, 144
Sutton, Willie, 12–13

tape recording
    of conversations with OCC, 84, 101, 210, 224, 322
Temporary Restraining Order (against the OCC), 137–42, 211, 322
Thornburg, Richard, 95
Thornton, Charles, 198
Title One loans/securitization, 15, 20, 49, 60, 62, 73, 77–78, 87, 89, 97–101, 103–4, 110–11, 205
Truth in Lending Act, 87
    Reg. Z, 87–88, 90
Turpin, Ellen, 2–3, 25–26, 28, 45, 146–48, 150–52, 154, 167–68, 172–75, 198, 326–28
    sister-in-law, Amber, 3

United National Bank, Wheeling, West Virginia, 27–28, 157–58, 176, 234, 236–39, 250, 257, 259–60, 331
U.S. Bank, N.A., Minneapolis, Minnesota, 331–32
U.S. Court of Appeals for the District of Columbia
    decision in the case OCC brought against Grant Thornton, 251–54, 297–98

U.S. Court of Appeals for the Fourth Circuit
    decision in the case Ellis brought against Grant Thornton, 261–66, 321–22
U.S. Marshals Service, 144–45, 161–62, 183
U.S. Senate Permanent Subcommittee on Investigations (PSI), 280, 285, 296

videotaping
    of examiners' workspace, 83–84, 101, 143, 321
Virginia Board of Accountancy, 187
Volcker, Paul, 305
Volcker Rule, 288
Vorono, Nancy, 41–42, 45–46, 198–200

Wachovia National Bank, 286
Warren, Michigan, 190
Washington Mutual Bank (WaMu), 275, 280, 286, 306–7
Watkins, Deborah, 50, 196
Waynesburg College, Waynesburg, Pennsylvania, 34, 40–42, 46, 181, 193–96
    lawsuit against Church, et al, 193–96
Websters Restaurant, 161
Western Schools, 187
West Virginia Board of Accountancy, 187
Williams & Connolly, 84, 143, 201
Wilson, Cindy, 156
Wimmer, Jeanie, 199
Wood, Billy, 107
Wooldridge, Gracie, 147–49
Workpapers
    taped back together by bank, 84, 210, 224, 322
Worldwide Church of God, 50
Wright, Mack, 17–18